THE GOSPEL OF
SOPHIA

THE GOSPEL OF SOPHIA

THE BIOGRAPHIES OF
THE DIVINE FEMININE TRINITY

TYLA GABRIEL, ND

our spirit

Our Spirit, LLC

2014

our spirit

2014
OUR SPIRIT, LLC

P. O. Box 355
Northville, MI 48167

www.ourspirit.com
www.gospelofsophia.com

Library of Congress Control Number: 2014953168

ISBN: 978-0-9906455-2-8 (hardback)
ISBN: 978-0-9906455-0-4 (paperback)
ISBN: 978-0-9906455-1-1 (eBook)

We pray that these, our dear friends and teachers, who have passed before us, yet who remain connected to us by the Light of Christ, continue to offer our loving service to the Goddess Sophia.

Henry Barnes ⋆ Haggan Besantz ⋆ Manfred Schmidt Brabant

Sergei O. Prokofieff ⋆ Rudy Wilhelm ⋆ Rene Querido

Kathryn and Ernst Katz ⋆ Manly P. Hall ⋆ Willie Sucher

John Davies ⋆ John Hunter ⋆Barbara and Werner Glass ⋆

John Gardener ⋆ Eve Hardy ⋆ Emily Thurber Kollie Roth

Kathryn Barber ⋆ Hans and Rosemary Gebert ⋆ Rosina Arndt

Hans and Ruth Pusch ⋆ Rudolf Grosse ⋆ Ernst Lehrs

Carl Stegman ⋆ Fredrick Hiebel ⋆ Beredine Joslyn

Norma Roth ⋆ Carlos Pietzner ⋆ John Root ⋆ Dr. Otto Wolf

William Bryant ⋆ Dan and Velma Birdsall ⋆ Adam Bittleson

and

Dr. Rudolf Steiner

Contents

Volume 1
The Biographies of the Divine Feminine Trinity
The Outer Teachings

Contents

Know Her.

FIRST SEAL
The Initial Revelation

No one can feel the spinning Earth or hold the ocean's life,

No one can know the creator God without Her selfless strife;

No rock or stone or tree or cloud can exist without Her grace,

For She's the one who made it all, the features of Her face.

The Vision of the Triple Goddess

No one has seen Her triple, flaming soul, so brilliant and yet subdued,

No one has known Her secret ways that labyrinth the soul,

No one can dance Her birthing song, so deep and suffering true,

Unless her names she chants again or gathers the spring morning dew.

She was standing before me, a crone with leathery skin and a crêpe neck, but eyes that sparkled with vibrancy and youth that pierced my soul with a knowingness of ageless wisdom. So deeply did her eyes penetrate me, and with such discomfort that I glanced away.

She pointed her crooked, ancient finger back over her shoulder to hot red fields of molten lava that were pouring forth as a rich cake batter might have spilled in folds upon itself as it emptied from a baker's mixing bowl.

Through intense heated air, I could see massive pools of percolating magma fed by liquefied rock cascading down a mountain. From the lava pools, four bubbling, red-hot rivers curved downstream and away into a distant, smoke-hazed horizon. In a silence where all is understood, the wisdom woman brought forth from her cloak an ordinary shovel and held it out to me.

With her other hand, she pointed upward to the distant falling streams of molten lava. I accepted the shovel and set off in the direction she indicated. With an intuition of knowing the destination and then floating into it with a kind of spiritual momentum, I looked behind me to see if the crone was following, but she had faded into darkness and invisibility with only the sound of her laughter lingering in the aura of fire.

As I started to ascend the mountain and headed toward the rim of the summit, I could see a fountainhead of the thick folding, churning streams of molten rock. Tightly holding the shovel as my walking stick, I seemed to use a type of dream-will to pole vault and weightlessly propel myself over the streams and pools of liquid fire. Yet, in little time, the intense heat had melted the blade, leaving only the handle.

But this was of no concern to me as I vision-willed myself to the top of the summit without the constraints of ordinary physics.

In a dimension of experience that was not framed in time and space, I perceived the source of the four rivers of molten rock: a huge black cube, suspended a few feet off the liquid-fire ground. Gushing streams of molten magma flowed out of four sides of the black cube to the rim of the summit and cascaded down the mountainside.

What was this mysterious dark cube? How could I reach it?

Feeling the presence of someone other than myself on the precipice of the fiery threshold, I turned my head, and there was the wisdom woman standing in her knowingness with a warm and loving smile.

"How could you be here?" I questioned her without words. "Without a walking stick?"

"How can I get to the black cube?"

Her silent language told me to turn to the cube and hold out the remaining shovel stick that I still grasped. Following her inner directive, I turned back to the cube, held out the shovel stick, which seemed to have become an enchanted wand, and struck the cube's ebony side in an attempt to analyze the strange formation. Instantaneously, in a whirl of mystical displacement, I found myself inside the cube, immersed in an enormous volcanic fountainhead.

And there she was, standing motionless in the middle of the fiery fountain of magma: the wisdom woman.

Her timeworn image had been transformed into a youthful, shimmering beauty who was holding an infant in her arms.

Her heavy pleated cloak that had hidden all of her features except her face and hands had become a gossamer gown of sky blue chiffon that barely made her naked figure modest. Her hair fell below her shoulders like opulent strands of silky ribbons in a multitude of hues and tones. Her skin was luscious luminescence. Her face was perfect symmetry. Her eyes sparkled with vibrancy and youth.

She approached me and, with a mother's tender love, placed the baby in my arms.

Holding the infant and gazing into its face, rushing imaginations flooded through me. The infant became a mirror of recognition.

"This child is me." My soul reflected.

I saw my life stream forward in time as the four rivers of magma gushed from the cube.

I was the child growing into what I had become, quite unconscious of the guiding forces of the wise woman who stood before me as mother, maiden, crone, hidden Goddess.

Once hesitant to look into the eyes of the crone, I now hungered to look into her wise gaze to give me knowledge of myself. Our eyes met, and her wordless language began to pour into my heart and soul.

"It is time to birth your higher self."

"You have traveled this path of fire and heat, given only a simple shovel," she thought into me. "By trusting forces beyond your physical experience, you willed yourself over fiery obstacles and up to the volcano summit."

"Then, trusting your intuition in a place where no logic seemed operative," she continued, "you awakened your consciousness to the time- and space-defying act of holding yourself as a babe."

Her parting thoughts to me resounded as I began to wake from my dream.

"It is time," she said.

"Time for what?" I asked.

She smiled knowingly. "It is time to birth your higher self."

Drenched in heavy sweat, I leaped out of my dream state, jumping out of my bed with my arms folded in front of me as though cradling a baby. My beating heart felt like a heavy baton beating on a tightly stretched drumhead.

I caught a glimpse of myself in the mirror across the room. My face looked magma red.

"My God, I'm sweating blood!"

I sat down on the bed and then tried to calm myself and make sense of this strange dream.

I was living in Hawaii at the time. I had come to the Big Island to participate in a series of Tibetan Buddhist initiations and empowerments in the highest Yoga Tantra teachings on the deity Vajrayogini, the Holy Mother Consort (dakini) of all male tantric deities.

These special holy teachings are at the heart of Tibetan tantric practices. The initiations were conducted by the three leaders of the Sakyapa tradition, especially the venerable Luding Khen Rinpoche. The present embodiment of Vajrayogini, Jetsen Khusala, also helped conduct the ceremonies.

My dream was no doubt the soul unwindings of the day's intense esoteric practices.

The revelations, visions, dreams, and experiences that came to me while immersed in these teachings were, I believe, part of my initiation into the deepening awareness of the Mother aspect of spirituality. As my initiations progressed, so did the vividness of my dream life.

When a Hawaiian friend offered to lead me through miles of underground lava tubes that visitors and most residents did not know about, I did not hesitate to accept the offer. The thought of experiencing my dream on an actual volcano field stirred my adrenaline and piqued my curiosity.

Bryan was going to take me to a place called Pele's Vagina, so named because of a natural invagination of the rock from which blood-red lava had flowed.

Pele's Vagina is a geological wonder, but also a sacred ceremonial chamber for Hawaiian women's birthing rituals. In early geological times, lava tubes were created when streams of magma hardened against the cooler sides of the tube to form a continuous and hard crust. The tube formed a roof under which molten lava oozed.

"Even though a tube appears harmless and dormant," Bryan explained to me before leaving on our excursion, "these lava tubes can be filled in an instant with hot magma any time a volcano is active.

"Just as women birth new children with the same womb, Pele can arise as she wishes and fill these old lava tubes with new hot magma," he warned.

I was intrigued.

"Let's hike directly up Puu'oo," I challenged Bryan.

Puu'oo is an 800-foot-tall cone volcano that vents a constant plume of sulfuric smoke high into the atmosphere. The hazardous climb to its rim is prohibited by law and punishable with a thousand-dollar fine per person.

Its lakes and rivers of molten magma deep below the cone continuously flow down the gentle slopes to the sea, making it the largest shield volcano in the world.

How I convinced Bryan to follow my crazy idea still confounds me today.

He knew that the black, cold lava crust of Puu'oo insulates the hot magma rivers that actively flow underground. In periods of strong activity, Puu'oo can vent thousand-foot-tall fountains, while the areas around her can well up into active magma lakes that rush to the sea in fiery rivers. Puu'oo's cycle of flow is extremely unpredictable, and her onslaught had already consumed three villages where friends had lost their homes to the advancing flows of lava.

We hopped into his four-wheel-drive and ascended the dangerously steep and rocky road. My anxieties were somewhat assuaged by my friend's adept driving as he maneuvered through what seemed like unending challenges of difficult terrain. Miles beyond where I thought no vehicle could travel safely, we came to a dead stop on a bed of lava gravel.

Before us lay a vast incline, a landscape of frozen black lava ornamented with huge chunks of hard glass boulders that had heaved up into bizarre and surreal sculpture-like formations.

As Bryan and I hiked out onto this volcanic wasteland that would take us to the foot of Puu'oo, I was enthralled by the musical sounds of the lava glass breaking beneath our heavy boots. It sounded like walking on thousands of crystal and glass shards or a film of freshly frozen ice, and unlike any musical instrument I had ever heard.

Pling. Shriek. Ring. Screech.

Lying around in countless shapes and images were lava sculptures that had been created by rushing rivers of lava that had moved down the mountainside and had cooled over time, leaving a natural gallery of carvings and figures to be interpreted by one's imagination. Some were china-thin plates of polished black glass. Others looked like contorted faces of grotesque demons peering from the moonscape ground. The rock field was full of hardened, black, ropey images of swirling forms.

Here and there we spotted black, desolate slopes where skeleton-like trees had miraculously remained erect among the rushing onslaught of fiery molten rock. Their strange starkness punctuated the cloudless blue sky.

The scorching sun baked the black lava, and the heat rose in ripples. Sweat on the surface of my skin mixed with the glass-like powdery residue that arose from the breaking surfaces beneath our feet. It felt as though we were walking on a different planet or in some realm of hell.

After we had climbed five miles or so, the terrain became more treacherous because we had reached the area where the hot magma rivers from past eruptions still slowly flowed beneath the surface crust of hardened lava.

As we walked, our boots broke the brittle boundary between the hardened crust and the flowing, hot magma below, leaving sizable depressions as footprints. It became increasingly difficult to see where we were stepping because all around us were cloud-like streams of vaporous sulfuric "vog," or volcanic fog that rose from vents in the lava crust beneath our feet.

"I knew at that moment that something magical would transpire from this adventure."

With each step, I began to wonder if the next might drop us into a scalding river of death. I was grateful more than once that I had decided, because of my dream, to take a walking stick. It saved me from falling on several occasions—falls which could easily have taken my life—as we threaded our way up the treacherous terrain.

When Bryan and I arrived at the foot of Puu'oo, the home of Pele, I was dumbstruck.

Here was the mountain I had seen in my dream. I knew at that moment that something magical would transpire from this adventure.

As I stood in awe of the bizarre and unearthly landscape, helicopters were circling above, filled with tourists observing the wonders of the volcano at a safe distance.

Bryan called out.

"We may be going too far. Look ahead at those people who are wearing hazmat. Maybe we should turn around." I turned to see a group of explorers wearing heat-resistant asbestos clothing and protective face masks.

My euphoria was checked when Bryan further explained that we could be reported for trespassing, causing our trip to end and resulting in thousands of dollars in fines.

But being young and daring, we threw caution to the wind and continued our climb.

Near the top of the slopes, we came upon a series of vents, or caved-in holes. Looking into them, we could see enormous underground caverns nearly filled with boiling lakes of magma fed by rushing rivers of fire beneath our feet. The vents were encircled by thin, fragile crusts that frequently collapsed beneath our feet. As we walked around the vents, large sections would suddenly cave in and drop into the flowing magma.

I realized, with no small amount of anxiety, that my trusty walking stick would not be much help if a large section of the fragile crust suddenly fell into one of the vents.

"Bryan, look at this," I shouted over the piercing sound of lava glass breaking under my heels.

I pointed to a particular vent that was extraordinarily large and looked like an opening to a cave rising up thirty feet in front of us. We circled it to find the closest place to peer inside it without crushing the lava crust under our feet.

"Here, let me use the walking stick to stabilize us so we can look into the opening," I explained to Bryan.

I stuck my head into the smoke and ash and saw an underground cavern. Fifteen feet below, there was a surging, heaving, exploding, boiling, spinning, whirling lake of magma.

A huge river of magma rushed into the lake. The force of the river was so great that the molten lava was being pushed uphill, swirling into a roiling cauldron of white-hot liquid rock about three hundred yards in diameter. Pockets of vapor exploded onto the roof of the cavern about fifteen feet above the surface, creating spectacular underground fireworks.

"Mobile and ethereal, it seemed like a consciousness was leading my attention further into the cavern."

Bryan picked up a chunk of hardened lava the size of a football and heaved it into the lake of magma. Before it reached the surface of the fiery lake, it vaporized. I moved closer, trying to discern the colors swirling within the searing heat, which was beyond white-hot, a sea of liquid fire contained within a corona of clear, luminous light. Mobile and ethereal, it seemed like a consciousness was leading my attention further into the cavern. Using my stick, I leaned forward, stretching as far as I could to see what was in the middle of the lake.

That's when I saw Her: Pele, the Triple Goddess.

The light had begun to coalesce into three separate forms, all hovering above the infernal lake. Three beings—three sets of eyes—came into focus, and they were all looking at me, into my eyes. And, it seemed to me, into my very soul.

On the left was a naked young Goddess, all red, dancing on a lotus flower, her eyes filled with compassion. She had three eyes, with one in the middle of her forehead. Her third eye was looking into heaven. As flames leapt about Her, She drank Her own blood from a raised skull-cup. She had a cross over her shoulder. A bell and drum sounded loudly.

I recognized Her as a form of Vajrayogini, a Goddess whose image had been imprinted in my mind from my Tibetan studies. I realized that this holy Mother consort was the creator of fire and earth, the mysteries of birth and the past. She is the dark Goddess who is actually brilliant red, but few have ever seen Her. It was She who was sought after in underground mystery centers where the secrets of fire were taught.

In the center was a pure, beautiful Goddess of light seated on a luminous throne and clothed in a long, flowing white veil studded with stars.

Her form was white with heat, so white that I could see right through her. Another veil covered Her eyes and most of Her face. From her heart came flashes of white light that were as wispy and soft as cirrus clouds.

She had many veils about Her that moved and flowed with the rhythm of the rivers of magma beneath Her, though She Herself was sitting still, hands firmly holding Her throne. She seemed to be waiting patiently and attentively.

Then, I suddenly knew Her as Eve, the mother of humanity. I saw Her great suffering as She left the garden of Eden and lived many lives, longing for creation in the purity of its beginning. She lived and died, gave birth and saw death. Her wisdom grew. She gave birth to Jesus as mother Mary.

My vision continued in what seemed like an eternity, only to be told later by Bryan that only a moment had passed.

In those brief moments, it was revealed to me that twelve years after Christ was crucified, Sophia (who was Eve, Mary, and the Spirit of Wisdom) was assumed into heaven and conquered death. She is still with us and continues to appear to the faithful who are pure of heart when they pray to Her. She is present for them at the moment of their death. She is the ruler of the present moment.

On the right was an entity of light that was not bound by one body, but seemed composed of creative swirls of energy resembling the wings of doves. Each swirl was filled with wisdom so profound that when I looked upon a specific one, any thought I had, any image formed in my mind, became an immediate picture mirrored back to me from Her creative response.

"Nothing I had ever before experienced prepared me for the fierceness, the explosive creativity that I witnessed that day on the mountaintop when I saw the unveiling of the Triple Goddess."

She was responding to my thoughts, filling them with the wisdom to understand this threefold being that I was beholding. The other two Goddess forms seemed to both surround and yet work through Her creative, swirling energies.

This third Being revealed Herself to me as the future, uncreated, yet continuously being created. She rules fate and destiny and is the nature of resurrection and new life born out of death. She was truly indescribable, because She could take any image and coalesce it into form, manifesting before my eyes that which I wished to know.

She seemed unlimited, constantly changing, more powerful and terrible than any other force, yet more compelling, alluring, and beautiful than my greatest imagination of feminine beauty.

When I could bear no more, I drew back from the vent and my vision. I was startled to see a look of shock on my friend's face. When I asked him what was wrong, he informed me that my eyelashes, eyebrows, and even the hair around my face had been severely singed from being so close to the intense heat.

I had been so enthralled by my vision of the Goddess that I had not even noticed that I was being scorched.

I was more astonished by the realizations that began to flood my mind. I began to understand who the Dark Goddess is and why people are afraid of Her and why some philosophers place her underground or in the obscure. I could see that She is a volcano Goddess who is fiery red hot on the inside (magma) and cold black (lava) on the outside. Her magma is hidden by the veils of heat and poisonous gases that surround Her.

She only shows Her true colors when She chooses and when an aspirant is ready. Her sister, the air, always cools her, and therefore She remains hidden from all prying eyes deep in Her concealed labyrinths. Her other sister, the ocean, rushes to extinguish Her fire with her cold, wet touch.

"Are you okay?" Bryan asked.

Still reeling from my vision, I murmured a grunt of affirmation and pointed to another area that we should explore. I remained silent as the vision began to unpack itself in my brain, unfolding its truth as I continued to walk with my friend.

"Let's walk down the slope," Bryan said as he pointed. "We can see where the underground rivers of magma flow to the sea. It's mind-blowing to see curtains of flowing magma meet the open air and crash into cold waves of the ocean," he explained.

Indeed, it was breathtaking. We watched as the hot magma reached the sea, exploding in all directions into tiny pebbles, floating pumice, or a rain of volcanic glass-like hairs. Eventually all would succumb to the relentless thrashing ocean and become grains of sharp, black sand that would continue to extend the islands' beaches.

As I reflected on all that I had seen and as my vision continued to reveal more of its truth, I awakened to other understandings. I realized that the advancing, cascading rivers of red-hot magma were the Earth's blood.

Pele is bleeding to create new land forms for her children to live upon. When Pele's blood reaches the ocean, Her magma explodes like bright bombs of methane fireworks shooting sulfuric rockets into the sky, fragmenting lava into sand, and birthing Her child as a new black sand beach.

Nothing I had ever before experienced prepared me for the fierceness, the explosive creativity that I witnessed that day on the mountaintop when I saw the unveiling of the Triple Goddess. I realized that even though I had spent my lifetime to that point committed to the study of knowledge, my journey to wisdom had only just begun.

My Hawaiian experiences revealed to me why man has characterized woman, in the aspect of the Great Goddess, as dark, black, and even evil. The Dark Goddess in her fiery red nature is the ruler of the past, and She is so fierce and powerful that no one has ever been able to see Her inner nature, which is below the surface of the dark, black earth.

> *"No longer did I feel the need to go to Her molten fields of creativity. I could feel her under my feet everywhere."*

Her molten magma is much like the "Veil of Isis," which "no one can lift and live."

But this ugly, black lava that is the blood sacrifice of the Mother Goddess is composed of a perfect mixture of elements that is the richest soil in the world. Plants love it. It is Pele's progeny, offered from her endless boiling oceans of molten magma. These oceans of magma literally carry the weight of the land we walk upon.

After seeing Pele's many wondrous forms in the fiery lake, I came down from the mountain with the vision indelibly inscribed in my mind.

My soul was transformed by the majesty of Her presence, and my being was permanently changed by Her power and beauty.

It took months to grow back the hair and recover from the magnitude of what we had done. Few people ever go into those realms of fiery, molten creativity without proper gear or without getting arrested and fined. I thanked Pele for sharing Herself with us and protecting us from danger.

Pele continued to reveal herself to me while I was on the Big Island of Hawaii—in my dreams, in a spirit birth, on the road, and in signs wherever I went. Through inner promptings that were vivid and real, She led me all over the island, showing me the way to secret underground hot springs, warm ponds, steam vents, caves, and lava tubes.

She took me up Mauna Kea, the island's 14,000-foot extinct cone volcano, and her sister, Mauna Loa, a 13,000-foot active shield volcano. She led me wandering all over Her sister islands. She taught me how to swim with sea turtles, dolphins, and whales. Pele taught me their language, the speech of the heart's true desire, the nature of harmlessness and purity.

Through Pele's vision, I became aware of Her nature manifesting over the whole world, in the past, the present, and the future. She revealed to me that Her inner workings are found in all things.

She is the Archetypal Mother of everything.

Her precious black jewel of the Pacific is truly Her home, but Her works are found everywhere as the foundations of the earth that bring us life. No longer did I feel the need to go to Her molten fields of creativity. I could feel her under my feet everywhere.

> ## "She is a being that is beyond time and space."

It was then that I decided to try to verbalize and share this vision of the Goddess given to me through Pele. It was difficult to use conversational language to describe this Being, so I began writing poetry to describe Her nature. I also gathered every poem, verse, or wisdom saying that related to what I had seen and experienced as my communion with the Triple Goddess, in the hope that this information would help others see Her more clearly.

I became a devotee of the Goddess, unaware that many before me had also had their vision of Her and became enthralled in uncovering her mysteries.

Reflections

The Gospel of Sophia is a life offering to the Triple Goddess, otherwise known as Sophia, the Mother, Daughter, and Holy Sophia. She is the Original Deity from whom all male sun gods were born and rules the past, present, and future.

Because She is a being that is beyond time and space, one must move outside of known dimensional space in order to get a glimpse of Her. This multi-dimensional revelation is reflected, as best as the author can perceive in her own limited understanding, in *The Gospel of Sophia*.

For the casual reader, this manuscript may seem overwhelming. This is a natural barrier between *here*—the safety of ordinary consciousness—and *there*—the realm of supersensible experience. The casual reader is not ready to step across the threshold of perceiving the Triple Goddess, so the deep philosophical nature of this manuscript becomes a spiritual boundary to keep the uninitiated from proceeding further than his or her spiritual capacities are prepared to travel.

For the reader who is prepared to cross the threshold and take up the study of *The Gospel of Sophia* one paragraph, one poem, and one page at a time, without a need to rush to the end—for there is no plot that wraps up the story in a neat and tidy way—one's life begins to change.

One's consciousness begins to expand.

One's soul begins to stir.

One's spirit begins to awaken.

There is a saying in Hawaii that "Pele giveth and Pele taketh away." This refers to the function of the Triple Goddess, who rules birth, death, and resurrection. She existed before and after the more well-known trinities of Father, Son, and Holy Spirit, or Brahma, Vishnu, and Shiva, or any other of the much later, male-dominated, sun-centered religions and cultures.

She is the unmanifested Creatrix who has participated in all levels of existence, including the human.

She descended as a Pure Virgin Soul and lived for eleven years as a human. The Holy Sophia is now growing with humanity as a sister soul.

As Queen Mother, She redeemed humanity by giving birth to the Christ.

She was with Christ through His three-year ministry and lived eleven years after His resurrection, teaching the apostles, in particular St. John the Divine at Ephesus in Turkey.

Mary (Sophia) overcame death herself after the dormition period, was assumed into heaven, and now sits on Her Throne of Wisdom next to Christ Jesus and God the Father.

Mary's apparitions have never ceased to appear to those with a pure heart. She nurtures, intercedes, and shows the way.

She is the principle of Wisdom (Sophia) that has been hidden for thousands of years, and She has now reascended Her lost Throne of Power, comprised of the collective wisdom of all nature.

By whatever name She is known—Eve, Mary, Sophia—She has resurrected the fall of the Virgin Soul into dark matter and has led Her through Wisdom to her higher spirit self.

We are all called to this wedding feast as brides in the great alchemical marriage.

Eve and Adam were Virgin Souls incarnating first in Eden and then on the Earth. They continued to incarnate in the many mysterious religions of antiquity until the time of Jesus of Nazareth. Eve became Mary, the mother of Jesus. Adam became John the Baptist. Together, they stand next to Christ Jesus as Adam and Eve redeemed.

The forces of Sophia the Daughter inspired Mary/Eve at the time of Jesus' baptism in the Jordan by John the Baptist and lived with Her for years after the descent of the Holy Spirit, even until Her Assumption into heaven.

As the tongues of fire descended at Pentecost, the Holy Spirit that had inspired John the Baptist moved the Apostles to spread the Gospel of Peace, and Sophia the Daughter dwelt in Mary and instructed St. John the Divine. The Holy Sophia wed the Holy Spirit in this World Pentecost.

The Most Holy Trinosophia is triple in function.

She is the Mother (Creatrix), Daughter (Spirit of Wisdom), and the Holy Sophia (Collective Consciousness of Humanity).

Maria Sophia is the first and greatest initiate to arise complete and pure.

She is the first of the Virgin Souls to return to Her spiritual home, New Jerusalem, a place which exists in the atmosphere around the Earth, much like Shamballa or Heaven.

Sophia has conquered death, resurrected, and has now returned to Her Temple of Wisdom and ascended Her mighty throne of birth, death, and resurrection.

Now the Triple Goddess calls out, not the ancient injunction of the Egyptian mysteries, "I am the past, the present, and the future; no one has lifted my veil and lived," but a new Invocation of Sophia (given by Rudolf Steiner):

"I am the past, the present, and the future; all must lift my veil to live."

A new global wave of awareness of the Goddess mysteries has crested with archeo-mythological research that elevates the Mother to Her rightful, primary position in both culture and religion. Once again, the doors of the Temple of Wisdom have been opened, and everywhere there are signs of Sophia's resurrection.

The author believes these sacred messages, some of which have been spoken and written from the beginning of human culture, should now be seen and spoken again in heralding Her good news. Some readers will need the intellectual platform of "The Review of the Literature" section or the biography of the Holy Sophia contained in the Fourth Seal in order to acknowledge the Feminine Divine. Their Imaginations cannot make the leap to the Triple Goddess without a "walking stick."

Other readers will resonate immediately with the poetry that describes the unfolding of the Goddess and will pay little attention to the philosophical and theological arguments, preferring to use the book as a meditation or study group guide for their reflections on the Goddess.

> *"Maria Sophia is the first and greatest initiate to arise complete and pure."*

To many readers, the *Sixth Seal* in Volume 2 on the practical applications of developing earthly and cosmic nutrition streams and the etherization of the blood will seem as far reaching as a personal vision of Pele and require deep spiritual insight to comprehend the material presented.

The reader does not have to understand each page of *The Gospel of Sophia* to receive its spiritual gifts. Each reread of *The Gospel of Sophia* will bring you to a deeper consciousness of Her nature. Even the author re-reads the very words she has written and is in awe of new layers of understanding unpeeling in her soul at each round of reflection.

They are the outpourings of love and devotion for the Great Mother, the Triple Goddess. All great thinkers have approached and courted Her with their penultimate expressions. The depth of any thinker is defined by his or her understanding of the Triple Goddess and Her twelvefold manifestations of space in Her sevenfold realms of time. The Goddess defines space and weaves time into the tapestry of life.

Take your refuge, solace, and sustenance from the forces of the Goddess and She will ennoble you with Her qualities and virtues.

Pele the Creator

Her ancient, boiling cauldrons of life create the firm earth beneath us,
While She vents Her plumes of sulfur high into the atmosphere above us.
Her roiling oceans of molten rock have thrust up the mighty mountains,
And have ripped open the expanding floors of the seven seas below us,
While her blood red rivers of magma rush to the surface to birth new land
Or explode the top off a mountain, leaving only volcanic rubble and dust
Or a plume of ash that can reach into outer space and blacken the sky,
While being heard by all in Her deep rumbling, the whole world round.

No one has beheld Her fiery beauty in Her hallowed halls beneath us,
No one has known Her virgin soul from times immemorial,
No one can stand upright on Earth without Her fiery hold,
No one can remember creation without sounding Her names of old.

No one has seen Her triple, flaming soul, so brilliant and yet subdued,
No one has known Her secret ways that labyrinth the soul,
No one can dance Her birthing song, so deep and suffering true,
Unless Her names she chants again or gathers the spring morning dew.

No one can feel the spinning Earth or hold the ocean's life,
No one can know the creator God without Her selfless strife;
No rock or stone or tree or cloud can exist without Her grace,
For She's the one who made it all, the features of Her face.

The rays of sun She takes and holds, and births the planet whole,
As She dances the rounds and rhythms long that tumble as we roll,
Through space She claims as Earth's own song, harmonies of the spheres,
That create the time and space we know down through the passing years.

She suffers long to bear our weight, both our bodies and souls,
Patiently awaiting the time when our spirit can hold its own
And not depend on Her unconsciously, without ever any praise,
Uniting again as One Earth, till our voices together we raise,
To exalt Her names, Her deeds of old, to know Her efforts true,
To find the way to unite again, one planet, one spirit, renewed.

SECOND SEAL
The Quest for Sophia

We are the stardust of a thousand worlds, swirling into the dance of life,
Filled with the dark light that has fallen into our bones and marrow,
Igniting the heart, the organ of fire and love that shines ever brilliant.

Finding Sophia

No one has beheld Her fiery beauty in Her hallowed halls beneath us,

No one has known Her virgin soul from times immemorial,

No one can stand upright on earth without Her fiery hold,

No one can remember creation without sounding Her names of old.

Throughout history, many thinkers have sought the mystery of Wisdom and tried to plumb Her depths. All ancient cultures initially worshipped the Great Goddess in one of Her many forms: Prajnaparamita in India, Hecate in Persia, Inanna in Babylon, Isis in Egypt, Shekinah of the Hebrews, Athena in Greece, Sophia of the Gnostics, Philosophia of the Scholastics, and the being of Anthroposophia to Rudolf Steiner.

Many original sources are offered in this book to demonstrate that the original concept of the Divine is a Goddess who is manifold (threefold, sevenfold, twelvefold) in Her expression.

She is the original revelation and the ubiquitous binding of all creation.

She is the Mother-Bride-Consort of the Father God-Christ Jesus-Holy Spirit.

She is the perfect example of what our own souls should become to be worthy and prepared for the uniting of our higher consciousness with our spirit source and future.

Sophia's path of development is humanity's path of development. We cannot rise at once to the level of christened beings, but we can prepare our souls for receiving the gifts of the hierarchy of beings who wish to commune with us consciously and feed us the ambrosia and nectar (bread and wine) of the gods, the nourishment of the grail.

It is this calling-path-quest that defines our spiritual nature. All great spiritual seekers ultimately find an epiphany of the divine. These apocalyptic testimonies come from every land and tradition, but they all have similar motifs and descriptions of this Being, whether as Natura, Beauty, Chaos, Creatrix, Mother, or Beloved Sophia, among others. These encounters often come early in development and drive creative souls all their lives, or they may come in the twilight of life as a reflection on the long path of destiny that now shines clearly.

"We all spring from Her night of silent unknowing where dreams come not—from that blessed nothingness that holds all and weaves together the loose ends of time and space."

She can be found as close as your heartbeat or as far as distant stars and natural wonders. Both are the same, the near and the far, birth and death, and Her gift of rebirth maintains it all and binds the extremes. We all spring from Her night of silent unknowing where dreams come not—from that blessed nothingness that holds all and weaves together the loose ends of time and space.

She is all one, but She is separate and different than the Father Ground of Being, the unmanifest fire that does not consume or illuminate, that original continuum of creation that holds all pasts and futures in the apparent present moment of being, beyond, far beyond in fact, far, far beyond all sense-perceptible matter or providence.

She is that one beginning note that holds all harmonies in balance without sound. Only such a One could be the Consort of the Father Ground of Being, who unites in the celestial marriage that births their Wonder Child: Humanity, the Christened Spirits of the Aurora of the Coming Dayspring.

We are all called on the path of the prodigal son. We fall from the heights of spirit into matter and wallow in the mire until the warmth and light of the sun calls us to rise to the heavenly songs of creation and the dance of sacred life.

Only Wisdom will be the ever-present helpful companion that can see us through the challenges of this quest and draw us forth from darkness and the muddy vesture of life.

Only Her presence can draw away the veils of chaotic matter blinding the higher senses with common fear of the future.

Only Her patient knowing lifts the veils of ignorance and confusion that parcel the world into separate beings who are alone and suffering.

Wisdom leads us to the Fountain of Virtue where sacred surrender joins us with the grace that accompanies blessed goodness. The world hangs like endless temptations, lush with blissful indulgences all about this excellent Fountain of Virtue to distract the seeker from the music of the waters of life. Wisdom refocuses our view and helps incline our heart's ear to resonate with the music of the harmony of the spheres and the instruction of the Teachers of Wisdom and the Harmony of Feelings and Sensations.

"Only Wisdom will be the ever-present, helpful companion that can see us through the challenges of this quest and draw us forth from darkness and the muddy vesture of life."

This Fountain of Virtue is the continual on-rushing of the gifts of the higher hierarchies that create all of the wise interactions of the beings in nature. Everywhere we look in nature, wherever we unveil Isis, we find behind the beauty of nature, the miraculous power of creation imbued with endless wisdom in its design.

Life is the search for the wellsprings of wisdom, the nourishing happiness that fills each person's thirst and hunger completely.

All true seekers have traveled this path to the unknown land, the New Jerusalem that descends from above and meets the aspiring Virgin Soul in the mid-heaven. *This land cannot be perceived with any of the physical senses.* It takes newly developed, supersensible organs to perceive and interact in these heaven realms.

Until now, the hierarchy has supported our bodies, organs, and senses. It is now our turn to take over the function of the seven chambers of the heart, the seven organs beneath our ribs, and the seven chambers of the brain in order to open these organs of spiritual perception. The human body is an exact replica of the universe—the hieroglyph of the universe—the microcosm of the macrocosm. We need travel no further than the perception of our own senses and the consciousness that arises to find the Heavenly Fountain of Excellence, which is a holographic mirror of the Fountain of Creation in the center of every galaxy and each atom.

When we look out at night into the starlit cosmos, we are looking into a mirror of our own mind looking back at itself from the future and the past—from behind and in front of us. We are presently becoming gods looking at our future spiritual natures developing towards us, making us into gods. We are one and many, and it is the many that confuses us.

The Taoists speak frequently of the ten thousand things that must be put in order to have the possibility of the golden moment of illumination, when the ten thousand things become the One thing, which is your self merging with your not-self. You are the ten thousand things in One. All suffering and joy are part of the ten thousand things. We believe that we must experience all ten thousand things before

> *"We need travel no further than the perception of our own senses and the consciousness that arises to find the Heavenly Fountain of Excellence, which is a holographic mirror of the Fountain of Creation in the center of every galaxy and atom."*

the mind can accept that it is the One thing we were searching for all along. We cannot attain Oneness until we have thoroughly exhausted our search for ourselves in all outer things—or at least, that is what the mind tells us.

Our search was long and hard and we did not falter until we had looked Beauty, Truth, and Goodness in the face everywhere. We have found the Grail in numerous forms. Religious experience is everywhere, in all beings and all things.

All strivings have led us to understand that loving one partner and creating a loving family is the highest of selfless callings. No other can embody the perfect form of the universe. The marriage of the eternally Virgin Mother with the Father Ground of Unmanifest Being births the Christ in us as the Alchemical Wedding of the Soul to the Spirit. The alchemical wedding is the formula for the transmutation and disenchantment of matter back into spirit.

Wisdom is what anoints the royal effort of virtuous purification that prepares the virgin soul for the celestial wedding to our Christened Spiritual Self—the mysterious conjunction that merges the alchemical red and white drops into the eternal magenta drops hidden in the heart of hearts. Lovers who wish to birth a miraculous child intuitively know this to be true. This is why we search for Wisdom wherever we might find Her.

The search must happen for all of us in our own way, but the end is clear; we are gods and goddesses in the becoming as our virgin soul weds our higher self in the light and blessings of the Father and Mother.

Sophia is Wisdom.

The human body is all-wise.

The universe is formed in the shape of a human body.

That body is Sophia.

She is the manifest world and all things in it. Sophia's naked body is the birth, death, and rebirth of all natural things in the known world. This process is Her breathing; from super-massive black holes that swallow billions of suns and make them vanish, to super-massive galactic ion jets that alternate and conversely spin out billions of suns from seeming nothingness.

On both sides of these sense-perceived cosmic activities, we find a place where matter disappears and reappears. This is where Sophia and God, the Father Ground of Being, cohabit—in the potential unmanifest.

God is unmanifested divine order.

Sophia is both manifest and unmanifest potential, or the *Creatrix.*

Sophia is the consort or beloved of God.

Sophia is God manifest in this world. Male and female created He-them—in his own image. The two are one.

The slow-burning fire has awakened from a slumber that was like death. She has walked again in the garden of delight. No tears need to be shed, for She waters her garden with streams that run beneath the Earth, refreshing all with a wondrous Earth-born spring—hidden, deep, pure, and fresh with desire to burst forth feeding the bounty of the Earth.

Goddess of Birth! Your sweet milk nourishes our body and soul and fires our spirits with courage and peace profound. She is in us, forging the moment to come into heaven's delight. No more separateness. We are One with you, dear Sophia. We long to hold you in our hearts, in that wondrous chalice of bliss that is union divine.

The Secret of Fire

I know the secret of fire; I have been burned alive
    many times to see Her face,
As She falls from heaven to Earth
    in a blaze of wondrous sacrifice,
Like Prometheus thrown down to the mountaintop
    where an eagle devoured his liver each day anew,
Chained by the gods for his gift of fire
    given to humans all too soon.

Fire in caves lit up the pictograms
    of soul images painted by midwives,
Whose sacred flame must never die,
    passed on through rituals of the woman soul
Or burned as offerings for gods on every altar
    to unite sacrifice with the spirit.

Life-giving warmth in the cold,
*   gray light in the darkness;*
Life-giving fire found on the sun,
*   or the deep flames of burning stars,*
All call the ancient name of Thee, Holy Mother Fire,
*   Queen of the luminous realms and destroyer of matter,*
The light-bringer, the conflagration of all living things
*   as they die and fall back into your silent arms.*

When the flames die down and turn to ashes
*   And only cold and dark remain —*
Where has this luminous wonder gone?
*   She roars, consuming, and then falls silent as death.*

Each votive candle lit in faith
*   burns as a heart's desire calling spirit into matter.*
Each leaf that falls surrenders into the slow burning
*   of all matter in its dying embers.*
Each life during birth ignites the magically conjoined elements
*   nurturing its fragile existence.*
Each human soul birthed as a helpless spark
*   needs years of warm enkindling to shine.*
Each human becomes their own sun in time, surrounded by
*   their progeny planets—flames born of love.*

Review of the
Literature on Sophia

The rays of sun She takes and holds, and births the planet whole,

As She dances the rounds and rhythms long that tumble as we roll,

Through space She claims as Earth's own song, harmonies with other spheres,

That create the time and space we know down through the passing years.

A recent review of the existing literature on Sophia, encompassing the associations with Isis, Ishtar, the Great Goddess, as well as the new philosophical, religious, and scientific views of Sophia was most encouraging and rewarding. It seems that everyone has a personal view of Sophia and Her place in their philosophy, science, or self-created religion. Sophia is found in a myriad of forms and expressions—from colleges created to study the Sophia/Mary connection to self-proclaimed prophets who say that Sophia is incarnated in a person bearing the marks of stigmata as a spiritual endorsement of authenticity.

There are Tibetan tulkus who claim to be the incarnation of Vajrayogini, the fiery goddess of wisdom. There are authors who have discovered hidden "treasures" about Sophia that have been revealed exclusively through them.

After years of study in humanities and religion, the author found that all sacred doctrines of a "trinity" derived from a universal worship of the Great Goddess in her many forms but primarily as a trinity of birth, death, and rebirth or Mother, Daughter, and Holy Sophia. It led her away from the male deities of traditional Christianity into a new-age "romper room" dance with the goddess in all Her Christian, pagan, and new-age forms.

She saw that there were only a few attempts to draw back the curtain to reveal that Sophia was a primal Creatrix who was always working in all aspects of creation. During her research, her blinders were removed, and she could suddenly see Sophia shining out from the very pages that she had read previously, where she had ignored Her principal part in creation and its maintenance.

She was shocked to have missed the golden thread of wisdom and providence that runs through all myths, religions, and philosophies. She had been looking for a synthesis of beliefs found in all world religions, and she found Sophia staring at her from the pages of every sacred text reviewed. She did not understand at first that it was simply the way she was raised that had prejudiced her mind from seeing the obvious.

Fortunately, unlike Joseph Campbell, Fritzhof Schuan, and many other thinkers, she discovered her short-sightedness before her twilight years. *The Gospel of Sophia* attempts to resurrect the goddess traditions by showing direct quotes from the world religions, mythology, and philosophy to drive home the point that Sophia has always been in literature and theology, waiting to be brought back from the death that She underwent from 2100 B.C. until our own time.

Some say that it was Lucifer, the great light bringer, who tried to kill Her and take Her far from the perception of the modern, thinking soul. This death was so complete that when male-dominated thinkers are presented with the evidence of Sophia's continued revelation to the human mind through literature and history, they deny it summarily.

The history and literature of modern philosophy and ancient beliefs all comprise part of the biography of Sophia's interaction with the thinking human being. Some of these thoughts have been resurrected by authors like John Lash, who uses the tremendous insights of the Gnostics to create an approach to the true nature of Sophia throughout time. These types of resurrection of Sophia are wonderful.

Sophia, in all Her many forms, must be brought from the grave of sense-bound thinking. Sophia was an integral part of Gnostic creation stories and She is given Her proper respect in the cosmic view of Her central role in spiritual life. Through such efforts to bring the historical significance of Her Wisdom and its applicability to modern questions into our consciousness, Sophia is given back Her crown of gold.

Authors like Arthur Versluis and Richard Leviton do a wonderful job of bringing forward new materials on the thinkers and their sects that placed Sophia as the principal deity of the past. These histories need to be resurrected to shed new light upon the central position of Sophia in the development of beliefs and philosophies.

The Internet has transformed the topology of Sophian studies as the majority of Sophian literature is now available to any independent researcher. Most of the sacred texts of all religions are free online. The opportunity for independent research is unparalleled in history. But even with all of this Sophian literature readily available and brilliant thinkers translating and making commentary on the texts, there is still a short-sighted view of the full threefold biography of Sophia.

The Limits of the Seer

There is a plethora of available material of Wisdom studies and the tremendous efforts and insights of modern thinkers to share their view of Sophia are astounding. Yet, almost all authors, commentators, theorists, and thinkers still arrive at the conclusion that Sophia is an unknowable mystery. The current literature draws a dividing line between that which the thinker is able to explain about Sophia and that which is "an unknowable mystery." This conclusion leaves Sophia again and again marginalized by the limits of the author.

The thinkers describe more their personal limits than a comprehensive view of Sophia in Her threefold nature. *It seems that the limit of the philosopher becomes the limit of the philosophy.* But a close examination of the development of the human intellect reflects the parameters of Sophian Wisdom as an evolving being. (See Appendix A for the traditional view of Sophia.)

"Basically, there is no philosophy of science. No one knows the purpose of knowledge."

In other words, the limited view of Sophia speaks more to the limits of the thinker than the limits of Sophia. As Sophiologists delineate their understanding of the Feminine Godhead, they reveal the limitations of the evolving intellect that conceives of Her divine nature. In fact, the limits of the ancient religion or philosophy were directly connected to their ability to meet and commune with these higher beings (or archetypes) effectively.

For example, prior to 2100 B.C., many ancient cultures were led by priest-kings who were still able to directly perceive and communicate with spiritual beings who worked in the human realm. These ancient teachings have practical wisdom woven throughout all aspects of the religious rites, rituals, and cultural expressions. The general population was only vaguely aware of their thinking, and when they did have thoughts, they were perceived outside of the human body, not locked into a private viewing of mental images in the brain. When an ancient Greek spoke of Athena, the Goddess of Wisdom, he saw Her outside of himself, weaving the wisdom of natural law and providence. Thoughts were commonly shared and perceived by thinkers as living archetypes that had a life of their own. Thinking was a shared perception happening in the ethers between here and the moon.

Aristotle saw these ordered thoughts as a ladder of ten ranks rising up into the living, active realm of creative archetypes. The modern thinker believes his thoughts are private and belong only to him. It is true that the "little" thoughts of most people never reach a thought that is an archetype. Their personal brain-bound thinking is not an active part of living archetypes. For this reason, humans are not yet clairvoyant—because they cannot control their thoughts.

The ugly thoughts that arise from personal desire have no true life of their own and die in the private realm of a brain-bound thinker. Yet, when the spirit inspires, it usually inspires numerous people in different parts of the world simultaneously, as often happens with new inventions. Therefore, Sophia is only limited by the thinker who is pondering Her nature and Her revelation.

We seek the current revelation of Sophia.

First, we need to resurrect Sophia from the death that modern, brain-bound thinking has put Her through and left human thinking in a soulless void of space.

Then, we need to seek Her revelation in our personal lives as an active force of Wisdom that heals and turns all things to love.

Sophia has always been wisdom turning into love in the human being; this is Her mission. Wise people love. That is the long and short of all philosophy, which is the love of wisdom. Wisdom's place in the world is to create natural order that leads all things to evolve towards love, or a universal acceptance of the proper place, nature, and order of all things moving towards perfect union. Wisdom is active in all things and is the source and end of all creation. The intelligent design of the universe is a humble picture of Sophia.

Sophia is also the destroyer and the Mother of Rebirth. Modern thinkers accept that part of Sophia which is death, entropy, and the natural laws that human minds believe to be unchangeable. Some thinkers place Sophia at the moment of creation, and that is an acceptance of Sophia as the Goddess of Birth.

> *"When the spirit inspires, it usually inspires numerous people in different parts of the world simultaneously, as often happens with new inventions."*

But most modern thinkers do not want to look at the rebirth aspect of Sophia. Modern scientists are under the illusion that no new matter can be created. Sophia shows that this is not true. The forces of burgeoning life, levity, and ectropy are living manifestations of active divine forces.

Scientists believe that natural law is immutable, a clock wound up by the Big Bang and now just winding down to death. This idea kills the ability for those scientists to see life properly. They look at life and see death. It is a preposterous game played by male-dominated thinkers who believe that to find an archetype, they should hunt it down and shoot it. Then they can name it after themselves so that it will never change, and they will live in immortality as the "discoverer" of this dead idea.

Scientists and all their believers, called secular humanists, forget that scientific theory changes daily and that no one is updating the textbooks or replacing the "old" theories with the new ones. Basically, there is no philosophy of science. No one knows the purpose of knowledge. We discover new aspects of the natural world and then fail to integrate them with existing knowledge.

Most nonscientists, who are secular humanists and do not necessarily believe in life after death or the spiritual world, are left with the corpses of old theories that lead to dead ends, a bleak world without spirit or meaning. Soon, depression sets in on the modern thinker, who may dwell on being a human on an insignificant planet on the edge of a small, no-big-deal solar system that is miniscule compared to the galaxy. Human life may then seem small, temporary, and an exercise in futility. When cosmic depression sets in, it is easy to say the universe is a dying clock and one lives an insignificant life.

Is that the philosophy of science—to dissect everything to death and then claim there is no life?

To pull up a plant, roots and all, to study its life?

To marginalize and disprove the nature of the Beings behind nature?

One could argue that without a "philosophy of science," science is a butcher who cuts up the meat but has no idea of how to raise the animals that create the meat. Only the study of life as a living, active set of new icons and symbols can solve these materialistic questions.

Sophia's revelations are all around if we could but open our minds and perceive them properly. She can be found everywhere, especially in the *perception* of the person seeking Her. She is, in fact, a marker of the development of the intellect of the person attempting to perceive Her.

Sophia is both natural and supernatural. We know that many of the laws of nature have yet to be found. There are many missing elements in our periodic chart. We have lifted the veils of nature that reveal the awesome forces behind the beauty and wisdom of natural and spiritual law. Humans have only slightly uncovered the dance of atoms, which is the same as the harmony of the spheres of our solar system. When we have discovered a small part of it, we turned it into weapons of mass destruction and nuclear power plants, both of which create deadly materials and wastes that we have no "philosophy" for which to manage the consequences.

We can disturb the dance of atomic material, but we never took the time to think about any of the results of our scientific progress. This indicates that we are no more than infantile thinkers who do not think of the effects prior to taking action on new scientific discoveries. The male-dominated, aggressive, war-like nature of science should be enough of a warning for the moral leaders of culture to limit what science dissects and tortures to find the secrets of Sophia. With this aggressive mentality of materialism, it is a wonder that we have sought out a loving, peaceful, and inspiring relationship with Sophia and Her emissaries.

Often, modern authors want to define Sophia and keep Her bound to the theories they have painstakingly written in their books. Each new author builds on the old and then we have wonderful books filled with historical elucidations of the past that are detailed and precise.

The interpretations of these historical accounts are often limited by the intellectual and spiritual development of the author. Misunderstandings about the so-called historical facts abound. Authors have opposite interpretations of the same historical evidence, and everywhere there is little cohesiveness in a definition of the Divine Feminine, Her nature, and manifestations, as well as Her relationship to the hosts of other beings who work with Her.

Great praise should be given to the historians who are now looking at mythology, archeology, and anthropology in light of the ubiquitous Great Goddess. Numerous encyclopedias of goddesses now exist and wonderfully researched books bring to light an enormous amount of support showing Sophia active in every pantheon, philosophy, and religion.

These resources provide a composite of Sophia in a way never before available to researchers if one can cull through the overwhelming amount of information. For example, it might be interesting to know that Athena was worshiped in three different forms by Athenians and to find the supporting materials available to develop a wide-ranging view of these three different faces of Athena. But what does the reader do with that information?

> *"Sophia is the limit of the mind's ability to cognize the divine."*

We can learn from the ancients. The Greek gods and goddesses were "seen" and "felt" and interacted with all of the Greek people. At the height of Athenian worship, every Athenian felt Athena in his soul and spirit as a threefold goddess of wisdom, beauty, and victory. If you stopped an Athenian and asked him where Athena was, he would point to the Acropolis, which he knew for certain was the location of her physical home. Athena's existence in her temples proved her presence outside of their own bodies in a common place of shared perception.

Eventually, the Greek people became more independent and felt that Athena had come to reside in their bodies as a threefold force of thinking, feeling, and willing. Certainly the perception of an entire culture was not wrong. Eventually, we see individuals like Aristotle begin to order the nature of thinking as a ladder that ascends the rungs of principles and forces into the realm of living archetypes. Even a modern, clear thinker like Aristotle speaks of living beings that humans can reach through thought. Thinking descended into Aristotle from a common world of thought; then he ordered it by rank and category.

Later, Christian thinkers like Thomas Aquinas would also write about these ranks as spiritual hierarchies of angels. This dynamic interaction with a living world of beings is now called by Sophiologists the "Soul of the World," and they try to equate it to the Holy Spirit or some such association. Whether it be the ancient Indian teachings about Vac, the Goddess of Sound (Word) who spoke the trinity of Brahma, Vishnu, and Shiva into existence, or the Persian teachings about the Flowering of the Mind creating breath, mind divine, and august love, or the Egyptian teachings about Isis, Osiris, and Horus, Sophia is the primal trinity who created all beings and maintains the natural and supernatural laws that govern those beings and their manifestations.

Sophia is the limit of the mind's ability to cognize the divine. That is why a trinity is used to define the highest male God: the Father, the Son, and the Holy Spirit. A trinity presents not only a paradox—which goes beyond the mind's abilities to cognize and must be accepted by faith—but also a second paradox within that paradox; and yes, again a third paradox also within the concept of the Holy Trinity.

When the ancients said—and they all did—that Sophia (the Great Goddess), the Goddess of Birth, Death, and Rebirth, was a trinity, they knew that the normal intellectual mind could not get past the first paradox. That is a given. The spiritual world cannot be cognized with the normal thinking intellect. This is represented by the paradox that hides the true nature of the trinity.

The ancients, and moderns for the most part, cannot explain Sophia. Therefore, they hide Her in a trinity of paradoxes. The powers of the Fates, for example, were seen as a trinity in most myths and legends—three sisters who ruled the lives and deaths of even the gods and goddesses. As part of their emanation, trinities have great mysteries that reveal the true nature of the divine. They have been described in all beliefs as the past, present, and future power of Wisdom.

What is this essential power of the divine that is represented in the trinity of gods or goddesses?

Why is the trinity such an accurate, yet "nonlogical" part of worship of the divine?

Sophia is threefold in one sense because She combines the forces of the surrounding stars with the forces of the sun and the forces of the planets.

Humans, like Sophia, are also threefold. That is why our resonance with the truth of the trinity is so profoundly accurate in its application. We tend to reflect these forces in our heads as a model of the spherical universe presenting the starry heavens all around us as thinking, or mental images of the perceptions of thinking. Second, we reflect the solar forces of the sun in our own hearts, where warmth is added to the body through the fiery process of breath, which gives rise to our feelings. The third force is given by the moon, which reflects the forces of the stars, sun, and planets and is found microcosmically in the seven organs that are sheltered under our rib cage as a model of the planets in our solar system that spin around our heart as the sun.

This trinity of forces in the human is quite complex. Sometimes, it is very hard for the individual to manage. Understanding these forces brings self-knowledge; managing them brings self-development.

The Divine Feminine Trinity is profound and far-reaching, with countless ramifications and applications to the human archetypes of body, soul, and spirit—or thinking, feeling, and willing. Logic is only somewhat useful when trying to balance the three soul forces. Desire is often the victor in many internal disputes as logic and duty are set aside.

> *"Sophia is only limited by the limits the perceiver brings to Her manifestation."*

The human is a trinity of forces just as Sophia is a Trinity. At the Temple of Sais there is an inscription that reads: "I am Isis, I am the past, the present, and the future. No man has lifted my veil and lived."

This claim to be a trinity that transcends time is a key factor for developing the faith one may need to understand the nature of a trinity.

One thing is certain; the clairvoyants of the past all saw Sophia (in whatever name) as a living trinity who extends beyond time and space. Essentially, existing as a trinity of the divine predicates that the trinity is beyond space because it can be three places at once, and it is beyond time as Isis who is the "past, the present, and the future."

Isn't a human similar to this threefold nature of Sophia? At the moment of birth, a mother knows that death may be the result. Later she can give birth again in the same womb. To the ancients, the birthing woman was the representative of the Great Goddess of birth, death, and rebirth, who is beyond space and time just as Her representative in a human mother replicates Her mysteries.

It is very difficult for a male-dominated religion, philosophy, or science to perceive the simple truth that remains a mystery. Try as they will, no comprehensive philosophy of science can explain human origins, their current capacities, or provide an accurate prediction about where humans are headed. Even the question "What is a human?" has yet to be addressed in any comprehensive way.

Since humans are a mirror of the Great Goddess, we should study the development of what humans have believed or thought about Her because it will be very instructive and illuminate both Sophia and ourselves.

Seeing Sophia as a Trinity is just the outline of the picture. Sophia's Temple of Wisdom is often described as sevenfold, and we can find the human and cosmic corollaries to this picture. We know from clairvoyant seers that the human brain has seven chambers, the human heart has seven chambers, and the human body, which is a copy of our solar system, has a sun (heart) with six planets around it (the organs).

Sophia is our created universe. Therefore, if we can understand the universe of Her created body, we can find it also in the human constitution because we are created in Her image.

Everything in the universe is replicated in the human body.

Everything we can see as we look outward is also found in the human being as we peer inward. We see the universe as ourselves looking back at ourselves. Whether we look at Sophia's threefold, sevenfold, or twelvefold nature, we are looking also at our own bodily nature. Sophia exists outside of time and space and already knows where Her creation is going.

Each individual is a multi-dimensional holographic mirror image of Sophia. That is why She can care for each of us separately and not disperse Her energies. Cognize, debate, and philosophize all you want about the being of Sophia; you can never reach a conclusion, because your consciousness arriving at that new conclusion just extended the collective understanding of Sophia's Wisdom.

The limits of the seer are the limits of what is seen. Therefore, the existing literature is somewhat a disappointment in its scope.

For instance, when the Christian theologian who first associated Sophia with the Holy Spirit came up with this idea, he probably thought it was a new and ingenious concept that solved many problems in his personal belief system. He convinced others he was right, and soon Sophia was looked at in this particular, limited way. Consequently, philosophers and theologians stop looking for Her in any other place and hold on to this limited view.

The conundrum is that the female spirit of the Earth keeps appearing to people at the source of springs, at holy places, and through personal encounters. Those that have authentic experiences of Her cannot accept the limited view given by spiritual authorities because their encounter is something quite different. Theologians absorbed the ancient cults of the goddess and subsume the holy sites into their repertoire of accepted rituals and traditions.

Subsequently, Mother Mary devotions abound. The Catholic Church makes Mary Immaculate and the Mother of God, then has her assumed into heaven physically. Millions of pilgrims visit these Gaia sites and commune with the spirits that existed before Christianity and will exist far into the future—and may have nothing to do with Mary, the mother of Jesus.

Sophia as the Mother of the Earth will never leave; She created this planet and keeps it in balance with the starry, solar, and planetary forces around us.

Sophia is only limited by the limits the perceiver brings to Her manifestation. Thoughts are often Earth-bound, sense-bound, and cannot cognize the possibilities of spaceless and timeless thoughts. Yet, they will have to if they wish to truly begin to see Sophia, Her accomplishments, and Her plan for the future.

The telling of Sophia's story is one that is beyond belief, a few times over. It is three biographies of a Divine Being that is equal to and perhaps greater than the male trinity. These biographies must be taken on faith, for without faith, you will not gain the wings to ascend to Sophia's active revelation and bridge the multiple paradoxes found in Her nature.

A complete biography of Sophia will pull from the familiar and the new and will point in directions that will someday become commonplace wisdom that enlightens the nature of human destiny and the path to godhood. Some elements of Sophia's biography will be far beyond belief but still can be weighed against the morality in one's heart to find out if they ring true. Some other descriptions of the future will be so far beyond belief that only the fiery courage to selflessly examine the ideas without prejudice will lead beyond the capacities of those who have not seen the golden thread of destiny in their own lives.

Only by becoming objective global beings who communicate with the hierarchy of beings surrounding us will we be able to hold such profound wisdom in our souls. It will take expanding the parameters of our belief system to reach into the revelation of the spirit that brings all life to Earth and can hold all death with the wisdom to know that life will be born again and resurrection is assured. This alone is the ancient wisdom that can lead us beyond the threshold of death and sense perception into the world of the spirit, which is inhabited by a hierarchy of beings who are deeply concerned with our spiritual growth.

Natural and Supernatural Forces

What researchers of truth need now are wings of soul that can take us across the threshold into the spirit lands where we can nourish ourselves each night through communion with the divine. These wings must sprout from our hearts as materialistic thoughts do not rise up or give us flight in thoughts or dreams.

Wings of soul give rise to spiritual thoughts that defy space and time. They engender the courage to temper our imaginations into wisdom that lights the fires of inspiration, allowing free deeds of love. Once those wings are earned, we become angels. Then we can journey beyond the limited logic of materialism and wing our way to insight that is born of spiritual wonders far beyond all sense-bound perception.

Sophia is an ever-changing whirlwind of wonder and power found in both the large and small. When authors write about Her, they cannot be other than limited and superficial. All of the books in the world are written about Her, and yet She is hardly known. The very process of knowing is one of Her intimate domains, where She is always changing and growing together with human development.

> *"The limits of the seer are the limits of what is seen."*

As humans evolve, so do our interactions with Sophia. She is, more or less, the collective intellectual evolution of humanity as She leads us all forward to merge with the future nature of humanity that She has already prepared for us. The primal cause and meaning of universal and personal evolution are designed by the Beings of Wisdom, the Kyriotetes, led by Sophia. Sophia orders the ranks of all beings, so any author is remiss not to introduce the ranks of hierarchies involved in the cosmic dance with Sophia. Beyond the ranks of the hierarchy, Sophia exists as a co-equal female Trinity coupled with the male Trinity of Father, Son, and Holy Spirit, or Brahma, Vishnu, and Shiva, or any other sun-oriented trinities.

There are numerous descriptions of Sophia as the female aspect of God during creation. This TheoSophia is ever present and found throughout creation as God's epiphany or reflection. She is seldom given co-equal status, even though the sacred texts tell stories of the way She was present before any of the gods and She was the first "non-created substance" upon which creation was written or spoken by God. Therefore, reality is the opposite of what is being told by the male-dominated thinkers who changed the stories.

"Great souls are twinned as male/female as they come into this realm of dualism. Every God has his Goddess in the greater scheme of things, and every light creates a shadow in this world of day and night, waking and sleeping, life and death."

What these authors are saying is that God the Father is non-created (unmanifested) and that it is Sophia's "word" that brought about creation. In this view, whether described as the Big Bang creation or creation via the spoken word, or creation as the dance of the Goddess, Sophia was there at the moment of creation and seems to have inherited creation from that moment forward. God was there to seed creation somehow and then disappear, leaving Sophia to tend creation as the leader of the Beings of Wisdom and Dominion, who rule and order the universe.

God the Father is often considered to be the ground of being, a holy ground somewhere unreachable, unattainable, and unmanifest. No one gets to look God the Father in the eye. This is also a description of super-massive black holes that are found at the core of most galaxies. These black holes are swallowing millions of stars into a place about which scientists can only speculate. Where do they go? And then, at the heart of other galaxies, there is a super-massive ion jet that whirls out millions of stars from seemingly nowhere. Where do these stars come from? These dynamic forces of creation and destruction can be icons for a new understanding in Father God—Mother Goddess dynamics. Galaxies have a heart that rhythmically alters between creation and destruction (and then creation again). This cycle is found not only in galaxies, but also in atoms, in cells, and throughout the human body.

This fantastic image of male/female dynamics in the process of creation in the material world is a beautiful leading image that shows the power of the unmanifested Father God in the black hole that swallows creation and the Mother Goddess in the effulgent fountain of new-born suns arising from a super-massive ion jet.

In the black hole's "active darkness" of wonder and speculation, everyone is transfixed. It would be hard to look directly at the yawning jaws of death without fear, awe, and reverence, the very qualities for which the male god is known. Sharing this same space is the female image of "manifested" creation as a super-massive ion jet that whirls out millions of stars into its galaxy. Both of these images are nearly incomprehensible; yet, they fit together perfectly. The rhythmic alternation from one to the other seems as natural as waking and sleeping.

A similar process of sweeping alternation between manifestation and unmanifestation is found in Hindu beliefs that tell a similar story. Hindus believe that creation undergoes alternating periods of outward, creative manifestation in rhythmic periods of time called manvantaras, or physical manifestation. The opposite periods of darkness, called pralayas, happen when matter becomes an amorphous "soup" that reorganizes the material for the next outward manvantara, similar to a caterpillar in its cocoon bursting forth as a butterfly. Pralayas are incomprehensible to the intellect because all matter as we know it turns into another type of substance of which we cannot conceive with a sense-bound brain.

These are natural and supernatural forces at which we can only marvel, considering their power and majesty. Is there a philosophy or religion that can explain these cosmic forces of birth, death, and rebirth? Perhaps not, but since we live in a holographic universe, we see that even the growing plant reflects these rhythms of growth and decay on a small scale. Every seed grows into leaf, stem, and fruit filled with new seeds that birth only after falling to the Earth and dying in the darkness of the soil, ready to burst forth again when spring arrives.

Black holes and ion jets also live in our hearts as the rhythmic falling into the void that accompanies each heartbeat, followed by a fountain of warmth and movement that fills the body with harmony and nourishment. We need more pliable icons that include supernatural forces in our cosmology of the human and the world. Then, surely, Sophia would come into view.

The same mathematical harmonies are found in cyclones and star clusters, sea shells, and galaxies. Humans are looking into mirrors whether we look inside or outside, and we see nothing but ourselves. Until our consciousness has evolved to that of an angel, we cannot be expected to see the world as anything else but created just for us, the center of the universe. This childish view is so unevolved that it is hard for a being of higher thinking to even imagine our limited perspective.

Imagine a scientist arguing with an angel that the angel does not exist. Who will win the argument?

Imagine a theologian telling Sophia that She cannot exist, or better yet, can take a secondary role as a mirror, or a part of the male trinity, or perhaps even the Holy Spirit.

Once we develop new icons that can lead culture to a broader view of the world and humanity's place in it, then a more accurate description of natural and supernatural forces will enable a balance of the trinity of Father, Mother, and Child forces that are active in the human and the cosmos. These icons and symbols are effective tools of self-knowledge that illuminate the nature of the human being as a composite of body, soul, and spirit.

"We have all been mothers in one incarnation or another."

Unfortunately, marginalizing the power of the Great Goddess is a standard response of male-dominated thinking. Any serious researcher of truth would take a closer look and discover that the feminine is primal in human embryological development. We were all female before the sexes were separated in evolution. Each newborn reminds us that the ten months in utero recapitulate key parts of human development, that all humans are initially female. It is nearly impossible to marginalize the female in physiological development.

Theosophists and Anthroposophists believe that before recorded history, there was an ancient time and land called Atlantis. Prior to Atlantis were other large eras of development called Lemuria, Hyperborea, and Polaria. These spans of time and their subsequent evolution are fantastic, to say the least.

During the period called Hyperborea, all humans were female. The sweeping pictures used to describe this time period defy general human imagination and point at central questions of sexuality and the roles of gender in spiritual development. Humans are made to be parthenogenic (female birthing female) in this view of human evolution and only later separated into male and female when the Moon separated from the Earth during Lemurian times. These images are icons and symbols of worlds that humans have seldom imagined. They are an integral part of the collective consciousness of human development that show a primal reverence for the feminine. These mysteries of sex are woven into the natural wisdom of the human body and its evolution.

Some authors say that angels and the spiritual hierarchy are not female in nature and ignore the primal forces of the "mothers" in the process of creation and its maintenance. We have all been mothers in one incarnation or another. We need to understand that the female sources of human wisdom and love commune with a living hierarchy of beings against which the male-dominated thinker has warred with savage brutality.

In the shame of death and destruction of world wars and endless killing, Sophia has been present to tend every wound and accept every soul into Her bosom. Sophia is night, death, hell realms, and prisons of the human mind where no one dares enter. If there is consciousness in any form or at any level, Sophia must be there to record and associate all that is manifest in relation to Wisdom.

Creation and destruction, male and female, black hole and ion jet all show the simple reality of dualism in the created world. Great souls are twinned as male/female as they come into this realm of dualism. Every God has his Goddess in the greater scheme of things, and every light creates a shadow in this world of day and night, waking and sleeping, life and death. The duality of this world is clearly described by ancient

Persians, through the teachings of Zarathustra, as forces of light and darkness, Ahura Mazdao and Ahriman. The Gnostics had cosmic twin aeons that birthed our world, Sophia and Anthropos. These teachings are instructive for creating living images that illuminate imagination with sense-free thinking concerning hierarchical beings that create our world.

These ancient teachings are excellent ways to re-experience what prior cultures have reported of their experience of the Feminine Divine. Hundreds of books on these topics are now available, many for free. This history of Sophia can be accessed through any search engine, and we can easily access the texts of sacred mysteries with a click of a mouse.

Analyzing a collection of historical perspectives of Sophia is one path to resurrect Her central importance in the development of human thinking throughout history. It is good to see so many authors working with new perspectives and respect for the Earth, the forces of nature, and the animals and plants we share with Gaia as our home.

Sophia Consciousness can be found everywhere, yet there is still no consensus on who the Goddess is, exactly why She was hidden and willfully maligned and destroyed, or where She is now and what She is doing. Nowhere in the literature were descriptions of Sophia found that illuminated the past or consciously resurrected the full image of the rightful place of Sophia. Besides Valentin Tomberg and a few Gnostic sects, no one has acknowledged that Sophia should be raised to the rank of a Divine Feminine Trinity. Nowhere was a comprehensive story written of the most wondrous biographies in history, the biographies of the Great Mother, Her Daughter Sophia, and the Holy Sophia of Wisdom. Through becoming the Mother, the Sister, and the Spiritual Consort of Christ Jesus, Mary/Sophia/Eve Kadmon became the Heavenly Witness of the Mystery of Christ, the birth of the Earth as a new star. Sophia is helping Christ turn the Earth into a sun for a future that will shine love on all beings.

Only Sophia the Goddess of Wisdom (Kyriotetes) and the Archangel Michael, who was known as the countenance of Christ, could endure witnessing the full meaning of the redemption of the Earth through Christ's sacrifice: that a God would become man. Sophia became human, over-lighting Mary for eleven years during Her passion and devotion in ministering the Wisdom of the hierarchies to the followers of Christ. Mary became the Vessel of Wisdom for Sophia for eleven years and taught John the Divine what he would write in his Gospel, Epistles, and the Apocalypse.

Mary was transformed through the Heavenly forces of Sophia the Daughter as She became Wisdom incarnate. Mary's body was taken whole into the heavens before Her many followers. Since then, She has never ceased to appear to believers throughout the world at chosen spots where the forces are ripe for listening to the direct revelation of Sophia.

Sophia the Daughter came to Earth as the second person in the Divine Feminine Trinity through the ranks of the Kyriotetes, the Heavenly Beings of Wisdom. Her story of suffering was coupled with Christ's passion, as She accompanied him in birth, death, and resurrection. Sophia the Daughter is the spiritual consort of Christ, and living witness and vessel of redeemed suffering, which constitutes the foundations of the New Mystery of the Incarnation of Wisdom. (See Appendix C.)

Mary's story is intertwined with all stages of Jesus of Nazareth's life and the full incarnation of the Christ into Jesus from the time of His baptism in the Jordan until his ascension into heaven. Mary was united with both the Eve Kadmon (Eve's Paradisiacal Spirit) and the Goddess of Wisdom. She had also received from Jesus, prior to his baptism in the Jordan, the wisdom that he had acquired from age twelve to thirty and the

> *"Only living archetypes taken directly from the spiritual world will unlock the doors to our higher spiritual self."*

wisdom of the other Jesus who had died at age twelve. Mary became Mary/ Eve/Sophia in one, and the spiritual vessel that mirrored the incarnation of Christ into Jesus of Nazareth.

This relationship is truly a Mystery of Wisdom that only a few authors have addressed. It is this side of Sophia that is lacking in the currently available literature. Anthroposophists like Rudolf Steiner, Sergei Prokofieff, Emil Bock, and a few others address the deeper aspects of Sophia in her threefold nature.

Sophia is the most complex of hierarchical beings. Her sacrifice of descending from the Trinity to the rank of a human is one of the untold stories of human spiritual evolution. To develop a clear picture of all the avenues that must be traveled to see Sophia in her depth, breath, and width takes years of open-minded study and contemplation.

Many researchers of Sophia's Wisdom are overwhelmed with the tremendous resources available about the historical Sophia and do not know how to integrate that material into a new, resurrected cosmology of Sophian revelation. How can a researcher make Sophia relevant without simply reusing old forms and descriptions? Where do we find Wisdom revealing Herself in our apocalyptic age?

We need new symbols and icons to represent a Living Imagination of the spirit and its workings. It is the Sophian Wisdom about the cosmic nature of Christ, how both Sophia and Christ are found in the human being, that forms the elements of this Living Imagination.

Only living archetypes taken directly from the spiritual world will unlock the doors to our higher spiritual self and its threefold nature.

Sophia is the leader of humanity who has already traveled the path through the soul aspects of the human being into the future aspects of the spirit. The highest soul qualities are developed with Sophia's help until they can become the chalice that receives higher thinking as nourishment.

This *earthly and cosmic nutrition stream* needs to be understood by spiritual practitioners and is described in detail in Volume 2 of this Gospel. Sophia is the collective group consciousness that accompanies all souls in their strivings into the spirit world to receive this nourishment. She is the guide that enkindles the flame of Christ in the human heart, giving it wings to rise to the Temple of Wisdom.

Both the normal stream of etherized elements and the second stream of Christ ether entwine and grow as the new Tree of Life sprouting from the heart and rising to the head. This Christened ether stream represents the Tree of Life, while the other ether stream represents the Tree of Knowledge of Good and Evil. As they intertwine and grow together as one, they rise up through the throat and brow and into the pineal gland, which can be seen as the Grail Castle.

Spiritual, supersensible realities are there for the trained seer to witness. Living streams of spiritual and material forces rising up as offerings to the pineal gland, where calcium carbonate crystals form in response to being bathed by these ether streams, represent a Living Imagination in a symbol filled with wisdom. This picture of the human and cosmic nutrition streams in the human heart is part of the new icons and symbols that can lead humans to see and hear supersensible truths that demonstrate the workings of the hierarchies in human physiology.

Everything in the world corresponds to human physiology. The human being is the image of the universe, the hieroglyphic monad, as some have called it. The outside world is a projection of human consciousness. This means that as consciousness evolves, so does the ability to see, hear, and understand aspects of nature that were previously supersensible, or apparently invisible. Someday, we will stop projecting our limited view onto perception and will simply perceive the living beings behind all sense perception.

It is all well and good to resurrect the past and see it in a new light. Likewise, it is worthwhile to research the true biographies of Sophia, but we must create a new living cosmology that is supported through the best that science has to offer. A new synthesis is necessary as a new beginning—one that does not marginalize either side of the story.

We must examine the world with different senses, new organs that will perceive beings, archetypes and living hierarchies that create and sustain our world. Science makes new discoveries every day that show some marvelous aspect of Sophia. Yet, without a cosmology in which to frame the discovery, it gets lost in the global information and communications network.

We need a new image of the human as a spiritual being who can operate in multiple dimensions simultaneously and who can learn to retrain her vibrations to harmonious resonant frequencies that penetrate and maintain the scaffolding of creation.

"Wisdom requires us to become a warrior, to regain lost ground, and then surge forward with a new banner that combines our eternal longing for Sophian Wisdom with tangible spiritual insight."

We can create a new vision of the divine as male/female trinities with co-equal natures who have sent their beloved children (Christ/Sophia) to the Earth to endure the divine becoming human to conquer the forces of death.

We can restore the primal rights of the Eternal Feminine through a synthesis of ideas that help define Wisdom as She appears to humans at different stages of evolution.

We can create a new cosmology that better defines our known universe and humanity's place in that evolution.

We can create new images of the redeemed Garden of Eden or New Jerusalem or Shamballa, true pictures of human spiritual development that directly relate to co-creation with the divine.

These new icons can bring insight into the living nature of the supersensible forces all about us. They will indicate the future direction of science, art, and religion and the spiritual development of humanity.

The shortcoming that we find in most literature on Sophia is the lack of leading images that can fire the imagination to deeds of love. Wisdom requires us to become warriors, to regain lost ground, and then surge forward with a new banner that combines our eternal longing for Sophian Wisdom with tangible spiritual insight. We who stand watch for Her return must give wings to our Imaginations and draw from the future guiding images that will one day be as commonplace as Sophia and Christ walking among us. Sophia is the Wisdom that illuminates Christ's cosmic nature and leads humans into their true spiritual natures.

View of Anthroposophia

One's consciousness begins to expand.

One's soul begins to stir.

One's spirit begins to awaken.

Rudolf Steiner pointed out that the Egyptians and the Greeks saw a being outside of themselves that they referred to as TheoSophia, the Wisdom of God. This being belonged to no single individual, yet was the common experience of every philosopher who rose up to meet her in the air between the Earth and the Moon.

Later, this being came ever closer to mankind. The great philosophers of the scholastic period developed what seemed to be a more personal relationship with this being. They called her Philo-sophia. With the advent of Anthroposophy, Rudolf Steiner created a body of work that describes the physical and spiritual nature of the world and the place of mankind as an evolving spiritual being within this world. Since the founding of the first Goetheanum, this Being has come ever closer to mankind. Presently, she is found knocking at the heart of each aspirant, interacting with the effects of living with the content of Anthroposophy as it helps our spirit evolve.

This Being, AnthropoSophia, is intimately aware of each spiritual struggle and success that the aspirant experiences. In a way, she is the midwife of our higher selves, helping us bear the pangs of spirit-birth into this new land.

AnthropoSophia is beyond the work of Rudolf Steiner and Novalis. She awaits the spirit-courage of each individual to forge his or her own path to the Spirit Self through the Consciousness Soul, that part of ourselves we call the higher self. In the future, she will evolve to become the fully active earthly and cosmic nutrition stream that feeds the soul and spirit of each person and the spiritual world: "Give us this day our daily bread."

AnthropoSophia is the pure virgin maiden who awaits the sacred marriage and sleeps not, lest she miss the coming of the groom.

At this point in spiritual evolution, any striving soul can build a bridge across the abyss of modern thinking to reach the land of imaginative archetypes that enliven souls who witness the spirit. Great thinkers have suffered to find insight on every common path or highway. But when their wisdom is housed together as a pillared temple of beautiful wisdom (Pansophia), we can all see the higher self that is the image of beauty found in the mirror of nature and self.

> *"At this point in spiritual evolution, any striving soul can build a bridge across the abyss of modern thinking to reach the land of imaginative archetypes that enliven souls who witness the spirit."*

Every striving modern thinker can find Wisdom as close as her own breath, heartbeat, or thought. AnthropoSophia is our spiritual mirror image that shows us that we are, indeed, the "fairest in the land." Wisdom illuminates beauty and births good deeds. Every precept is filled with beauty, wisdom, and the forces of good in nature and ourselves.

We no longer need to enjoy nature as a Sentient Soul, nor understand nature as an Intellectual Soul. We need to commune with nature as a Consciousness Soul that artistically finds moral application for the terrific forces hidden in her beauty. Humans must rule nature for good, not ill. That is the challenge of the Consciousness Soul Epoch: to understand the forces of birth and death and apply them to further positive spiritual development.

The forces of eugenics (birth-mysteries) unlock genetics while the forces of mechanical occultism unlock the forces of physical immortality (death-mysteries and the future). Physical, material forces will try to convince mankind that it is bound by matter instead of the moral insight that humans are consciousness and are not limited by genetics or death—because humans are immortal spirits supported by hygienic occultism (life forces).

This simple wisdom has been lost to many modern thinkers because they have cut their connection to the spiritual world, where they came from before birth and will return to after death. This materialistic blindness is a tragic illness that keeps the spirit world in dark shadows for many people who do not know the face of Wisdom, Sophia, or the love of Christ.

Through the great apocalyptic challenges of modern times, many people have seen the truth and distilled their wisdom in simple words. Each of the writers quoted in this book has found his and her way through the darkness of Kali Yuga to the New Age of the Archangel Michael (started in 1879).

Wisdom lives and breathes everywhere, if you look closely.

People are awakening to their Divine Natures.

Life is a balancing act; what you end up seeing depends on where you place your focus.

Isis-Sophia
by Rudolf Steiner

Isis-Sophia,
Wisdom of God:
Lucifer has slain her,
and on the wings of the world-wide Forces
Carried her hence into Cosmic space.
Christ-Will, working in man:
Shall wrest from Lucifer
and on the boats of Spirit-knowledge
Call to new life in souls of man
Isis-Sophia, Wisdom of God.

The Temple of Wisdom

The First Goetheanum
Art by Claudia Gimenez

Pillar One

The Many Faces of Sophia

Humility

You are the temple palace that calls forth the scene
Upon which all history awakes as an innocent dream.

Sophia has had many faces and many names throughout history, but one of the best names is *mirror*.

She has been called the Mirror of God the Father, God the Son, and God the Holy Spirit, often being confused with being one and the same. Some great thinkers believe she mirrors the epiphany of the unmanifest Father God bringing into existence the knowable world in all of its variegated forms. Gnostics believe that at the moment of creation, Sophia and Her Consort were both swirled into existence as two parts of the same being.

Sophia (Wisdom) and Her Consort, Christ (Love) are two sides of the same coin—or the face and the reflection in the mirror. Incarnation into the dualistic physical world, by necessity, causes the spirit to split into two parts that continuously long for reunion. This duality of being comes into manifestation as the twin forces of nature—birth and death.

When Sophia and Christ are reunited, a third possibility comes into existence as the force of resurrection. The uniting of the two poles of female/male, space/time, birth/death, and the many other polarities found in nature creates the possibility of resurrection—new births that lead to reunion with the divine and immortality.

The mirror-like reflection that Sophia provides to any of Her counterparts unites the poles and brings forth creation out of nothingness as a true act of Wisdom and love that transcends duality and manifests a trinity of birth, death, and rebirth.

This triple force of nature was often attributed to the Magna Mater or Great Mother of the ancients. But if we do not linger for a while on the dynamics of the polarity of nature, we may miss some of the subtleties. For instance, the mirror of Sophia reflects back the reversed image of the consort or beloved.

Sophia and her consort are not the same being, nor do they look alike. Sophia is actively engaged in being a mirror, not projecting an image as does her consort when he looks into her nature. When he sees himself looking back at himself, we call this self-knowledge. He does not see the nature of the mirror, its characteristics, or the true mirror there in front of him. He sees only a reversed image of himself. This is a most important distinction.

Sophia is not an exact replica of the other. *She is a mirror.* Her human consort may not understand Her mechanism of reflection at all and may be quite busy simply studying the aspects of himself that She reflects. And again, even the reflection is reversed and can be quite confusing when trying to interact with the image. Is Sophia just the reflection of, or the same as, Her beloved? Do they grow together and change over time?

If we see Mother Nature as an aspect of Sophia and examine the description of a mirror in relationship to nature, we gain further insight.

When a scientist performs an experiment on an element of nature, we know that a principle of quantum mechanics is that the observation of the scientist may change the substance and nature of what he is observing. This is much like the mood of the person looking in the mirror determining the image that he sees.

Perception changes as the consciousness of the observer changes. When you are in a great mood, it changes the perception of how you feel when you walk away from the mirror—a lighter, more buoyant image. If depressed, the image may look depressed. So Sophia, as the personification of Mother Nature, may mirror back that the harmonic motion of an atom is beautiful to behold. On the other hand, another mirrored image of the atom could include the forces that can create a chain reaction leading to a nuclear explosion. This teaches us that one can witness the forces in nature, but it is up to the observer to decide what to do with the perception.

This is similar to the image of Sophia as a mirror. She can reflect many different faces to the beloved without changing Her nature. Two parts of the same whole may not be exactly alike. One coin may have two images that are naturally joined but are quite different.

One could argue that any discussion of Sophia, the Being of Wisdom, is simply an exercise of the evolving human intellect. As human consciousness and the intellect have developed over the centuries, so has the understanding and image of the Being of Wisdom. Therefore, anyone who tries to describe Wisdom is simply expressing the limitations of his own intellect or imagination.

Even cleaning the mirror and learning how it is made and what substances create the ability to reflect light back to the viewer will not necessarily change the image the observer sees. The observer's attitude directly impacts the perceived image and its effect on the observer. If Wisdom is seen as necessary to understanding God, nature, or the creation of the universe, then the Being of Wisdom enhances the image as the human being increases in knowledge and wisdom.

The image of a holographic mirror is also instructive. Imagine that Wisdom is a multi-dimensional holographic mirror that reflects the observer looking at herself and the surrounding world. Then, the mirror breaks into many pieces. The observer would still be able to *see* her entire image in each individual piece of the shattered mirror, for each represents the whole. Each atom of nature is just that, filled with Wisdom and power, informing the observer about her own wisdom and power. Once the consciousness of the observer evolves and develops, so will the image of Sophia as Wisdom.

> *"As each human grows in consciousness, so Wisdom grows."*

The great religious leaders and thinkers of the past had limited linguistic expression for Wisdom, so they chose images, symbols, and parables to express their relationship with Sophia. She has been referred to as a mirror, a ladder, the Temple of Wisdom with seven pillars, the pala of wisdom spread out in the sky as the Milky Way, and thousands of other images and symbols that describe the human's developing consciousness with his *other part*, the vast Wisdom of nature that informs him of his place, his relationship to the whole. These images and symbols have changed throughout history in mythologies, fairy tales, parables, religions, aboriginal beliefs, and scientific theories.

Super-massive black holes and galactic ion jets alternate in the heart of galaxies and are known to create or destroy billions of stars in their center. This icon of galactic polarity broadens the natural human intellect. It enhances the picture in the mirror, the image of Wisdom. As the beholder grows and evolves, so does the image that Sophia reflects. The observer gathers one piece of the holographic mirror after the other in his attempt to understand Wisdom. The image of himself also grows larger and more encompassing. Now, the full picture can be seen, and the surrounding landscape also comes into view.

As the observer steps back from the mirror, he sees an even grander perspective, and his own image takes a less prominent position. Eventually, the observer may ask who and what is this mirror? Why is it that the observer can only know himself through seeing his image in a mirror that is clean and directed at him? So the question might arise: "Who is this mirror and why is it somewhat selfless in its design? Does the mirror also grow in its capacities, and what does it gain from the relationship with the observer?"

Often Sophia is seen as that which was there before creation began, the cosmic soup of undifferentiated matter many call the "primal waters" that are responsive to the urges of creation. In this way, wisdom is seen as the result of creation but not the active force; thus, the analogy of the mirror.

"Sophia is the skein of time upon which history is written, or the primal ocean of waters that separates each element as a birth of another child."

Wisdom is imagined as selfless. It is not usually thought of as the prime motive force. Wisdom receives creation, then becomes Mother of the created, responsible for them until they reunite with the unmanifest, the source of the picture of wholeness.

Sophia is the skein of time upon which history is written, or the primal ocean of waters that separates each element as a birth of another child.

She is found throughout all of creation, but philosophers have resisted stating the obvious: that She is a Creatrix or co-creator of all things known by human consciousness. This is analogous to God looking in the mirror, seeing creation, and being happy with what He saw.

Sophia, as a mirror, is selfless. She takes on the shape of God even though She is the vehicle for self-reflection of creation. God is subjective and Sophia is objective. To co-create, they must unite. Most creation myths start with the primal waters of a feminine deity who was in existence before God had the impulse to create a world for awakening humans. God is the unmanifest, while Sophia is the manifest universe. As the body of God, Sophia is the one who *fell* into existence. God is somehow untouched and unscathed by creation and, in effect, has left this world to Sophia to rule and complete the intent of creation. Sophia and humanity are thus bound together in this mutual mission of redeeming the world we have *fallen* into as we reunite the duality of Wisdom and Love.

Humans try to find the truth and wisdom in the world to create an aligned vision of unity and redemption. Each small step of knowing that leads to broader consciousness changes the person who embodies those higher principles. The image of the observer looking into the mirror of nature changes with each interaction that leads to higher Wisdom. As humans unite the duality between themselves and the world, they are led to a sacred marriage of Wisdom and Love through human consciousness.

Sophia is already the known universe, and She alone knows the mechanism of the mirror that can reflect all as though each individual was the only one looking in the mirror. In these matters, Sophia does not lead the observer to consciousness but is intimately interacting with the growing perspective of the awakening consciousness. She witnesses each and every change. She knows how it links to the past and the evolution of the consciousness of Her beloved observer.

The growth of the observer is just as precious to Sophia as the growth of a child is to his parents. The universe is deeply concerned with the growth of consciousness because it is composed primarily of consciousness; the evolution of consciousness, in fact, is the goal of creation.

As each human grows in consciousness, so Wisdom grows. One could imagine it as the collective consciousness of all humans growing with Wisdom. What one individual accomplishes is available for all others who come along that path. The trailblazers of consciousness have left a path—symbols carved on milestones and stories told to people along the way—that reveals the archetypes of nature in the world and human soul.

We can read about the revelations of Wisdom that great religions, myths, philosophers, and thinkers have left behind, thereby broadening our view of what Wisdom is and our relationship to Her.

If we can hold the image of Sophia as a mirror of nature, wherein we can see our own image evolving, then we can include in our consciousness the sum total of our development. The essence of knowing about our evolving consciousness brings a more fully developed perception of ourselves to the image in the mirror.

We can only know who we are through the reflection we see of ourselves in others. Others hold the full picture of who we are searching to become. In effect, we become the mirror to others and likewise they to us. We can reflect back to others their animal or divine nature based upon our own understanding of Wisdom.

Only Wisdom can reflect back to the beholder Wisdom. As a cosmic mirror, Sophia is a device that humans cannot comprehend except as an abstract concept. A holographic cosmic mirror is quite beyond logical, linear thinking. But we are each similarly a mirror to all other humans that stand before us, for we reflect back to them who they are. We can even choose to reflect higher or lower aspects of the person using us as a mirror as he views his own self-consciousness. We can hold perfectly still and let him see himself in stark contrast, or we can choose a fainter light that may not reflect the furrows and lines on his countenance so clearly.

The mirror analogy can go both ways, and it is quite useful to see the world as a *looking glass universe* with holographic principles underlying it. Some astrophysicists say that we are looking into a spherical mirror in all directions and that ultimately we are looking at ourselves. The universe is filled with two hundred billion galaxies, and our brains are filled with two hundred billion neurons. There is mirroring going on in many ways in our perception of the world. Mirroring is a form of creation.

When the primal waters were still, the divine could see its reflection in the water. One might ask, "Which came first, or did they both manifest at once?" Gnostics would say that God was unmanifest but envisioned creation in its whole from beginning to end and then "He" *made* it.

Perhaps the perception of the universe in God's mind reflected off of the primal waters of Sophia, and this act was creation. It seems logical in the scheme of things, a simple, effective plan. God's self-conscious perception of His *Imagination* kept the perfect form in His mind and allowed the reflection to come into being and suffer the fate of manifestation, a broken holographic mirror of the image of the divine.

Sophia might have mirrored the divine plan, but we should not forget that She was not created by God. She becomes the mirror that must re-*member* that the parts fit back together as one whole mirror reflecting the divine plan with its re-union.

Sophia is the mirror, but each of us is the beholder who can see ourselves reunited with the divine. The observer can only realize this after having seen the duality and reunite the extremes in a whole image of himself, wherein the higher and lower natures of those selves recombine at a higher level.

> *"The author does not believe in the current theory of the Big Bang; she believes in the Big Reflection."*

This is the process the alchemist used when he incorporated a mirror in the transmutation of matter from lower grades of materials into higher ones. The mirror reflects the stage of development that the alchemist had developed and allowed him to use his own body as the crucible for the stages of alchemical transmutation. The *means* was the mirror; the *end* was self-development or the wedding of the higher self to nature or the soul of the alchemist to his higher spirit. The fire of transmutation burns off the dross of the lower self, which muddies up the picture of the human becoming an angel, the goal of the philosopher's stone, also referred to as *turning lead into gold*.

Mirrors use lead or silver backing to create a clear reflection. The glass of mirrors is often made of silica, which we can imagine as the silica of the human body creating the form of the human mirror. But it is the clarifying of the glass that creates its ability to reflect accurately. By refining or polishing the glass, it becomes clear enough to see through easily to the reflective surface of lead or silver in the backing. Creating a mirror is a process; the mechanism of reflection can become a science.

Reflecting as in a still pool of water is another form of mirroring. The pool needs darkness on one side and light on the other. The pool needs water or some substance that can selflessly give itself away. The pool needs calm to reflect clearly. And most of all, the pool needs an observer who is objectified and separate from the mirror effect.

These conditions for reflection can be said to describe space, the reflective matter that we see through our limited thought, in the dark night sky. When we look at ourselves, our image is limited by what we *envision* we are.

We choose to see ourselves as hieroglyphs of the universe, holographic copies of the consciousness that saw its reflection at the moment of creation. The author does not believe in the current theory of the Big Bang; *she believes in the Big Reflection.* Sophia as mirror has many useful avenues to explore because we are all reflections or mirrors in one way or another.

Sophia reflects the level of consciousness of the person describing Her. That is why the description of Wisdom takes on new and ever-evolving perspectives throughout history. As human consciousness grows, so grows Sophia.

Many people think Sophia is the Holy Spirit, the Comforter sent by Christ. Some think Sophia is the Pentecostal experience. Others think Sophia is Mary, the mother of Jesus who bore Jesus in Immaculate Conception and later was assumed into heaven in a bodily form.

Sophia grows along with human consciousness. Tibetans see Wisdom as the consort of all ten thousand Buddhas, as well as every monk who prays to Her. Wisdom is embodied in the hundreds of apparitions of Mary or female beings appearing all over the Earth. These *visitations* of Wisdom have never stopped. Those who look carefully into the mirror may see a divine woman looking back at them. These apparitions bring messages from the divine, and many people are healed at these sites. Visions of Sophia abound and, in some cases,

> *"The divine sees itself in us, and we see ourselves in the divine."*

last for years and are witnessed by many. Why do these *chosen ones* get to see the divine picture, but many others cannot? Why does the mirror of Wisdom seem to work better for some than others?

We are limited by the lens through which we see the world. We objectify the world when we use a lens. Perhaps we should throw away the lens and simply merge with that which we are trying to perceive. Likewise, with the Sophia mirror analogy, perhaps we should notice that what we bring to the mirror is what we are going to see. What we believe the mirror can do limits what we can see and do with the mirror. And in the final analysis, we are the mirror for others, and therefore it is logical that we are the mirror of—and for—the divine.

The divine sees itself in us, and we see ourselves in the divine. We are the source and end of all that there is, each one of us. We simply have to be a mirror and realize that our level of Wisdom is reflected back both to the divine and to others, and also determines what we see in others' mirrors. If we wish to be the "mirror, mirror on the wall," we need to reflect back that whoever is looking into us is "the fairest of them all."

Every single moment of existence is the "moment of creation," limited only by the amount of Wisdom that we can embody. When we look into the mirror of nature and all we see are the angelic beings working through the forces and natural laws of the world, then we are Wisdom.

Sophia has come along with us through each step of the process as our reflection of the divine has grown with our consciousness. Our lack of consciousness broke the primal mirror of creation, but our redeemed perceptions of the divinity of nature raises our consciousness to our rightful place as co-creators with God and Sophia.

"We stand perfectly in between the worlds above us and the worlds below us."

We are God and Sophia both at once. We create the concepts that we overlay on the percepts of the world, thus creating our own world. This world we create is heaven or hell as we choose to see it. Every moment is the Big Reflection, and we live in the world we choose to create.

That is why it is possible for some people in great pain to still have a wonderful disposition. They take responsibility for creating their response to what they see in the mirror of their self-reflecting consciousness.

We are who we believe we are; we see what we want to see. God and Sophia are the duality of the world, and yet we are both of them. We are the body outside of the mirror looking at the mirror, and we are the mirror itself.

Remove the mirror, and we will see a unified world where the divine and the mundane are wedded in a reunion of spirit and matter. This awareness is the nature of our evolving self. The world has many parts, like a broken holograph, but it is essentially one.

Objectification of the world or ourselves is temporary and evolves over time. This means that we never look the same in the mirror as we evolve. Perception is in the ever-present now; concepts are created afterwards.

Once we stop creating limited concepts, or limiting who we think we are going to see in the mirror, then we will find ourselves immersed in a world where beings stand behind all forces and aspects of nature.

Each of our organs has a being giving it life, structure, and form. We do not consciously beat our own hearts or drive our lungs at night when we sleep or tell our kidneys to filter fluids. Other beings do that work for us. If, for a moment, we could perceive the true nature of the activity of the divine beings in our own bodies, we would become like them in the reflection of their nature. We would commune with them, and they would show us all the Wisdom actively working in our organs and every aspect of our beings.

We do not need to look any further than the human body to see divine Wisdom. Just as there are worlds outside of us in the expanse of space, there are smaller worlds inside of us, down to the electrons of each atom.

We stand perfectly in between the worlds *above* us and the worlds *below* us. At each moment, we affect the worlds inside of us just as the worlds outside of us exert their own influence on us. We are the holographic mystery of the universe revealed to plain sight. We do not have to go anywhere to find heaven or hell; we create them.

The Black Mirror

In alchemy, there is the tradition of a *black* mirror. This black mirror has to be made carefully by the alchemist with all the known metals and minerals and planetary substances that make up the physical body. Made in secret, no one can look upon it. It must stay away from light and be kept near the head at night to capture dreams.

After long preparation and contemplation, the alchemist must bury the black mirror in the ground of his backyard. This then signals the spiritual world that the student is ready for the master to appear, and so the master *appears* to the student. From that point on, there is a personal teacher for every single step of the way towards transmutation or enlightenment. This master is especially suited for the student and has watched with anxious eyes the student passing through all the stages of renunciation and preparation for this *union* with his specific spiritual teacher.

Once the master has appeared, the black mirror can be taken out of the ground and used occasionally to answer questions and give advice. It then becomes the launching pad for astral travel and communication with spirits.

The black mirror can only be used at night when the light of day does not allow the *light from the darkness* to come forth. Over time, it enables the practitioner to see more and more of the whole picture of the world. The mirror speaks and acts in every way like a person, a masterfully wise and old person, much like a mother who tends every step of growth with love and interest. This master of wisdom in the alchemical tradition is actually Sophia. She is the person who accompanies each alchemist in the process of transmutation and evolution toward angelhood through the use of the black mirror. We are Sophia's creation and She is our Mother. We are Her children, and no one could love or tend to us any better.

The black mirror is the "night" wherein we dream of who we truly are and get to look into the teachings of Wisdom.

All of our spiritual efforts are reflected in our dreams. Every character in every dream is an aspect of our self. Our dreams show us how we are seen by others. In other words, our mirrored image of our self surfaces in our dreams every night.

Everyone dreams, but only some of us remember the dreams. Dreams give us the possibility of self-reflection in the way we were seen by others throughout the day. Our dreams can tell us who we are. Other people are always reflecting back to us who we are in the day, but often we are too busy to see it until we reflect on the day's activities in our dreams.

Our dreams are Sophia working on our evolution, just as the alchemist said the master appears to teach the student only when the student has prepared the mirror with great care. No one was allowed to look into the black mirror of the alchemist, just as no one can look into your dreams.

If we can see who we are through our dreams, Sophia's mirror is working, and we become co-creators with the divine beings who work in our lives. This realization is like looking in the mirror and asking, "Who is the fairest of them all?" and the mirror answers, "We are the fairest." This awareness empowers us to grow into the divine kingdom that awaits our return.

Humility

Holy spark of human life flames in Thee,
The ground of being, Creator Mother rests in Thee;
The wonder of Thy creation amazes all
Until in labor and pain on knees we fall
To grasp for life and health and precious ones,
Our three graces, and our glorious sun,
Gifts beyond measure, heaven's unfold,
Before our sacrifice and heart's true gold,
The treasures of Angel's elation
That rides on the tide of our creation.
The soul's bold courage of heart, humility born
For She is too delicate for the world to scorn,
And found another, as delicate as She
Together they live and strive to be free.
Then the dream awoke and found one day
They had flown higher and further away
Than their dreams had told them might come to show
The path through the maze, the right way to go.
Humility knows through Her Mystery of love
The way to transcend to the land above
Where the Lord of Earth meets the Queen of the Sky
And together they bear the Christened I,
The ego of both, wed one to the other
A union of opposites, the Father and Mother,
The twin flames that unite to birth
All human suffering, joy, and mirth;
That moves us round the mill of the soul
Where our joys and sorrows are all made whole.

Pillar Two

Sophia the Creatrix

Compassion

Now cold, distant, and alone, except for the touch of compassion

From the teeming worlds yet unborn within the womb of time.

Sophia evolves along with the practitioner and is intimately concerned about his or her growth. At first, She can appear as the Mother of Creation, the Creatrix. It is She who imbues Wisdom into human bodies and consciousness.

The oldest of beings, She loves us like Her own newborn infant, knowing everything about us and loving us unconditionally. Sophia and Christ have parented our budding consciousness for the sake of advancing the universe, and they are ever-present, ubiquitous, and personal.

Great thinkers and writers have described meeting the being of Wisdom, personified as nature, providence, or higher consciousness. These encounters often happen in one of a few ways. For instance, Jacob Boehme, a true follower of Sophia, encountered her physically three different times. Those encounters transformed his life and inspired him to become one of the greatest authors of Wisdom teachings. Boehme also had an experience of looking at a pewter bowl in the sunlight that turned into a mirror. A shaft of light brought his full and total illumination, which then inspired his writings for the rest of his life. So an encounter with a "reflection" began his new perceptions, and then three meetings with Sophia inspired one of the greatest writers on the development of human consciousness in the Western esoteric tradition.

For Boehme, Sophia was a physical being with whom he directly conversed and who he loved faithfully for the rest of his life. This is a direct revelation of an active and powerful being. Boehme was said to have been given the ability to read and write multiple ancient languages, though he had no previous training before his simple *moment of illumination*. His work is very instructive on the nature of the being of Sophia.

Pierre Teilhard de Chardin also encountered the being of Sophia and wrote his most beautiful poem to Her. He, like many others, had a direct, physical encounter with Sophia as a person.

> *"Sophia and Christ have parented our budding consciousness for the sake of advancing the universe."*

The scope and description of Sophia is profound and encompasses the doctrines of Christians and pagans. In fact, so many descriptions about this encounter with a physical being of Wisdom were found that the author stopped gathering them, and assumes that every enlightened person will one day meet the being of Sophia.

It has been noticed in the literature review that encounters with Sophia often happen throughout a person's life at different intervals, or they come at the end of life, usually in a set of three visitations. These encounters are so universal in all religions, myths, philosophies, and animism that it is amazing that many people do not know about them. They often have the same description, and, subsequently, inspiration flows to the person after encountering Sophia.

Frithjof Schuon was one of the greatest thinkers in the Traditionalist Movement, who ended his life living in seclusion with his wife in Ohio. He lived in a tepee and painted a new image of Sophia each day since his direct encounter with Her. As one of the great philosophers of his day, he understood all of the traditional religions in ways that most people cannot ever comprehend. Yet, he dedicated his life to Sophia, once he encountered a true, living being of Wisdom, revelation, and spiritual insight. This shows that everyone, even the greatest among us, is humbled before the presence of the Being of Wisdom.

In the end, aren't we all looking for the Wisdom we can glean from life?

She speaks in the patterns of destiny that lead us to thoughts that encounter Her.

She is found in every pillar of the Temple of Wisdom, where we all work each night to build our own part of the spiritual edifice.

We encounter Her in the Wisdom of nature, from the perfectly clear quartz crystal to the turtle sunning on the log in the pond.

If we are searching for Wisdom, we do not have to look further than our nose, toes, or pineal gland.

The mystery of the human body has hardly been revealed, and everywhere in nature we see the miraculous and wonderful labyrinth of life. We have barely found our way on this globe, with the secrets of the ocean only slightly known. Every day, science discovers new and amazing things that augment the picture of who we are in the mirror of consciousness. Each newborn child is an unimaginable miracle of hope and love for

"Like a wind bringing nourishing rain, Wisdom will rush into anyone who invites Her into their development."

the whole world. And Wisdom often pours through the mouths and actions of children and people we might not think are wise.

Like a wind bringing nourishing rain, Wisdom will rush into anyone who invites Her into their development. Sophia is there for all heart-felt, genuine advancements in consciousness. She fosters self-reflection and witnesses self-knowledge. There are no secrets from the Being of Wisdom. She is as concerned with your spiritual development as you are. She will not and cannot take the steps for you, but She will encourage you to take the next step leading upward on the path.

Compassion

We are the stardust of a thousand worlds, swirling into the dance of life,
Filled with the dark light that has fallen into our bones and marrow,
Igniting the heart, the organ of fire and love that shines ever brilliant.
We are the hope of love and freedom that the gods have born
In timeless caverns of old, resounding the thought of creation,
Now cold, distant, and alone, except for the touch of compassion
From the teeming worlds yet unborn within the womb of time.
We have forgotten our celestial home and the paths we have tread,
The promise of grace that is ours for the asking;
Until we remember that as a mother loves her child so dear,
We too are progeny of the divine, held softly in the arms of time.

We are so blind to the future, though we create it every day,
We are numb to the feelings of divinity that reside in our moral deed.
What comet need light our way to see the path we have come from heaven?
It leads to the creation of our little heaven—our heart of love,
That is the starry path of destiny reaching beyond time and space
To our spirit-child, whose anxious dreams have yet to be born.

It is hard to know and act in concert with the hosts of angels
Who care for our needs in each moment of our lives—
As we care for the spirit-child of love whose needs we serve.
Could the gods be less kind or concerned about our fulfillment
Than we are about our budding spirit-child?
We stumble through lessons that make us stronger each day
That challenge us, once we leave the world of dreams.
Waking is such a trauma—a world where dreams are crashed against the shore
Like so many shells that have come too close to shore and soon become sand.

What clam can see the beauty of a white sand beach created by its sacrifice?
What person can know the gifts we give to the gods who feed on us?
If we knew the gifts we create by loving each other, we could see eternity,
The higher shores, where time crashes like the ocean
Grinding our gifts into a beach for the gods to walk upon.

You are my starfish, the beauty of the sea of heaven
Whose every movement and angle shines like a neighbor sun
Filling my world with warmth and light from your heart.
This star of love has fallen onto my shore with news of future worlds
That beckon to us, calling the names of those yet unborn.
Shine your heart-fire like a sun and light the way ahead
For your love is hope that constant is, the joy of my tomorrows
The sacred ground upon which I tread towards the ocean of spirit.

Pillar Three

Sophia as Wisdom

Purity

These gifts are rarer than any found in this world,

Dazzling and pure like heaven itself.

Many descriptions of Wisdom offer the loftiest views of the spirit that words can describe. In the Old Testament, Wisdom was described as a human woman. Solomon, the wisest of men, sought Her above all else. Why is it that the descriptions of Her include so many faces from Creator to Lover? Could it be that the changing face of Sophia evolves with the person seeking her?

> *"The greater the thinker, the greater his image of Sophia."*

Perhaps as we look into Her mirror of nature, we see an image that relates to our changing and evolving minds. The perceiver defines the perceived by the capacity of his own consciousness. This would account for the many different *faces of Sophia* that are described by authors, philosophers, and great thinkers. The greater the thinker, the greater his image of Sophia.

If the thinker imagines just the limits of nature, Sophia then appears as the Goddess of Nature. If he can incorporate spiritual ideas into his cosmology, Sophia can become the Goddess of Creation, the Creatrix. If the thinker seeks out beauty as an ideal, Sophia can become the Goddess of Beauty. For those passionate seekers who wish to develop their soul feelings of love for Sophia, She changes into the Virgin of the World or the Beloved or the Bride. If the advanced mind can envision an all-encompassing Goddess, it can picture Her as the Mother of God or the Queen of Heaven.

Sophia is often seen as three Goddesses in One, encompassing a grand view of Her majesty. Some great lovers of Wisdom have imagined a Trinity of the female aspects of Mother, Daughter, and Holy Sophia called the Most Holy Trinosophia. It tends to be a close description of the ubiquitous being of Sophia, who can be found everywhere, nowhere, and all places in between.

This long tradition stems from the aboriginal view of the Mother—the Great Goddess of Birth, Death, and Rebirth—which predates any mention of a male trinity of gods. The thinker could easily see that from the mother came birth that later became death and fell back to earth, to be absorbed and born again later. This natural cycle of life was the highest thought or image of the divine that could be attained by an intellect so developed.

Over time, the Threefold Goddess took on many forms and names—but remained the same. She taught us about the mysteries of birth, death, and rebirth, teachings found in all cultures.

The Mother is Divine because She is the cause of life. This animism still holds true, even after the advances of science. The many-faceted Goddess expanded to represent the knowledge the ancients found when they looked into the starry sky and saw a circle of animals (zodiac) in images circling around us. Each section of the sky that represented an animal force became another headdress of the Goddess. So we see images of the Goddess with every imaginable head of an animal. Again, as consciousness expanded, so did Her image.

The Milky Way became the star-studded cloak of the Goddess, and star-like *milk* was given to the ancients through the Wisdom of the timing of the celestial cycles. From the heavens, Wisdom came to the ancients through long years of devoted observation and learning. The mathematical secrets of the precession of the equinoxes marked the level of intellectual development of any particular culture.

The Goddess of Wisdom instructed humanity through the seasons and the stars. Eventually, humans understood the cycles of the moon. Ancient wise women danced and sang of the birth of children, plants, animals, seasons, and cycles. Speech arose from these activities, and pictures were drawn to educate the young.

Only much later were the male-dominated, sun-oriented religions of a male trinity conceived. It was the female from which we arose. Even embryology shows us that we are parthenogenic, that we all are generated from the female form.

Birth is the domain of the moon; the cycles of birth are lunar bound. Long ago, a stellar Wisdom spoke to the ancient clairvoyant peoples. The Madonna culture of mother and child was ruled by the lunar forces, creating a matriarchal culture prior to the third millennium before Christ. This civilization knew no war nor even had words to describe such aggressive behavior.

> *"The Creator is unmanifest, but Sophia is manifest creation— the Creatrix."*

Helen of Troy was the representative of the Goddess that had fallen into the hands of a patriarchal culture—fought over for control of beauty's power. Most of the goddesses of the Minoan culture eventually became male gods in the Greek culture. The majority of the Greek gods were male/female or had a goddess as a wife. The later sun-cultures primarily had gods with wives, given secondary positions. But even the male-orientated gods needed a female to legitimize their power. The Trinity of Brahma, Vishnu, and Shiva is a good example of a trinity taken from the original female trinity: three gods married to powerful goddesses.

If we are not to fail Sophia in advancing our image of Her, we will want to be cognizant of Her biographies and not move backward in our perception of Her. We must move forward with confidence, taking into consideration all that the great thinkers have ever conceived of Her.

It would be proper at this point in evolution not to limit but to enhance the image. For instance, what if we stopped relegating Sophia to second place in creation or some part of the Holy Spirit? What if we could consider that Sophia was there with the Creator? The Creator is unmanifest, but Sophia is manifest creation—the Creatrix. She is also a hierarchical being. Just as Christ is the manifestation of the combined work of the Elohim, or Beings of Form, Sophia is the manifestation of the combined work of the Kyriotetes, the Spirits of Wisdom.

Sophia and Christ are like twin spirits who work together for the redemption of humanity. They are counterparts. They are united. As Christ came to the Earth to incarnate, so did Sophia. They came together. It is a complicated story that will be described later. Let us say for now that as Christ is the Son, or second person, in the Male Trinity, the Daughter of the Goddess is the second person in the Female Trinity. The Holy Spirit is the third person in the Male Trinity just as the Holy Sophia is the third person in the Mother, Daughter, Holy Sophia Trinity.

It would be hard to justify that once we have researched history and found the primacy of the Female Trinity, we would discard it. The only choice of evolution would be to encompass at a higher level the current revelation of Sophia as a co-equal to the highest "God" that we can conceive. The celestial

"We looked into the mirror when we were young and saw very little. Now, we see the marks of growth and pain in the lines left there to remind us of our passing time."

dance and wisdom of the union of these two Trinities would fill volumes.

It was always so, but humans were not evolved enough to perceive the truth. One could say that truth changes over time, and Wisdom evolves. Sophia was taken away for a time and hidden while both star and moon wisdom were repressed. The great books, religions, myths, and fairytales have long held these secrets in plain sight.

The suppression of Sophia caused the suppression of women as male-dominated cultures led humanity into war and selfishness, with little consideration for humans, nature, or the planet. Male, ego-centered pride has let loose the Seven Deadly Sins instead of remembering the Seven Heavenly Virtues or the singing of the Seven Harmonic Spheres.

When we look into the mirror of nature and perceive Her changing form, we realize that evolution is the right and natural thing to do. Our consciousness evolves as our ability to widen our perception evolves. Our image of ourselves in the mirror evolves. We create nature in our own image; so we have become the creator.

Who is the divine behind your view of the world? Is it majestic and all-encompassing?

Sophia is Threefold as She manifests the past, the present, and the future. She will certainly continue to evolve and, through grace and mercy, She will take us with Her.

We looked into the mirror when we were young and saw very little. Now, we see the marks of growth and pain in the lines left there to remind us of our passing time. We can see youth's folly and old age's wisdom in the glimmer of its reflection. All of these possibilities are in you, in the present moment, through Sophia's perception of you.

She is a timeless and spaceless being who knows you better than you know yourself. She sees who you have been, who you are, and who you will be. It is like Alice "Through the Looking Glass." Once you step through to know the image that Sophia has of you, you will never look the same, and your *perception* of yourself will change permanently. Once you have been to the mountaintop and seen the view from those new heights, you never forget.

Purity

You have renewed the wellsprings of life,
And planted the eternal tree of wonder
That ceaselessly streams forth a fountain of love,
Giving life, love, happiness, and strength.
These gifts are rarer than any found in this world,
Dazzling and pure like heaven itself.

Heaven's gate swings wide open if you are mine,
No reward could equal what you've given freely
And dedicated in the foundation of your gift eternal,
The sacrifice of your being in true commitment
And surrender to what we have together as one.

My heart cannot hold the width of your love,
No ocean is as deep as your touch of life,
No mountain so high as the goals we've set,
No death, nor life, nor resurrection can equal
What we share throughout eternity.

Finding you is the meaning of life,
Loving you is the purpose of existence,
Creating together through spirit union
Has breathed the breath of life into my heart;
Igniting the two as one in the heavenly dance.

Pillar Four

Wisdom of the Trinity

Generosity

Come Sophia! Give us the spirit-wings of fiery imagination
Which carry us across the threshold into the kingdom divine.

You are the *Trinity of Sophia* because you have a physical body, soul, and spirit all happening in you at the same time.

Your physical body is made up of forces from the past.

Your soul is active in the present.

Your spirit is your future coming to meet you.

You are a trinity, and nothing less than a trinity of the divine could be the *image* that you were originally created *like*.

But of course, is any human complete by herself alone? It takes another person to help you *see yourself* and reflect your existence. No one is complete without love, and the highest manifestation of love is marriage for the sake of procreation—when humans become divine and can truly create a miracle of life. So, too, the soul needs a counterpart, and the spirit likewise. Therefore, how could Sophia, or your own beloved one, be complete without the other?

The Trinity of Mother, Daughter, and Holy Sophia must have the divine counterpart of Father, Son, and Holy Spirit. It is the logical conclusion, let alone the divine image. If a human longs to find her counterpart, why would the gods and goddesses be any different? We are made in their image. Shall we not allow them the natural love of the other? Is it not just the limited view of the evolving human intellect that does not see this natural course of life?

Sometimes we look into the mirror and see a monster looking back. We see things that we do not want to see. We see the unresolved issues of fear, doubt, and hatred that remain in our astral body. This visage of *black* or *dark* aspects of the soul can also be found in Sophia. Over time, Sophia has also been associated with death, darkness, and dreamless sleep. She was called the witch, hag, whore, and Kali the Destroyer. Often She is colored red for birth, black for death, and white for rebirth.

Sophia is not always a walk in the park. She is the Goddess of transcendental wisdom dancing in the flames. She can be terrifying, especially when She is bringing you self-knowledge that is difficult to face.

Sophia gives, and She takes away. Death is hard for us, but Sophia is timeless, and She sees the timeless pictures of us from life to life.

Many people do not want a Goddess of Wrath. Sophia is God's mercy and compassion and His judgment and wrath. This broader image of Sophia is necessary if the seeker wants to see all sides of himself. Sophia shows us ourselves, both the beautiful and the ugly.

The view or perception of Sophia is only limited by the view or perception of the thinker. If there is a part of nature that is not included in your view of Sophia, then you might expand your concept of Sophia to allow a greater perceptive capacity.

Sophia, or Wisdom, is essentially your cosmology of the world. A good cosmology of the world would encompass all time, space, and the intent of creation, whether that is evolution or de-evolution. Do you know why you are here, who you are, and where you are going? These ideas would be part of a cosmology.

> **"Do you know why you are here, who you are, and where you are going?"**

If you do not have a cosmology, then when you look in a mirror, you know not what you see.

In fact, when you look out into the world, you do not know what you see. You are then simply a lost person in the present with no navigational tools to direct you. You do not know if you are an animal or an angel or something in between. You will not know where you are going because you will not know where you have been. As such, the ship of your soul is lost at sea and cannot navigate by the stars.

The metaphor of Sophia as a mirror is instructive. It shows us that

She creates a *threshold experience* as we try to *see* Her in nature. This experience is one wherein we can peer across the threshold into the spiritual world. At this moment, we are closer to the spiritual world and its inspiration and influences.

Sophia acts as the ferryman to get us across the River Styx without losing consciousness. She accompanies us as Beatrice to Dante on his own journey. Just like all heroes and heroines of the past, including Psyche, Heracles, and Orpheus, we must consciously choose to cross into the underworld to win the prize. We must learn to cross this boundary in meditation, sleep, and death, while maintaining consciousness. That is how we evolve our consciousness into accepting our higher spirit that the future is sending to us.

Once we cross the threshold, there is no time or space. We begin to see ourselves for who we truly are. Sophia is our personal guide and will not force anything upon us. We grow at the rate that we choose to grow. Sophia is simply there, like Quan Yin, to help each soul cross the threshold into heaven (enlightenment). We are Her children, so She cares for us more than anyone else can. She is the midwife of our spirit, our physical Mother, who watches each toddling step we take with parental interest and love. Therefore, it becomes clear that when we take any spiritual step, She is there.

She becomes our spiritual companion, like the Archangel Raphael watched over Tobias when he went in search of a cure for his father. Tobias was not aware until the end that the servant his father sent to accompany him was an Archangel guiding his every step. We, like Tobias, are ignorant that every time we have an Inspiration or Intuition, we are actually communing with and through Sophia to our guardian angel and thus to all the hierarchy.

Again and again, we ignore the picture in the mirror that actually tells us that we are becoming angels. We forget our knowledge as we cross the threshold in the way the River Styx makes us forget.

We must now find the forces to hold onto the consciousness we carry over the threshold to the spiritual world as if it were gifts of food and drink for the gods. *Hold on to it.* If we could do that, we would be able to bring stronger spiritual forces back across to manifest the will of the divine on Earth. We would evolve into the angels we are supposed to become. This is the dance of life, with Sophia as our partner: a loving, personal, passionate quest for beauty, truth, and goodness. It is very simple, but all-encompassing.

This personal and passionate love for the divine has inspired humanity since Eve gained knowledge of good and evil in the Garden of Eden. It is intimate and secret, and it blooms. Each of us is given the chance to relive and redeem the Garden of Eden challenges in every moment of life.

The angel with the fiery sword guarding Eden is the boundary to the spiritual world. We go to Eden each night when we cross the threshold of sleep. We can relive Eden's challenge every day if we like, or we can cross over to where the Tree of Life still blossoms. When we look into the mirror, we can ask the question, "Is this Eden, or are we cast out again?"

We are citizens of two worlds—Heaven and Earth. Our consciousness can reside in one or both. We decide where to place it.

Sophia is the one who can help us develop the super-sensible organs needed to be able to perceive and remember what we learn in the spiritual world across the threshold. Sophia is the doorkeeper of the entranceway and threefold in Her duties.

She sees us born from the spiritual world, return to it every night, and finally return to it after death. If we become active citizens of the spirit with Sophia, we will be able to accept Christ's gift of eternal life and develop our souls into everlasting spirits.

Generosity

I love you from life to life
Through Sophia's flowing of destiny
Making the hierarchies sing with joy
Over our union, brought together again,
Weaving the picture of immortal souls
Wedded together in karmic paths of spirit
Showing life as a grand puzzle
Whose last piece is our reunion.
We separated, but now we are found.
Together our spirit-light pierces the dark
Revealing Wisdom descending from above.

You are the chalice, I am the wine,
You are the bread, I am the paten;
Together we are the feast that feeds the spirit
From the Wonder Fountain of immortal life
Nourishing all who come to the table of love
To receive the communion of nectar and ambrosia,
That lifts our spirit to pure realms of burgeoning life
Raising the offerings of souls into spirit lands
As fiery currents of human-born light blazing the artic sky.

Come Sophia! Give us the spirit-wings of fiery imagination
Which carry us across the threshold into the kingdom divine.
Sing forth the praise of holy spirit-inspiration,
As the harmony of the spheres rings true in human hearts.
Blaze forth the courageous deeds of spirit-intuitions
Spoken from the holy, sacred ground of the living divine.

You are the three in one that I find in myself—
You are my other half, without which I am not whole.
You have united my soul with my spirit twin
As Wisdom weaves through our love, uniting all.

Pillar Five

The Cosmic Dance of Christ and Sophia

Temperance

And mixed and churned and rose anew into the magic alkahest;

That soothes my soul and sparks my mind and gives my spirit rest.

Christ is the Lord of Karma and the savior of this realm, while Sophia is the Wisdom we need to arrive at understanding and help our budding Christ Self evolve. It is not possible to understand the cosmic aspects of the Deed of Christ without Sophia's Wisdom. We should emulate Sophia Christos (Wisdom of Christ) in our spiritual development.

The wisdom Jesus developed was given over to His Mother. Mary of Jerusalem joined with her higher self and Sophia the Being of Wisdom to hold cosmic Wisdom alongside human wisdom in her heart. Mary, who accompanied Christ throughout His ministry, passion, and resurrection, was the reincarnated original Eve. Mary merged with her paradisiacal self that had been "held back" when Adam and Eve first incarnated, called the Eve Kadmon.

After Jesus gave his wisdom over to Mary before His baptism in the Jordan, the *human incarnation* of the Being of Wisdom (Sophia) began to over-light Mary and dwell in her soul and spirit. (See Appendix C.)

John the Baptist was the original Adam reincarnated. Mary was the original Eve. Together these two, Adam and Eve, John and Mary, helped Christ redeem the Fall from the Garden of Eden.

After the baptism of Jesus, Mary held in her heart the consciousness of the original Eve, the Eve Kadmon (the paradisiacal Eve), and Sophia, the Being of Wisdom. Mary also held the collective wisdom of Jesus of Nazareth, Zarathustra, Hermes, and Moses that was passed over to Her from Jesus.

Mary became the vessel for Sophia to incarnate in human form so that cosmic and human wisdom could come together in one person. This over-lighting of Mary is simultaneous with Jesus of Nazareth becoming the vessel for the Being of the Christ to incarnate. The Wisdom that Mary held in her heart helped her "be conscious" while witnessing the suffering that Jesus Christ endured through the Crucifixion.

Both Christ and Sophia utilized and redeemed the perfect Kadmon vehicles (paradisiacal spirits) of the original Adam and Eve who were held back in paradise when the physical Adam and Eve incarnated. These paradisiacal bodies were necessary to help Jesus Christ and Mary Sophia to physically rise to heaven.

It was necessary for Adam and Eve to gain the Knowledge of the Tree of Good and Evil in order to understand that the sacrifices of Christ and Sophia brought the Tree of Life back into human reach.

The Tree of Life holds the secrets of immortality. Christ died on dead wood that was turned into living wood as the cross of death became the Tree of Life. His deed turned evolution around; now we can return to heaven, our home. But first we must eat of the Tree of Life and accept our immortality.

When Christ redeemed death with his body and blood, all seekers of the spirit gained immortality. At the same time, Mary/Sophia suffered tremendous pain, helplessly witnessing the death of Her counterpart.

It was the divine plan for Mary to witness this cruel death with the help of Sophia because the pain was beyond what a human could endure. Yet, the deed of redemption had to be witnessed in full consciousness by a redeemed soul: Mary. Consciously witnessing the death of Christ was the other half of the deed. Only Mary, with all of Her new "wisdom capacities," could endure being such a conscious witness.

After Mary witnessed the death, resurrection, and ascension of Jesus Christ, she was able to totally redeem her physical body and ascend into heaven without death. Mary conquered death and was assumed into heaven to sit with Her Son, who becomes God as She becomes the Mother of God and Queen of Heaven.

Mary has never stopped appearing to the faithful. Just as Christ sent the Holy Spirit at Pentecost, so Sophia appears to the faithful as the Holy

Sophia. Her appearances have increased since She rose into heaven. She appears to each striving soul when needed as a loving teacher of Wisdom.

Christ had to die to conquer death and enter the realms of the dead to redeem them. His blood fell into the Earth to redeem the lifelessness of the material world. Now, He is active in the etheric realm, resurrecting the Living Imaginations of humanity and appearing to those who are in distress and need.

> *"Christ is leading us the way back to heaven from whence He and we came."*

Mary/Sophia is also active in this etheric realm as the archetype of the fully redeemed human being and is present "now and at the hour of our death" to help us across the threshold. Sophia is at the threshold of death as mediator and teacher. Christ is on the other side of the threshold as the Lord of Karma. Christ can alter the ebb and flow of karma and is certainly not limited by karmic debt because He conquered death and aligned His spirit with the karma of all humans. Christ transcends time and space, just as Sophia does.

Each person has a drop of immortal life in her *heart of hearts* donated to her through Christ's deed. Every time she evolves further, more drops appear. These drops continue from life to life because they are immortal drops of love. They may be increased through conscious effort that drives courageous deeds of freedom and love. In Seal Six of Volume II the methods and mechanisms used to develop the capacities for increasing the drops of immortality in the heart are described. Essentially, the pure loving soul that is striving towards the spirit creates these drops naturally. The vases that the Buddha and Quan Yin hold at their hearts contain these drops of immortality.

Christ is leading us the way back to heaven from whence He and we came. His love and compassion is beyond anything humans can ever imagine. Sophia's Wisdom is equally as profound. Together, as counterparts joined in union, there is nothing the human can conceive that will match the beauty and goodness beyond anything They manifest.

We can imagine ourselves, with our soul and spirit as bride and groom, uniting in the divine marriage in New Jerusalem or the Temple of Wisdom.

Every night in our dreams, we are building a community. Every day in our meditations and prayers, we develop our evolving spirits. Sophia Christos is the symbol and example of our re-*membered* selves growing over time. We gain Wisdom through perceiving the sacrifices of the divine. This Wisdom fires the Christ-light in our soul to grow and help all those in need through love born from true freedom.

The female and male Trinities are co-equal and co-incident. That is why when the Trinity of Father, Son, and Holy Spirit resolved to send Christ (through the combined Elohim) down to Earth, the Trinity of Mother, Daughter, and Holy Sophia decided, likewise, to send Sophia (through the combined Kyriotetes) to accompany Christ. This cosmic plan envisioned that Wisdom/Sophia would need to witness Love/Christ as He conquered death and united with the future personal and spiritual development of every human.

Both of these Trinities exist separately from the nine ranks of hierarchies even though they work through them. Existing above and distinct from them, Christ and Sophia help create the hierarchies. (See Appendix B.) They both also use the forces of the second hierarchy—the Kyriotetes, Dynamis, and Elohim—to channel Their personal energies.

Christ used the Elohim to create a physical body in which to incarnate once in human history. Sophia used the Kyriotetes in which to incarnate and accompany Christ's mission into the human realm. Christ entered a human body for three years, whereas Sophia over-lighted Mary for eleven years.

From the wisdom of Rudolf Steiner, in his *Fifth Gospel,* we know that Sophia was "born" when Mary, who had been Eve, received into her consciousness the "wisdom body" of Zarathustra that Jesus of Nazareth had merged with from age twelve to age thirty. This wisdom body refined the Wisdom from the many incarnations of Zarathustra through the consciousness of Jesus of Nazareth, who resided in the Adam Kadmon body, the perfect physical body that was kept in heaven when Adam was first created.

Mary/Eve received this wisdom as an expression of Michaelic Wisdom that had come to the Earth and been worked through by Zarathustra and Jesus. (See Appendix D for the incarnations of Zarathustra.) This body of Wisdom was the most developed intellect of any human. After Jesus gave this "wisdom body" over to Mary before the baptism, she held that Wisdom in her heart as she witnessed Christ's ministry.

Mary also had the wisdom of Eve and her many incarnations since the

Garden of Eden in her soul. Mary (Mary of Jerusalem) was inspired by and in direct contact with the "other Mary" (Mary of Nazareth-Eve Kadmon), who was the mother of Jesus of Nazareth (Adam Kadmon). Mary of Nazareth was the Eve Kadmon, the pure (virgin) physical body that was created at the same time as Eve but remained in paradise until she incarnated for the first time as Mary of Nazareth (Eve Kadmon), who gave birth to Jesus of Nazareth (Adam Kadmon). Later, she died around the time when Jesus of Jerusalem died at age twelve and passed over into Jesus of Nazareth.

"The secret of the 'two Jesus children' and the 'two Marys' was protected by the Masons and others for centuries."

The secret of the "two Jesus children" and the "two Marys" was protected by the Masons and others for centuries. The second Jesus child was, of course, the soul known as Zarathustra, who had also been Hermes and Moses. This human soul is one of the greatest leaders of humanity and goes back to the fifth migration from Atlantis. His "wisdom body" was necessary to share with the pure Jesus of Nazareth child (Adam Kadmon).

The Zarathustra child (Jesus of Jerusalem) died at age twelve, and Mary of Nazareth (Eve Kadmon) died shortly thereafter. The Jesus of Nazareth child then became endowed with the Wisdom Body of Zarathustra and was adopted by Mary of Jerusalem.

As Anthroposophists know, these great truths of history were shared by Rudolf Steiner, a clairvoyant who researched these topics. Steiner believed that we all have the capacity to conduct spiritual research and test truth. Indeed, the study of Anthroposophy and other esoteric streams gives us the spiritual research tools needed to test these truths for ourselves, independent of gurus, masters, and priests.

After Mary/Sophia received the wisdom of Jesus of Nazareth, she went through the three years of Christ's ministry by his side. She was with him during the three years that the Christ Spirit came to inhabit His body more and more. She and the other two Marys were often the ones listening closely to and believing Christ's words. The three Marys seem to find a central place in all of Christ's activities. While the apostles fled, the three Marys stayed under the cross to witness the entire Passion of Christ. (See Appendix C.)

The question of who witnessed the death of Christ is a pivotal issue for all of human development and is a key to the archetype of the divine human. Christ died after being in the body of Jesus of Nazareth for three years. Mary/Eve ascended into heaven eleven years after the crucifixion and fourteen years from the time She came to hold the Wisdom of Jesus/Zarathustra/ Sophia. John the Divine and the other two Marys (Mary Magdalene and Mary of Bethany) witnessed both the crucifixion of Jesus and the

> ***"We now see the original Adam and Eve under the cross."***

Assumption of Mary. Over-lighting John the Divine was the spirit of John the Baptist, who had been beheaded earlier. John the Baptist was previously the original Adam (not to be confused with the Adam Kadmon), and he had a particularly strong bond with John the Divine. John the Divine had the spirit of the original Adam (John the Baptist) hovering over him and, as we have learned, Mary was the original Eve. (See Appendix E.)

Now we can see the original Adam and Eve witnessing the Crucifixion and discovering what the Knowledge of the Tree of Good and Evil has brought to humanity: the death of the divine in human form. The death that ensued from the expulsion from Eden is now redeemed by the death of the Adam Kadmon, the Second Adam, Christ Jesus.

John the Baptist (Adam) acknowledged Christ before his beheading and now can witness from the spiritual world that Christ Jesus (the Second Adam) is redeeming the death that came into the world through the expulsion from Eden. John the Baptist witnessed this through the eyes of John the Divine.

Mary/Eve stands under the cross now as the original Eve, redeemed by the New Tree of Life. Eve is joined with the Eve Kadmon (Mary of Nazareth), the being of Sophia and also with the Wisdom Body of Zarathustra and Jesus of Nazareth.

Mary/Eve, as she stands beneath the cross, becomes the first human to reunite with her ideal past (Eve Kadmon) and her ideal future (Sophia) at the same moment that a God (Christ) becomes human through the ideal vehicle (Adam Kadmon) and dies a human death for His children's spiritual future.

This cosmic evolution unites the second hierarchy of the Kyriotetes and Elohim: Wisdom and Love as the divine gift of eternal grace.

Christ had to die for the divine to enliven the etheric body of the Earth and human beings. Mary/Eve lives for eleven years after the Crucifixion with John the Divine as her new son. Mary was the first Eve and John the Divine is over-lighted by John the Baptist, who was the first Adam, thereby reuniting the original Adam and Eve. Mary and John travel to Ephesus where Mary eventually enters dormition (a sleep-like condition) and then is assumed bodily into heaven. John witnesses this Assumption of Mary. He lives on until he is 105 years old and is imprisoned on the island of Patmos, where he writes the Book of Revelation.

> *"With or without a cosmological map, we are all the boat of consciousness sailing toward the evolution of the spirit."*

Others who witnessed the crucifixion of Christ were Joseph of Arimethea, who caught Christ's blood in the Holy Grail, an event that Nicodemos witnessed in his sleep. From out of the ranks of the hierarchy, only the Archangel Michael could witness the crucifixion. Michael is intimately connected to Christ and is known as the face or countenance of Christ. The other hierarchy had to turn away from the crucifixion because they could not understand it or were horrified by the cruelty of man.

The evolution of humanity was reenacted and redeemed through Christ's ministry. The deed of Christ is the turning point of time—the Mystery of Golgotha. To understand that moment is to understand all of history, the present, and the future. The depth of the deeds of Christ and Sophia are revealed as an unending Mystery unfolding itself throughout history and human evolution.

We are each a reenactment of the Garden of Eden. Its restoration can be found in our perception of the world. For instance, all that has been described in strange details and hints may mean nothing to you, or it could mean the world. You could use it as a tool to open the Mystery of yourself, or you could ignore it. Either way, it will end up the same, but perhaps with different timing.

With or without a cosmological map, we are all on the "boat of consciousness" sailing toward the evolution of the spirit. We may resist, but eventually we will have to grow up and develop archetypal symbols, images, and parables that instruct us in the collective Wisdom of our elders. We may stay adolescent longer than is necessary, but after many incarnations, we all awake and resume the path up the mountain.

All spirits know good from evil and up from down. Perhaps we get a little lost with right, left, forward, backward, but we still learn to walk, talk, and think. After that we have to assume some self-responsibility for our development.

The hierarchies have done so much for us in the past; it is time for us to do some work ourselves. In other words, we need to work out how we came to be here and where we are going. If you resonate with the archetype of the Christian esoteric path, then what was written here should "wake you up" a bit. If not, just read the material for the "ringing of truth" that accompanies spiritual reality and revelation.

Temperance

What whirlwind grand from time beyond has changed my little world?
And brought me now to lands afar where dreams and hopes are swirled
And mixed and churned and rose anew into the magic alkahest;
That soothes my soul and sparks my mind and gives my spirit rest,
In blessed places that quench my thirst for spirit ever new
Where love abounds and spirit reigns, and union found by few;
With horizon wide, filled with light that calls a new-born day
That holds our love, a chalice clear, that feeds our work and play.

You are that storm that calmed the night
And brought the wisdom cloak of light;
You wear it well, this mantle of starry life
Earned through suffering and forgiven strife
To mark your soul with knowing sight
And clear for you the path of light.

You are that strength, my refuge strong,
I have wandered the world for so long,
To find you, to hold you, and give you my all,
Until both of us merge under Sophia's call,
That unites our souls through chance divine
And breaks our molds and desires so fine,
Which kept us pure, reserved through time
As our spirits blossom and grow sublime
Through love eternal, not bound by time or space,
Born ever anew in this sacred, holy place
Which we build together, with Her blessed grace
Until we know Christ and see Sophia's face.

Pillar Six

Sophia as Revelation

Diligence

To calm our strife and conquer all fears,

To accept the grace that Her presence has given.

We are all supposed to be a "faith of one" and find our own north star by which to navigate. Revelation is open for everyone, not just the developed intellect or prophet. In fact, often intellect gets in the way of perceiving revelation.

Intuitions first arise in the heart as impulses of love, then are reflected in the brain. Usually true and good impulses of love will lead us to help others selflessly, and we come full circle to Christ. You don't have to have names or dogmas or belief to interact with spiritual beings from the hierarchy. You should believe in what you experience as true, good, and beautiful. But if you need archetypes to organize your cosmology, it is best to use what clairvoyants and mystics have described for ages.

The old traditions have great wisdom. Seek in those sources all that you can about yourself. You will find that you are the mirror of these divine hierarchical beings manifesting in your life. For instance, all of us are reincarnated souls who hold pieces to each other's stories, just as the story of Adam and Eve is united with Christ and Sophia. One is cosmic, and the other is a reflection of it.

What is true rings out in many ways and creates many harmonies. All of them can be true at once. Whether Christian or not, the archetypes and beings remain the same. If you have strong associations with the ideas, then the soul can come alive and experience these ideas as ideals inspiring your life with the images and archetypes that resonate with you.

In Christian terminology, all nine hierarchies are governed by the Kyriotetes, the Spirits of Wisdom. They order and tell the other hierarchy what to do and when. They are below the Spirits of Will (Thrones), Harmony (Cherubim), and Love (Seraphim), but still order and direct their activity.

"Each seed is a mystery of Sophia yet to unfold."

Love, Harmony, and Will Power are the highest sources of hierarchical power and influence. The rulership of these forces is the domain of Sophia the Goddess of Wisdom, who uses the combined influence of the Spirits of Wisdom as a vessel for the Daughter Goddess.

One could say that to know Sophia is to know the order and design of all things earthly and divine. Sophia is the weaving force of divine will that ties together the effort of each individual creation. She is the Mother of All who understands the workings and meaning of the symphony of forces that must unite in just a particular fashion to create the substances that build and sustain life. Sophia is present everywhere in the Wisdom of nature, working to create sustainable ecosystems. She is the revelation of life in all its forms.

Life is a delicate balance of substances that must combine in an alchemical transformation to bring forth new life. Each seed is a mystery of Sophia yet to unfold. Her Wisdom has created this thin atmosphere on the surface of a spinning planet that must be perfectly balanced between the sun, moon, and planets.

Humans understand only a small amount of what nature tends to in every moment of life. Our knowledge and comprehension grows exponentially, yet science is diversified into shattered views of the whole. Every day, we discover wonders of nature that seem like magic forces at work, supernatural forces that will become the commonplace science of tomorrow.

Revelations of Sophia's wondrous wisdom are woven into every atom, cell, and life system. Sophia continually raises the veil between humans and nature to reveal the wisdom, beauty, and power that burgeon forth from every aspect of creation. The thinly separated membranes between plants, animals, and humans are dissolving. We see higher connections and correspondences between substances and effects between the component parts, but still cannot put the puzzle together. Sophia is being undressed in all areas of science, but She still is not seen.

It is true that humans have done poorly with some of the responsibilities that come with knowledge. This responsibility should lead to Wisdom, not just to discoveries in nature that can be turned into directed will force.

For example, electrostatic energy is everywhere and free to use, so humans designed and built electromagnetic engines to capture and direct this force of nature. This one secret of Sophia has created our visible world, as spirit is primary to matter. Knowledge of the atom unleashed all kinds of potential to use it for both good and harm. The invention of gunpowder, rockets, weapons-grade lasers, and much of the new combat technology that we see today chronicle the challenges that humanity has had since the fall of Troy in using nature's forces. Nature seems to no longer be worshiped, but bent, forged, and twisted into evil human machinations.

Sophia has as many faces as needed to lead all of nature to a higher calling, the will of the divine. Natural law is one of Sophia's tools to *order and rule* the world, and humans are only now beginning to understand it. Sophia has natural and supernal laws that go far beyond human sensory perception. Each new century rolls out thousands of new scientific theories about the laws of Sophia. Then those theories are replaced with new ones, and scientists act like the old ones never existed.

The secular humanism of modern science is not a cosmology that is comprehensive or workable. The revolving door of scientific theory is a shaky foundation for a cosmology. Science lacks revelation and a cosmology in which to place it once revealed.

The humble alchemist, working steadily in his laboratory with meditation and prayer, often comes to a direct revelation of Sophia, a direct meeting with Her that is real and tangible. These encounters are common, often take a similar form, and can inspire a person for an entire lifetime. Visitations have been well documented, the experiences filling volumes with the Wisdom that She has imparted.

Sophia seemed, in some cases, to become as real and tangible as a living person. Some seekers believe that they actually "wed" Sophia; She becomes as close and personal as their Bride. Jacob Boehme had such a revelation of Sophia that inspired his many books. There is a long list of others whose encounters with Sophia, early in life or at different times throughout their lives, or just at the end of their lives, are the most important, pivotal moments in their biographies. Why does Sophia appear *human* to these seekers?

Sophia is the highest hierarchical being to *incarnate as a human being* (over-lighting Mary) during this great round of time. Christ, as we have outlined above, is Her counterpart who united with Her before and during their time on Earth and ever after. Sophia became human, just as Christ became human, except She did not go through the human birth experience.

Sophia knows all aspects of life and death as a human. United with Mary and the memory of Jesus of Nazareth, She welcomed the Kyriotetes into her body until it was so purified that it could be bodily assumed into heaven.

The Holy Sophia is human also. She understands all of our strivings and shortcomings as we develop our intellect and higher consciousness. She is as close as any human being, standing in front of your countenance, looking into your eyes, and seeing into your heart.

Sophia is also divine and knows where we are and where we need to get in the long run. She accompanies us across the threshold each night and makes sure we get to Her Temple of Wisdom to build our spiritual abodes.

As the cosmic ruler of all time and space, She knows the past, present, and future without limitations. She weaves the threads of destiny that Providence guides into a coherent and unified image of the future, where all beings evolve into their higher spirit nature, or Christened self.

Christ is the way and the path; Sophia is our guide. She keeps track of every step forward, recording and adding it to the whole. She is the lens to see our personal angels and receive the gifts they are bringing. She is our Mother, our friend, our confidant of the spirit.

No one is closer to our spiritual development than the Mother who helps prepare our souls to be the Virgin Bride of our Spirit through the grace of Christ. Sophia helps unite us with Christ, our higher self. As a bridesmaid, She shows us how to trim our spiritual lamps so that they shine brightly throughout the night. As a mystery of perception, She finds the hidden truth that reveals the power and majesty of creation in every moment. This *Revelation of Sophia* has the power to transform even hell into heaven.

Maker, creator of the universe, the source of natural and supernatural law, Sophia is intent on helping humans become angels, angels become archangels, and so on throughout the ranks of the hierarchies.

Diligence

Why do we seek the sound of perfection
When it rumbles so close in the heart?
Why do we pray for the blessing of heaven
When the divine drives our heart's own pulse?
Why should anyone look further than the beloved
For proof of the Almighty lighting our hearts?

Our little selves tremble that our hearts beat alone,
Though a joyous chorus sings in our home,
This life seems hard and unrefined
Compared to beauty we cherish in our minds.

You are my heartbeat, my breath defined,
You are my future—the furnace that refines,
You are my daylight, my hopes and my dreams,
You are the answer to every question, thought, or scheme.

Hear the voice thunder, your whispered promise of love,
Hear the Earth quake at your coming from above,
Hear the future call—the fates of our restless nights
Dancing illusions swirling through our streaming sight.

We are the wedding of soul to spirit,
Through all tides of time and life,
Reaching for perfection, the sound that will heal,
Holding to Her nature those love-dreams we feel.

You are the one I have always awaited,
You are the soul who has held my passage,
From anger and hatred to love divinely shared,
To make our path known and filled with Her care.

I thank you; I'm whole now and totally devoted
To unify our efforts and join all our dreams,
Calm our strife and conquer all fears,
Accepting Her grace that is always near.

Pillar Seven

Angelic Hosts of the Hierarchy

Patience

The author of surrender, the spontaneous ubiquitous binding of all, giving birth from the past as a gift to the future through freedom now.

There are some who consciously resist natural and supernal law and disobey the *order and rule* of Sophia. These hosts of angels are called Luciferic. They rebel at all levels of the hierarchy and remain behind as evolution continues. Some have called these Luciferic hosts evil, but there is no permanent evil in creation, only "rebellion" for a period of time.

Sophia is a Being beyond time, so these beings do not worry Her. Often they falsely inspire seekers who bring too much ego into their self-development.

But Lucifer and his hosts have redeemable characteristics, too. Like Prometheus, Lucifer has brought the light from the heavens to the Earth. In fact, human intellect is a gift of Lucifer the Light Bearer. For this reason, when we seek Sophia, we must be aware of the temptation of Lucifer.

Sophia will inspire us to pursue selfless acts of love and freedom, whereas Lucifer's inspiration is selfish, and based on pride, envy, and the other deadly sins. Not surprisingly, much of modern history is the inspiration of Lucifer, the Father of Lies.

Sophia can, in our time, unite with the intellect, leading it to truth and knowledge that can be tempered over time into powerful knowledge and practical wisdom. We must see the whole picture to understand what it means to be "inspired by Sophia," and not just powerfully wield the modern intellect, which so easily becomes materialistic.

Sophia's intent is not to give super mental powers to her followers. She grants us peace and courage that comes with spiritual faith that the universe is created out of Wisdom. The seeker needs only to align with Sophia's will to join the synchronicity and oneness that comes with supernal Wisdom. She has cleared the way. She has made the connections in time and space that we cannot begin to imagine. Her Wisdom is intent on uniting all spiritual flames into a beacon of light that illumines the darkness around us.

> *"The trinity is the highest representation of the spirit that the intellect has designed."*

Each seeker meets Sophia from his or her point on a personal spiritual path. She arranges the next step and points the way up the mountain. She cannot do the work for the seeker, but She calls him forth, challenging him to ascend the path to higher realms. She gives wings to soar into the realms of archetypes to commune with the living sources of all things earthly and divine. She revels at our growth and is thrilled by our advancement. When we learn a lesson, She may even be happier than we are. The ultimate teacher, She always sees the highest and brightest in us and can help call it forth.

Christ is love and compassion. Sophia is wisdom and illumination. Together, They teach the best way to love and serve the whole in the wisest fashion through synchronicity, grace, and mercy.

Synchronicity happens as the wisest and most economical way to connect the parts of the whole so that harmony and grace weave merciful karma between people, regardless of time and space. Synchronicity is happening always; sometimes we are *in sync* enough to participate in the *will of the divine*. Generally, no accidents happen. Or if they do, the Lord of Karma will still prevail and mend all wounds.

A master magician, all of the tricks are on Sophia's side. She has ways to link time and space through sub/super-time and sub/super-space, weaving together streams of consciousness that baffle logic or the materialistic mind.

She knows more about our human nature than we do. We are very predictable creatures to such a being as the Divine Feminine Trinity, who works through a high rank of the hierarchies and has experienced all of the pain that a human could endure. She has traveled the pathways of soul and spiritual development. She has worked with and monitored the spiritual development of every human being. She is similar to the *human collective spiritual consciousness of the planet.* Sophia is not only the world soul, She is far more. Perhaps we could imagine Her as the vessel within which all human spiritual development takes place. Paradoxically, She is watching from the outside of this vessel, yet She created the vessel.

> *"When you resonate with Sophia's vibrations, you become a vehicle to incarnate the spiritual intentions of the hierarchies."*

Within the concept of the trinity, we can find three distinct paradoxes. Logic of the intellect cannot even get us beyond the first paradox, and then we find another paradox and yet another within one trinity. This abnegation of logic does help explain the nature of the spiritual world. Logic and thinking do not work in the soul or spiritual world as they do in the material world. While good for the materialist, logic falls apart in the soul world as soon as love arises.

Love is often not logical. Neither are spiritual impulses. The trinity concept implies that A is not B, but A is B. Then B is not C, but B is C, and so on. Three beings are one and the same, yet separate. The trinity is the highest representation or symbol of the spirit that the intellect has designed. This concept is quite useful in describing the economy of the spiritual world. When one entity can be in three places at once, much can be accomplished. Synchronicity often appears as though the spirit were working hard in three places at once to make one event come together in a synchronistic fashion. Now let's add the fact that this trinity transcends time and space and can have all natural and supernal laws available to do its bidding—then synchronicity happens threefold.

Human thinking usually tries to limit perception to digestible bits of percepts bound by time and space within a recognizable, familiar framework called a concept. That type of perception will only get you through the material world. But if you could add a *sense of timing* that often brought you to just the right place at the right time, you might be more useful and more economical with your time.

If you could move through space without any hindrance and fly anywhere you wanted as quickly as you like, you might feel the economy of purpose you would possess. As a trinity of being, Sophia has these advantages. She is ubiquitous synchronicity working through the individual for the good of all.

When you resonate with Sophia's vibrations, which exist beyond your human concept of time and space, you become a vehicle to incarnate the spiritual intentions of the hierarchies. As Sophia's tool, you can become an agent of grace and mercy. This is the nature of Sophia's revelation in the willpower of the human being.

When we act out of pure Intuition, we become Sophia's will.

When we receive spiritual Inspiration in our hearts, we become Her feeling.

When we fill our minds with fiery Imaginations of the spirit, we become Her thinking.

The threefold nature of humanity unfolds synergistically with the threefold nature of Sophia.

The human being is a trinity of thinking, feeling, and willing, and this balancing act prepares us for the reality of the spiritual world.

Patience

When love comes, we are always joined together,
freely giving the gifts from heaven above.
We are moved to deeds filled with warmth of heart
burning for the causes of good.
Your love embraces my broken temple, sacrificed to the
Goddess, built anew.
A bridge between today and tomorrow is raised again
by grace given from beyond.

Our imperfections are refined in our hearths of love, rising to new joys
　　ringing with their home—the divine.

Your gracious mercy and holy union carry me again across the bridge to lands
　　filled with wisdom-light and sacred songs of praise,

While we unite as citizens of this New Eden, this Spirit Land of peace and
　　illumination,

That joins the opposites, cancels oppressing space and nagging time and finds our heart
　　as the world's center,

A new temple, sacred ground only present for those who are timeless through love's
　　freeing power.

You cannot be prepared, calculated, or deserving of this love, for it is the active agent of
　　selfless deeds,

The author of surrender, the spontaneous ubiquitous binding of all, giving birth from the
　　past as a gift to the future through freedom now.

When love comes, my soul soars and sees all through the eyes of my beloved—the holy
　　sight divine—the wedding vows of the royal couple,

Birthing a spirit child from beyond, a dweller of that other realm, who
　　we create together through our love,

As our sacred union of devotion becomes a reverent deed to heal all others throughout
　　all worlds.

The cosmos is gathered into the bundle of our heart-rose, a grail, born of celestial vision
　　and beauty,

An example of love's gifts of light, grace, and goodness, which fill our lives each
　　moment we forget our self and give love freely.

When love comes, no challenge or threshold of change shall ever separate us again and
　　become one who forgets the boundless divine;

For when love comes, you shall be ever upon my lips, held warm in the grail temple of
　　my heart—the altar of Our Spirit.

THIRD SEAL
The Twelve Labors of Sophia

She is the universal solvent that makes that which is hard soft;

light, dark; forward, backward; and the present, timeless.

She is the intimate lover's embrace that unites the Three Worlds into one.

She is the dawn and the dusk, and all in-between states of being

that remember what was and will be.

The Mother

Sophia as the Creatrix

It is only into Her arms that we can willingly surrender

and sleep, or die, or suffer long;

Only Her emptiness can hold what we bring from life

and plant in the fields of Spirit.

Sophia as the Great Goddess can be found throughout all lands as the primal deity of worship. Initially worshipped as the Goddess of Past/Present/Future or Birth/Death/Rebirth, only later did She devolve to a Trinity of Father/Son/Holy Ghost, devoid of any divine feminine influence.

The ancients also worshipped the Goddess with many different animal heads. Typically, between ten and twelve different animals comprised a pantheon of Goddesses. These became the star clusters of Earth's zodiac—eagle, snake, fish, goat, lion, tiger, bull, horse, mouse, ram, and so on. The Goddess was the Great Tree wherein the stars hung like fruit. Later, She would wrap them as a pala or star-studded wisdom cloak around Her shoulders.

When the ancient clairvoyants looked at star clusters in the zodiac, they saw images that reminded them of the ten months of human gestation. These stages of human embryological development are symbolized both in the zodiac and later in the formation of the convolutions of the brain.

The Great Goddess was the being of Wisdom, who designed the human being as a distillation of the cosmos compacted into a holographic image of the divine. Each zodiacal sign represented the mother participating in the stages of creation.

The ten months became the ten labors of Heracles, who was originally known as the Heroine of Hera, the Goddess who ruled birth in the Greek pantheon. The "ten labors for Hera" are the ten months of the embryo's recapitulation of human evolution. This is the alchemical transformation and birth of a soul emerging into a human form.

All mothers are alchemists. Sophia as Mother is the only One who holds all secrets of transformation and metamorphoses in the kingdoms of nature. She embodies all mothers through these great labors of humanity birthing its consciousness.

In time, the Greeks turned the original female heroine of Hera into the male Heracles, whom Hera hated and hounded throughout his life. The male Heracles had ten labors (two were added later to make twelve) that were located on the Earth and associated with physical animals. He was assigned the labors as a punishment for killing his wife and six sons in a fit of rage.

In ancient Greek literature, the subsumpiton of the feminine sources of the divine is often only thinly hidden. Heracles was deemed to have cheated in performing two of the labors by relying on outside help to accomplish the task. Afterwards, two more labors were added. Then after the twelve labors, he had to live disguised as a woman among only women for seven years to finish and fulfill the labors placed upon him as punishment.

> *"All mothers are alchemists."*

Heracles had to become so much like a woman that no woman would know he was a man. His physical labors were not enough; he had to tame his own "animal nature" inside of himself to complete the labors. In the same way, a mother in labor is a heroine. Once her labors are complete, she still must tend the child with seven years of intense "female" care, just as Heracles was required to imitate a woman for seven years to finish his labors.

In effect, a mother becomes a creator goddess through birth. She also takes on many faces throughout courting, wedding, pregnancy, labor, birth, and the rearing of a child. The mother knows the cares of the creator. Death is often at the same doorway of birth, and the temporal nature of a helpless baby is profoundly awakening.

The female human has many faces, just as Sophia does, whether it be a trinity, a sevenfold configuration, a decem (10 months), or a zodiac

(12 months). Sophia sets and establishes all of the rhythms of life, death, and rebirth. Likewise, the human being mirrors Sophia's rhythms and resembles Her throughout the various life stages.

The infant female child evolves into the mother of other female infants, thus continuing the stream of life. One human female life can take on the twelve labors of Heracles and the Mysteries of birth, death, and rebirth. Profoundly beautiful, the revelation of Sophia follows the natural laws of metamorphosis and life cycles found in the evolving human.

The Mystery of Rebirth

Rebirth is a cyclical pattern attributable to Sophia. The great heroes and heroines made arduous journeys into the realms of hell (death) and returned (rebirth) to tell about it. Psyche journeyed to the underworld of Hades to redeem her betrayal of Eros and win back his love. Hermes, Orpheus, Heracles, Dionysus, and Aeneas all descended into Hades to overcome the fear of death and redeem a part of their immortal souls.

The Great Goddess of rebirth is a cornucopia of life burgeoning forth and then later falling back into that source at death, to be later born anew. Sophia is the cycle of time, the magical web of existence where everything is remembered, though seemingly forgotten. From life to life, the memories of incarnations weave this web of life, death, and rebirth.

Sophia is pictured as the Three Norns under the Great Tree Yggdrasil who spin, measure, and then cut the thread of life of all beings. Isis, too, was seen as the past, the present, and the future. The Triple Goddess was primary to all other deities in almost all cultures.

"Creation is not a big bang. She is a Big Birth."

Sophia is the Triple Goddess and more. She encompasses the wise aspects of all archetypes. Therefore, wherever you look, you will see Her weaving Her presence in the wisdom of nature and manifesting as the Queen. That is why an amorphous, changing, ever-growing image of Sophia, encompassing all aspects of feminine incarnation, is necessary for the enlightened thinker. Each human soul evolves through those changing archetypes of life and emulates them as higher principles.

The "New Labors of Heracles" is described as a thirteen-stage evolution of the soul into a higher archetype of the manifold human expression of Wisdom, Sophia. *The Gospel of Sophia* attempts to gather and synthesize words that can be spoken aloud to invoke, visualize, and embody the Goddess. This process of reading wisdom selections aloud is offered to the reader as a way to *become what you visualize*. The method of sutra (visualize), mantra (invoke), and tantra (embody) has been used effectively in the East for thousands of years. Based on the manifestation of the female archetypes in time and space, this is a helpful way to embody many of the qualities of Sophia.

As the consciousness of the thinker contemplates the divine and evolves, so further she develops an all-encompassing definition of the divine. New insight and inspiration must be added to the complete picture of an omniscient, omnipresent, omnipotent deity or deities. By standing on the backs of her ancestors, the observer gains a broader perspective. Otherwise, gods and goddesses will typically war with one another for control over human culture. Sophia Herself is all-encompassing; worship of Her has not been used for aggressive cultural control.

From the perspective of an animistic aboriginal, the mysteries of birth were tied to the female giving birth. Creation was as close as childbirth, yet it was little understood and approached with respect as a mysterious force, like the stars above. Nature was worshipped as a Mother.

In modern terms, Sophia is worshipped as the Mother of the Church, or the Holy Mother, or Mary, or Gaia Sophia. Throughout the evolution of thought, Sophia grows with the consciousness of the thinker. As Her revelation continues, it will unfold from a tightly closed bud to a gloriously unfurled, full blossom. This is why She is called the Rose of the World, as an image of the unfolding evolution of the divine growing alongside humanity. One day, the image of a Mother/Daughter/Holy Sophia Trinity will be as easily cognized as the image of Gaia—the living being of the Earth. Sophia is the future coming toward us to unfold our blossoms of higher soul and spiritual organs; She has imprinted the future of evolution inside the heart of humans. Her Temple of Wisdom (the human body) encompasses the archetypes of the divine that derive from the past, emanate from the future, and are visible in the present. We do not yet have all of the spiritual organs we will need to commune with these beings from the future, but they will unfold naturally. In later chapters of this book, the processes and the methods to develop those new spiritual organs will be highlighted.

Sophia is the bridge of time that enables the perfected future aspects of ourselves to manifest now. She has already planned the pathways to the future, where our higher spiritual self is whole and perfect. Existing beyond time and space, She has power over what human minds cannot yet comprehend. Only when we perceive the profound economy of the tapestry of Providence as She weaves human karma can we begin to understand Sophia's perspective.

Sophia as the Queen of the Kyriotetes orders with Wisdom all kingdoms of the hierarchy.

Sophia as Trinity is higher than the nine hierarchical ranks of spiritual beings.

She was there before time and space and will be there when time and space dissolve back into Her womb.

She is often pictured as the "waters" or the "face of the deep" or the "primal mix" of creation. Most religions mention Her, but few dwell on Her presence at creation.

"The universe is much more than intelligent design; it is heartfelt and patiently tended with a purpose that informs its participants through holographic connectedness."

Often, God the Father is seen as the unmanifest, while Sophia is the manifest world. There is an inference that the Holy Spirit was present at creation with the Father God and that some part of the Holy Spirit may be female (Sophia). Gnostics believe that Sophia and Christ were born simultaneously as space and time, while the Father God remained unmanifest. One way or the other, the creation event was female. Whether contemplated as a big bang of compact space exploding in all directions, or any other cosmological theory, Sophia was there.

The revision of female creation myths to male creation myths in Greek mythology is a clear example of the primal feminine forces of creation being subsumed. Male gods, who dominated by force, became the leading images of culture and commenced a war-centered history.

Prior to 2101 B.C., there was a ubiquitous belief in the Great Goddess. Archetypes ascribed to the Goddess-inspired culture demonstrated little or no war archetypes and no cultural archetypes to support domination of other cultures.

The theft of Helen from Greece by Troy began a new age where the Goddess was embodied in human form—Helen of Troy. Also in Troy was the palladium, a meteorite that was naturally shaped like the winged goddess, Pallas, and held sacred by both sides. Though Helen was clearly taken back by the Greeks, the palladium was claimed to have been won by both sides. During this era, Sophia was envisioned as a mortal human, and an animistic meteorite became the center of historic transmission of culture from Asia Minor to Greece and Rome. Likewise, the female in creation has been pushed to the background and minimized, although in some cases not entirely obscured.

Some modern thinkers live in sandcastle theories that do not last much longer than the next generation's tide. Astrophysics is principally speculation. Human understanding is very limited and even less cohesive. Often myths, religions, and fairytales get us closer to the truth than theoretical science.

"We are carefully tucked into our little bed of ground like seeds lovingly planted in the dark of the earth dreaming of a day when the tender warmth of the sun will draw us forth into the light."

Can humans create life? Can we understand light or life? Is there a definition of what a human has been, is, and will be? These are all fundamental questions that science does not explain.

Why was there creation to begin with?

Ask a mother why she would have another baby after she has gone through nine months of pregnancy and then the labor of birth, afterbirth, and care of a child. Yet she chooses this path, with joy, again and again. Once scientists understand a mother's overwhelming desire to create at all costs, then, and only then, will science begin to understand creation.

Creation is not a big bang. She is a Big Birth.

Sophia was created before any of the heavenly hierarchies, and She is part of the Trinity of Mother/Daughter/Holy Sophia that rules from outside the realm that human comprehension can reach.

The Sixth Rank of Angels, called the Kyriotetes (the Spirits of Wisdom), are in charge of the order and rule of all nine hierarchies. Wisdom is present at every rank of the hierarchies and the Kyriotetes work through the Being of Sophia. She uses the combined forces of the Kyriotetes as Her vehicle of expression. Many view Sophia as the wellspring of all natural manifestation, both life and death. She is sometimes given credit for being equal with God, His Mate, or His creation, but there are few revelations that indicate that all of those possibilities are true.

It would seem to reason that Sophia is a mirror or the epiphany of God, some type of substance upon which creation was "written" or "spoken" from out of some super-abundant source of creation. This male-female polarity is but one possibility.

Embryology shows us another possibility called parthenogenesis, wherein all humans are female early in development. In other words, we all originate from one female source before subsequently developing into male and female forms. This simple fact of a natural process should give some pause to male-dominated, sun-oriented religions.

Modern science shows that there is a striking polarity between supermassive black holes and supermassive ion jets alternating at the center of most stable galaxies. Matter is seemingly destroyed by the

> **"Only a free deed of love could have created the wisdom of the natural world."**

black hole, then created by the ion jet. There was no big bang in this cycle of giving and taking, birth and death. There was rhythmic exchange between manifestation and non-manifestation.

Call it the Father God of the ground of unmoving space (black hole) and the Mother Creatrix of irresistible time (ion jet). Both sides are equal. Both must be willing to surrender their natures to each other so that creation can arise through their efforts.

Only a free deed of Love could have created the Wisdom of the natural world.

The universe is much more than intelligent design; it is heartfelt and patiently tended with a purpose that informs its participants through multi-dimensional holographic super-connectedness. In other words, our bodies are the hieroglyphic monad—the Mystery revealed and concealed—the secret that lay behind Isis's Veil. We must all lift the veil and see ourselves as the locus of the divine within the temple of the human body, the Temple of Wisdom (Pansophia).

Each new aspect of creation is found in the Temple of Pansophia. Each night, the higher thinking, feeling, and willing of humanity perpetually adds to the construction of this temple. This building is the body of Sophia, the living being who knows the personal development of every human.

Sophia is similar to the collective super-consciousness of humanity, except that She is from both the hierarchy and the Divine Feminine Trinity.

She knows all the travails of cosmic and human birth, and all things in between.

She was there before creation, during creation, and tends Her children until the end of creation.

She is both within the stream of time and beyond its rushing currents.

She rules space in all of its permutations and dimensions.

Without the cohesive consciousness of One Being ruling and governing the Earth and the heavens, worlds would collide.

We are carefully tucked into our little bed of ground like seeds lovingly planted in the dark of the earth, dreaming of a day when the tender warmth of the sun will draw us forth into the light. Out of the deep sleep of humans, Sophia is awakening as the Goddess of Creation more and more each day. If scientists could understand just one facet of the Goddesses, such as the Titan Thetis, who could morph into any form in creation, they would have a new archetype to embody the wonders of nature that are continually being discovered.

Humans have tortured nature until Her secrets scream louder than ears can endure. Quantum physics shows that the Creatrix is hard to pin down and even harder to explain with the concepts and theories available to limited human understanding. Some scientists look to ancient religions for clues, images, and stories that explain the breathtaking miracles of nature and supernature.

For instance, the ancients often began their concepts of creation with a polarity of waters above and below, and of earth and sky. After brooding between light and darkness, typically an egg is formed. From this, the Earth is created in some fashion.

These images may seem oversimplified, but they provide the foundation of a very potent archetype upon which to build. Polarities create a spheroid of life, an egg. From this, a boundary is created between inner and outer, which subsequently hatches something new, built from the interior substance while interacting with the exterior.

Surprisingly, these types of archetypes apply both to embryology and astrophysics quite accurately. In fact, there may be more scientific knowledge in this simple myth than, contained in the current theories of gravity and levity.

The star and the embryo, both the grand and the small, follow Sophia's natural laws and lovingly strive to become more of the essence She has given them. It is for the love of creation that we become human and long to become divine.

It is fair to say that modern scientific theories of creation or cosmology are no more accurate than ancient ones. Now that the female has been extracted, the universe is seen as a clock winding down, a machine supposedly wound up by a big bang. Scientists explode matter in experiments to find out how matter began, and they found out that exploding matter began matter. So shallow, this concept cannot be taken seriously, especially in light of new discoveries about what is in the center of galaxies.

Essentially, humans are between and in the midst of the large and the small.

We are creator gods and goddesses, but do not yet know it.

We have a solar system in our bodies.

We have the future in our organs that hold the evolution of new capacities and senses.

We are just hatchlings crying to be fed.

While we cannot yet fly, Sophia is the Mother Bird who can soar to faraway realms to bring us back the delicacies of the world. As the creator of our bodies, the vehicle of consciousness, She has given us the most precious gift in any universe or any dimension: free will, to use our Temple of Wisdom for either divine or devolved purposes.

We can evolve naturally, or rebel and fall behind as the Luciferic hosts have done. In so doing, these backward beings have helped create the illusion of time and space as a temporary theater of experience for evolving humans. Creation made room for humans and spiritual hierarchies to evolve. Nothing stays the same. All things evolve, else they fall behind. Human consciousness evolves, and collectively we advance our definition of the divine as it reveals itself. One person's progress in thought is the ladder of the next person behind her. Each new human idea conceived creates an elemental knowledge that continues to live beyond the life of its creator. This morphic thought-field is then available for any other human who can rise to understanding.

Thought is not personal. When humanity is ready for new concepts, the spiritual world rejoices. Humans simultaneously rise up to the new archetype and create a space inside of their soul to embrace it. Higher principles of thinking are not personal. They are the common property the universe uses to create the material world that we see. It is safe to say that material things are essentially slowed-down thought.

Sophia's part in creation is a commitment to the created. How could a mother not love her child? The Great Mother is always there, changing faces to enhance our experience of creation. As we evolve in Her likeness, She grows with us, through us. We could have no greater example to extol and emulate than Sophia the Creatrix. We are co-creators with Her.

The Creatrix

The Eternal Now swallows all pasts and births all futures,
Creating a chalice that forms for a moment to harden and then dissolve
     the substance of life, the rush of passion.
It is Novalis' Night, the Akasha of the Hindus,
     the Zero Point of creation and remembering.
She is our one Mother—the Mother of all sentient beings,
     accepting death and giving birth and life anew.

No one can cognize Her labyrinthine ways,
    for She quiets all meager thought in Her embrace;
No one has seen Her, for She extinguishes all light
    in the darkness of Her womb;
No one has spoken truth about Her because all words
    are mute before Her terrible silence;
No one has stood before Her, for She dissembles the upright soul
    into beds of blissful sleep,
Healing all words wrongly spoken, all deeds not good and true,
    all imaginings that limit.
She is the universal solvent that makes that which is hard soft; light, dark;
    forward, backward; and the present, timeless.
She is the intimate lover's embrace that unites the Three Worlds into one.
She is the dawn and the dusk, and all in-between states of being
    that remember what was and will be.
She is the shared presence of timeless, eternal love that shines
    from a mother's eyes to her child,
The knowing Wisdom of all things working together for good,
    in paths of simple beauty.
Each freely surrendered moment unites us with Her cause
    and shows us Her infinite fields of Wisdom;
That spiraling, milky cloud that beckons our soul to spirit's tunnel of love,
    swirling in blissful passion.
She unites the eternal drops in our soul's heart into a shower
    of fragrant blossoms blessing the spirit;
She is the one, the many, the levels of hell and heaven
    opening before our tender, seeking soul;
Calling us by name, with the most personal and divine voice
    that joins our soul to all others.
The hosts of angels never fail to do Her work
    and prepare all hierarchies for their sacred futures.

God Himself is incomplete without His Holy Consort,
     the Beloved Epiphany of life, death, and rebirth;
Completely alone, yet united with all—the Secret Lover
     whose soul is pure and spirit is loyal and true.
She is our Virgin Soul, immaculately conceiving the divine will
     through grace and understanding.
She can move all things through total stillness, and Her voice
     creates the Music of the Spheres sounding together.
The joys and sorrows of all who wish to be a part of Her unfolding
     accepts everyone as they are.
It is only into Her arms that we can willingly surrender
     and sleep, or die, or suffer long;
Only Her emptiness can hold what we bring from life
     and plant in the fields of spirit,
Only Her care can birth the dreams that drive our conscious lives
     to new heights of free deeds,
Only Her whisper reminds us that our lives are echoed versions
     of who we dream we are each night,
Only the hope of knowing that She will accept everything
     we bring Her each night, ignites our tomorrows.
Who can hold us so tenderly and yet free us so gracefully,
     or let us make our childish errors without blame?
Who else can guide our path by being already at the end,
     where our home has always been waiting?
Only She who is triple in Beauty, Power, and Love,
     who always was, is, and ever will be;
She is the fulcrum of existence, the ever-present power of love
     through freedom without compulsion;
Always knowing, always caring, always forgiving —
     the Midwife of self that births all selves,
Our hearth, our home, our heaven, Our Mother.

Sophia as the Mother of All

Mother, the source of all creation, the fruit of spiritual hope,

You offer your sacred ground of being, to suffer and to cope

With all the darkness, doubt, and anger of this lonely world

Drawn into one miraculous space, where emptiness has swirled

And flowed into a sea of blissful fecundity.

Tibetan Buddhists believe that we have been or will be the mother to all other beings and, likewise, they to us. Thinking this way, it is easy to develop compassion for all others. This sentiment is instructive in understanding why Sophia is seen as the Mother of All.

We can see by association that as a Creatrix, Sophia assumes the role of Mother of All almost by default. As the ancients drew closer and closer to Sophia, they better understood the forces of nature. Each cycle of time brought Her closer to their intellectual world.

The Creatrix Goddess and creation could be objectified and kept at a distance, but not so with the Mother. Every person can understand the connection to the Mother, so much so with the Mother of All. Humans cry out instinctively to their mother to care for them the way only a mother can. Birthing children is the highest honor of life and the central task of human existence—each mother as her own special creatrix goddess. Motherhood is universal, once reincarnation is understood. We have all been mothers many times, in many incarnations.

Motherhood is as essential as the desire to live. A mother will give up her life for her children, and she will help them live the best life they can lead. Biological, psychological, and spiritual, the motherhood bond is learned from the natural world but made supernatural by humans.

Love is beyond biology when given freely. From nature, we learn the cycles of life and death, yet humans defy death through reincarnation. With seeming supernatural law, they can defy natural law.

Sophia goes beyond creation in the human being because we ourselves become creators through free will. This replication of creation is like a holographic universe. We are all creators. Some of us have more "wisdom" in our creation than others. Through our children, we also create new worlds. Our personal creative efforts build possibilities that can nourish others. We are gods and goddesses of an order. By following Sophia's example, we can become loving Mothers of All.

In aboriginal cultures, the mother was the central seat of social life. The first initiation mysteries were the Mysteries of childbirth, often with midwives holding tribal healing knowledge. Birth was the key to life or death. Midwives developed the first images to record the cycles of time so that human births could coincide harmoniously with nature. Lunar cycles were the first measure of time in the Mysteries of the female birth cycles. Only much later did planting cycles derive from solar observation. The first thrones were birthing thrones; the first temples were round, signifying the pregnant belly. The wise women of the past watched over the thresholds of birth and death; they were *The Mothers.*

The Mothers also are the archetypes that live in the nine layers of the Earth and the 28 steps on the stairway of consciousness between the Earth and Moon. The Mothers control magma as it surges up from the mysterious realm below from which they, too, arise. Volcanoes spew forth mountains of lava that build the ground we walk upon. The rivers of molten minerals and rock that flow throughout the Earth congeal and are thrust skyward.

The Mothers continued to create, drawing down the waters above into the waters below. Thus, the oceans were created and life was born. The Mothers designed it all with archetypes from deep within the Earth and realms between the Earth and the Moon.

The Sun is the ultimate mother in this world, constantly enlivening all She shines upon.

The Moon is male, the father of crystallization and death on the Earth. He effects tides and cycles of solar, planetary, and stellar influence.

The Mother creates, from sources yet unfound, a perpetual fountain of life that reflects the archetypes of the divine into this material world.

Birth and death are realms of the Mothers, who give all and then receive all as it dies and falls back into the source of its life. Through rebirth, the Mothers then give new birth from the dying. They are the night and dark, all that is forgotten or thought lost. They can hold the dying and still remember.

"The tapestry of time is the biography of mothers giving birth to other mothers in a never-ending lineage of love."

The Mothers hold the life of all that has been, and coherently gather the threads to weave the image of our personal lives into all that will be.

The tapestry of time is the biography of mothers giving birth to other mothers in a never- ending lineage of love. The Mothers love and suffer all, just as Her lava ground creates the earth we walk upon. It is Her blood spilt for our foundation. Her watery fountains of life are also a wellspring of creation. She continually gives so that we, too, may give.

The ancients could see that they were placed here, watched over, and taught by the loving Mother of All. Of course, they had to observe and obey Her laws as best they could. The more they knew of the Mother of Life, the Mother of All, the more they could fit into their environment effectively, "commune" with nature, and even bend Her to their will for power and might.

The power of the Mothers was a force to be worked with for control of nature and the environment. These Mysteries were a tradition passed on from one wise woman to the next. Women met in secret, teaching each other the mysteries of fire, the secrets of procreation, and the knowledge of the Mothers.

When ancients, aided by collective clairvoyance, saw the forces of nature at work, they listened as if their own mothers were instructing them in a valuable life lesson. Nature spoke to the ancients and told Her secrets. Thoughts or archetypes existed externally from the seer and were shared commonly by all.

The Mothers taught their children both sides of life and death. To the ancients, nature did not seem cruel, for they could see its necessity—the basis of life. Indeed, it seemed as if the Mother of All watched over every aspect of living and dying. Cycles of life were a reality. The seer was in the lap of the divine, feeling truly that the Mother of All was watching over them with loving care.

Mother

Mother, the source of all creation, the fruit of spiritual hope,
You offer your sacred ground of being, to suffer and to cope
With all the darkness, doubt, and anger of this lonely world
Drawn into one miraculous space, where emptiness has swirled
And flowed into a sea of blissful fecundity.
Your love for the newborn citizens of this earthly plain,
Has taught you the spiritual Wisdom we must regain,
Through labor, sweat, and blood you have suffered long,
To birth the innocent babe, who someday will be so strong
That his love and strength will carry you along.
It's an honor to watch and feel the adamantine bonds of love,
That only a mother and child can receive from the gods above.
Such terrestrial ties show us the path of compassion that lies
Clearly before us all, with our enlightened eyes.
So rejoice in finding happiness, and the end of suffering's grips,
Reach out and take heaven's immortal nectar to your lips.

Sophia as the
Goddess of Wisdom

You are that Temple palace that calls forth the scene

Upon which all history awakes as an innocent dream.

We dance destiny's rhythms, Her cloak in time and space,

We shall come to know our rightful spiritual place.

As humans evolved, so did their thought processes about the divine. As the ancient forces of clairvoyance weakened in the light of individual thought and philosophical development, the divine faded into a far distance.

As the ancients spent more and more time thinking about the divine and examining their own thought processes, the connection to the Mothers, or the Creatrix, was veiled.

During this era, Sophia moved further away from human cognition. Direct experience of Her, which had once been so powerful, became lost in time and space. Though Her form was seen everywhere, there was no name to embody Her many qualities, so the ancients called Her Wisdom and hid Her behind all mysteries in nature.

Wisdom, for them, meant what their predecessors all referred to as the Mothers, the Mother of All, or the Creatrix Goddess. It became a symbol and metaphor for individual human evolution. It also became a search for Sophia, the Being of Wisdom, who is much sought after but seldom found.

Much like the Mysteries of the Mothers, Wisdom is a path to secret knowledge that will advance one's personal evolution. To understand creation and the natural forces of nature is to obtain power, but to attain Wisdom is far beyond that, for it exists beyond this world of gross material matter. It is to be possessed and treasured by the thinker more than silver or gold, diamonds or jewels. In fact, the thinker is consumed by finding a path to Her and develops philosophies to meet Her face to face. Philosophy, after all, means "the lover of wisdom."

The Wisdom tradition of the Hebrews is a beautiful path of relationships evolving with Wisdom. At times, Wisdom is the cause of the search for spiritual awakening. At others, She is the Virgin Beloved found through yearning and longing for the wedding day.

In the wisdom teachings of the Hebrews, She becomes everything from the Creator to the Beloved. She is personal to Solomon, Baruch, and David, who speak of Her in a thousand ways, with words unparalleled in literature.

The love of Wisdom is higher than any attainment on Earth, yet will perhaps cost you everything you know and hold dear to heart: your spouse, your family, your wealth, your name, and anything tied to this world.

Wisdom brings wings to the soul to mount the heavens on the other side of the threshold. Ancient clairvoyance took the seer of the past into the world of living thought where the seeds of all ideas reside. This natural ability connected him not through thought, for thought was just becoming individualized and personal, but through direct experience with the spiritual beings who resided in all things and could be found in the wisdom of nature and within the human being.

Thoughts existed outside of the human body and were accessible to all. Anyone with the ability to rise up to thought could join in the living presence of archetypal ideas, which are the seeds of the material world. All of humanity experienced these beings in nature. Through animistic reverence, people saw them manifested in fire, lightning, storms, and the countless forces of nature that are driven by *seeming* consciousness.

Father Abraham, the Father of the Hebrews, Christians, and Muslims, was the "father of mathematics" because he developed the inward intellectual paradigm to express these forces. True mathematics sheds light on the frequencies of planetary vibrations that interpenetrate each human through their corresponding organs. Mathematics leads to the "music of the spheres," which harmonizes the seven centers of music that resonate in our chakras.

The ancient seer perceived the thoughts of nature both as living beings in his external environment, and within the human body as reflections of the heavens in the microcosm of the human temple. The books of wisdom refer to this understanding of the sevenfold nature of the human temple as the Seven Pillars of the Temple of Wisdom, the first order of creation.

This Temple was dedicated to Sophia, the Goddess of Wisdom, traditionally present at creation. Often this reference serves as the foundation for Christians to claim that Sophia is the Holy Spirit or Christ, since Christians adopt Jewish creation stories. So was Christ there at creation? Or perhaps the Holy Spirit?

Clearly, Sophia was there with the Father God of the Ground of Being, who does not manifest because Sophia is the very Wisdom of creation. Every primal act of movement was done with and through Wisdom, who had been given the complete plan of creation by the Beings of Harmony (Cherubim).

> *"The divine is not comprehensible to earthly human thought."*

Sophia (as the Kyriotetes) had been empowered by the Beings of Divine Will (Thrones) to create all worlds as the Kyriotetes, those Beings of Wisdom who sustain the control and order of all forces in the hierarchy.

Sophia the Mother is equal to the Father God of the Ground of Being. Therefore, the Being of Wisdom, Sophia, is also part of a Trinity of Goddesses who we call Mother, Daughter, and the Holy Sophia.

The nature of both of the Trinities of Male and Female are beyond human comprehension. The Mystery of the Three in One is not a logical equation that can be solved. Even with quantum physics, we only begin to understand. With string theory and zero-point physics we get a little closer, and with the Akashic Theory of Memory and Time by Irvin Laszlo, we can begin to understand the nature of the Trinity.

Basically, the Trinity concept implies a double paradox compounded.

If God and Christ are one and the same but separate—then what?

If God and the Holy Spirit are one and the same with Christ—then what? Who is who?

Essentially, we have another paradox in that Christ was and was not there at creation and likewise the Holy Spirit. Plus, Christ said He would send the Holy Spirit after He left.

Then where were Christ and the Holy Spirit before they manifested on Earth?

If God is in "heaven" and "not of this Earth," and Christ said that He was going to "My Father's kingdom" and there He would be, then who maintains creation?

All of these conundrums cannot be logically figured out with our brain-bound thinking, even with new fancy theories.

The Divine is not comprehensible to earthly human thinking.

Only the Divine within us can experience the Divine, and only when the three parts of the human being come into alignment: body, soul, and spirit. This is much akin to the Trinity. Humans reflect the Divine Image and the Mystery Wisdom of the Trinity in their nature as body/soul/spirit and thinking/feeling/willing.

The Trinity is the uniting force that weaves between the hierarchies. Each of the three ranks of the hierarchy is coordinated by one of the Beings of the Trinity. This is true for both the Male and Female Trinities, Father/Son/Holy Spirit, and Mother/Daughter/Holy Sophia.

So, too, with the human being; we have both inner and outer counterparts to the Male and Female Trinity. Thinking, feeling, and willing are the inner aspects of the human being that relate to the Male Trinity. Imagination, Inspiration, and Intuition relate to the outer being and higher development of the human consciousness and the Female Trinity.

> *"Christ and Sophia are the merging of love and wisdom."*

It is Christ who, together with all the hierarchies that He passed through in His descent to the Earth to become human, creates and sustains the physical, material vehicle for consciousness or the human "I" or ego.

It is Sophia who, together with all the hierarchies that She passed through in Her descent to the Earth to become human, nurtures the new and developing seeker into the creative fields of the higher natures of thinking, feeling, and willing as Imagination, Inspiration, and Intuition.

Christ is the perfected human, and Sophia is our aid in becoming Christ-like.

Christ gave the three gifts of standing upright, speaking, and thinking to humanity before He incarnated in a physical body. Rudolf Steiner speaks extensively about these pre-earthly deeds of Christ.

As Christ descended from the ranks of the Elohim (Spirits of Form) through the ranks of the archai, archangels, and angels, He used these hierarchies to make the gifts to humanity.

Sophia descended from the ranks of the Kyriotetes (Spirits of Wisdom) down through the hierarchy of the Dynamis (Spirits of Motion), the Elohim (Spirits of Form), and the Archai (Time Spirits).

As Christ descended to the Earth to become human, so did Sophia descend closer to humanity as She assisted Christ with each of the pre-earthly deeds.

Both used the hierarchy as vehicles for the transformation and evolution of consciousness.

Spiritually paired, both have a component in their respective Trinities that place them beyond the manifestation of the combined hierarchies.

Christ and Sophia are the merging of Love and Wisdom.

Athena

The Greeks believed in Truth, Beauty, and Goodness and sought them in all that they did. They embodied Wisdom in the Goddess Athena, who also is a trinity of beings.

Athena was known as the Goddess of the Harvest, the Goddess of Victory (Nike), and the Goddess who sprang fully armored from the head of Zeus. In Athens, the Acropolis contains three temples dedicated to her triple nature. For the Greek philosopher, truth is synonymous with wisdom, beauty is synonymous with power, and goodness is synonymous with victory and love.

Athena the Armored had an owl on her shoulder that knew all things and whispered that wisdom into her ear. She wore an image of Medusa on her shield as a symbol of power, and her husband was Hephaestus (Vulcan), who crafted Zeus's thunderbolts.

She held in her outstretched hand the palladium, described as a winged goddess purportedly made of meteoric iron that never rusts.

Next to the temple to Athena the Armored is a small temple to Athena-Nike.

Nike was the winged goddess who represented victory and love. It was said that whoever "held" her in their possession would always rule. She is much like the palladium, a winged goddess who represents the favor of Athena, the Goddess of Wisdom. In fact, the Goddess Nike, the Winged Goddess of Wisdom, Beauty, and Love, is an early precursor to Athena the Armored.

The primary goddess on the acropolis is Athena of the Harvest. The priestesses of Athena the Harvest Goddess (much like Demeter), gathered each year to celebrate agricultural bounty and plan for a new year based upon a lunar planting cycle, which as we have already seen was derived from the Feminine Mysteries.

All three representations of Athena that developed over time give us a good example of how the Female Mysteries were eclipsed by the more dominant male war gods. In a single culture that was focused on the attainment of Wisdom, we can see evidence of the slow evolution from matriarchy to patriarchy.

Athena the Armored was the new male version of Wisdom who holds Nike (the palladium) in Her hand and Athena the Harvest Goddess in Her shadow. It is interesting to note that both the Greeks and the Romans claimed to possess the palladium as proof of being the new home of Wisdom. Indeed, the Greeks were so concerned that warring conquerors would steal Nike the Victorious that they cut off her wings so that she would be incapable of flight to other lands.

It is easy to see in this example of mythology-turned-history where the interior Feminine Mysteries of Wisdom were subsumed by the exterior male mysteries of war. This is also seen in the male-dominated Christian religions where God the Father is unmanifest and rules the past, the Son God Christ is manifest and rules in the present, and the Holy Spirit is "in the making," drawing us forward into the future. This is the Triple God.

A trinity of Gods then resolves the paradoxes of time and space. But this simplified system leaves many questions unanswered and several paradoxes unaddressed. The blending of these two Trinities of male and female resolve the dilemma, as both the manifest and unmanifest elements of the Trinities combine to create our dualistic universe.

The Greeks did not seem to mind living with the paradoxes of the three Athenas on the Acropolis. They prayed to whichever goddess seemed most appropriate for their needs.

They did not seem bothered by Athena's transformation to the characteristics of male warfare. They believed that the wise or clever warrior would win the battle if they worshiped Athena (the threefold goddess), for she sprung from the head of Zeus, the most powerful.

Athena had the owl of wisdom for counsel.

She held the palladium of victory in her hands.

She was the combined influence of the True, the Beautiful, and the Good.

In her shadow, Western philosophy was born.

As the mathematical thinker was born in Aristotle and spread by Alexander to the far corners of the known world, the message of the Goddess of Wisdom, Pallas Athena, was also taken with them and measured against all that was known about Her in other cultures.

This spread of Greek thinking advanced Sophia's influence throughout the male-dominated cultures of the Mediterranean and both the Near and Far East. In order to gain perspective of the new and active revelation of Sophia, the awakened thinker now had to understand the past natures of Sophia as Creatrix, Mother of All, and the Being of Wisdom. Wisdom entered thinking first through Father Abraham, then via the mind of the ancient Greek philosopher. The biography of the Holy Sophia, in fact, begins with this evolution: from clairvoyant perception of living thought-beings outside of humanity to the recognition of Wisdom within our own thinking and the external laws of nature.

Being of Wisdom

Sophia, the Being of Wisdom, descended through the hierarchy from the realm of the Feminine Trinity, moving closer to humanity as She entered each new hierarchical rank.

In 2100 B.C., She fully entered the realm of the human domain as a human-like being, just as the first individuated thought was being born in Father Abraham and other abstract thinkers. Sophia took great interest in the development of each human intellect and its effect on the collective consciousness of humanity. She nurtured the Hebrew people and the development of their God—who was given the name "I am." This is also the name of each human intellect.

The development of the individual consciousness impacts the development of the whole. As each human ascends towards higher spiritual principals that give the soul wings, Sophia is there with them step by step. She is the Mother, the midwife, and the nursemaid of human consciousness. She bridges the span of time and space because She is part of the Divine Feminine Trinity, whose essential nature creates and sustains time and space.

This time paradox shows that we all have an ideal spiritual body that is like that of an angel. Becoming this angel is the mission of human evolution. The question then arises, "Why can't we simply go outside of time and space (with Sophia's help) and embody our future angel bodies right now?"

The answer is quite simple. We can and do.

Every time we raise ourselves to spiritual thoughts, feelings, and deeds (Imagination, Inspiration, Intuition), we give Sophia an opportunity to draw back the folds of space and time and unite our present self with our angelic future self.

This embodiment, otherwise experienced as synchronicity, may only come in flashes of truth for the new researcher, but for those devoting their lives to Christ through Sophia, it is a way of life.

Christ stands at the Earthly side of the threshold and Sophia on the spiritual side, mothering every birth of a spiritual self.

> *"Sophia is always and everywhere, beyond time and space."*

No spiritual deed ever happens without witness from the spiritual world. We ourselves have our own memory of our spiritual merit, but the spiritual world has its own.

Sophia is the one who writes and reads the Akashic Records. It is She who holds us up by the hand until we learn to stand.

It is Sophia who teaches us the *language of the spirit* as we learn to speak as children in the Kingdom of the Spirit.

It is Sophia who helps guide our way along the path to the Kingdom of the Spirit.

Sophia is always and everywhere, beyond time and space, and yet acts coherently in all dimensions. That is why the ancient Hebrews found Wisdom so inexplicable and seemingly unattainable.

Their lack of clairvoyance caused Wisdom to be hidden, if not slain. When the light of the heavens appeared in thinking, Sophia was drawn back into the human presence. The Hebrews and Greeks courted Wisdom and sought Her blessings in every possible way. These blessings were tangible fruits of the spirit that made Abraham, Solomon, Aristotle, and other thinkers wise in the annals of history.

Dominant cultures were driven by a desire to seek Wisdom beyond the human body with clear thinking. Awakening to the outside world and seeking knowledge brought great power as the forces of nature were twisted into engines of war.

Knowledge dominated culture and war dominated the landscape.

The principal aim of the budding roots of science was to awaken to the power of natural forces. Humans wanted "to know"—*scio*—and, thus, science was born.

The Greeks essentially gave us a foundation of knowledge that did not lead us to the Beings behind nature but rather to the forces behind nature. They articulated a new mythology of human concepts that described forces instead of Beings in nature.

Sophia then descended further into the ideas of Greek philosophy, named after the original lovers of Wisdom, philo-Sophia. The philosopher stood just as far above Democrates' atom as he was below the Gods of Olympus: exactly in the middle of the universe as a thinking being who can control some forces in nature and still worship those he cannot understand. Basically, we have not advanced much further than the Greeks in many respects. We are still living in the shadows of Greek philosophy and Roman law.

If you wish to evolve, seek Wisdom at all costs. Pursue Sophia as She develops in the mind of the natural human intellect, because that is Her home.

Each human can read and study the thoughts of philosophers over the four thousand years since Sophia was born as the Holy Sophia. Today's thinker has access to most of the sacred literature written down by those who experienced direct clairvoyant interaction with Sophia and those who struggled to reconnect with Her after human intellect impeded clairvoyance.

Study the ancient cultures; many descriptions of Sophia remain. Study of such literature, as outlined in the *Fourth Seal*, is highly instructive, for it shows that Sophia has communicated with the great sages and seers of the past.

The beauty of Sophia is that She has never been unfaithful to the sages or the seekers of Wisdom. The descriptions of Her majesty are among the greatest writings of humanity.

The Father God may be invisible, but Sophia has never stopped appearing to humans on the path of spiritual development and She will continue to do so ever more as we unfold our higher spiritual bodies that She has prepared for us.

She gives the Greek philosopher wings to rise up through the soul to experience the spiritual archetypes.

She bestows on us the radiant white robe that we adorn before entering the Temple.

She guides us along the path to gain the Wisdom necessary for our spiritual advancement.

The wings of Sophia are our higher thoughts that rise up to the realm of true spiritual Imaginations in the light of Wisdom.

The white robe of Sophia is the washed clean astral body of desires—the vessel for true spiritual Inspirations that harmonize with the hierarchy.

The path of Sophia is the path of Wisdom, which can be found by surrendering our will to the higher spiritual Intuitions of Sophia.

When all three are earned—the wings, the robe, and the path to the Temple of Wisdom—then "Wisdom has made Her temple of seven pillars" and we accept the angel body that Sophia has prepared for us as we spiritually evolve.

Temple of Wisdom

Marble-columned Temple of Wisdom strong and true
Embodies the canon of proportions as Beauty's sacred dew,
Each turn with grace so wholesome and exquisitely fine
Surely Sophia as Goddess in you I find.
Your loving glance flamed my cold, dead heart
And your touch divine, burnt my limbs apart
Into a conflagration of falling love unheeded,
Into the garden of the ancient ones we seeded
A love from ages untold, rolled into one
Before my eyes as brilliant as the noon-day sun.
Yes, we are one and together we are All,
When we wed our will with the Mother's call.
We answer in union, wrapped in sacred, divine bliss
Sweetly surrendering to our Angel's heavenly kiss
Which awakens anew the love of ages gone
To sing the minstrel's tune and dance the holy song.

You are that Temple palace that calls forth the scene
Upon which all history awakes as an innocent dream.
We dance destiny's rhythms, Her cloak in time and space,
We shall come to know our rightful spiritual place,
To receive the blessings of good work and conquered fears
As we accept the love She is giving to quell our every tear.

Sophia as the Goddess of Nature

Truth and Poetry bespeak one source, you see,

For Nature speaks in all that She can be;

The windward rush, the crashing sea,

The northern lights, a redwood tree

All call the ever changing name of Thee.

Humans live in fear and awe of nature. The more we delve into and examine nature, the more we fall back, staggering in wonder.

Nature evokes reverence from those who observe Her splendors and see the symphony of life and death repeatedly occurring in the arms of the Mother.

Mother Nature is the source and end of all of our efforts. Worship of Her can be pure animism and still be completely rewarding. There is no need for philosophy while watching a massive thunderstorm roaring overhead and striking lightning to balance the war in the heavens. Children cower at thunder, and all humans stand in fear while watching a tornado approach with windstorm fury.

It takes only one erupting volcano to show humans that they cannot stand before Her power without bowing down to the ground in submission.

We cannot withstand or fully understand nature; we can only accept Her design and fate. Sophia as Creatrix, Mother of All, and Wisdom can easily be seen as Mother Nature. All that we do is done for Her in Her domain and with Her tools that She has loaned us in hopes that we might ascend into angels.

Nature loves evolution, and all things in Her domain are performed with Her laws and forces. Humans bend nature to their will. They forge Her beauty into mortal power. But we only borrow Mother Nature's forces with a superficial understanding. Life is Her greatest wonder in its ubiquitous burgeoning throughout the seemingly infinite worlds of nature.

Mother Nature, in Her entirety, is incomprehensible for the human intellect. Science develops new theories continuously to replace the previously limited theories that grow old in the light of Her effulgence and endless Wisdom. Humans can look into the smaller spaces beneath us, into a seemingly infinite number of miraculous worlds turning dynamically together to make the building blocks that create "our world." At the same time, we can look outside of ourselves to a seemingly infinite universe with hundreds of billions of galaxies and a universe that defies explanation.

As mortal beings, we stand in between the two; yet we do not usually think to define our station in the universe. Many have no idea where they came from or where they are going in time or space. And yet Mother Nature keeps order and degree, position and place, time past and future. If She did not do this work every moment of every day, we would not exist at all.

People are beginning to wake up and look outside of the nest as newborn chicks that long to take wing and mount the heavens above to survey grander skies.

But at first, humans took the fire brought down from the heavens and used it for both good and evil. Fire, celestial and earthly, in the sun and stars, is a gift from the Mother.

When She sent the fiery meteor from heaven to Earth, Mother Nature gave humans both fire and hard metals that could be forged into tools. No observation of Her ever went without reward. The more humans observed nature, the more expansive their definition of natural law became. Is there any end to this ever-expanding definition of Mother Nature? Can a human mind ever comprehend the inner workings of nature completely?

Spiritual researchers have found that the seven major organs in the body are related to the seven major planets in our solar system. Each has a particular metal, tree, herb, note, color, etc., with the same planetary signature and resonance as a planet. In this way, Mother Nature has situated the entire solar system in the organs that are under our ribs.

Our heart is the sun. Our liver is influenced by the signature of Jupiter, our lungs by Mercury, and so on, in this dance of the planets. Our rib cage holds these planets orbiting within a microcosm of our own solar system.

Our head is a representation of the globe of the starry sky. There are about two hundred billion neurons in our brains and as many galaxies in our known universe, which is basically the brain of Mother Nature that thinks us into existence. She tends to both the minutest protozoa and the grandest galaxies with wondrous detail, efficiency, and care.

Her laws also include many supernatural laws that are as yet to be observed. Modern secular humanist science theories limit their proven knowledge to observations made with the five senses.

Humans currently use twelve senses, and many more organs of perception will be developed in the future to help us perceive other supernatural laws of Mother Nature.

Science often limits itself to the material world. It fails to explain the realms of the human soul and spiritual experience. Like sleep, these cannot be so easily observed or explained. The soul and spirit nature of the human being can transcend the material world, as in spontaneous healing or stigmata. If we look at the visible and invisible worlds of nature, humans are only beginning to cognize the subtle workings of Mother Nature. No person has lifted Her veils completely and lived to tell of it. Great inventors and scientists have revealed only the hem of Her garment, while the true vision of the inner workings of nature has only just begun.

"No person has lifted Her veils completely and lived to tell of it."

In the distant past, the priest-kings who led great cultures were inspired by Mother Nature through natural clairvoyance. Direct communication with the beings behind natural forces was available to the great initiates. Most of the teachings of the Mystery Schools of antiquity revolved around revealing natural law as the working of a Being in nature. For example, mighty pictures of nature were embedded in symbols and stories to make these forces visible to the initiated.

Initiates guarded these secrets with their lives. A novice might spend years preparing to enter the Mystery Temple, with renunciation and austerities as prerequisites to receive the revelation of the workings of nature.

When the novice finally received the knowledge in this rarified condition, natural clairvoyance enabled him to directly commune with one or another being of nature. To the Eleusinian initiate, it was the knowledge that the moon reflected the sun's rays and that the sun's rays give life to all living things.

Sunlight brings life to all. We supposedly know this now as a scientific fact, but modern humans seldom consider such realities. To the ancients, this knowledge was power that demonstrated the beauty of nature. By giving the initiate the key to life, the wisdom of nature placed him in the exact middle of all universes as a meaningful creation that is now itself empowered to create.

Modern humans have lost the natural clairvoyance that connects them to the beings of nature because we have developed materialistic brain-bound thinking. Solitary awareness also makes it possible for a thinker to deny the existence of the divine. This was a necessary step in evolution to objectify our thinking so that we could act in total freedom.

There is no compulsion in nature to make a modern thinker believe that nature is a living being. Some modern thinkers even deny "intelligent design." It is somewhat comical that a modern human can stand before the universe and say that all of nature is an accident or a *big bang* that will someday wind down to nothing—just entropy and death. The same human thinker can believe that there is nothing after death—just the grave and ashes.

> *"Humans cannot yet be trusted with the power of nature."*

This type of pride is an expected outcome of humans becoming brain-bound thinkers. Thinkers will deny that their feelings and desires create a soul, or that their higher, non-brain-bound thinking creates a spiritual body. Yet Nature understands and loves newborn thinkers. It is all part of Her master plan.

Some people have not lost connection with the beings of nature. Some have developed the clairvoyant capacity to reunite with them.

In both cases, the development of moral forces of consciousness must accompany the non-brain-bound thinker into the active, living world of Mother Nature. Nature has placed guards at Her door because the power that often accompanies Nature-Wisdom is awesome and inconceivable to the normal human intellect.

We see these forces when we compound natural elements to make unnatural elements that endanger the world with nuclear reactions.

For this reason, humans cannot yet be trusted with the Wisdom of Nature. Having not yet succeeded in properly utilizing the forces we have already discovered, we have a long evolution ahead of us before the higher forces of nature are revealed. Nature provides all that we need for life in abundance, but humans apply those gifts in irresponsible ways. We take it for granted. We dissect and burn instead of co-exist and sustain.

A few great thinkers have lifted some of the veils of nature and showed us a cooperative and sustainable path to take. Rudolf Steiner, John Keely, Nikola Tesla, Theodor Landsheidt, Irvin Laszlo, Walter Russell, George Washington Carver, Mishio Kushi, and many others have shown us ways to work with the forces of nature through morally responsible technologies. Many researchers of truth have found the pathways to the soul and spiritual nature of the world through ardent study, meditation, and prayer.

Mythologies, philosophies, religions, and consciousness movements have attempted to connect us with the beings behind nature. As the mind evolves, these symbols and parables also evolve, but many of the enduring aspects of Mother Nature remain throughout the perennial philosophy. This is the biography of Mother Nature—Natura.

The lovers of Wisdom were led to Natura and the developing intellect analyzed nature until veil after veil fell away and Sophia's form was revealed. She is the leader of the Kyriotetes, the Wisdom of the hierarchy who rules all aspects of manifestation.

Sophia is the commander of this material world. She makes all the rules. Only Christ, Her beloved, may break them. As the Lord of Karma, Christ rules all worlds: material, soul, and spiritual. Together, the divine couple oversees this universe of dualities. It takes the union of both to complete creation.

Nature has created the human body as a holographic image of Herself. All of nature outside of the human body is ensouled and therefore provides the substance for humans to become ensouled.

All of nature is filled with spirit, which gives the opportunity for humans to become inspirited.

Who can look at the sun with clear thinking and not be amazed by its life-giving nature?

Who can look at the Earth and not be filled with gratitude for the perfectly balanced, narrow band of life that we call home?

Who can witness the birth of a child and not be convinced that the divine spark of life is wondrous?

It seems only natural that the being of nature is a "Being." There is intention behind creation, and the human role cannot be underestimated. We are gods and goddesses in the making, if we would but acknowledge it and take our spiritual place in the universe. Scientific theories search outside of the human body for knowledge, when all that is necessary is to look within ourselves as a Temple of Wisdom.

There is nothing outside the human body that is not found within. The human temple is the model of the universe: "as above, so below."

As we see Sophia evolve from Creatrix to Mother, we still have a sense of personal connectedness with the divine.

Sophia is visible, tangible, and concerned with each human. As She became Wisdom, She was drawn more and more away from human perception until She was invisible to human brain-bound thinking.

She was slain by the forces of materialistic thinking, and hidden from all but the few who sought Her day and night.

Wisdom was carried far into space and deep into the human body. There, Isis Sophia was slain, dismembered, given false names, and accused of heinous crimes. The female principle was degraded, dragged through the mud, made into a prostitute, and subjected to every other imaginable horror.

In the end, She was accused of being responsible for all sin coming into the world, and Her sisters were cast into slavery, with many still there. The Feminine Mysteries were defiled. Gods and men subsumed divine titles and warred against nations. Nature was burned and destroyed until the natural balance was tilted towards human greed, power, and manipulation. The dark age of science had come, and all things natural were demoted and marginalized.

Fortunately, the image of nature as a clock running down has now been replaced with a new leading image of the Earth as a living Being called Gaia. This revolution in consciousness has raised a new standard around which to rally. The Earth is alive—a living Being! In fact, this one concept alone has turned millions towards a resurrection of nature, Mother Nature. The tide is turning. Consciousness is evolving into a living relationship with Mother Nature. The primacy of natural wisdom is arising again. Modern humans are beginning to question why the Earth and women have been treated with such disdain, when in reality they are both sacred beings worthy of spiritual respect. Although the unnatural machinations of society still reign supreme, the rise of Gaia, the Great Goddess and the feminine, is underway.

Mother Nature has always been in control, even though human nature has twisted the roles and played God. We did not do God's job well. Had the same image of nature continued under the oppression of the warlords, the Earth might have responded with cataclysmic natural responses, which would surely show humans that they were indeed only playing God.

When brain-bound thinkers peered out into the universe with their telescopes and found no god there, they pronounced that the "godless" universe is simply a clock running out of energy. Brain-bound thinkers, in effect, declared themselves to be the only gods in the universe. This limited theory of the cosmos lacks Imagination, Inspiration, or Intuition. We are indeed gods, baby gods in the becoming. Recognizing Mother Nature as a divine Being begins our exploration outside of the nest. Perhaps in time, we can learn to fly and free our minds to evolve consciousness.

The forces of nature that follow the laws of nature are only now being revealed to scientists, but either they are misinterpreted or the new discovery is not connected to other fields of knowledge. The veil is thinning between humans and nature. For example, DNA research now helps historians and archeologists solve their mysteries by simply taking blood samples.

The lines between the fields of knowledge also are disappearing. Embryology can inform astrophysics, and mitochondrial DNA research can inform literature. Discoveries in all fields of research indicate that our previous theories were way off the mark, and the fuller picture makes it clear that a hierarchy of Beings created and sustain this world, both visible and invisible.

These Beings seem to all speak a language humans have forgotten, one of vibrations and frequencies harmonizing in resonance. The ancients called it the "slow-burning fire." For indeed, all things are on fire and emit energy in the form of vibration. There are many new discoveries that show the fantastic simplicity, beauty, and wisdom of nature's spectrum of vibration.

Sound has been found to create light in a process called sonoluminescence—"and God said let there be light." Before, it was unimaginable that sound might create light, until an inspired scientist tried to see if the Bible was right. Truth is unimaginable until it is imagined; then it seems quite natural and always known. Some say that we were imagined by the Divine in Her own image.

The scientific "laws of nature" seem to be created just to be broken. Most laws of nature that we think we see manifesting may only do so because we are looking. The observer changes the observed. Consciousness is the key to observation through enhanced perception. Consciousness changes perception, which can change the object being perceived.

The object of perception does not change necessarily, just the consciousness of the observer who now can see beyond previous limitations. Consciousness can understand that time dilates over space; therefore, time creates space and space creates time. Space is illuminated by light, and consciousness is akin to light. Light is known to act like both a particle and wave. It has many properties that science has yet to observe with the current limited consciousness.

Rudolf Steiner pointed out in his *Astronomy Course* that the speed of light is not a constant. Measuring the speed of the leading edge of newly emitted light creates misleading theories. He tells us that light in a continuum can travel infinitely fast. It is present simultaneously throughout the continuum of expression. Therefore, how naive to imagine theories based upon a fixed speed of light. This is a perfect example of brain-bound thinking chasing its own tail.

Recent discoveries have proven that Steiner was right. Light in a laser has been measured moving hundreds of times faster than the previously known speed of light. If science would apply this new discovery to astrophysics, all that scientists seemingly understood about light, time, and space would have to be rewritten. Many similar discoveries are continuously being made, yet little effort is used to combine the gleaned knowledge of nature to create a comprehensive picture of the wisdom of nature.

Extensively studied by the ancients, the forces of nature were called tatvas, ethers, or etheric formative forces. These forces were used in magic to control nature, often as secrets known only to the initiated.

These forces are based upon the simple dualities of nature. Warmth, light, sound, and life are the four ethers that best explain the laws of nature.

Warmth and light are expanding forces (levity) that ray outward, while sound and life are contracting forces (gravity) that condense.

The continuous alternating of these two sets of forces creates the foundation for all exchanges of energy that build life.

A full understanding of the origins, growth, and inner workings of the ethers constitutes true co-creative magic with nature. These dynamics are unveiled secrets of Sophia found in the wonder-working magical forces of the ethers. They are pictured in the images of the Tree of Knowledge of Good and Evil and the Tree of Life.

These same symbolic and allegoric images and teachings also manifest in the DNA of each human cell. The mitochondrial DNA leads us back to one of three Eves in Africa (*Out of Africa Theory*) and the Fractured X research similarly traces our lineage back to a few *primal Adams*. In many cases, a story or symbol carries Wisdom that cannot be transmitted otherwise. In each cell is the Garden of Eden with the Tree of Knowledge and Tree of Life in the midst.

Eden has been tracked back through our DNA to the very ancestors who gained the fruit of the Tree of Knowledge of Good and Evil.

Each new thing these Eves ate became another branch of the female mitochondrial DNA. We know the history of our ancestors by what they ate—the fruit of the Tree of Knowledge of Good and Evil. If Eve could eat it, then it was Good and brought life, but if she could not, it was evil and brought illness. The fruit brought the knowledge of good and evil.

Is this sounding familiar? When we bring the proper "fruits of the trees" to the cell, perhaps the mitochondrial DNA will let it back into Eden to bring new life to the cell.

Losing or regaining the Garden of Eden happens each time you eat— actually, every time you perceive. When you look into the mirror of nature, you have the chance to regain paradise through cleaning the mirror and seeing perception for what it really is—a chance to reimage the world through a lens of Wisdom that is not locked in by time or space. Our original duty in Eden was to tend the Garden and enjoy. That is still our *only* duty. We just need to clean the mirror, recognize that we are divine, and then act like it.

But you will not know how to act if you do not have good examples. The old example is Adam and Eve being blamed for humanity getting kicked out of the Garden. Perhaps the new example of the Adam Kadmon and Eve Kadmon can unite Wisdom and Love and, through freedom, regain Eden and the Tree of Life, which is Sophia Christos. These are just some of the many faces of Natura that can inspire icons for a new spiritual science.

It was the alchemist's job to study the secrets of nature. The ancient teachings of the Goddess had gone underground to escape the persecution of the male war machine now wed to the Holy Mother

Church. Alchemists continued the traditions of ancient India, Persia, and the religions of the Near East. Egyptian magic synthesized the Mediterranean traditions. The birth of modern science arose from the "black earth" (*al-chemi*) of Africa.

Observation and consciousness were key to the alchemist if he wanted to seize the beauty of nature and coax Her into the processes of transmutation. He refined both material and spiritual substances, knowing that consciousness influenced matter. Only by turning lead (brain-bound thinking) into gold (sense-free thinking) could the alchemist prepare his consciousness to witness nature as Her veils are drawn back.

Sophia as Natura was the inspiration of the alchemists. Finding the gold of their hearts was the goal. The elixir of life was the consciousness that knew the alchemist as an immortal being partaking in the life of divine Natura.

As human consciousness grew and evolved, Natura appeared to many philosophers. She took on incredible visages and faces to manifest to each person. The limits of their knowledge were the limits of their direct experience with the Being Natura. This Being was coming closer and closer to the thinker, who was also becoming a seer again.

The scholastic philosophers of Chartres wrote about the goddesses who sit at the poles of the Earth, keeping the cadence of the spinning globe. Later, science finds nine deep Arctic Ocean currents that cause the spin of the Earth. The Norse called these nine sisters the Mill Grinders who grind out salt, meal, and gold. Natura was the Queen of all of these hierarchical and elemental beings, as far as the human mind could conceive.

The thinking philosopher, in a quest for the Goddess of Wisdom, became the thinking scientist who wished to find the secrets of Natura without knowing Her as a Being.

These scientists discovered forces and named many parts of Natura, seeing Her as laws of nature and not as Beings of Natura. They observe with their limited senses the dance of Natura, but cannot hear the song to which She is dancing. Scientists observe the effects of natural forces, but do not notice that there is no *philosophy of science* to create a framework in which to fit knowledge. As they develop modern materialistic science, scientists have no *true cosmology*. Natura is taken away, hidden somewhere beyond the stars, where scientists believe they cannot probe. Before long, not even "intelligent design" is believed, let alone "wisdom design."

Eventually, the entire universe is distilled into a distinctly male-dominated thought—the universe came into being as a *big bang*. Only an inconceivable violent ejaculation could satisfy the male-dominated materialistic scientists. Truly, the most ridiculous scientific theory in history is all that scientists have to stand on as their cosmology. According to these modern theories, humans are an incidental by-product of a big explosion. There is no meaning to anything in life because it all happened by chance and essentially is just a big clock that is winding down to death. This frame of mind is unimaginative.

Nihilism is the logical philosophical pathway for a modern materialistic scientist.

Scientists cannot believe in God or the Goddess because neither will cooperate and lie down on laboratory tables to be dissected.

Nature's tornado will not submit to scientific experiments in a laboratory.

Nature is found to be a terrifying force that must be dealt with severely, the "bloody tooth and fang of nature," cruel and heartless.

The more materialistic scientists observe nature, the more materialism they find; whereas the spiritually motivated scientific researcher finds a natural realm of intelligence, order, and spiritual economy.

If the scientist's ego is big enough, he even believes he has conquered nature and controls some part of Her. Awarded the Nobel Peace Prize, he names that small part of observed nature after himself with ultimate arrogance and pride. "I have tortured the secrets out of nature and named them after myself," says the proud scientist. Then a few years later, another scientist "proves" that the former scientist was "wrong," his own theory correct, and renames that part of nature after himself with pride while the previous theory is forgotten.

Sophia as "Mother" aspect of the Divine Feminine Trinity has not changed in Her consistent care and love for humanity; it is the consciousness of the beholder that has changed. It was necessary for humans to evolve from being clairvoyantly cuddled and cradled by the Great Goddess as Creatrix, Mother, Wisdom, and Nature to the independent, ego-centered thinker.

Humans, like children, need both nurturing and independence in order to discover who they are.

We have alienated ourselves from our origins just so we can turn around and tread the path home again with New Wisdom gleaned from our experiences. Materialistic thinkers, whether they practice in the laboratory or boardroom, are simply children who have run away from home and do not want to admit they are wrong and need their parents' influence and love in their lives. These thinkers would be laughable if they were not at this moment trying to torture nature into some new twisted form that brings power without wisdom.

Many thinkers do their jobs unconsciously as human components in the machinations of a larger, unconscious leviathan. They, or the system of which they are a part, may never question the foundational issues of morality and philosophy, least of all develop a cosmology of life instead of one of entropy and death.

Modern materialistic science has divorced spirit from matter, the divine from creation. This is tantamount to the child who tells his mother that he was not born from her and that in fact, she is not truly his mother and that he will prove it. This is the logic of many scientists, and obviously it does not work out well.

They spend the rest of their lives in a very compartmentalized aspect of scientific research that never again associates with other fields of science. Why this type of piecemeal science? It is caused by the lack of a philosophy or cosmology of scientific inquiry. In other words, what is the point of doing scientific research? What is the motivation for the research, and who is the beneficiary?

These questions are not asked. Consequently, huge amounts of knowledge are accumulated, and not one speck of wisdom is gleaned. Knowledge without reference to a cosmology is, at best, useless. At worst, it leads to more weapons for the war machine and corporate interests.

If the intent was to "meet our maker" or "better all of humanity" and the research was to help all humans, not just military and industrial interests, then science would turn towards religion and art again to accomplish its purposes.

Once isolated research is analyzed and synthesized,

> *"There is intelligent design found in nature if there is intelligence in the beholder."*

we would find that the hems of the garment of Sophia have already been discovered by scientists and ignored, perhaps because they were not looking for Her. New discoveries should be added to a living cosmology of beings that provide a more comprehensive picture of Sophia as Mother Creatrix of Nature.

As human intellect has developed over time, we have lost Sophia the Mother in shreds of scientific data. Those millions of pieces of data uncovered by the scientific mind all create a mosaic picture of the Creatrix Sophia that has yet to be pieced together. Personal, egotistic interests have taken Wisdom and tried to steal Her power without recognizing Her Beauty.

The honest scientist admits that as more knowledge is revealed, more reverence for nature is instilled in the beholder. The true open-minded scientist of Natura can only be left in awe and wonder at the Wisdom he or she finds from the largest to the smallest components of nature.

There is intelligent design found in nature if there is intelligence in the beholder. There is wisdom in the design of nature if wisdom imbues the observer.

Natura

Truth and Poetry bespeak one source you see
For Nature speaks in all that She can be;
The windward rush, the crashing sea,
The northern lights, a redwood tree
All call the ever changing name of Thee.
The Oracles at Delphi, by vaporous tongues unsealed,
The poems of Homer and Hesiod, the nature of gods revealed,
The Wind of Dodona sounding the Oaks so tall,
Like Druid magic circles, speaking Nature's call;
These are voices, still there for us all.
Merlin is still with us, watching from his home,
Under the Stone of Bardsey, by Nimue cast alone;
Not dead, nor too old and tired to speak,
Just enchanted, limited, and growing weak.
And Arthur lives too, sleeping in Avalon,
Until the time is needed, a Kingdom to be won.

From Broceliande, news of Fairy Quests came,
Was Merlin wrong to trick and send them on these games?
Do we conquer Nature, or seek Her for some fame?
Do we forget her Beauty, or try Her might to tame?
Can't we listen? The surge is deep and strong.
For without Nature, you cannot live for long.

Christian Rosenkreutz listened and made a book called M,
The open book of Nature, your higher self within.
Alchemy tends the fire so true,
As time measures the moment's due,
And gives to each its process and kind
As we manifest the will sublime.
In us, about us, around us and through
Nature's ubiquitous harmony speaks to us too;
Just listen, then dance, then sing joyful strains,
To build the future's hope and extinguish all our pains.

The Daughter

Sophia as the Goddess of Beauty

You are the hopes of which dreams are made,

The joy of youth, the wisdom of ages,

The innocence of a child, the knowledge of sages,

The breath that moves the spirit bright.

The transition from the Mother Goddess to the Daughter Goddess is most important, because this is where the human ability to perceive and understand aspects of the Triple Goddess is dramatically increased.

Sophia the Mother—as Creatrix, Mother of All, Wisdom, and Nature— can easily be seen in the outside world as physical creation ensouled with a spiritual nature. Her four aspects seem to be outside of oneself and not particularly personal. For this reason, the Mother Goddess sent the Daughter Goddess into the Earth realm to experience what it means to be human and to manifest Herself in a way that we can perceive Her.

Sophia the Daughter descends from the Divine Feminine Trinity through the hierarchies until She over-lights Mary for eleven years. As She descended, Sophia the Daughter Goddess brought all the forces of the Mother Goddess with Her as capacity. As a human, She stood before the crucifixion just as helpless as Mary. The plight of the human being needed to be understood completely and redeemed for all times by bringing the Wisdom to understand Christ's deeds.

The Daughter Goddess descending to Earth is mirrored in Christ, the Son of the Father God, descending into Jesus of Nazareth for three years. Human physical and spiritual development depends on a member of the

Trinity becoming human and joining Their personal karma with the karma of humanity in order to conquer death as a human being.

There are thin boundaries between the Mother, Daughter, and Holy Sophia, and sometimes the distinctions are hard to understand. One must remember that, although there are differences, these three are still one being.

Both the Male and Female Trinities are depicted as three-in-one because humans, at this point in time, cannot perceive worlds or beings that are beyond time and space. The spiritual world is not limited by human perceptions. Physical space and linear time do not exist beyond our human dimension. In order to depict a being that transcends human space and time, a three-in-one representation is used.

In our hyper-materialistic age, the Mother Goddess and Her aspects of Creatrix, Mother of All, Wisdom, and Nature can easily be dismissed. But when the human heart loves another, the Daughter's aspects of Beauty, Virgin, Bride, and Beloved are replicated in the human soul, which can then begin its journey back to its spiritual home.

The perfected vehicles of these aspects of the Daughter were created by Sophia and implanted in the etheric realm around the Earth for anyone who can rise up to them.

By simply loving, the human heart can connect to the divine.

To anyone who loves another, the four aspects of the Daughter are close, personal, and very real.

To learn to love is to pass through these aspects as a Labor of Love that is birthing the higher soul nature of the one who loves.

The Labor of Beauty (Daughter) and the Labor of Love (Holy Sophia) are major thresholds that the aspirant must consciously understand on the path back to the divine. Both Labors are prerequisites for the following three.

The aspirant must believe completely that she is beautiful, or she cannot go further with the other three Labors of the Daughter. The aspirant must know that she and the world are made of the same beautiful forces of creation that are found active in the human. Her human physical body, no matter its shape, size, color, or appearance, is the most beautiful creation in the universe. Her human soul

> *"We learn to love others by learning to love the divine in ourselves."*

is capacious enough to hold all of creation. On wings of beauty and love, her human spirit ascends to the divine.

Without knowing this deeply in her heart, she may not know the Goddess in her soul and spirit. Beauty resides in the human heart and communes with all other beauty in the world.

You cannot love another if you do not love yourself. This is not an injunction to selfishness and egotism, but just the opposite. To love the divine and others, we must see the intrinsic beauty of our own self. We learn to love others by learning to love the divine in ourselves; then, it is easy to perceive that divinity elsewhere. The more one loves the divine in herself, the more she can love others. We are the beautiful children of the divine.

Beauty has a two-fold nature: celestial and earthly. Celestial beauty is the original force of nature, the willpower that started it all. The Father God saw the beauty of creation in the Mother, and then She manifested it.

Pure perfection of beauty is both manifest and unmanifest. One part of beauty is untouchable. It never came into the material world, but remains intact in its first expression of purity. Humans long to find such beauty everywhere.

Beauty also is found in all material things as the substructure of its existence and is wed with power. This beauty and Her power can be used by humans for good or evil. That is why Celestial Beauty remains aloof and hard to grasp. Only a pure moral being can witness Celestial Beauty because he has cleansed his soul to be a quiet mirror to reflect it.

Celestial Beauty is ever pure, untainted, and intact throughout time.

Earthly beauty is a reflection of Celestial Beauty, but is limited by the beauty of the beholder's soul and spirit. Earthly beauty is relative; Celestial Beauty is absolute.

We rise to whatever level of perception we can. We are limited only by our ability to perceive and understand.

A great saint might bathe in the beauty of the divine in all of Her glorious aspects and then share that capacity, which might be recognized by others as great healing or teaching.

Perhaps you, the reader, feel limited that you have not arrived at that place yet. Please know that only your free will keeps you from taking the steps necessary to *see* ... to *become* the saint ... to *perceive* the triple goddess in the world and yourself.

To witness true beauty is healing, and the aspirant must first heal the soul to perceive beauty. This chasm can be bridged by purification, devoted study of the divine, and self-initiation.

Celestial Beauty can reside in the aspirant's soul and then it matters not what one looks like because others will see you as truly beautiful. The humble, devoted soul is beautiful to humans and angels alike.

In her heavenly realm, the Daughter is seen as Celestial Beauty. As She descends through the spiritual realms to meet us in our human, physical plane, She is seen as Earthly Beauty. As we take Her into our soul as Beauty, Virgin, Bride, and Beloved, we meet the Holy Sophia through love and begin our conscious ascent back to spirit.

Descent of the Daughter

The second person of the Divine Feminine Trinity, the Daughter, descended through the hierarchy from the Kyriotetes, Spirits of Wisdom, into the human realm, just as Christ descended from the Male Trinity into the Elohim, and from there through the ranks below, likewise, into the human realm.

The Son of God (Christ) and the Daughter of the Goddess (Sophia) descended together, and both rose back into heaven through ascension and assumption. Christ and Sophia are spiritual consorts, a divine couple that shows the path of redemption through love.

Christ is Love. Sophia is Wisdom. Together, the divine union is complete, and Eden is redeemed.

Sophia the Daughter manifests through four of the twelve aspects of the cosmic Labors of Sophia. Just as *Sophia the Mother* embraces the labors of Creatrix, Mother of All, Wisdom, and Nature, *Sophia the Daughter* reveals Her countenance as Beauty, Virgin, Bride, and Beloved.

The remaining labors of Love, Mother of God, Queen of Heaven, and Holy Trinosophia are the four aspects of the *Holy Sophia*.

As Sophia passes through the twelve signs of the zodiac, redeeming the animal nature of humanity and laying down the path of ascension, She defeats the lower nature of humanity that can appear as astral animal desires and passions. She also develops new characteristics in Her relationship with the human intellect. This part of Sophia will be described when we examine the other four labors that comprise the biography of the Holy Sophia.

Sophia as Daughter not only has a personal relationship with Christ but also with the Christ in each of us. Our higher self depends not on dogma or institutions but lives in the temple of Our Spirit, unbound by visible laws of nature.

As the twelve labors, or facets, of Sophia that we are examining unfold, we see that these aspects relate directly to the evolution of human consciousness and intellect. As our understanding of the Divine has expanded over time, we have collectively used a variety of changing pictures and descriptions to articulate our relationship with this incredible Being.

At first, we approached Her in primitive ways: fear, reverence, and awe. Then we overcame those primal responses and greeted Her with more sophisticated qualities such as respect, worship, and love. As our civilizations, consciousness, and intellect advance and flourish, so does our relationship with Sophia.

The image of *Sophia the Mother* was incorporated into many world mythologies, religions, and philosophies. Human culture evoked ideas of the divine in awe-inspiring, megalithic structures like pyramids, ziggurats, temples, and churches.

Most early writing, illustrations, and calculations were created to worship the Wisdom and beauty of nature. One could say that originally, all activities of human life and intellectual accomplishments upheld a prevailing belief in the divine aspects of nature. Nature and divinity were inseparable.

As the human intellect evolved and our image of the world around us became more physically oriented, so individual consciousness evolved too. As consciousness awakened and enlivened, our connection to the spiritual worlds began to dim. Man's necessity to gain freedom of thinking, feeling, and willing caused a deep separation between the thinker and the spiritual world, cutting him off from higher realms and casting him alone into the Earthly realm. This awakening consciousness has long been severing the connection between the Creatrix and the created. As such, we have forgotten our divine lineage. Our divine language lost, we have forgotten how to speak with our Mother.

We are left with a sensitivity and awareness of nature's beauty and a longing for reunion with divine Beauty. For many nature lovers who begin to re-*member* their connection to the divine, the wonders of Mother Earth are so profound that one can never take in enough of Her splendor. Beauty has a living, visceral effect on the beholder that *takes him away* even without his permission.

Many people have known this feeling. Upon seeing the majesty of a natural wonder like the Grand Canyon or the sequoia forests, one is often swept away to a rarified place of awe and reverence quite beyond normal perception. As part of this experience, the beholder wonders whether such beauty exists inside of him. He has an intuitive knowledge that all of

Mother Nature is found within the human. This longing for reunion with the beautiful is a living knowledge and memory of our spiritual home.

All humans yearn to be reunited with beauty, truth, and goodness. These are familiar qualities—we know them from the realm we lived in prior to descending to the Earthly realm. They are the source of our being. As Socrates said, all knowledge is a *remembering* of the archetypal world we lived in before we were born. There is our true home, the land of the spirit, where all is pure and alive with light, sound, and vitality.

Even though we are made to drink the draught of forgetfulness before we incarnate on the Earth, we do not truly forget our divine home. We still have a sense of beauty, some of us developing this sensitivity to a high degree. This love of Beauty is found in all aspects of life, regardless of the vocation we pursue.

Beauty is ubiquitous in nature and human design. The full scope of beauty is much larger than "the eye of the beholder"—a "standard" that makes something useful, artfully crafted, and naturally suited to its environment. Beauty shines through architecture, engineering, medical research, poetry, art, physical appearance, or anything where the true or the good can manifest.

When all three—truth, goodness, and beauty—combine, the divine is present.

There is an unimaginable beauty in an ear of corn—its harmony, resonance, and structure, how it sprouts and reaches down into the earth to receive its mineral nourishment and up to the sun to receive its light sustenance. When a clever scientist, who does not understand the wholeness of corn as both a physical and etheric life force, manipulates and denatures that wonder into a genetically modified "substantially equivalent" product, we all suffer the consequences in the disease of our natural bodies by consuming something that is devoid of vitality or etheric life.

> *"Most of this world is a shadow of the spirit wherein living beings and forces are hidden."*

The moment we dissect Beauty and the perfect completeness of nature, whether a kernel of corn or an atom, in order to arrogantly change truth, goodness, or beauty, nature falls away into something sub-nature or man-made.

Humans need to appreciate nature without defiling it in cruel misuse and evil design. We have only begun to understand the devastating effects of manipulating natural forces. The end results of terminator seeds to weapons of mass destruction are all the same, yet corporations and their scientists still pursue a trail of corporate greed, which ironically ends the same for all humans, even the very scientists manipulating nature and dissecting Her beauty. This is why the real power of Beauty remains hidden, revealed only by the development of a higher sense, feeling, or perception of beauty.

Unfortunately, when the undeveloped intellect sees Beauty, it tends to envision the potential for power, control, and egotistical manipulation. We should remember that Beauty is not a pretty "thing" of which to take advantage, but is the vehicle of Mother Nature to convene the cooperation and association of hierarchical and elemental beings dancing in harmonious union to create the manifest world.

Scientists do not yet understand that Beauty is only the *hem of the garment* of Mother Nature. With our five senses, we only see the degraded aspects of spirit that have congealed into this material world—the after-effects of life manifesting in a dying world.

Beauty can never be fully understood or imagined with brain-bound thinking. Once we begin to dissect Beauty with materialistic science and philosophy, She falls away until all that is left is a semblance of Her true nature. Scientists often are only measuring spiritual forces, such as volts, amperage, and gravity, as they splinter into material form, while the true nature remains supernatural, unperceived by the limited senses of the materialistic scientist.

Most of this world is a shadow of the spirit wherein living beings and forces are hidden. Science probes the effects of natural forces but seldom ferrets out the causes. It often claims to understand a force when in fact it only proposes a theory that is usually disconnected from other, more comprehensive aspects of knowledge, thus revealing nothing substantial except the singular effect that is being observed.

Light, water, electricity, gravity, thoughts, feelings, and many other defining forces in the world are, in fact, invisible. We see their effects, but not their source, cause, or place in the whole of nature—a cosmology. No one has seen electricity; it is invisible. We see only its effects in a spark that lights up the air. Scientists can measure and manipulate these forces in fantastic fashion, but do not have a single theory or clue about what electricity is, where it comes from, or what it is doing here.

This is true for most forces in nature that scientists fail to relate to the other forces in nature, just the field-specific knowledge in which they are immersed. So cloistered within the scope of their own research, most scientists are truly blind to the big picture.

Electricity is a beautiful force of nature, found in lightning, lightning bugs, the human nervous system, the Earth's atmosphere, and anywhere else that nature organizes itself. Atoms are electricity that develop magnetism due to their unique flow of particles.

No one has ever seen an atom in motion. A cyclotron researches the particles of atoms but has yet to perceive one. The effects of these scientific studies are turned into data that seems to help no one. Until scientists know *why* they want to spend billions of dollars to create new theories of atomic structure, genetically modified organisms, or weapons of mass destruction, we might consider a science that studies life in all Her many forms. Science has neglected its moral duties just as society has done by throwing beauty to the swine.

Beauty is a *Being* that shows the divine correspondences inherent in natural law and creation. She is not to be confused with desire, which is so misunderstood by modern people, especially in contemporary life, where beauty is a food or drink in which people indulge with gluttony and greed.

Beauty has been raped and pillaged by those who wish to consume Her, to steal Her innocence and purity.

Modern beauty leads to pride, envy, and jealousy instead of wonder and respect. New fads intend to shock and startle the beholder instead of assuming beautiful states of grace, balance, and harmonic proportion. What is ugly and overtly sexual tends to be confused with the sense of beauty. The weird, bizarre, and disgusting saturate modern culture until people believe that evil is beautiful and that humans should allow all forms of *new beauty* to be considered equal to what the ancients considered beautiful.

Beauty is a Being, not an appearance. Mankind has lowered and degraded the being of Sophia into gross misrepresentations of the divine that drag Her through the muck and sully Her name. Through the decline of human intellect and the prostituting of beauty, human sense organs have reverted into common and gross organs of hedonism and selfish pleasure pursuits.

Originally, these organs of perception were constructed differently. They could perceive Beauty in all natural things. Even death is beautiful if seen from the right perspective. These sensory organs provided ancient humans with a group-soul experience that clairvoyantly connected the individual with the source of its life—the spiritual worlds filled with a hierarchy of beings. Over time, these organs have become the personal vehicles of the individual to use as he pleases.

The thinking individual can stand before a beautiful phenomenon of nature and say boldly, "This is all created by forces in nature that have no living intelligence. I am a thinking man. I say there is no god, goddess, intelligent design, or any other conscious force or being directing the universe. I, as a thinking man, say that there is no life after death. There is no meaning to life except self-gratification and selfish pursuits of desire."

When put in such words, any clear thinker can see that the man who was just speaking is similar to a preschooler telling the principal that he does not have to listen to him. "I am my own boss, and no one tells me what to do!"

How foolish and limited to listen to the philosophy of one who could take such a naïve approach to consciousness. The fact that modern man cannot answer any of the questions concerning the creation of life, evolution of consciousness, or personal self-development reveals the puerile condition of the materialistic thinker.

Such nihilism subtly infuses secular humanism as a default philosophy for a modern materialistic science that has no cosmology, philosophy, or reasonable projections of the future of human consciousness. Scientists make monumental discoveries every day that no one will learn about, especially other scientists in other fields.

Every scientist is like a captain of a ship with no one at the helm. This begs the question: are they bad explorers or simply pirates? That depends on what cosmological flag they are flying. As we know, the world view of the scientist defines what they perceive in their laboratory. Will the ship be full of geologists studying the land or pirates looking for gold?

An elevated version of the developing human intellect would see that some unknown force stands behind nature, but to anthropomorphize that force would be adding religion to nature. This world view might allow *intelligent design* in the universe but still deny the existence of life after death or living hierarchical beings and elementals.

The modern view does not seem to notice that there is no philosophy of science, education, or psychology that drives scientific research. Science does not know what it is seeking. Therefore, it certainly will not find supersensible forces or beings because these words and concepts do not exist in their scientific vocabulary.

This implies that no one can understand the results of science because there is no examination of the many diverse directions in which scientists (in their pirate ships) are sailing. Most scientific discoveries are by special-interest industries and kept secret, certainly only shared for profit. If no one can purview the scope of scientific research and discovery, then who exactly is in control of twisting and torturing nature? Currently research is underway to discover a single particle of a mysterious substance called "dark matter." Scientists announced recently that if they are successful in isolating and capturing a single particle, then the entire Earth could possibly explode at that very moment. Who gives them the authority to conduct such deadly research and gamble with the lives of humanity?

"Beauty is all around us if we choose to perceive it."

This type of anti-thinking is often the foundation of scientific research. A scientist devises a theory and then tries to prove it right or wrong. Unfortunately, he should have asked why and for what reason the task is undertaken.

Wouldn't it be wise to share ideas or research that may potentially harm human beings before work is undertaken to develop them? Before denatured substances lead to local or global eugenics? Shouldn't we closely examine the human and natural implications of allopathic drugs, GMO foods, cloning and DNA manipulation, food irradiation, chemical-biological-mechanical weapons, brain micro-chips, and robot-human technologies, to name a few from an exhaustive list? How foolish that scientists and politicians think man-made denatured substances, whether individual plants or animals, will be confined to specific political or geographical areas.

Knowledge is neutral. It needs wisdom to temper its direction. Thinking does not rule research, but a form of *anti-thinking* that somehow forgets that humans should be involved in all equations.

Most of what people have been taught in school has been proven wrong in the last few hundred years. Science is always out of date, misquoted by the very people who mistakenly believe in the latest theory. It is, in fact, an intellectual misdemeanor in modern society to be anything other than "scientific." The person who perceives intelligent forces or beings behind nature is deemed to be irrational or outrageous.

Isn't it amazing that modern thinking has painted itself into a corner and reversed the facts of the matter?

Each individual must sort out his own thoughts, observing their source and substance. He needs to look beyond the obvious and determine where he stands in relationship to the world. This is the first step of objective thinking—to know one's self.

The ability of the modern thinker to completely sever himself from the sources of life that create the outer world (including the human body) and consider himself disconnected from divine origins creates the dis-ease of materialism that leads to physical, mental, and emotional illness. This happens when life is lived contrary to the Laws of Nature instead of cultivating an art of life that dances in harmony, ease, and coherence with Natura.

The condition of living without knowledge of the beauty of nature, Beauty as Sophia, is spiritually profound. It has adverse effects upon the organs of humans to perceive the working of the worlds of supersensible beings around them. Alone and desperate to make sense of the world, the modern thinker subsequently falls prey to illnesses of the body, soul, and spirit. Of course this sense-bound intellect was necessary in the divine scheme for man to realize himself as a free being. But once the strength of personal ego has been born, the individual has free will to make a decision to return to divine sources—this time with clarity of one's place in the divine order of things, which naturally brings health and wellness.

The decision to perceive beauty is truly in the hands of the beholder, in keeping with the development of an autonomous thinking human.

Beauty is all around us if we choose to perceive it, but that decision is left in the domain of the free will of the beholder.

Beauty is a personal experience and, like all Facets of Sophia, can only be known by the limits of the perceiver.

Beauty is ease, wholeness, and completeness.

Some would say that anyone who witnesses a brilliant sunrise or sunset and afterwards does not believe in a higher power is not well in his soul. Any two people could witness the same natural phenomenon and have opposite experiences. Humans are very busy projecting their limited perspective upon the world, thus inadvertently projecting whatever condition of soul their mood happens to resemble. The young often overlook beauty in the natural world because they are preoccupied with technological devices that lure them into virtual worlds, which are not connected to the living forces of nature.

Beings in nature surround us everywhere. We just do not perceive them. Modern people have denatured much of that with which they come into contact, including their food, clothing, and shelter. Many children have no experience with nature. They miss the opportunity to see the very laws of nature that build up their organs and develop their minds. The lack of observation of the natural world also blinds scientists to the very forces they are supposedly seeking, causing shortsightedness in the approach and the lack of *beingness* in the final analysis.

Even processes of nature are seldom seen as living forces but defined as individual parts that randomly create the whole. George Washington Carver once said that the most important thing he ever witnessed was his daily observation of tadpoles turning into frogs in the pond behind his house. When Beauty in Natura is found, wisdom flows. Carver learned through the process of observation to contact the metamorphosing *spirit* of the tadpole. Thus he opened a world of correspondences that led to his historical scientific discoveries.

It is safe to say that Carver witnessed the Beauty of Natura that indicated the power and force of Her truths and the goodness they can provide for humanity. He was the example of what a scientist should be: humbled by nature and morally bound to human good. The modern thinker must first decide whether the vehicle of thought, and the thinker who is thinking, is in any way connected to higher thinking. He must ask, "What is this force of thought, and how do I direct it and not be swayed so easily by personal desire?"

Thoughts can be beautiful or ugly. The thinker alone determines how much of his thoughts are beautiful. In some cases, there is simply no thinking at all. Once the thinker actually scrutinizes the basics of the process of thinking and of his thought, he will realize that they form the basis of what he actually perceives about the world.

The positive thinker who only looks for the good and true will find exactly that. Humans with terrible disabilities may still have the best outlook on life and seem unimpeded by their handicaps, whereas a perfectly healthy person may have an awful attitude towards himself and others.

When life is a projection of the beholder, beauty then is in the eye of that beholder. The beautiful thinker finds beauty everywhere. Ugliness too finds its own. As resonant vibrations sound together, like draws together like. The modern thinker can also stand up and say, "I am an exact copy of the universe and all is divine in the long run." That *outlook* or *outpicturing* creates an entirely different universe than that of a nihilistic, materialistic thinker.

This approach will quickly find Beauty in the stars, the solar system, the planets, the human body, and everywhere else. History will become a revelation of human development. A thinker, who starts from the premise that he is a living image of the divine, will experience all life as sacred. No amount of thinking can ever quite convince the materialistic mind into

"Intellectual thinking can only take the mind so far."

seeing himself as an image of the divine, but as we have seen, that materialistic thinker is also incapable of gathering all the data from science and creating a comprehensive cosmology that refutes what the ancients have always known.

Intellectual thinking can take the materialistic mind only so far; after that, it is the development of the supersensible organs of perception that limit or open the way to perception of nature as the Being of Beauty, another aspect of Sophia.

It takes the warmth of the heart to fire the Imagination of the higher mind to conceive of an interconnected natural world populated with hierarchies of beings and elementals. Dead, cold thinking cannot arrive at the proper conclusion and, in fact, is subject to the very death that it attributes to the universe. If thinking remains only in the sense-bound brain and lacks a living imagination, it will always be falling apart and away from nature, in bits and pieces, never moving towards wholeness and beauty, but towards its own demise.

If you believe your thinking is dead, then it will begin to resemble death. The modern thinker who cannot see beyond this one life will have great trouble perceiving the many facets of Sophia as She evolves over time and is described by humans whose intellects developed likewise.

Sophia as Mother God is evident in nature everywhere. If the modern thinker only sees a dying world, then his relationship with Her will halt. It takes the ability to perceive with new organs of perception the Being of Sophia as the Daughter Goddess. Sophia as Beauty draws closer to one who can perceive Her as Creatrix, Mother of All, Wisdom, and Natura.

By understanding Sophia as Beauty, we are taking a step closer to a personal relationship with the Divine Feminine Trinity.

Although seldom discussed, the Daughter Goddess is an open secret for all clairvoyants to perceive. It takes the forces of *Imagination* to truly perceive and believe in a Being that has become personally associated with you.

When the aspirant allows the beauty of nature to reflect itself in his or her soul, the Daughter of the Goddess manifesting as Beauty becomes personal. When this happens, the soul and spirit are beautified. They rise up to a higher plane to witness Beauty in Her own court. This becomes personal. A relationship is begun. For many philosophers and wisdom-seekers, this relationship never ends.

In fact, it can be more important than any other relationship on the Earth. A love affair with the beauty of nature leads to philosophy, the study of the Being of Wisdom. From there, Sophia as Creatrix, Mother, Wisdom, and Natura unfolds as the "Rose of the World" to an ever-blossoming and unfolding Sophia—Goddess of Beauty. It begins with the thinker finding beauty in his own thinking as a gift from the most beautiful thinker—She whose thoughts brought the human thinker into existence.

The philosopher begins to love Wisdom more than anything on the Earth, even though it was the process of observing the laws of nature on the Earth that led him to perceive the being of Beauty in his own thoughts.

Wisdom and the thinker begin to unite, and a loving relationship begins. The Being of Sophia as Beauty arises in the mind of the beholder. A higher type of desire is then born. The thinker realizes that Earth-bound thoughts will not transport him into worlds where other beings associated with Beauty live. Beauty Herself loves to be perceived by the novice aspirant who for the first time lifts Her veils and *sees into heaven.*

Beauty is like the apparition of Helen of Troy, by legend the most beautiful woman who ever lived, who Mephistopheles conjured up for Faust but warned him not to touch. Faust tried to touch Helen, even after he promised to restrain himself. He paid the price for trying to possess beauty.

Similarly, the thinker, upon seeing Beauty, often wants to grasp Her and hold onto this prize. This is exactly what a materialistic scientist does upon witnessing a new force. Yet we should not be led to believe with egotism that we can possess Beauty. We cannot. She is a force that moves through the world, existing for anyone to perceive. She holds more power and wisdom than any one person can ever hope to possess.

Beauty will teach us in slow measured steps the path to Her Mysteries that hold great power. She reveals Herself in all natural things. These keys unlock the Mystery of Wisdom hidden in seemingly powerless objects. The secrets of the resonance of mathematics and geometry found in every plant, animal, and human would overwhelm the thinking mind, for only the heart can begin to hold such Wisdom.

"Often, for a human, it takes years to see the beauty in a situation or circumstance."

Beauty requires of Her lovers sensitivity, harmony, and clear thinking. She is as personal as your own thoughts, yet mighty enough to hold all the thoughts of all thinkers of all ages. She creates the higher desire to look for Her everywhere, in all things, people and situations. She demands that selfish thinking centered on personal desires of gratification not come near Her presence.

Beauty cannot be held or possessed. She is limited only by the perception of the beholder.

She reigns throughout all creation, death, and rebirth, each aspect with its own particular grace and beauty.

Beauty is not bound by time or space, but Her relationship to them creates graceful proportions and profound lessons of providence. Often for a human it takes years to see the beauty in a situation or circumstance. It may take years of effort to finally draw back the veils that hide the Beautiful and reveal the Wisdom that only time distills. This panoramic view gives us higher objectivity, the ability to perceive the function of providence over a longer period of time.

When an aspirant courts Beauty, she begins to resemble Beauty through her association and relationship. When true love sets in, Beauty is then seen everywhere just as a lover may see her beloved's face in everyone around her.

It is very difficult to restrain the desire to privately possess Beauty. These are the thoughts of a novice who does not understand that Sophia is omnipresent and appears to each individual personally, collectively, and cosmically.

Sophia, like humanity, is a holographic image of the universe. She can be one and many at the same time, without diminishing Her capacity. This is similar to Christ existing in each of our hearts and yet also collective and cosmic in nature and manifestation. Sophia and Christ demonstrate similar characteristics.

It is a characteristic of the male-dominated perspective to want to possess beauty, whether in the form of things or people. Often Beauty is seen as a symbol of power and authority. She can be prized highly by those who attempt to manipulate through money, power, and control. Too often people intend to rob nature of Her beauty before someone else does, to spoil beauty just for the sake of doing so. There is also evil intent in the choice to destroy beauty simply because it is beautiful.

All of these avenues toward Beauty are possible with the modern thinker. Thoughts can rise on the wings of Beauty to witness the archetypes of Truth and Goodness in the realm of the eternal or can go the opposite direction.

Often the male aspirant is looking for the *White Goddess* and the female aspirant is looking for the *Knight in Shining Armor* with whom to fall in love and worship. Just as often this doesn't work out and the search for the Holy Grail of the Goddess goes awry. The desire to find the *other part of our soul* ends in seeming unrequited love.

Beauty has its day, goes the saying, but eternal Beauty never fades, even in the realms of darkness and death. The search for the divine may end at this stage, when the aspirant believes he has petitioned the divine and She remains elusive and hidden.

Beauty appears in many forms, from birth cries to death pangs, from laughter to sorrow. The Great Goddess appears as a maiden, mother, and crone—no less beautiful at any particular stage. Just as the maiden is beautiful in her freshness and purity, so is the crone equally beautiful with her wisdom wrinkles. Beauty is much more than skin deep; it is soul- and spirit-deep. In the light of spirit, even the darkness of suffering may hold beauty.

We know little about Beauty and much about desire, but when the Goddess of Beauty comes, the mind is still and Her Inspiration rings joyously in the soul.

To the early Greeks, Beauty was joined with Her other two components, Truth and Goodness. Bound together, all three qualities existed in the thinker's outer and inner worlds. If we were to go back to that era, thousands of years ago, we would find that:

Truth was the highest goal that the thinking mind could comprehend.

Beauty was the noblest feeling the heart could experience.

Goodness was the loyal duty of the good citizen and philosopher.

In ancient Greece, the body, soul, and spirit of the thinking philosopher were united in the love and pursuit of wisdom. Beauty was not personal, nor was it connected to earthly desire. Therefore it could not be *held*, only *beheld*.

Beauty was not the personal reward of fulfilled sensual pleasure or desire; She was the outcome of the search for Truth (Wisdom) on the path of moral development.

She was the shared higher values, morality, and Wisdom of the divine.

She gave the Goddess Venus, the daughter of Uranus and the Sea, an opportunity to show some part of Herself. Venus was associated with power. Older than Zeus and the Olympian Gods, she was married to Vulcan, the Titan who gave Zeus his thunderbolts. In this way, Power and Beauty were wed in the Greek pantheon.

Celestial and Earthly Beauty in Mythology

Mythology has embodied beauty through beings such as the Greek goddess Aphrodite (also known as Venus), Helen of Troy, and Psyche. Each is mythological and depicts the descent of Celestial Beauty into earthly (human) beauty. These stories are archetypal and can be used as examples of beauty misunderstood and often abused.

Aphrodite has two different natures, one celestial and the other somewhat more earthly as she becomes an Olympian. Often the celestial part of Aphrodite is ignored and misunderstood. The Olympian Aphrodite is seen as promiscuous, more earthly, and almost mundane. Few people understand this dichotomy.

The same is true for Psyche, who was seldom discussed by common Greeks. The story of Cupid (also known as Eros) and Psyche is the story of celestial beauty coming to rest on a human and the drama that ensued. Psyche lures and conquers Cupid with her earthly beauty. Cupid, the god of beauty and love, is overwhelmed with earthly beauty and, by chance, puts Psyche through the trials of initiation that Heracles and many other Greek heroes had to endure later in history.

Psyche was the first human raised into the stars and given immortality amongst the gods and goddesses. She descended into Hades to bring back to Venus (Aphrodite) the beauty of Persephone, the seasonal wife of Pluto. Persephone, the Earthly goddess of Spring and budding nature, had to share her beauty with divine Venus through the human Psyche. Psyche was not able to handle the beauty of Persephone. It caused her to go into a death-like swoon. It took the love of Eros (Cupid) to awaken her.

These lessons of beauty and love constitute a psychology of the soul with many profound insights into the motives of both love that liberates and fear that hinders.

Helen of Troy was not a single person, but the position of the highest priestess from the Mysteries of the Divine Feminine that lingered after 2100 B.C. She spanned a period of nine hundred years and was wife to both humans and mythological heroes. Helen was taken to Troy, where the first defensive walls in the Mediterranean were built to protect the sacred sculpture of Pallas Athena, called the palladium. Fought over for centuries, this talisman was believed to give its possessor ultimate power.

Helen was also like this sacred object, protected behind those same walls. She was fought over due to the interference of the three goddesses who were arguing over who was the "fairest." Eventually, Paris, the son of the King of Troy, chose Venus as the "fairest" of the three goddesses, and Helen was given to him as his reward. The Trojan War was fought over the issue of celestial and earthly beauty, the palladium and Helen.

As we follow the Daughter of the Goddess through Her four labors, we will see the issue of celestial and earthly beauty arise again and again.

The main issue is this: Can humans see that they are celestial beauty come to rest in earthly beauty? The intent of creation is to raise earthly beauty back up to its home of celestial beauty just as Sophia as Daughter descended into the Earthly realm and reascended back to the celestial.

Aphrodite

The Greeks worshipped two forms of Aphrodite: Aphrodite Ourania, the daughter of Cronus, and Aphrodite Pandemos, the daughter of Zeus and Dione. Thus, we have a *celestial* Goddess of Beauty and Love and an *earthly* Goddess of Beauty. This dichotomy of celestial and earthly beauty underscores the divisions of both attainable earthly beauty and unattainable beauty.

One Beauty can be understood by the thinker. The other is still a mystery in the unfolding that cannot be cognized.

Country-dwellers understood Beauty through the plants and animals they tended, the cycles of the year, and the wisdom of nature lore. Wisdom stood behind the ability of an herb to heal or the proper breeding of animals. She held mysteries and power.

The beauty of human propagation and the physiological aspects of childbirth held great power. The ancient Greek clairvoyant was surrounded by these earthly facets of Sophia as the Goddess of Beauty.

The *celestial* Goddess of Beauty was much less understandable or attainable to the Greek thinker. Aphrodite Ourania was conceived when Cronus cut off the genitals of Uranus, his father, and threw them into the sea.

Aphrodite arose from sea foam at the edge of the sea, on a shell. Thus, she is the sister of Cronus, and her mother is the sea. Humanity was said to have been born from sea foam. That is why Aphrodite is called the Goddess of the Dawn and the creator of man. Her son Eros, more commonly known as Cupid, was born from an egg, carrying a bow and arrow. Wherever he shot his arrows, creation arose. In some versions, Eros was depicted as the creator of the visible world. Feared both by gods and men, his arrows had the power to compel desire, especially the physical desire for love and beauty.

Aphrodite (Venus to the Romans) had carnal relations with most of the Olympian Gods and had over a dozen children, even though Zeus had given her to Hephaestus (Vulcan) in marriage. The ravaging of Beauty is a celestial and earthly theme throughout Greek mythology. The gods and goddesses are openly hedonistic and unfaithful to their marriage partners.

Zeus is notorious for tricking and mischievously disguising his way into the arms of many lovers. There is a divine precedence for wishing to hold beauty, not just behold it. The Greek heroes, often half-god by birth, were also notorious for abducting other men's wives out of admiration for their beauty.

Helen of Troy

The classic version of Helen of Troy tells the tale of beauty so highly prized that almost all known leaders in the Greek world compete in bidding for her hand in marriage. They swear a pact of allegiance that all suitors must honor her husband of choice. This type of power in service to beauty is unimaginable.

The Trojan War was launched because this pact was broken. The entire Greek world spent ten years trying to conquer Troy and win back Helen for her husband Menelaus, the Mycenaean King.

All of these stories border on myth and need sorting out to understand, but do show the depth and breadth of the issue of earthly and celestial beauty.

Helen of Troy, who was first Helen of Sparta, was abducted by Theseus and held prisoner on an island until her twin brothers, also children of Zeus, were able to free her.

Helen, her sister Clytemnestra, and her brothers Castor and Pollux, were all born from eggs, just like Eros. In fact, Castor and Pollux are identified in art by the eggshell they wear on their heads. Helen, as a daughter of Zeus, was known for being the most beautiful woman on Earth, but her twin sister was not noted for such beauty.

Castor and Pollux were members of the Argonauts and knew Heracles. Helen stands on mythological ground, as do her twin brothers. She represents much more than a single woman who is beautiful and desired by every king and hero.

Helen is a representation of the matriarchal culture being subsumed by the male-dominated war-culture of the Greek world. The walls of Troy were built to protect the palladium, the most treasured sculpture of Pallas Athena. Most likely, this sculpture was a meteorite that resembled a winged goddess. Helen of Troy and the palladium were both sacred treasures of Troy and ferociously fought over as the prizes of the Mediterranean.

After the fall of Troy, Odysseus and Aeneas claimed to have taken the palladium. Helen was returned to Menelaus. The first walls in the Mediterranean region were erected to protect the remains of the ancient and ubiquitous worship of the Great Mother that was represented in the palladium. Helen was an earthly archetype of beauty that represented the celestial beauty of Aphrodite, and thus the priestess of the Great Mother cult.

The references to Helen being born from a swan egg conceived by Zeus and Leda is an obvious reference to Aphrodite and Eros, who are both associated with shells. Helen transcends human beauty, and thus inspires kings and heroes to consider her the highest prize worthy of ownership. Her beauty solicits uncontrollable desire, just like Cupid's arrows and Aphrodite.

Helen is the representation of the Mystery Wisdom of celestial beauty that was still alive at the time of the Greeks.

Aphrodite was born on Cyprus, whereas Zeus was born on Crete. The Olympian gods, with Zeus at the head, subsumed the Mother Goddess cults of the Minoans and the Phoenicians. This is illustrated in the myth of Zeus and Europa, in which Zeus takes on the form of a white bull, abducts Europa in Tyre, and brings her across the waters to Crete, whereupon Europe was born.

Aphrodite was older than Zeus, and her Mysteries more ancient. They held the secrets of human creation. She represents the matriarchal culture of a celestial station being abducted by male-dominated cultures and debased into the mysteries of desire, sex, and manipulated beauty.

Beauty was stolen from Her throne in the heavens and dragged down to Earth, made common by those who wished to possess Her power. She was bound, bought, and sold without any respect for Her position. Helen was the Greek embodiment of the fate of beauty.

One part of Beauty still stayed distant and aloof with Her forces of nature that create the world in the image of Wisdom. When the lover of Wisdom sought Beauty, he imagined that wings were given to thoughts that could mount to the heights where the living archetypes reside.

Beauty on Earth was another matter altogether. The Greeks wished to surround themselves with unparalleled beauty in architecture, sculpture, paintings, music, writings, thought, and life-style. The winner of the Olympic Games was judged not by speed or distance achieved, but by the beauty, grace, and harmony of movement that accompanied the athletic effort.

The winner had displayed divine aspects of Beauty and therefore was celebrated for four years as the embodiment of the beauty of the gods on Earth. In Greece, the embodiment of Beauty was a way of life.

Beauty was born from the sea, or an egg, or the co-mingling of the *ichor* (blood) of the Greek gods and goddesses with mortals. Somehow She has an otherworldly aspect to Her origin, with the chance to be immortalized in the Greek pantheon by being raised into the starry script of the zodiac.

Castor and Pollux, the twin brothers of Helen, were both given Greek immortality by being raised to the stars. Heracles, another son of Zeus, was raised to the starry sky as testament to his immortal deeds.

Psyche, the wife of Eros, was also raised into the sky and immortalized through overcoming her suffering and labors.

The issue of humans becoming immortals in the Greek pantheon is indicative of the path of Sophia incarnating on Earth.

Sophia takes on a human form and descends from heaven into a realm where She must grow along with the developing consciousness of humankind.

Sophia (*Heavenly Beauty*) became an *earthly beauty* and took on human characteristics, except without the mortal limitations of a physical body.

Sophia crossed over the threshold of consciousness from the divine into the human—a sacred ground of spiritual development we often imagine as a temple. There, surrounded by the Wisdom of Sophia in the Temple of our body, we can see Beauty and rightfully communicate with Her without breaking the spell that binds Her in this realm.

> **"Sophia is the Sleeping Beauty archetype that can only awaken with a spirit kiss from our purified souls."**

Sophia is the Sleeping Beauty archetype that can only awaken with a spirit kiss. Nature is a sleeping beauty that can awaken unlimited powers yet undreamt, but clearly active all around us. The treasure chest of future seeds holds many mysteries of human evolution. Sophia is the guide to show us those seeds of potential that lie inside of us.

Each of the Greeks who started as humans and gained immortality may have drunk of the same nectar of immortality, but each suffered specific trials to earn the right to rise up to the land of the immortal gods.

If we look closely at the stories of the people who have trodden this path to immortality, we typically find a common golden thread. The story line: a hero or heroine with divine blood obtained through magical means is destined from birth to meet a great challenge.

The very beauty of their *birth-effect* sets them apart, yet ultimately becomes their own curse. A jealous god or goddess notices the divine birthmark and levels a curse that causes the beautiful soul to undergo trials, challenges, labors, and great acts of courage and power. Heracles is the perfect example of this storyline. Orpheus, Aeneas, Odysseus, Theseus, and scores of other heroes have faced these challenges, which involved a trip to the underworld to perform an arduous deed and then return. The oldest of these stories in Greek mythology is of Eros and Psyche, which was probably borrowed from the Ishtar Mysteries of Assyria and the Inanna Mysteries of Sumer. In these, the female protagonist descends into the underworld and, with a partner's help, returns to the upper world.

These Mysteries continued with the Eleusinian and Ephesian Mysteries of Greece and were made public through the work of Lucius Apuleius in his book *Metamorphoses*. Apuleius is not condemned for revealing the contents of the mysteries in his story because this story is universal, found in most ancient cultures in one form or another. *Beauty and the Beast, Cinderella, Rumpelstiltskin,* and many others echo in their themes the wisdom of this prodigal son story that seems to be the plight of humans.

Psyche

Psyche, through no fault of her own, was born beautiful. Inadvertently, she attracted the wrath of Venus due to the fact that so many men were distracted from their sacrifices to Venus in their overwhelming desire to marry Psyche. It was even rumored that Psyche was the human incarnation of Venus, or at least a child thereof.

Highly offended, Venus sends her son Eros (Cupid) to reap revenge, but when he sees Psyche, he immediately falls in love with her. He then secretly contrives a plot to abduct her. Through an oracle, he convinces her parents that if they leave their daughter on a cliff at a monster's doorstep, the beast will devour her, and she will then be endowed with fierce power. The parents believe that she will turn as terrible as a dragon, so fearsome that even Zeus and all of the gods will be afraid. So that is exactly what they do.

For being beautiful, ill-fated Psyche is fought over by many men, just as Helen of Troy was fought over by all of the Greek kings (Sparta, Thebes, Memphis). In the end, she is offered to a monster.

Fortunately, Psyche is carried on the wind from the mountaintop and down into a beautiful valley where a fountain springs up in a heavenly courtyard. Approaching the fountain, she can see a perfect palace inside the cascading water, glistening in the sun. She enters the palace and is served anything she desires by invisible hands.

When the sun sets, she is approached in the dark by her husband. He gives her a choice. Either she may see him in daylight, but never be with him in bed, or he can come to her bed at night, but she will never see him in daylight. Psyche chooses to bed her lover and not see him in the daytime. All is perfect with this arrangement until she invites her three sisters to visit. They instill doubt in Psyche's mind, so she lights a candle to see her lover. At that moment, she is amazed to discover that the most beautiful young god imaginable, Eros, the God of Love, is her own lover. But the candle drips on Eros and he flies away suddenly, betrayed, his heart ailing.

Psyche appeals to Venus and begs forgiveness, but the goddess commands her to perform three nearly impossible tasks. She completes the trials with the help of ants, river reeds, and Zeus himself in the form of an eagle who fetches the resurgent waters of immortality for her. Psyche is then told to bring back the part of beauty that Venus does not have—the portion that only Persephone in the underworld possesses.

Psyche successfully returns from the underworld with a box of Persephone's beauty. Opening the box out of curiosity, she falls into a deathlike swoon. When Eros sees this, he realizes just how much he loves Psyche and comes to her rescue. Satisfied, Venus determines that the human Psyche has earned the right to drink the nectar of immortality. So Eros and Psyche are wed in heaven. Their daughter is named Joy.

This story is a beautiful example of the fall of Sophianic Beauty from a celestial being into a human, earthly being. From one realm, Venus is brought down into the domain of earthly beauty due to jealousy. She then sends her most-powerful son Eros to exact revenge, not realizing that Eros (desire) could also fall prey to the power he wields.

This is justice for Psyche, who had not committed any offense to begin with and now gets Eros the god of love to fall, out of control, in love with her earthly beauty.

This is a powerful message: beauty has now been given to humanity.

The gods envy humanity because we have free will; we may choose whether or not to be swayed by Beauty's grace. Mortals can behold Her without attempting to grab, possess, hold, own, control, or manipulate that beauty. The way to do this is first to realize that celestial Beauty already has taken up Her home in the Temple of our own bodies.

The ancients knew that they could not fully understand the Mother aspect of the Trinity: Sophia the Creatrix, Mother of All, Wisdom, or Natura. They could stand back and worship Her as a being that was everywhere and nowhere, yet controlled all birth, death, and rebirth. They stood in awe and reverence and communed directly with Her hierarchy of beings who obey Her commands and work under Her dominion.

When the Daughter aspect of the Trinity, revealing Her aspect as Beauty, began to draw near enough, humans tried to grab and possess Her.

Once humans had evolved enough to find the beauty of their own thinking, Sophia began to manifest in beautiful thoughts and philosophy was born. The thinker had developed the ability to mirror the very thoughts that comprise the world.

The same Beauty in nature could now find a home in the thinking of humanity that was liberated from material perception. The spiritual world has remained consistent, but our consciousness continues to change as supersensible organs of perception develop over time.

At one time, it was important for the ancients to see the Beauty of the divine directly. In our time, it is important for humans to see the beauty of our own thought processes that we use to create our perception of the world.

It is the changing human perception that sees Sophia as the celestial being of Beauty transforming into an earthly beauty found in the human temple. Ultimately, one finds that Sophia has taken one step closer, existing now in both the outer world and the more intimate inner world of thought.

Pure Beauty

You are the hopes of which dreams are made,
The joy of youth, the wisdom of ages
The innocence of a child, the knowledge of sages,
The breath that moves the spirit bright
To heights of love pure and unfounded.
There you stand, filled with the Goddesses' grace
The song of the creator yet unsounded.
My soul can't believe the depth of your love
Which moves the heart and shatters hate,
The boundaries which have held us fast
Have melted by the fire of my beloved mate,
And burst asunder the limits of the past

As futures unfold before our strength of being
Holding the secrets to our karmic link
A new joy of which only now I am seeing.
Your kind acceptance and gentle ways
Shall bless my blighted, troubled soul,
And together as one we shall be joined
Until we are all made new and whole.
No words can speak the desire I hold
For every thought adds to Beauty's song
That we sing together under heaven's grace
And joins us to the celestial throng.

Sophia as the
Cosmic Virgin

While a blue jay and a robin share the tree together,

And sing their sweet harmonies of the new hope of Spring

That makes the sleeping rose bloom beside the lonely heather,

While all nature sounds, burgeons and bursts with a ring.

The next labor—Sophia as Virgin—comes even closer than Sophia Goddess of Beauty to humanity as a co-creative process determined by the development of the thinker, either to be celestial or earthly.

Through Sophia as Virgin, the thinker takes wing. He must rise from the gravity of earthly perception into the Pure Virgin thoughts of the spiritual realm. When traveling into the beautiful harmonies and grace of the divine world, all tainted and sense-bound thinking are left behind.

The thinker who wishes to ascend to higher realms must cleanse and purify the lower desires from the soul. In the ancient mysteries, this preparation might have included a purified lifestyle devoid of sex or eating meat, for example. One must be committed for many years before the actual rituals of the Mysteries were open to him.

Prayer, fasting, study, and morality training were prerequisites for most any spiritual order. The taming of the lower desires was preliminary to exposure to Wisdom. Otherwise, the aspirant may not appreciate what he was about to behold or have the requisite spiritual sense organ development to perceive the higher beings active in the rituals.

The image of the virgin bridesmaids in white gowns awaiting the arrival of the groom's party in the middle of the night is a clear Mystery reference describing this next process of human intellectual development with the being Sophia.

At this point, She has already passed through the stages we now walk. She was the Bridesmaid and Cosmic Virgin to Christ Jesus. She knows the path back home, to the future that awaits us beside the divine couple in heaven.

We prepare our soul as the bride, our spirit as the groom, in the divine marriage of our soul to our higher self.

Sophia and Christ have set human and cosmic examples for all to follow. Christ gives life to our soul, and then Sophia mothers it. The washed, cleaned, and purified virgin soul is then ready for the spiritual marriage to the higher self.

Essentially, Sophia and Christ already know the beginning and outcome of our personal self-development. They help our efforts like a father and mother would do for their child. Sophia is the midwife of our soul development, while Christ holds our spiritual self in readiness. Our role simply is to prepare for the wedding and the feast that will follow.

Renunciation from desire is universally accepted as a path to the spiritual world. Poverty, chastity, and obedience as spiritual vows demonstrate the commitment to win the war against desire, pleasure, power, and control. The dragon of desire arises as a composite image of all the animal forces in the zodiac that a clear wisdom-thinker must conquer. As the thinker tames the animal desires and comes to rule space through the twelve labors of conquering the astral desires, he becomes free and, in fact, a god or goddess.

The human ego, or *I consciousness*, is the ultimate proof that humans are made in the image of the divine. This demonstrates that consciousness is indestructible just as scientists believe matter to be. The individualized *I consciousness* perceiving the outside world and mirroring it in human perception is Beauty and Wisdom working in nature. The fact that a human *I* can objectively consider these thoughts is evidence of the divine in humans. Understanding the simplicity and purity of the human being's virgin soul is the first stage of acceptance into the teachings of Wisdom.

As we have learned when we reviewed Sophia as the Being of Wisdom, true seekers will give anything or do anything to find Wisdom. They would give up their lives and everything they have, including everyone they know, just to be with Wisdom.

Throughout history, Wisdom seemed to find those humble individuals who sought and tried to embody Her during their lifetime.

Only a soul that has been purified through the baptisms of water, air, fire, and earth can achieve reciprocal communion with divine Wisdom, Sophia. This preparation and renunciation is necessary on the path of spiritual development in order to temper higher thinking, feelings, and moral deeds.

In the story of Inanna's (Sumerian Great Goddess) descent into the underworld, for example, she was required to leave her jewelry at one stage, her crown at another, her scepter, her cloak, her clothes, and the rest of the material world before she reached her goal.

Then she was hung upon a hook through her heart and left to die.

Along the spiritual path, everything of the physical world, including our bodies, must be left behind. Inanna was ultimately resurrected from her plight, just as aspirants seeking Wisdom can purge themselves of lower desires and thoughts. Through strict self-discipline, they must train themselves to work with higher forms of human thinking and feeling. They must be willing to resurrect from earthly desire to heavenly grace.

Nothing of the physical world may be brought into the spiritual world— no impure thought, no unresolved desire, no evil word or deed. Only the pure virgin soul of the humbled aspirant may cross the threshold between the physical and spiritual worlds consciously. The Norse called this rare threshold the Bifrost Bridge, a rainbow that spanned from Earth into the heavenly realm of Asgard, where the gods and goddesses resided. Bifrost would not uphold an earthly foot of any nature treading upon him. Heimdallr the Watcher kept guard to assure that no unworthy being attempted to cross.

As such, only the virgin soul can cross over to the spiritual realm, carrying nothing of this world with her that might sully the pure realms of spirit.

Travel across this threshold is similar to the descent and return from the underworld. The heroine must follow rules: be prepared to pay the ferryman, feed the guard dog, and take care not to imbibe of any food or drink from the underworld. Under those conditions, she may return or be resurrected from death and become one of the immortals, an initiate of the Mysteries.

In the case of a heroine rising into immortality through labors and deeds, she then carries her story to the stars. From then on, the legend remains to guide and instruct all who aspire to follow.

The Greek hero or heroine conquers the lower world to rise into the higher world. This is also true of the aspirant who wishes to behold the celestial form of Beauty in the realm of living archetypes. Only the purest of souls can cleanse and prepare themselves to directly perceive the higher hierarchies. When this happens, he becomes a Virgin Soul of the Mysteries, a *Sister of Sophia*, and is instructed directly both day and night.

As we can see, the relationship with the Divine Feminine Trinity is all-encompassing and directly connected to human spiritual development. Sophia as the Virgin is the veil between the physical and spiritual worlds. Only the pure virgin soul can witness Sophia manifesting in either realm as the Cosmic Virgin.

In the Earthly realm, the virgin soul can see the effects of Sophia's Wisdom in natural law and providence, for She rules time and space in harmonious order.

Whereas undeveloped souls will see no Wisdom anywhere, the virgin soul allows Wisdom and love to pour through her soul, and grace and mercy to rain down eternally from the celestial realms. Only the emptied soul has the hollow space to let such beings flow into her, for once the virgin soul is purified and empty, she can become a resting place for the spirit.

The virgin soul is like the Holy Grail of the heart, purified by the flames of desire and tempered into a true vessel for the spirit to come to rest.

When the virgin soul is prepared, it becomes the sacred Temple of Wisdom, acting as the eyes and ears of the divine in the Earthly realm. As we ascend in our purification and development towards the spirit, we become the sense organs of Sophia. These must first be consciously formed and purified before the heart is transformed into the holy of holies.

"It is the slow burning fire of the alchemists that refines gold from the dross."

In spiritual development, the purification of the desire body is called the taming of the astral body. Astral refers to the starry influence of the twelve directions or zodiac, the starry circle of animals. This realm of fixed stars is reflected in the dome of the skull, which is the star-studded home of human thoughts.

The Chinese saw this dome as two dragons chasing each other. The dragons represent the lower animal desires that drive animal-like behaviors. Once they were brought into balance and control, the *human* element could then reign in the mind.

This is indicative of the taming of the astral body in any spiritual tradition. The idea is that humans can become angels through their thoughts or beasts through their desires. Buddha also taught that all desire creates suffering, and if we cease to desire, we cease to suffer.

There is no doubt that training the mind to concentrate, contemplate, and meditate is necessary to prepare the virgin soul. It is not enough that the soul be empty; it must also be filled with purity, simplicity, truth, goodness, wisdom, and all of Sophia's other heavenly virtues.

As in the image of the wise bridesmaids who properly trim the wick of their lamps and have them filled and ready for the celebration, so too the aspirant who wants to directly contact Heavenly Beauty needs to be ready, for we know not in what hour She might arrive. This watchful diligence is another characteristic of the virgin soul who is ever prepared and anticipating the appearance of the divine.

This preparedness is essential so as not to be left behind without light when the time comes. It is the *slow-burning fire* of the alchemists that refines gold from the dross. We must know that love comes when it wills. We are its servant. As a bride awaiting the groom, the virgin soul must be chaste, pure, open, and committed to finding and wedding the divine within the self and the world.

To tread on spiritual ground, we must cross a burning bridge and go down to the waters to drown our every desire. There we must look up to Sophia, the Cosmic Virgin. She beckons us to rise on wings of tears and suffering that beat the cold air of despair, and to mount ever higher as memory of the cruel Earth melts into rain as we rise to the warm, radiant light.

Before the coming of the new day, we are offered a brilliant white linen gown to wear. As the light of the sun fills our souls with loving warmth, we may feel alone. Suddenly, we notice that we are surrounded by others who also wear the white linen and stand in awe before the Wisdom of the Divine.

It seems as if the *lamp of light* that we had brought, what seemed so insignificant before, spreads its light to all other lamps of the virgin souls who stand united. Together, the lamps radiate a brilliant light that *answers back to the light of the sun* as a warm embrace of love and tenderness from thankful children.

Sophia the Cosmic Virgin is there for each of us as we mount the steps to the Temple of Wisdom. Concerned with every step we take, no matter how small, She measures our growth and development.

No one could be happier than Sophia when we tame our astral

bodies and don the white linen of the virgin soul. Heaven rejoices in this accomplishment, when another prodigal child steps forward.

Turning towards heaven and purity is contrary to the allures of power, sex, money, and hedonism. It is a great and bold task to turn toward purity and Wisdom instead of immediate gratification that often wishes to steal the pure and innocent, corrupting it with personal desires. This is unfortunately an earmark of our age, the corruption of the young, pure, and innocent. We can see it everywhere. A passion for desiring the gifts of youth is rampant.

"Communion with spiritual beings is a type of earthly and cosmic nutrition stream."

At every turn, the pure is being spoiled. Mother Gaia has been raped and defiled. The human bloodstream has become a dumping ground of unholy poisons and passions. Great spiritual beings struggle for our souls; the battle rages on. Humans know little of spiritual development. For many, the purification of the astral body is not even a consideration.

It takes a great soul to be humble and pure, the prerequisites for beholding Sophia as the Cosmic Virgin. The yoga sutras of Patanjali give many instructions to reach the divine, but the last instruction is simply: *be pure.*

Being pure is being the virgin soul. When the pure soul rises into the divine realms, she seeks the pure spirit as a resonant partner. Virgin soul to Cosmic Virgin, the two arise together working to create a vessel to perceive other pure beings.

When spiritual beings commune, they interpenetrate each other, so only a pure and clean vessel could hold those who wish to communicate and share the substance of the spiritual world. Nothing unclean is allowed in this Holy Temple; therefore, only a virgin soul who has something to offer the spiritual world is of any interest.

The spiritual world, and the beings that create our world, are interested in higher thoughts, feelings, and deeds. These beings wish to take what we have to offer. In return, they give us spiritual nourishment.

Communion with spiritual beings is a type of earthly and cosmic nutrition. When this symbiotic relationship begins to develop in the virgin soul, a true relationship is formed, one as intimate as with a beloved spouse.

Upon First Meeting

The Earth quaked beneath our feet,
As the stone rolled away from the eye of love.
Molten flames leapt from your eyes, igniting my heart-
Peace descended like the distant song of a dove,
While a blue jay and a robin share the tree together,
Singing their sweet harmonies, the new hope of Spring
That makes the sleeping rose bloom beside the lonely heather,
While all nature sounds, burgeons and bursts with a ring.

I know those piercing eyes, that gait so strong and firm,
This holy visage personal has pronounced its covenant term.
A magic fate has wrought this glimpse, and living now in turn,
Has come around to teach again, and find what we have learned.
Beauty comes twice to haunt, and bid me heavenly fair,
Like royal fairies, cast in the castle's alchemical air,
Turning and returning, to threshold's precious touch,
So few others can realize, and know love as such;
To see the King and Queen, and know the Feast Royale!
Climb the steps to heaven's heights, and ring the wedding bell.

Wing your way, goddess princess fair,

Speak tender truths of your home over there,
Out of sight from earthly eyes in the now,
But clear to the sight that shows us how
That bonds of old, covenants secretly made,
Still possess power and must be paid.

Straight I'll go to the city sublime, wherever love holds sway,
I'll turn the day to night, and take the holy dream away,
Drinking the nectar of the grail, the Holy Waters Divine,
Returning again to hold our hearts, to touch that gentle time,
Joining the two as lovers, and singing the heart's sweet song,
To live in fire and forge new hope, to right all earthly wrong.

Sophia as the Bride

We reach upward, intertwine as one through the growth of time,

Weaving an ivy garden bower of gentle summer fruits

Offered to the Gods and Goddesses who join in our rejoicing

As we together echo the divine and whirl into the spiral of life.

Lovers of Beauty go to great lengths to find Her primal, virgin form. They want to be the first to experience Her magical wonders. This does not always bring Her close, for Beauty is just as elusive as Wisdom. Secret and hidden, Her ways often are recounted in the content of ancient Mystery Schools of initiation.

Indeed, one who longs to behold Beauty's inner sanctum is asking to undergo initiation into the *Mysteries of Fire* and the *living forces of the Creative Word*. So sacred and coveted, these secrets were only revealed to those who would risk their lives to learn them.

Often, a near-poisonous drink was given to the candidate to induce an altered state of consciousness so that the veil between the physical and spiritual might be drawn back and the divine beheld directly. This initiation-death would last for three days while the hierophants closely watched over the condition of the candidate. If the moral development of the candidate was adequate, he might behold one or another of Sophia's facets. Only once would this happen for each candidate. If he passed the test, he would move on to become an initiate of the Mysteries. It took years of preparation and development before the candidate was ready for this experience.

Today, in order to know Sophia as the Daughter of the Goddess who manifests as the spiritual Bride, one must undergo a process of preparation, renunciation, and training much like the experience in the ancient Mystery initiation centers.

Sophia as Bride is a condition of the human soul. In knowing Her, the thinker has taken ownership of his thoughts as living, active beings that manifest both in nature and human thinking. These beautiful forces and beings of Natura humble the beholder, inspiring wonder, awe, and reverence. A feeling of devotion overtakes the soul in the true sense of the word *religion*—to relink to the original source.

We wish to link with Sophia as Beauty because we inherently know that we are made of the same substance, forces, and beings. When we behold Beauty, we see our own self; that is the wonder of Sophia as a multi-dimensional holographic image of the divine. We are part of Her. She teaches us the truth each time we recognize a beautiful piece of Her workings in our self or the external world. Beauty is always present. As the beholder of each new perception of Beauty, each person must simply be ready to accept another piece of himself.

Purification is the first step. Once we have cleansed our soul of the lower self's desires and personal attachments, we can then begin to see our higher self and experience the manifestations of Sophia in all Her many faces. To prepare to meet the higher aspects of our self and the world, we need to become purified and beautified. Only then will we be ready to claim our birthright—to unite with our spiritual self from a distant kingdom that awaits our arrival.

The Bride of the soul weds the Groom of the spirit. Together, they birth the higher self, the spiritual self. This alchemical marriage unfolds as the future of humanity, but those who are awake and ready for the bridal feast are welcome any time.

All true traditions and cosmologies describe in their myths, histories and literature this wedding of the physical and spiritual. We have read about the heavenly wedding of Cupid (love) and Psyche (soul or wisdom). We know the price she paid to become ready for her marriage to immortality.

Traditions around the world repeatedly feature the wedding, the uniting of two individuals, as the central theme of the human developing into a spiritual being. It is apparent in our traditions and cultures that we believe that some part of the human being is missing the other. Future development will bring the next step, the ultimate intent of evolution. Each person needs to find his or her own path to his or her higher self. If not, evolution is hindered, unfinished, and incomplete.

One might ask: "Why were humans made incomplete to begin with? What would be the point of starting out incomplete?"

This is, of course, the grand question that lovers have been asking since the Garden of Eden. The answer is simple, but it usually upsets people to hear the answer. That is why preparation is necessary to hear and understand the truth.

Just as the Bible indicates, there were at least two different creation stories. In the first, Adam is androgynous and incomplete. In the second, he lacks a partner. In both, Adam was not a singular male figure as the Jewish version tends to paint God the Father. Male and female (androgynous) he created them, says the Bible. Yet this version is often overlooked because it begs too many questions. In the second story of Eden, Adam is created male but incomplete. He must give his rib to birth another part of himself—Eve. Even then, they are not complete, because they must obey God and follow some rules, for no apparent reason.

> *"We are beings continually vibrating between opposites in rhythmic undulations that draw us together, then apart."*

If anything, this was a set-up. God also created the snake to tempt the two of them into becoming *like god*, which generally would seem to be a good idea. Evolving from human to god would seem like a logical, good path to follow. So, what is the underlying message in this Hebrew story, which was taken wholesale from the Chaldeans, who took it from the Sumerians, who took it from other sources in the East?

The common message is clearly that humans are not complete. The other sex has a missing component.

Ultimately, everyone has a physical self that longs for reunion with the spiritual self. Most materialistic thinkers find this message disconcerting, for of course they believe they are quite perfectly whole and need no one to help them become complete.

This is understandable. The modern materialistic thinker wants to find himself alone in his thoughts and, therefore, be king of some world. However sad and unenlightened it is to rule as king of a lonely brain-scape of materialistic thoughts, it must feel good at least to be king of something.

This brain-bound thinker can think anything he wants about another person or thing. Because he is king of his thoughts, no one will ever know. He can visit the Grand Canyon, behold it, and own it in his mind. He buys a postcard and a brochure. He even hikes down to the bottom of the canyon and back up again. He has *done* that *beauty*. He puts a check in the box and moves on to the next beauty to conquer. If he has enough money, he can then buy all the beauty he wants. He can travel to the most breathtaking spiritual locations and do the most amazing rituals to invoke the Goddess. The spiritual materialist is certain that money can buy beauty and probably something that looks like love or spiritual development.

The aspirant, on the other hand, learns through trials and suffering that he is certainly not complete. There is no room for arrogance. He realizes that there are too many unanswered questions, too many wondrous marvels to behold, and far too many beautiful people to love. The world is incomplete, dynamic, and always changing in its array of beautiful facets. One cannot check off Beauty from a list. One cannot conquer such variety. It is much grander than that.

The forces of nature are never static. The stark contrast between life and death clearly demonstrates the dynamic nature of all living things. Living forms burst into life through mysterious forces of levity and longing for life. Then just as suddenly, they pass just as a blossom dies for another season. Nature draws opposites together to create motion and life, just as the night to day and sleep to wakefulness.

We are beings continually vibrating between opposites in rhythmic undulations that draw us together, then apart. It is this creative tension that weaves the patterns of life.

Just as nature is known for its dynamic polarities—light and darkness, levity and gravity, birth and death—so, too, does human nature encompass polarity.

Male/female polarity, including the alternating cycle of love fulfilled and then subsequently lost, has inspired art, literature, and the course of history. The love of the divine has created mythologies, religions,

architecture, art, and literature. The striving for love, or the *other*, has been an unquenchable force that seems to have no limit to its energies or capacities. Love drives heaven and Earth. We are told that all the hierarchies participate in
divine love.

The longing of one for the other quite literally makes the world go round. For example, the cold portion of the Earth longs for the warmth of the sun, and thus the Earth revolves. One could literally see the entire created world as the necessity of opposite forces to separate and then reunite.

When a life arises, duality becomes a unity. In these natural processes of life, there is always a bride and groom, a female and male. For instance, in nature, silica represents the forces of levity and the feminine, while calcium represents gravity and the masculine characteristics. *Male and female He created them*, so that life could go round. Adam was whole unto himself, male and female, but evolution created the necessity for duality (Adam and Eve), so that the possibility of union at a higher level could arise.

The duality of the divine can also be found in the union of the unmanifest Father Ground of Being with the Creator Goddess, the Creatrix. It takes the (unmanifest) black hole and the (manifest) ion jet to birth the full evolution of material existence in a galaxy: creation and destruction, birth and death.

This duality has divided spiritual thinkers over the last four millennia as they try to understand the feminine role in creation.

If humans are made in the image of God, then the divine would need to be male and female.

If our own image is divine, then being male and female must be a representation of the divine—or at least as divine as is possible in this material world.

The bearing of children is a miraculous evidence of the divine; life is too fragile and precarious not to see it as a miracle. Humans can barely begin to understand the workings of birth, let alone death. We stand as children before the forces of life, and we have little clue about the mysteries that drive our own actions. What human would say he understands the forces and ways of love?

Love beckons us to realize that we are incomplete and that life can only be born from becoming complete through interaction with others.

We know who we are by the feedback and reflections from others. Without the input and communion of others, only the first stages of self-development can take place. However, the selfish, materialistic mind believes it can be happy in life, all on its own. We must remember that no man—or woman—is an island. No one can get to heaven on his or her own.

The measure of a person's life is in relationships with others. We are dependent on others for the first and last years of life. Nature is completely interdependent, based upon sharing at all levels. Natura is not selfish. Only a human trapped in his limited, materialistic brain is alone and can be completely selfish.

To long for the other—to desire to see, hold, and share another in the fullest way possible—is the state of the soul called the Bride.

As the virgin soul, the aspirant purified his lower nature, renounced personal desire, and trained to become a worthy candidate for initiation. Becoming the Bride means that the candidate is ready to embark on a new path toward life in the spirit. In this journey, nothing may be brought from the previous world that was not pure, clean, and washed in the suffering of probation and preparation for this sacred celebration.

There is only one spiritual wedding. This is the beginning of a new life with the spiritual part of yourself, as intimate as a loving marriage. You marry yourself, not Sophia or Christ. At this wedding, you receive the perfected aspects of your spirit that already await you in the heavenly realm beyond space or time. Sophia is your guide. She is with you as a bridesmaid to celebrate this momentous day.

Christ has given us our spirit seed and made available all the future aspects of ourselves that will be needed to become like Him. Christ and Sophia are wedded twins. They descended together into this realm to demonstrate what a spiritual marriage is supposed to resemble.

Sophia as Bride is also reflected in the Mother Goddess wedded to the Father God, and the Holy Sophia wedded to the Holy Spirit. The wedded duality of spirit seems to be a model of a manifested world where the spirit splits into two parts that forever long to reunite. This is the same type of longing a groom feels for his bride, and the bride for her groom: the loving potential of a beautiful future filled with children and happiness. We attempt to replicate on Earth the heavenly marriage we know from our religions and beliefs.

Sacred marriage is found in every mythology, religion, and culture. Marriage is a convention of propagation, but it also fills a soul need that is both biological and spiritual.

As we already mentioned, to develop and evolve predicates that the aspirant is not selfish or ego-centered, but rather humble and willing to help others relieve suffering. This is a first step towards union with others. It constitutes a necessity in spiritual development.

Whether it is a human or a spirit that wishes to communicate, one must create the preliminary state of consciousness of being selflessly open to listening and holding the being of the other in one's heart. This is the soul mood of the aspirant who is longing to unite with her higher self as a spouse. It is a lifetime commitment, too. The aspirant must prove herself faithful and true. The spiritual world is not fickle. Be sure that a spiritual wedding is for a lifetime.

To spiritually marry another person, one must be willing to put the other before oneself in all respects. If we wed Wisdom, then Wisdom would be sought in all matters. We would plan our future with Wisdom in mind, hoping that She would shine in the eyes of our children. Wisdom would be loved exclusively with our entire body, soul, and spirit. Our life would be devoted to Her; all things would be performed for Her benefit. After some years, it would even seem as if Wisdom walked with us and would be ever present in our thoughts, feelings, and actions. We would live our lives for Wisdom and She would reward us many times over. This is the manner of a spiritual marriage. The aspirant, as a virgin soul, makes the commitment to be always a faithful spouse to the divine.

The mood of the aspirant is anxious. This must be met with patience. Desire must be tempered by the heart, a restless mind settled with calm and focus. We are the Bride, hopeful that we will appear pleasant and gracious to make all aspects of the wedding celebration beautiful.

Everything must be prepared, planned, and perfected, for everyone will be observing. Even the divine will be asked to witness the union of the couple.

Earthly marriage is the most beautiful of ceremonies. It tries in every way to be like the heavenly marriage that we all long for but often cannot remember. God is asked into many marriage ceremonies as the ultimate witness and binding of this spiritual event. After the wedding, the couple is free to go forth and reproduce through love. This earthly representation of the spiritual marriage of the divine male/female is a profound replication of what every human knows to be true: it takes two to make the world go round.

Johann Goethe beautifully portrays the soul as Bride in the material world seeking the spirit as Groom in the spiritual world in his fairy tale entitled *The Green Snake and The Beautiful Lily*.

Here, the soul is seen as a wandering prince who is looking for the Beautiful Lily (the spirit). He believes she lives across a river, yet he cannot seem to reach it.

In the beginning of the story, the prince accidentally crosses over the river the wrong way—from the spiritual land where the Beautiful Lily lives into the world, where he must wander and look for her.

The Beautiful Lily also bears an unfortunate curse; anything she touches turns to stone.

Eventually, a kind snake makes the ultimate sacrifice. It gives its own life to create the bridge across the river so that the prince may cross and return to the land of the spirit where his beloved resides. The prince marries the Beautiful Lily, thus removing the curse, and all the characters in the story are redeemed.

This story represents the soul seeking the spirit and not being able to cross the river to unite the two. The snake is the selfless spirit of Christ. He sacrifices Himself to bridge the two worlds and enable passage. Christ stands at the threshold to the spiritual world, for only those who are ready may cross. Only those who are ready may wed their spiritual self.

The story above underscores the need for life experience, suffering, preparation, and training to ready the Bride. She must obtain patience, calmness, and focus to create the spiritual celebration of heavenly marriage. Just as the *Woman Clothed in the Sun* in the Apocalypse must endure great hardships and face the beast head on, eventually She gives birth to the new king and is taken away to a high mountain for protection.

As the Bride, each of us will face the same challenges as we try to birth our higher self. We must face the dragon (astral body), yet be ready for the sacred marriage to the Lamb (higher self) in New Jerusalem (Temple of Wisdom), our new home in the heavens.

Christ is the Lamb. The Woman Clothed in the Sun represents all of humanity birthing our higher selves, while the Lamb with seven seals descends from heaven. Eden is redeemed through New Jerusalem, just like the prince who wanders the Earth trying to find the very place from which he started.

At birth, we, too, descend from the spiritual world. Upon leaving this earthly realm, we will return to the spiritual world, but only after we have birthed our higher self as a newborn child.

New Jerusalem is the home of the wedded soul and spirit. It provides all life and nourishment needed through the *River of Life* and the *Tree of Life*, which are in the midst of New Jerusalem. This bridal bower is not on Earth. The seeking soul must search in a place where no trace of the Earthly may follow.

New Jerusalem descends from the sky as the groom comes to meet the bride halfway. Here is the process: the bride rises. Then the groom descends to meet her in the redeemed Garden of Eden. This is no longer a garden of desire where humans are tested, but rather a garden of rewards for the tried and true soul who has completed the requisite preparation for this glorious fulfillment of spiritual effort.

Christ has redeemed Eden as the Second Adam and brought this sacred ground back into the reach of human beings. He also removed the angel with the fiery sword from the entrance to Eden and has become the guardian of that doorway into the divine Himself as the Lord of Karma.

> *"We must go back the way we came, but this time with consciousness and free will."*

We were expelled from Eden for trying to be like the gods by eating the fruit of the Tree of Knowledge of Good and Evil.

To return to Eden, the Bride must eat the fruit of the Tree of Good and Evil. This super-etheric sphere of life has many names—Eden Redeemed, New Jerusalem, Shamballa, the Temple of Wisdom, or Pansophia.

In old Jerusalem, Christ walked on Earth and was little known or understood, but in the New Jerusalem, Christ is present, enlivening the etheric realm and joining Wisdom to Love in the Celestial Union of the Divine.

Wisdom comes from understanding good and evil. Once the spiritual discretion is developed enough to know the difference, the path to New Jerusalem becomes evident.

We must go back the same way we came, but this time with consciousness and free will. Just as Seth went back to the Garden of Eden to gather three seeds from the Tree of Life, so too each Bride is tasked with the same challenge.

The seeds are the transformed aspects of thinking, feeling, and willing that have become spiritualized into Imagination, Inspiration, and Intuition. In the legend, these three seeds were put into Adam's mouth after he died. His body decomposed, but his head did not. Afterwards, his head became a stone that emitted light, warmth, and nourishment to all who came near it. Noah used the Head of Adam to feed all the people and animals on the ark. This stone was called the Stone of An—an obvious reference to a type of Holy Grail.

The same thing happens to humans as the transformed elements of the soul become higher aspects of the spirit. Essentially, we create a Holy Grail in our hearts that is reflected in the head.

Human physical bodies are male or female, but human souls are considered female because they can birth a spiritual child.

Either man or woman can develop the soul capacities and sensitivities of a mother to coax the spirit into birth. There is no clear sexual duality in the spiritual world, where only supersensible natures reside and the general characteristics of higher hierarchy tend to be slightly feminine due to their co-creative powers that resemble a mother.

> *"In the far future, we will no longer propagate through male/female comingling."*

In the first degree of some initiations, all candidates are considered "sisters" of the order and then rise to the second degree, which is characterized as androgynous.

The third stage is seen as beyond duality or gender.

The forward push of spirit falling into matter is often seen as male.

The return of the prodigal child is perceived as female, a Sister of Sophia.

Initially, according to Rudolf Steiner and other Theosophists, humans once were in union with all things.

In the second stage, humans multiplied through parthenogenesis: female giving birth to female without fertilization from a male.

The third stage began the separation of the sexes as the Moon left the Earth during ancient Lemurian times.

In the fourth stage, humans experimented with cross-breeding humans and animals. The final forms of the human being were established as male and female during Atlantian times.

Today, in our era, male and female characteristics are confused, disintegrating, and devolving. We are not evolving towards androgyny or asexuality. We are devolving into DNA manipulation and inhuman forms born with biological vehicles but no soul or spirit to inhabit them.

In the far future, we will no longer propagate through male/female physical comingling. We will create our newborns through a higher form of group speech that uses the formative forces of nature to build etheric structures that will become bodies for incarnating human souls.

Humanity's sexuality evolves dramatically over relatively short periods of time. As the most adaptable life forms on the Earth, we have come to understand pieces of the DNA mystery that control aspects of sexuality in just the past few years. Through medical operations, humans can play god and change their gender. Through preference, humans can change their physical desires into any aberration that an ego can devise.

These factors do not affect the feminine characteristics of the soul or the masculine characteristics of the higher self. The soul is, by its plastic and pliable nature, the mother of human consciousness. The forces that drive a soul to take action are invisible, unknown to an observer.

No matter how much intimacy is reached, one person cannot directly perceive another soul's experience. The soul's experience is unique, but spiritual experiences are shared with all other spiritual beings. All of the suffering of the soul is personal and of this Earth, but spiritual development is common to all. It feels like coming home on your wedding day with the perfect groom or bride ready and anxious to love you for the rest of time.

Shared by all of the hierarchy, this experience is like a birth or resurrection. It feels like standing before a sacred altar, declaring eternal love and faithfulness to your future spouse before the divine and everyone you know. For once, your true feelings can be shared and experienced by all. Therefore, your soul should be as clean as driven snow: your gown a brilliant reflection of your efforts to seek the beautiful and pure, your veil a reflection of the veil of nature that hides secrets of Wisdom.

The wedding kiss is the moment when the Bride becomes the Beloved and the Tree of Life blooms.

The marriage of the Bride of the soul to the Groom of the spirit is exclusive. It happens only once, as we have learned. Only your soul can marry your spirit; otherwise, the soul remains alone and longing for the spirit its entire life.

It is a soul illness, in fact, not to long for the other side of life, the invisible and supersensible mysteries that penetrate every aspect of your being.

The hierarchy dances in and through us. Lacking the desire to understand the hierarchy of spiritual beings and their communion with us is tantamount to spiritual illness. The healthy soul understands the *ways* of the divine because those same *ways* created the soul. Examine your own nature, and you will find that all laws of nature (and super-nature) are no further than the very thought you formed to examine the question. Thinking is the force in the universe that creates and sustains all visible matter, and yet it is as close and personal as a beloved spouse.

> "*Often, great souls have a specific partner with whom they reincarnate together through many incarnations.*"

Only you can marry the Christened higher self that has already been created for you. There is only one spirit mate for each soul, even though it does take other souls to help us evolve enough to wed our own higher self. This is not to say that there is only one person who is right for another on the Earth as a beloved.

There may be many souls who could be a suitable mate for a person, depending on the individual. Often, great souls have a specific partner with whom they reincarnate together through many incarnations. The greater the soul, the more likely that he or she will work together with another. In this way, with the familiar resonance that the twin-soul might provide, they are capable of accomplishing more within a particular lifetime.

It is a principle of spiritual economy that some souls reincarnate together. This has been seen many times with great spiritual beings incarnating into a spiritual lineage. These twin-souls unite together in the spiritual world and share their work. Subsequently, they long for each other when they reincarnate. The masterful forces of providence reunite them to do greater work for humanity. This does not mean that everyone follows this path, but it is common among spiritually developed people.

The personal intimacy of a bride and groom is incomparable to ordinary relationships. Planning to have children and build a home together for the rest of your life on Earth is profound. It is a true spiritual idea that becomes the ideal.

It is with this same intimacy that Sophia comes to us as the Cosmic Virgin, preparing us for taming the astral body of desires and showing us step-by-step how to become the most beautiful spouse possible.

She is like your best friend and mother who wants to see only the best for you. There through thick and thin, suffering and joy, births and deaths, She never turns from you and is interested in every tiny advancement or successful effort.

Sophia is the gauge whereby you can measure your self-development and preparedness for rising to the spiritual wedding. She will know even before you do if you are ready to be called to the wedding, whether your lamp is trimmed and your white linen clean and fresh.

As a bridesmaid, She walks with you as She continuously weds Christ, so that their union can help mid-wife your birth into the spirit.

We are born as young virgins into the spirit world and, as a bride, we are flush with innocence and inexperience. These aspects of our newly burgeoning spirit self are like the actions of a baby watched lovingly by its mother. In this same way, older married couples watch marriage with some wisdom gleaned from experience. They consider the bride and groom to be as fresh as newborns.

When the Bride soul meets the Groom spirit, a new world is born— one that begs for adventure and challenges the future with new hope, the possibility of a love that will outshine all others. Every wedding is hope for new life. The couple makes a vow. The rings of eternity are exchanged. A new life that will never end begins.

Once the soul weds the eternal spirit, there is no more death. Life holds no sting for the Bride. She has found the never-ending fountain of life and can drink, bathe, and draw her life from this eternal source.

The Altar

We stand together at the altar of life in service to generation
Weaving the tides of time through our love's bounteous strain.
Union is the highest perspective of bliss, wisdom, and joy,
As compassion ages in the treasure chest of the heart-grail.

Intangible effulgence rises through touching what will be;
The ever-present unknowing of Fate's fleeting feet
Dancing from caress to wonder and back again to rest
There upon the kissed brow of my beloved's blush of youth.

Psyche's bottled beauty from Persephone dreams us to sleep
With wonder and hush, born of death and dreamless sleep
Where the only surety is that which is born of the seed of love;
Only Joy, the child of Psyche and Eros, redeems the separation of love.

Our progeny are sure to go beyond our limits, to reach with love
All those places, half-remembered, but never forgotten: our home,
The heart, heaven, mother. This hearth of the soul gives wings to spirit,
To bridge the span of space, the lengths of time bordered by rainbows,
The Aurora of Dawn—which is every dawn that longs for dusk;
Every morning chasing the night, causing light-worlds to bloom and burgeon;
Every night, yawning to hold the warm luster of the day's brightness,
Together united, separate in our souls, bursting with life.

The Moon holds her mirror, a small image of brilliant day,
A wandering dream-lover beckoning a nuptial caress to fill herself

With those parts of the Sun she does not possess,
Ensuring that his presence lives on in lands far beyond his gaze.

We reach upward, intertwine as one through the growth of time,
Weaving an ivy bower filled with sweet summer fruits
Offered to the gods and goddesses who join in our rejoicing
As we together echo the divine and spin into the spiral of life;
Resonating as Our Spirit, born of Sophia, fired in Christ's love.

We rush through time and space, shining as a comet of love,
Defining our only limits as the image of creation's radiance.
We glow, burn, and shine through time's resistant substance
Leaving our impress as footprints on destiny's spiritual sands,
Building our tomorrows on best-laid plans, that may last or crumble.
We live, we love, and offer it all on the altar—the anvil of the heart,
On the path that is love's illumined trace, made by the twins of love divine.

Sophia as the Beloved

Wait, my beloved, for like the wandering stars, our fate also is ruled by a greater Destiny that knows, in time, all mysteries shall unfold their secrets.

In the tradition of alchemy, when the mysterious conjunction transpires and the Queen and King wed into the androgynous co-creators, the Bride becomes the Beloved. By the kiss of love and the vow of commitment, the soul acknowledges that the spirit will care for it and nurture it all of its days. This completes the alchemical Great Work.

This joyful day is the beginning of a lifelong love of the Beloved, the being of Beauty that we have desired for so long.

We have found the other half of the self.

Together, the higher soul qualities of the bride comingle with the newly found spiritual qualities of the groom.

This dance of the spirit is as exhilarating as newlyweds dancing their first dance together as one; the dance has been practiced, but the experience is altogether new, different, and unique. The newlyweds must work together gracefully and show the moves they have practiced so carefully. The floor is cleared for the first dance. Everyone in the spiritual world is looking on with support and love. The Bride becomes the Beloved. A new life begins where both participants are fresh, awake, and ready to learn.

Sophia as the Beloved is a profound example of love, its phenomenal power to endure the destructive and divisive forces of suffering, pain, and death. Always faithful and loyal to the vows of eternal love, Sophia the Beloved never leaves the side of the evolving aspirant.

Once the Bride becomes the Beloved, there is no end to the gifts Sophia provides. With the power of heaven and Earth, She can bend those forces and beings to Her will. She is there for you.

At this moment, you have come into your spiritual inheritance. She wants to lavish the best upon you and see to your every spiritual need. So pleased that the aspirant has risen to heaven as the Bride, She rains down her affections upon the consecrated Beloved.

The virgin soul has become the new queen who someday will rule this domain. For now, she will sit at the feet of the Lamb (higher self) and let Sophia instruct in the ways of Wisdom. Often, this happens during nightly dreams. The soul rises to a heavenly edifice or city. There, she is instructed about the workings of the divine.

This connection to the aspirant's higher self is always faithful from the spirit side, yet not always so faithfully tended by the soul. Often, it falls away from daily contact with the divine. To the spirit, this is as sad as a divorce.

The original inspiration and love of Wisdom and Beauty never goes away. The mirror of the mind, however, may wander, become distracted, and fail to connect with the spirit. This does not dissolve the marriage, and no divorce is possible. Once the soul has married the spirit, the individual ego will never forget the bliss of union with the divine. The longing will continue until the aspirant again begins the climb to the spirit.

Sophia as Daughter of the Goddess manifesting as the Beloved has three sacred couplings that show us the proper road to Wisdom in relationships.

As Creatrix, She is wed to the Father Ground of Being. She manifests all things in this realm while reflecting the unmanifest Father Ground of Being. Together they span the material and spiritual worlds.

As Daughter of the Goddess, She descended from the Divine Feminine Trinity into the realm of the Spirits of Wisdom just as Christ descended from the Male Trinity into the realm of the Spirits of Form. The two cosmic beings met in the spiritual realm and were faithful consorts throughout their descent and resurrection back into the higher realms. Both suffered greatly as humans. They understand our plight, and their spiritual coupling has given us a cosmic image to emulate.

As the Holy Sophia, She descended to Earth. She acts through humans as they spiritually evolve, collecting and nurturing each personal experience with the divine.

The Holy Sophia weds the Holy Spirit at the moment of Pentecost when Mary and the apostles received the gift of the Holy Spirit, sent by Christ as

His continuing presence of comfort and love. The tongues of flame descending on the apostles showed the divine fire of Christ that had been prepared by Sophia. The Holy Sophia acts as the collective soul of the spiritual strivings of humanity, while the Holy Spirit nurtures the Christ in each individual.

> *"When the soul and spirit merge, futures burst forth."*

Sophia has much to teach us about maintaining the eternal vow of fidelity and love that is made between the Virgin Bride and the Spiritual Groom. The more love and faithfulness that surround this union, the greater the good that may result.

Divine marriages abound in literature, myth, and religion. Often the offspring of such unions are the hope of the future that carries the message of resurrection and renewal for a new golden age.

These spiritual realities gave birth to myths of children born with capabilities greater than their parents. Horus, for example, is the powerful offspring of Isis and Osiris. In another example, the Black Madonnas commonly found throughout Europe depict a mother holding a child adorned as a king. This is an archetype of the newly born spirit self that will be greater than the mother or father, the soul, and the physical body.

The newborn king is the Christened part of our spiritual self birthed into the world with the loving help and wisdom of Sophia and Christ.

Once this celebration of the spiritual wedding has been enacted, there is no guarantee that the soul will not descend to hell again or find new sources of suffering. Discovering the spiritual self and beginning the process of an eternal marriage is no assurance that we will continue steadily on the journey forward in full connection. In time, we may lose the map that shows the path back to heaven.

It is true that from one lifetime to the next, the soul may wander many paths and forget the sacred vows, how it felt to be a virgin soul in the blushing beauty of youth. Fortunately, the heart never forgets those feelings. It always wishes to find them again.

Not always is the heart in agreement with the brain, especially in this age of materialism. The passionate love of the spirit may wane through the more mundane details—the bills must be paid, the house cleaned, the garbage taken out—but the heart always remembers a vow of love.

No time or space can prevent the heart from feeling that the other part of her nature is summoning her to realms where eyes and ears have no power. The heart knows when it is home and when it stands next to its spiritual mate.

When the soul and spirit merge, futures burst forth.

They echo endlessly.

Time and space dissolve.

The heart's eternal nature resonates with the universal pulse of life.

These moments are never forgotten, no matter how dark the way or how seemingly lost along the path one may appear.

It often happens that an aspirant wishes to love the spirit but knows not which spirit is which. He has not developed the supersensible organs necessary to commune with the spirit clearly. It is easy to confuse who is who and which aspect of our multifaceted being is which.

Sophia is so close to us that we might assume She is our personal guardian angel, but She is not. The higher self looks like Christ, but it is not; there is a subtle but important distinction.

The soul looks like Sophia and passes through many of Her faces, but it is not Sophia.

Sophia Herself has three faces in the Divine Feminine Trinity and at least twelve facets that manifest in the human soul, but She is not one of the beings in the Male Trinity.

It takes three separate biographies to describe the nature of the three beings in the Divine Feminine Trinity. Still, we cannot fathom Her depths.

In other words, Christ and Sophia bring tremendous forces to bear on our personal self-development. They help us develop, step by step, the forces we need to understand our earthly self and our spiritual self as they blossom into a world filled with new supersensible beings and realities.

> *"The love between the soul and the Beloved spirit kindles new fires and invites a new dawn."*

This marriage to the higher self is the ultimate phenomenon that happens to a human being, evidenced by the person developing into a wise, humble, and loving being. The soul becomes like its spiritual partner in the heavenly worlds. It starts to take on virtuous characteristics in her personal nature.

After spending time as the Beloved in the spiritual world, the soul begins to see the spirit all about him. The Earth lights up with joy. Wisdom and love are found everywhere.

These spiritual effects are universal. The higher one develops, the more *moral character* and *levity* enter the human soul, demonstrated by a nonjudgmental, accepting, and kind attitude of soul that draws everyone into its warmth. The more the soul loves the spirit, the more the spirit blesses the soul with patience, compassion, and the higher virtues.

"Love is a river that brings Imagination, Inspiration, and Intuition into the soul."

The love between the soul and the Beloved Spirit kindles new fires and invites a new dawn.

The love of the Bride Soul and Beloved Spirit comingles and unites into the birth of the higher self, a newborn child of Wisdom.

This infant will grow quickly if the soul regularly focuses on rising up to spirit. It is not alone. Many spirits await there to help lift it higher, to give it all that it can hold.

One fitting analogy is that the soul has lit a single candle. It has climbed the long flight of steps to the upper room where now it lights a vast space with a tiny flame.

Soon, others gather around. Their candles add to the light. The room is revealed as a beautiful temple where Wisdom has created every element as a living wonder. Each candle holder then lights other candles throughout the temple until it is bright as day.

This is the path of gradual ascent that accompanies a faithful and loving communion with the divine. The next morning, the soul remembers the illuminated wonders that accompanied its sleep. Both the soul and spirit are refreshed and renewed.

In this way, this reciprocal relationship with the divine feeds our soul and spirit. Lovers know this process well. They revitalize each other through their love, a fountain of eternal youth that flows infinitely, never running dry. This is the true nature of the elixir of life that provides immortality. Love is that fountain. We can find it and choose to drink from it. When we do, unceasing love will flow through us.

Married love is exclusive love, but there is a higher form of love: universal love. This type of love pervades all aspects of life as an unending source of energy. It is not exclusive at all. Given freely, it cannot be held by anyone.

This eternal fountain is the source of the divine itself perfectly unmanifest, yet present everywhere. It is the fundamental ground of being that continually brings forth life without diminishing.

Love is not logical.

It is not dual in its nature.

It comes from nowhere and can build entire worlds from nothing.

Love is a river that brings Imagination, Inspiration, and Intuition into the soul and spirit of the seeker.

Love is the cause of all effects.

Love comes from beyond the visible world.

It is the ever-present master force that binds all things together without coercion.

Love creates affinities, unites differences, and brings forth life while comforting death.

Love is the eternal in the world.

It races everywhere it is needed and slows enough to allow us to catch up.

Love is not an emotion, for emotions swing between sympathy and antipathy.

Love is ever-steady and faithful.

It is not a thought, for its manifestation is beyond what human thought can envision.

Without hands, love shatters and builds worlds.

Love creates life and children.

It may only flow into the future, for love is ever new, fresh, and becoming.

Love is not the past. Only through grace and mercy does love come to show Herself passing into the future.

Love is not tangible, and has built the world and spanned all space.

Love is pure. It cannot be bought or sold. Nothing can contain it.

This is universal love. Undefinable. Unimaginable. Surely to be praised and worshipped for lifting humans from exclusive love of the few to love of all.

Like the sun, love shines upon all equally and personally manifests as the one and the many.

Love is the cause of creation, and creation never stops. Thus, love never ends.

As we compare the personal steps of drawing closer to Sophia as She refracts light into Her many facets, we evolve in our understanding of Her. We grow from a selfish, less mature approach of exclusive love into a more sophisticated view of love that encompasses all beings in nature and super-nature.

The personal, secret love of the Beloved needs to branch out and include others in the dance of the spirit. Once the higher self is born and can move about in the spirit world and communicate with spiritual beings, the individual can expand his or her ability to love everyone selflessly.

This is a difficult task. It requires steadfast meditation and prayer. The single Beloved can be easy to love; to love an enemy is much harder to do—a much greater spiritual task.

Wisdom leads us to love all others and develop the capacities of tolerance, compassion, and courage to do the right thing. Love is a tough task-mistress. She asks us to love beyond the realm of our familiar comfort zone. As mere human souls on the path to the spirit, these challenges are difficult, but worthwhile.

We can spend a great deal of time being happy with our newly found spiritual selves and developing soul capacities that can metamorphose into new spiritual organs of perception that find meaning in life's challenges. Bathing in the glorious life-filled light of the spiritual world is mesmerizing and fulfilling, but the soul still lives in the solid world of matter where people everywhere need love and support.

To My Beloved

The heart can hear the beat of love at any distance,
Sounding in the timeless chamber of its home of origin,
Where feelings of wisdom shelter its fragile nature
And echo the heaven's harmony of union and bliss.

Two halves make up my heart, one mine, the other yours
And incomplete it was until its spirit-twin was found
United in the fiery stream of passion's embrace,
Welded together for purposes beyond our little worlds.

Like an instrument that resonates in concert with a sounding tone,
Joining in symphonic union to surround all that we do together,
Blessing our efforts with melodic strains of love and laughter
That fill our home with heart-warmth and joyous songs.

We join our efforts to do the will of the divine,
To lift our spirits to realms sweet and sublime
To raise the children to bask in heaven's light,
To know they are loved every day and every night.

This is my quest, to bond our hearts forever,
To risk all and everything in our vow to never
Be untrue to each other, or unkind in any way,
To live life to its fullest each and every day.

You are my inspiration, my sweet taste of bliss profound,
That opened all my senses to a new world of creative sound,
That repeats the love song of Sophia for all Her offspring divine,
And joins us in the wedding dance that makes our hearts to shine.

The Holy Sophia

Sophia as the
Goddess of Love

Lightning bolts of love spark

from your fiery heart-wheel.

Sophia as the Goddess of Love is the first step into co-creation with the third person in the Divine Feminine Trinity, the Holy Sophia. Her four aspects manifest as Goddess of Love, Mother of God, Queen of Heaven, and the Most Holy Trinosophia, in the same way that each of the other two personages have four facets or labors that illustrate some of the ways we may experience and perceive Her.

Sophia manifests as three in one, a Divine Feminine Trinity that cannot be understood by the human intellect alone. It takes the fiery passion of the heart and the indomitable, unstoppable forces of human willpower to join higher thinking to create the true, the beautiful, and the good.

The Greeks were correct in saying that humans have three domains, all active at once. Understanding the human being as threefold is essential to constructing a cosmology or world-view in harmony with nature, both the seen and unseen.

Human thinking and feeling are somewhat *unseen* because they occur in the private enclosed area of the human vessel. Human willing, however, can be *seen* when active and moving toward achieving a goal. But willpower also has a hidden component. People often do not understand their willpower or the forces and laws active in their own bodies.

Some spiritually cognizant people are just now beginning to control thought, generally through spiritual development and mental training. Feeling still runs rampant in modern materialistic habits of excess and indulgence. We are assaulted by media and superfast versions of everything, including emotional relationships that overwhelm the will.

This threefold nature of humanity—thinking, feeling, and willing—causes tremendous confusion that can lead to neurosis in thinking, psychosis in feeling, and aberrant behavior in the will.

On the other hand, the threefold nature of the human being gives the opportunity to overcome these forces and align them with the example of the Trinity of the spiritual divine, both female and male.

We have seen in the picture of the Daughter of the Goddess many ways to bridge the dualities we find in our soul and spirit. The world itself is built from these same dual forces. We need to take the next step into simultaneously balancing three parts of our being and harmonizing the natural forces that flow through our three soul capacities.

This juggling act is difficult. Many people fall prey to turning off or tuning out the different parts of the threefold soul.

First, we find out that we are missing parts of ourselves, and we must quest to find them, working hard to understand and tame these wild parts. Then we are accelerated through super-materialism, on a dead-end journey that scientists tell us ends in a cold, meaningless grave. Materialism says there is no spirit, no meaning to life, no life after death.

On the other hand, spiritual people tell us that we can develop the three gifts of thinking, feeling, and willing into new organs of perception that enhance and illuminate everything around us. These supersensible organs can directly communicate with a hierarchy of beings around us, within us, and through us.

"In the moment they love, humans are divine."

The hierarchy actually perceives us through these new supersensible organs of perception. Angels know our higher thoughts. Archangels are aware of our refined feelings. The Archai witness our moral deeds. Many great people throughout history have utilized these higher sense organs and bestowed on us the spiritual gifts of great literature, architecture, art, and culture.

These organs can see into the spiritual world. They enable us to develop the forces of Imagination to commune with living archetypes and then return to express their natures in the Earthly realm.

These visions of the spirit, called Imaginations, are not fantasies, but are perceptions of beings that have consequence and substantiality—

entities who build and essentially lift the spiritual nature of the experience out of the Earthly realm. These visions have inspired the visual, musical, literary arts, and all man-made pursuits that are beautiful, graceful, and harmonious.

When humanity develops the supersensible organ of Inspiration, the higher levels of the hierarchy can sound the music of the encircling planets into the vessel of the human being. Supersensible forces and beings then move into the heart to build new capacities of spirit that inspire the aspirant.

The spiritual world also listens through these Inspirations. It can sense the forces of archangels active in higher human feeling. For example, each time a person is inspired, he is actually listening to the spiritual hosts produce the music that weaves the web of life.

When both forces of Imagination and Inspiration combine with willpower, Intuitions are born. Imprinted in them are forces that build, destroy, and sustain all creation. These Intuitions appear as *knowing* in the human soul.

Intuition comes to birth as love.

Intuition is pure love. Humans have the capacity to create images of the divine as great Imaginations, to hear divine music through Inspiration, and to perform divinely inspired moral deeds through loving Intuitions.

When a human loves, all three soul forces are active. The loving person is using spiritual forces to serve as a divine vehicle in this world.

Love is the highest human capacity. It links all aspects of the human being as a threefold unity, a trinity. In the moment they love, humans are divine. Of course, this love is the universal love we have discussed previously; not some personal, possessive desire disguised as love.

Love is an endless fountain of nourishment, support, and comfort.

The small human ego does not love; it simply likes or dislikes. More often than not, it chooses to like that which is most similar to itself.

Desire, too, often masks itself as love to the undiscerning.

Sympathy and antipathy rule the soul like the forces of a rollercoaster, racing up and down and side to side with no center and possibly terror at every turn.

The common soul follows whatever the fickle eye sets its longing upon, never realizing that desire can be satiated but for a fleeting moment. Desire passes, like the rollercoaster ride. It is anything but stable. We have heard about the allure of Beauty and the unfortunate path we may tread if we *grab* beauty and try to *hold* desire.

The misunderstanding of love is the greatest challenge that humanity has ever faced. So far, mankind is losing the battle in the Earthly realm to hatred, war, and personal desire.

Love both starts and ends with selflessness. Individual love is based on selfish desire, personal gain, and self-protection. For many, love is an emotional equation, a calculated balancing act. They only love while they are being loved. When the individual soul believes the other does not love her anymore, or does not love her with equal interest, the balance tips and she, too, ceases to love. This kind of love begins and ends in selfishness. The irony is that this type of love was never really love at all. Far from it.

How difficult it is that no one can teach love to another so that they might understand.

You can only give love away. It cannot be held fast, accumulated, or hidden away in a safe place. Love is infinitely available to the one who wishes to give it, and yet humans imagine that they create or control it, showing no more understanding than a newborn who knows not why people give her love.

All humans are worthy of infinite love, but most do not know how to give or receive it. Instead of simply giving it, they spend a great deal of their life trying to find it in the first place. Love is a simple gift. When you give it away freely, you will experience bliss and unity of soul and spirit. A uniting force, love joins the threefold soul forces of thinking, feeling, and willing, transforming the Earthly human into a heavenly angel.

Love is the meaning of life. It is created by the hierarchy called the Seraphim, the Beings of Love. As the highest of the nine hierarchies, the Seraphim are the most powerful, pervasive, and supreme hierarchy.

Love reaches far beyond the confines of our solar system. It unites with the Beings of Harmony, the Cherubim, and the Beings of Pure Will Power, the Thrones, to manifest and maintain the divine evolutionary plan. Existing outside of time and space, these beings live in the forces of the Trinities and directly communicate with Them.

This highest rank of the three groups of hierarchies, the Seraphim, Cherubim, and Thrones, are a Trinity onto themselves.

There is a second Trinity of hierarchies comprised of the Beings of Wisdom, Movement, and Form. The third Trinity of hierarchies are the Time Spirits, Archangels, and Angels, who work with both the Trinities of Father/Son/Holy Spirit and Mother/Daughter/Holy Sophia.

Each human being also contains the same threefold force of a trinity, just as the divisions of the hierarchy and the supreme Trinities that maintain the manifest world. The human being has three physical components (physical, etheric, astral), three soul components (sentient, intellectual, consciousness), and three spirit components (spirit self, life spirit, spirit human) to match the nine hierarchies. In this regard, the human is clearly an image of the divine.

Sophia manifests in a Divine Feminine Trinity. We have examined the Mother aspects of Sophia as Creatrix, Mother of All, Wisdom, and Natura. We have likewise examined the aspects of human evolution that awoke to and perceived the Daughter aspects of Sophia as the Goddess of Beauty, the Cosmic Virgin, the Bride, and the Beloved. Each description brought Sophia closer to us as She became the personal guide and assistant on the path of self-knowledge and spiritual development.

Sophia is the image of Beauty that leads us through the realms of heaven and hell, just as Beatrice led Dante.

She changes Her face to meet our needs and match our level of development at any moment in time.

A shape-shifter, She appears as the goal of the quest, then is realized to be the servant who carried the bags throughout.

Sophia was there all along. We could not see Her because we were simply not developed enough to perceive Her.

She is the song of life, unheard until the soul is perfectly silent: the small, still voice. But once Her sweet song resounds, the spirit quickly takes up the dance, immediately swept up into the temple of wonders that play the harmonies of the divine.

At this point, let us examine Sophia as the Holy Sophia, the third person of Her Trinity. There are four aspects that describe the Holy Sophia, a most mysterious Being who is similar to the Holy Spirit, the Comforter, that Christ sent to the Earth after His ascension into heaven.

The Holy Sophia embodies the spirit of the Mother and Daughter aspects of the Divine Feminine Trinity. She is co-equal to and an undivided aspect of the Trinity. She is one and the same as the Mother and the Daughter.

This double paradox is beyond what the human mind can imagine. It takes the entire threefold being of the human to understand the Holy Sophia and the Mysteries of the Divine Feminine Trinity. Only Intuition, as the activating force that harmonizes thinking and feeling, can begin to fathom this Trinity and the manifestation of the Holy Sophia.

The Holy Sophia is connected to the future of our spiritual development. She is the last part of Sophia to be understood as the human spirit rises to the divine. One who has ascended to understand Sophia's twelve facets can comprehend the unfolding of the Holy Sophia.

The Holy Sophia manifests as the Goddess of Love, the Mother of God, the Queen of Heaven and the Most Holy Trinosophia, the third face of the twelve facets of Sophia. To understand the Goddess of Love, one must understand what love truly is.

The foregoing description about the nature of love is far beyond what most are capable of feeling for other human beings. It is closer to what they might feel in their hearts for the divine. To someone who has not experienced them, these pure streams of love are indescribable.

True love is like light seen for the first time by a person bereft of sight. One who gives divine love is carried into a heavenly realm, right here on the Earth. Heaven comes to Earth. New Jerusalem descends closer to those who know how to love freely, co-creating with divine will. Without this experience, the spiritual seeker will not be able to understand most of Sophia's higher aspects manifesting in the great Wisdom of the cosmic Sophia Christos Mysteries.

The Holy Sophia came to Earth because humans had evolved enough to begin to think independently. Abraham was the model example of a person who introduced brain-bound thinking into the personal domain. Prior to 2100 B.C., free, independent thinking was little known. The culture was led by priest/kings who still had a clairvoyant perception of the divine. Wisdom was imparted through communion with the hierarchy.

As humans developed independent thought, the hierarchy saw the need to guide and record the efforts of individuals in their personal, self-motivated mental development. People no longer acted as a tribal group-soul, led by a great spiritual being who gave them the knowledge and wisdom they needed to thrive in their environment. Leaders like Manu of the Hindus, Zarathustra of the Persians, or Hermes of the Egyptians laid down for their cultures both the civil and spiritual laws.

Individual thinkers were very rare in those times. The Hebrew people, who were instructed to possess no images of the divine, were being prepared for the dawn of the modern intellect. As thought developed, so too did the Being of Sophia, who entered this earthly realm with human capacities but without a physical body.

The Holy Sophia also had the full power of the Mother and the Daughter forces available to Her as She became the mid-wife and nursemaid of those whose intellect blossomed into independent thinkers.

Rudolf Steiner tells us more about this mysterious Being, the Holy Sophia, than any other philosopher. He calls Her TheoSophia, PhiloSophia, and AnthropoSophia. He points out that the Holy Sophia develops over time both in the thinking human being and in the development of Her own spiritual aspects.

At first, he says, She is young and develops the lower aspects of the physical, etheric, and astral bodies. Each of these seven-year human developmental periods takes the Holy Sophia 700 years to develop. She must develop all of the bodies of the human so that She can understand the human in every way possible, except for the fact that She does not possess a physical body and will never experience mortal death.

Sophia moves faster through Her development than humans. During Egyptian times, She developed the Sentient Soul; during the Greek era, the Intellectual Soul. In 1415 A.D., She caught up with humanity at the third part of our soul evolution, the Consciousness Soul. Today, She has evolved beyond the Consciousness Soul and is now preparing the Spirit Self for humanity.

The Holy Sophia is now active in the spiritual world, leading humanity to its next stage of evolution. The group-soul consciousness has been left behind. She fosters a personal self-development, intimately aware of each step of the aspirant's own path to develop the intellect into Wisdom.

The Holy Sophia is just in front of us beckoning us forward to our spiritual inheritance. She fully understands the soul's trials and tribulations, as She personally witnessed the passion and resurrection of Christ as the redemption of all human suffering.

She is our collective spiritual development, guiding us, giving each soul the comprehensive and compassionate love that only a mother can give. As the mother of our spirit, She holds our hand and steadies our steps into the spiritual world.

She never sleeps. She is always ready to help, delivering the forces of cosmic Wisdom and love. Anyone who experiences synchronicity or a unique providence that illuminates her experiences is feeling Sophia.

She loves the spiritual striving of each soul. Like a mother, She recalls our first step. She will be there when we consciously step across the threshold into heaven. Working on both sides of the threshold, She is our ever-present traveling companion on the journey to our higher self.

The Holy Sophia has taken the same vow as Quan Yin, which is not to enter heaven until all other beings have been helped to enter before Her. She wants every soul to rise to the spirit, to arrive in time for the wedding feast. Her most powerful tool is love. She is love. She gives and teaches love. She records its effects. She always supports the labors of love, anywhere that love alights.

Love is the active force of the Holy Sophia, who grows more powerful as humans spiritually evolve. No one but She is more interested and supportive of one's personal and spiritual development.

To love another is to *suffer* the other's pains and help him carry his load. The Holy Sophia learned about love from the author of love Himself, Christ Jesus. She witnessed all aspects of Christ's mystical life: His descent from heaven, His suffering and passion, His descent into hell, and His resurrection and ascension.

> *"Wisdom is the foundation upon which true love is built and the flame of the spirit ignited."*

Throughout all of these events, the Holy Sophia was there with Christ, sharing in the experience, writing it into the book of living memory that never fades from the realm of the super-etheric. His deeds fed Her own development. Once He had left, He sent the Holy Spirit to wed the Holy Sophia.

In that sacred marriage, love and wisdom united. The Comforter and the Holy Sophia are ever-present for each human who can rise to perceive them. It was the Wisdom of the Mother of Christ to gather in the upper room as Jesus had told them to do. It was the living presence of Christ, the Holy Spirit, that lit the tongues of fire above the apostles' heads and gave them the ability to speak as angels.

Wisdom is the foundation upon which true love is built and the flame of the spirit ignited.

Composed of the most beautiful Wisdom within the spin of an atom, the world is maintained carefully so that harmony and balance reign. Upset Nature's delicate balance, and unimaginable forces may be released. We need to respect Nature's rhythms. Then the power behind Her beauty will unveil the forces needed to advance civilization and culture on Earth, instead of destroy it.

Love will blossom from Wisdom.

Humans have been given free will, but we do not know how to use it with moral clarity and spiritual purpose. Like eager children, we sit at the mother's feet to learn about beings and forces that we can barely comprehend.

If we learn to perceive with supersensible organs, we would see Wisdom everywhere. She would teach us about ourselves and the world. Wisdom has created all natural things, yet is a hidden mystery. Science continually discovers new forces and gains knowledge, yet the basic questions remain unanswered.

Today, Wisdom is still as scarce as She ever was. We have yet to accept our inheritance of infinite Wisdom found in our own nature, let alone develop the higher forces of love that carry much more strength and power.

According to spiritual scientists, the present environment has been formed from the forces and Beings of Wisdom. They created this realm as an opportunity for humans to evolve into gods, if we eat of the fruit of the Tree of Knowledge of Good and Evil and open our eyes. Eve was right to have eaten the fruit and begin her path to becoming a goddess.

Wisdom is like spiritual nourishment. It is sweet fruit growing all around us if we only knew what tree from which to harvest. Presently, humanity is co-creating the love that will comprise the future environment. When we give love, we build the future. Humanity will be surrounded and nourished by this love. Abundant love will flow through all. Groups of people will combine to use magical forces of the Word, Holy Logos, to bring newborns into that realm of love.

By that time, humans will have evolved into angels. We will no longer be bound by space. Humanity will no longer need to sleep a third of its life away in the sunless dark. This future realm does not take place on Earth, but in a higher realm, as our older brothers and sisters arrive to help raise us from earthly darkness and travail into light.

Some humans will not evolve into angels. They will remain behind to try again. For a human to become an angel, he must be able to let the divine flow through him as love. Love alights first in the mind as an intuition. Our thinking is set on fire by the heart. In turn, it ignites the human will power into actions of love. The coordinated and aligned threefold human soul can then rise into the threefold nature of its spiritual being: an angel, an archangel, and an archai. Theosophists call them Manas, Budhi, and Atman. Steiner calls them the Spirit Self, Life Spirit, and Spirit Man. It will take the slow passing of millennia to develop these aspects of the spirit. In the present time, the advanced soul will be the one able to experience the forces descending as Imagination, Inspiration, and Intuition.

As the aspirant wishes to understand the Holy Sophia aspect of the Divine Feminine Trinity, she must develop herself into a worthy vessel or grail that can receive and hold the spiritual archetypes of the activity of the Goddess of Love. Again, this is no earthly or fallen Olympian Goddess of Love, but the Goddess of Love who loves each one of us separately and collectively. The original aspect of Aphrodite was the creator of humanity who stood virgin, beautiful, and naked before the Greek mythographer. She birthed herself from the genitals of Uranus, the sky god, which had been thrown into the ocean. The ocean was her home because she, like other ocean titans, could shape-shift and take on any form, which explains why she could be the form of the most beautiful goddess.

Aphrodite, the Goddess of Love, comes as an offering of the ocean, bringing only the true, the good, and the beautiful to humanity. All beings fall in love with Aphrodite upon sight because she is the representation of the perfect human in all its glory, ascending into heaven. As the heavenly gift of love to humanity, Aphrodite is the story of the Holy Sophia come to the Earth. People have tried every trick to catch this heavenly beauty, but love cannot be held by anyone.

Humanity's intellectual development is a love affair with the Holy Sophia. Every time one advances in significant thinking, the Holy Sophia passes through him. She embodies his unique efforts so that the thought or idea will be perfectly memorialized for all who rise up to the super-etheric realm. Steiner refers to this idea as spiritual economy.

The spiritual world does not destroy any good effort. It actually records it in the Akashic Fields found everywhere in nature. The Holy Sophia is responsible for making sure that no human spiritual development is ever lost or unaccounted for, but is instead recorded and remembered. Therefore, when Christ perfected each of the nine human bodies (physical, etheric, astral, sentient soul, intellectual soul, consciousness soul, spirit self, life spirit, and spirit human), the Holy Sophia was there to witness the imprinting of those bodies into the super-etheric body around the Earth, sometimes referred to as Shamballa or New Jerusalem.

Each night that an aspirant sleeps, he has the opportunity to visit that realm and learn from these perfected vehicles as personal teachers. St. Augustine, Francis of Assisi, Meister Eckhart, Johannes Tauler, and others utilized parts of these to transform their personal bodies into higher forms. These vehicles are there for anyone to use, if they have acquired the supersensible organs to perceive them and the moral advancement to embody them.

Thus, the perfected love of Christ is there for the Holy Sophia to embody. She participated in His life when She was the equivalent of twenty-one years of age. She had attained the age when the human ego is developed, twenty-one, as Christ enacted the Mystery of Golgotha: the birth, death, and resurrection of the Son of God.

The Holy Sophia was present with Christ, a witness to His birth, death, and rebirth. She was intimate with Jesus of Nazareth and the Christ Being who descended into Him. She experienced the embodiment of Jesus by the Christ as a human, as the Mother of Jesus did, with great suffering that leaves the soul helpless in this earthly realm.

To be truly human and witness the Mystery of Golgotha makes the Holy Sophia one of few hierarchical beings who could look upon the crucifixion and not turn away. As the human and divine experience of Christ was emblazoned into the super-etheric realm for all time to come, She was loyal. She stayed to witness.

"By simply lifting the veils of space and time, we can reimagine the entire world."

Christ's experience never leaves the Earthly realm. That is why some people can bear stigmata, exist without eating, levitate, heal, or perform any of His miracles. All of these examples are like new living archetypes that commune with the person who has spiritual ears to hear or spiritual eyes to see. This is what the Catholic doctrine of the Communion of Saints means, helping the worshiper become more like a saint. The examples of the saints inspire the soul to reach up to the spirit. The same idea occurs in Tibetan Buddhism through deity worship. The aspirant tries to follow the model of a deity or "enlightened one" in his spiritual practice so that he may ascend to the realm of the saints, Tushita Heaven.

Jesus told his followers that he had prepared the way for each person to have a home in heaven. When Jesus became Christ, He unlocked the future where the perfected vehicles of humans reside; humans were created with the end in mind.

The creative hierarchy is not limited by time and space. They created humans. They did so from beginning to end. There is an intelligent design to our destiny, where the hierarchy is leading us, because They are already there. We cannot see this because we experience a limited space-time dimension. In the spiritual world, we are mere babes. Most of us cannot stand, walk, or speak.

It is the loving intention of the divine to help us grow, to fill the positions that already await us, if we do not limit our self-perception. For instance, each time we have a true, spiritual Imagination, we reach into the future and access our spirit self in the realm of the angels. For a moment, we become a light-filled being of Imagination that is connected to other angelic forces. Just for a transitory moment, we revel in the light. Then we fall back into color and darkness. Perhaps we can create memories of the experience, but this is difficult in the limited earthly realm. In that moment, we can be a god or goddess. We can be co-creative with spirit. By simply lifting the veils of space and time, we can reimagine the entire world.

When an aspirant has that moment of divine Inspiration, her life changes. The encounter is a visual and audible contact with divine spiritual beings from the realm of archangels. It imparts Wisdom. This type of encounter may happen only once or repeatedly in a person's life, yet will drive and motivate her for a lifetime.

Inspiration arrives as music accompanied by images that are beautiful, true, and good. This is the realm of the archangels who welcome our participation with great joy and happiness. We receive Inspirations from the future. They come to us through the vehicles we will use when that time arrives.

> *"The Holy Sophia is the biographer of your spiritual self."*

By lifting the veil of time with Inspirations, we see a glimpse of our future spiritual nature. These mysteries are truly inconceivable with the sense-bound brain. They can only be envisioned with qualitative, not quantitative, spiritual perception. The heart can begin to approach a better understanding but, in general, until the aspirant experiences the dissolution of the bonds of space and time, it is hard to imagine.

The ultimate experience of human comprehension is to have a truly visual, auditory, spoken experience of spiritual Intuition. This event is unmistakable to those who have had it, because the resulting Wisdom gleaned is unbound by space or time, and thus true and accurate in its nature.

An Intuition is unmistakably the voice of the divine informing the aspirant about something that is to come from the future. It is generally true, but not always good or beautiful. One must obtain the proper moral level of spiritual development to access such accurate information about the future. Personal desire cannot enter into these realms at all; it requires multiple levels of discrimination to understand what you might believe you have perceived beyond space and time. In fact, if Intuition acts as personal self-desire, it could harm the person trying to manipulate it.

> *"A human can only exist in this realm for a tiny moment, yet be filled with years of insight."*

True Intuition should always appear through love and work for the betterment of spiritual purposes. It should provide the experience of new forces of love and life that help fulfill the divine designs. When an aspirant has a truly valid Intuition, she has entered the realm of the Archai or the Spirit of the Times, the Zeitgeist. Far beyond space and time, where there is not a single hint of the Earthly, these Beings pervade a dimension where Christened Beings exist. Here, there is direct communion with the higher hierarchies through consciousness. A human can only exist in this realm for a tiny moment, yet be filled with years of insight. This is why Intuition can drive a person's life; an archetype of this magnitude is worth human reverence. Truly, the divine reveals itself through Intuitions. The fact that humans can hold such a perception in their being shows that they, too, are created in the image of the divine hierarchy. Their mission is to evolve into the higher hierarchical positions. By developing the capacity to embody the higher qualities of the hierarchy, they will learn to transcend space, time, and everything sense-bound. They can exist in a state of consciousness where pure thoughts, feelings, and will carry out the harmonious work of the divine.

As each human soul develops spiritual qualities, the Holy Sophia works through Imagination, Inspiration, and Intuition. These steps are not sequential. Often, they may break into consciousness at the oddest times instead of during meditation as expected.

Love comes through us to help others whenever we call Her, but

Intuitions may be elusive and hard to achieve. Often clairvoyants report that they can only have Intuitions if the divine wills it to be. Their psychic abilities are limited by their own development, and they are humble enough to know that the Intuitions are not "their own" but belong to the divine and are shared only with moral individuals.

The seer who wishes to reach into the future and embody the spiritual aspects that are awaiting investiture must possess a highly developed morality. Only the motivation of love can help stimulate Intuition, for only love has the moral force to inspire the actions that accompany an Intuition. One must have love of the spirit and courage in the will. It takes a selfless person who is devoted to the divine to experience authentic Imagination, Inspiration, or Intuition. These tasks of the spirit are easy to talk about, but nearly impossible to do as a mere human. However, the Holy Sophia remembers your efforts toward each of these realms and nurtures you in all of your spiritual efforts.

The Holy Sophia is the biographer of your spiritual self. She has written the journey of your quest. She remembers even the most obscure parts of the story that you have forgotten. In this way, She is the best spiritual friend and mother that anyone could ever want. Her followers knew this: Vladimir Soloviev, Jacob Boehme, Gottfried Arnold, Jane Leade, Teilhard de Chardin, and many others. These Sophiologists openly wrote about their personal relationship with Sophia; some claimed that She came to them and "married" their souls.

> *"Finding the Holy Sophia is discovering the golden path to your higher self."*

Both men and women from all backgrounds had the same experience. A Being of Great Wisdom, Sophia, appeared physically to them and wed their souls. From that time on, they were married and shared a divine communion. These devotees were authentically filled with the spirit from their relationship with the Divine Feminine. There is a long list of great thinkers who worship the Divine Sophia; their devotion is profound. To them and others, the Holy Sophia is truly alive and inspiring more great thinkers all the time.

One such thinker mentioned earlier in the book was a renowned traditionalist philosopher who, one day, gave up all further writing and publishing so that he could live in a tepee to be close to Mother Gaia. He spent all of his days with his beloved wife, who he considered an embodiment of the goddess, and painted a new picture of the Goddess Sophia each day. This change of heart brought the great thinker into true appreciation of his wife, the Earth, and Sophia.

It seems that all of the tremendous effort and striving of the mind over a lifetime arrives at a simple life: worshipping the Divine Feminine. The prodigal child returns to the mother, a nurturing and long overdue homecoming. Many of the most astute minds have arrived at the same conclusion. The spirit is feminine. She is present. Alive. Know Her. Worship Her. Later in this book, literary selections from history are presented that show the beautiful ongoing relationship the human intellect has maintained with the Holy Sophia as She has unfolded throughout time.

"Love is the universal panacea and alchemical fire that tempers the heart into gold."

At first, the human intellect was barely a child, just as the Holy Sophia was developing through the stages of childhood. At the Mystery of Golgotha, She came of age and was then loved by the philosophers who saw Her everywhere. As intellectual ability expanded, so too did the vision and perception of Her facets grow. The pure thinker realized the nature of Wisdom. He found the Being of Sophia.

The aspirant may directly encounter Her nature as guide, goddess, and beloved. Finding the Holy Sophia is discovering the golden path to your higher self. Little did you know that you have been walking this path your entire life.

Sophia brings Wisdom from Her vantage point of seeing our efforts evolve into forces of love and gratitude. The path was always there. She has repeatedly been pointing it out, but we did not have the spiritual organs to hear Her voice and understand Her language. We simply did not have the ears to hear. Her nature is to always leave the human race free to choose the divine. Without this important choice, there would be no personal evolution. So She urges and encourages with Her love, but our own soul must climb to the mountain from whence we can rise into the heavens.

Originally born into every soul, the love of the divine is forgotten once we incarnate on solid ground. It is easy to believe that the physical realm is the only realm in which we exist. If we accept this idea, we lose a part of our soul. Love will not flow easily through us.

Love flows through a grateful soul. Anyone alive who can stand, speak, and think should be grateful for the gifts with which nature has endowed them. A lack of gratitude leads to isolation and illness.

Love is the universal panacea and alchemical fire that tempers the heart's gold. No interaction in nature is without love. All life, death, and rebirth are gifts of the divine through love. Nature knows the call of love, but many humans refuse to listen. They claim to be deaf to love's call.

Nature loves incessantly. The wind loves the wings of birds. The grass loves the sun. The ocean loves every creation therein. Yet humans often have difficulties in loving themselves or one another.

Love works strongly through the forces of levity to elevate the soul into spiritual vibrations that are more harmonious than earthly ones.

Levity gives wings to the soul to rise to the heavenly mountain on high.

Wings are the will of the divine raising each hierarchical rank up to the next.

Humans become angels when we are given the reward of our well-earned wings.

We are given a heavenly instrument to play music at the next level, and finally we are given a voice to sing the wonders of creation into being.

These ideas are not distant religious doctrines. All that is required is for one to take personal responsibility for his own spiritual self-development and not leave it in the hands of a priest, rabbi, or guru, however respected they may be. The greatest spiritual teachers learned their craft directly from the spiritual world without the intercession of a priest, intermediary, guru, or religion.

Just as we can tap into the future perfected bodies of the human being, and the realm of spiritual economy, we also can see the past manifest in the kingdoms of nature that surround us. The kingdoms of minerals, plants, and animals developed long before humans entered the Earthly domain. These kingdoms are comprised of sacrificed materials from the higher hierarchies, who donated substance that is held in a type of suspended animation. Humans then take advantage of the appearance of solids, liquids, gases, and fire working within nature.

The sacrificial offerings of the higher hierarchies are a loving gift sustained over incredible amounts of time and space. In effect, the vibrations of spiritual beings are "slowed down" in space/time to create an arena in which humans are born and evolve. When humans raise their own vibrations through free will, they can ascend towards the light. Once humanity evolves beyond the animal, plant, and mineral kingdoms, they will dissolve back into universal substance. The beings that held them together and interpenetrated them with infinite Wisdom will then no longer perform this function. During each cycle of manifestation (time period), the higher hierarchy also has evolved while passing through stages of their own development. It is fair to say that when you look at a rock crystal, you are looking at the shadow of a god. You are looking back into time. Space holds a variety of times simultaneously, but this awareness is based upon the consciousness of the beholder.

Looking into the depths of outer space, astrophysicists tell us, is equivalent to looking back in time. According to modern science, the further outward we look, the further back in time we go. This premise leads to inadequate scientific theories that try to understand the whole by examining the parts. The beingness of the whole will never be fully found in the parts until an expanded awareness of time and the definitions of space further evolve. Over time, humans will become aware of these simple but profound realities by carefully examining their own developing consciousness.

> *"Providence is love over time with the wisdom to find the seeds of karma in the ocean of destiny."*

The greatest force and beingness in creation is love. That is why Christ's teachings can be distilled into one law: *to love.* Love God. Love yourself. Love others. This is the supernatural spiritual law that only alights in this realm through efforts of compassion, long suffering, and understanding.

Love is undefinable. Its scope of power knows no limits in time or space. It lives on after death and into future incarnations. Love knows, through vibratory resonance, the soul nature of the ones we have loved before and will love in the future.

We often reincarnate with a group of similarly minded spirits who have established karmic patterns together. It is as though some friends and lovers were cuttings from the same tree, a mother tree of sympathetic resonance that is morphologically tuned to patterns of thought and oral traditions. We are often called back into the same patterns of life again and again until we learn to recognize the pattern and adapt. Providence is love manifesting over time with the Wisdom to find the seeds of karma in the ocean of destiny. In this realm, the spirit's greater designs weave Wisdom and love into karma's life patterns that help fate take its course.

This is the realm of Christ, called the Life Spirit, where continuous love flows as a River of Life from a central fountain nourishing all who enter the city. This is the super-etheric realm, or Shamballa, where the Tree of Life grows. This is a source of love.

Sophia as Goddess of Love leaves the aspirant speechless to describe the labyrinthine designs of Her flowing through every aspect of life. She gives such infinite attention to every detail of the Wisdom of creation that the mind cannot hold Her visage. She is beyond conception, visualization, or description.

We must rise higher to see the full panorama of the Temple of Pansophia, that sacred structure we imagine as our universe.

When our universe has been examined from the scientific point of view of visual data, infrared imaging, electromagnetic imaging, spectral analysis, and other forms of "perceiving," conflicting information has arisen. Ask each scientist, and he will give you a different answer as to the nature and shape of the universe.

One idea that is relevant to our studies is the "horn of plenty" shape of the universe. Other groups possess data that indicates the shape of the universe seems to be the general shape of a human body, or a triangle, a dodecahedron, a horn, or a torus field. All of the shapes also show complicated energy patterns that expand to a certain point and then mysteriously fold back in self-contraction in a paradoxical manner.

Imagine a balloon. It starts as just a dot. It can be blown up bigger and bigger until, at some point, it deflates in upon itself and magically is reduced back to the center dot. Then it begins the expansion process all over again, continuing the cycle indefinitely. This Imagination takes projective geometry to calculate and provides insight into the inner workings of the etheric formative forces of warmth, light, sound, and life.

The horn-of-plenty shape of the universe is like a conical basket that expands from the inside narrow tip of the cone and passes along the inside edges, expanding in a circular shape until it reaches the outer rim of the cone. At that point, it falls back and contracts along the outside to the tip of the cone. There, it turns from outside to inside and begins the process again.

Imagine a three-dimensional Mobius curve. For scientists, this may seem more like a puzzle to solve than a theory to hypothesize. Even if several compartmentalized fields of science have theorized about the shape of the universe, there has not been an attempt to align the data points and synthesize a conclusion. This highlights something simple: the universe is not as it appears and defies all known laws of nature. It cannot be tested in a laboratory. Too often, the outcome of multiple research projects is conflicting data that resolves nothing.

The universe is the body of the Mother Goddess. She is unimaginable, undefinable, and inconceivable. She is our Mother who loves each of us as Her child. We resemble Her in every way. So, is it surprising to find the first visual data about the shape of the universe is the shape of a human being?

"Love is the ultimate source of sustainable and renewable energy in the universe."

Perhaps it is simply the case that when we look into space, we are looking into a mirror.

When we look into a microscope, we are looking into a mirror.

Consciousness can only perceive the level of consciousness attained.

Increase our consciousness, and we increase our consciousness in the universe or within our bodies.

All science should be measured against a common standard: the human being.

A human-centered cosmology would produce a universe where humanity has meaning and purpose, knows both his origins and future. Consciousness dissolves space/time barriers and allows us to look into the past and future. When our consciousness expands, we gain a higher perspective from which time and space shrink and telescope.

In a universe that does not waste energy, the most effective energy in life is love. Love specifically supports and uplifts life. It gives humans the strength to endure suffering and pain and rise to higher qualities and virtues.

Love can be blind to pain. With its softness, it smooths over the roughest suffering of a lifetime.

Without love, everything earthly can be seen as pain, entropy, and mechanistic laws of nature, devoid of purpose.

Once love has opened the heart to new dimensions, when the mind is aware of new possibilities, anything is possible, even becoming divine. Love is the flow of all good things. It leaves pain and suffering behind and continually mounts to new heights.

Love is in the supermassive black hole of destruction and the ion jet of creation—joined equally.

Love holds no respect for cast, creed, or station in life. It rules both the human and divine.

Without love flowing through them, even the gods would lack the power or courage to face suffering.

All existence comes into being through spirit falling or dying into matter, but all existence is maintained with life through love. Existence kills; love brings life. This means that one with abundant love can give it to another to sustain, feed, and nourish him without ever diminishing his life energies.

Love is the ultimate source of sustainable and renewable energy in the universe.

The forces of nature love what they do because they are beautiful and filled with Wisdom.

"Life loves what it does; this love drives the universe."

The galaxy loves the spiral design of the flowing disc and tessellates it lovingly until nesting a beautiful form like a Mandelbrot set, perfectly amidst Julia sets (spirals).

These archetypes are found in flowing water. The laws that design one also design the other. Mother Nature uses the ultimate super etheric vibrations to encode nature's life forms with similar harmonic tones. These pervade the known universe. Beyond the limits that we can perceive, nothing else exists. The shape and structure of the universe is a morphologically resonant field that creates the human body as an image of itself.

The nested Mandelbrot set common to most galaxies is a hieroglyph of life. It centers on balancing seven centers of energies (foci, or chakras) through one consciousness. Again, this pattern is found in solar systems containing life. It is reflected in the seven chambers in the human head, heart, and organs.

The same scale of music with these intervals creates the planetary gravitational harmonics that drive our solar system and our seven-fold system of bodily chambers and chakras. We hear it in the musical scales. We see it in the seven-fold nature of color manifestation in the Earthly realm as the rainbow.

Nature loves to repeat Herself. She uses the same archetypes, but with infinite diversity. All things in nature wish to grow and become more of themselves. This is the first rule of life—propagate or the species dies. Natural law loves to replicate and create more of itself, just for the sake of life. Life loves what it does; this love drives the universe.

The beauty of a Julia set, found in galaxies and flowing fluids, is an aspect of the Beauty of Sophia. To see the same Wisdom in the small and, conversely, the large, is to know spiritual economy.

Sophia is love. The Holy Sophia is Her personal, intimate, tender love. In the holographic universe of wisdom, beauty, and love, large and small are the same. The human being is co-creator with this loving universe; we maintain our own kingdoms in like fashion.

Because modern culture has divorced us from our ancestral Wisdom, we may not understand Wisdom in our lives. We may not recognize what is beautiful due to the assault against Her image, but we all still know love when it moves through us and brings divine sustenance into our lives. Love is an unforgettable quality. It flows around us; we have the choice to access it at every turn. Love is undying, and every act of love is eternal.

Love flows together with divine mercy and grace. Between these qualities, all the forces of health, energy, and nourishment that any soul could need exist. The three spirit forces do not need to be earned. They are given freely and abundantly to humanity without measure.

Much like the characteristics of love that we have described, all three gifts flow through a human being from the divine. Grace and mercy are endless fountains of life. They sustain goodness that defies explanation, yet have an immediate effect upon an individual's soul and spirit.

When one receives these spiritual gifts, he is filled with gratitude and becomes capable of passing these virtues on to others. These are eternal fountainheads of the Water of Life that deliver immortality to the spirit. The gods themselves drink from these waters. They flow through their being to all others in need. The hierarchies participate in loving symbiotic relationships that feed their needs so that they can feed ours. Truly, our gifts to the gods are a type of spiritual nourishment to them, just as their love, grace, and mercy are food and drink for our spirit. *Love feeds all* is the lesson of the Holy Sophia as She manifests as the Goddess of Love.

Love

Your fiery heart-wheel sparks lightning bolts of love,
Igniting every monad of my being,
Beckoning me into the milky spiral of love's flow,
As we fall, swim, and drown in our thickly sensual veils of ecstasy,
Until all time bends and swirls into a tunnel of procreative power
That reaches both the beginning and end.
Where are we, spread so evenly over the skin of the universal beloved?
"Who is who!" rings out, and is answered by many spirits watching
And moving through our glance, our touch, our union.
The bliss of emptiness piercingly ripples through my thoughts
And joyously illuminates it to fantasy unbound,
Whirling through my feeling, aflame with the wonder of love.
It moves the cause of our affection, the truth of our joining.

You are the aurora of love who dawns in the wedding dance of the Beloved,
The eyes that are the calm port in a world of spinning madness,
Drunk with the dew of life that lingers on your freshly kissed lips,
Flowing in between, and through, and in and out—
Secret places, warmed by heart-fire, inward and deep,
Where all wounds reach and end—new joys begin,
That gentle mercy, that arises when we touch and lingers when we hold,
Grace that dispels unhappy memories and enkindles effulgence of spirit,
Born again through the love for which we've been waiting,
A love that moves beneath our feet, and spans the heights of heaven,
And turns us round again, to dance together as one.

Sophia as the Mother of God

Vessel of the Spirit, Holy Grail of heart and love,

We find You all around us, Hell below, Heaven above.

It is ever You we search for, it is ever You we find,

Teach us to seek You everywhere, Your mysteries to unwind.

The Holy Sophia helps birth the divine in your spirit. She raises it up to the realm of heaven, its home.

She has birthed Her own spirit self, and works in the realm of the angels to bring us the same assistance. As a member of the Divine Feminine Trinity, She holds all of the memories, powers, and capacities of the other two members of the Trinity: the Mother and the Daughter.

The Holy Sophia has become a Being far in advance of humanity. She is ahead of us and developing much more swiftly than humanity. After developing Her Consciousness Soul, Her Spirit Self is now evolving.

The Holy Sophia is the vanguard of human spiritual development. She is perfected in Her lower vehicles by having access to all of the perfected vehicles of Jesus Christ and Mary Sophia.

She is evolving back through the realm of the higher hierarchies to the Divine Feminine Trinity. As She does, She mothers the birth of Her higher vehicles. With access to these higher natures, She is able to manifest the qualities of the risen Christ; this is why She can appear everywhere at once and seem omnipresent. No longer bound by space, She moves through humanity's spiritual development and the unfolding of the higher vehicles. Still bound by time, however, She must help us catch up to Her.

The image of the Holy Sophia as Mother of God is quite complicated. It is not the same as the Mother of All.

The Mother of God is a clear statement about the primacy of the Divine Feminine Trinity. This can lead to many misconceptions and can be illuminated by remembering the nature of the Male Trinity and its part in the creation, destruction, and sustenance of the world.

The Father Ground of Being is often a misunderstood aspect of divinity. Christ told us that His father was not of this world, that he ruled a different kingdom where earthly matters may not enter. He also said that both He and His Father are one but separate. He said that after going back to heaven, when no longer in this world, He would send the Holy Spirit. He also said He would appear wherever two or more gathered in His name. This is very confusing. To date, theologians have yet to explain these paradoxical statements. However, if you listen with intuition and love, Christ was perfectly clear.

The Father is unmanifest in this world; thus, He has a different kingdom. Christ came from that kingdom and returned there at His ascension but can be invited back at will by his followers. Where is this kingdom, one might ask? It is everywhere, but nowhere in this earthly kingdom. Every atom of force or being has a part of the Father Ground of Being imbedded in its core. It is the foundation for manifestation but does not manifest.

The Father God is the cause but not the effect of creation. All creation derives from this spiritual nodal point of hyper-spirit that is unmanifest in sub-space. Every atom is connected to every other atom through this singular note of existence that is unsounded.

We have described it here as the super-massive black hole found at the center of most galaxies. Even a galactic ion jet of creation originates from that black hole.

In every atomic particle, there is a black hole that is the door to the Kingdom of Heaven.

This zero point physics theory was elaborated upon by Ervin Laszlo, the brilliant Hungarian philosopher and scientist, along with many others. The field effect has been named the Akashic Field, after the Hindu term referring to the subtle ether that records everything that occurs in the known world and renders it accessible for all time. This God Particle, as it is called by some, has been described by many, but found by none. It will never be found. It is not a material substance and defies all known laws of nature, for God is unknowable.

The kingdom that Christ referred to is at the center of each particle as the universe spins around in one form or another.

God does not manifest; only His Holy Consort manifests. She, as the Creatrix Goddess, generates the universe of life, death, and rebirth in a material form.

Sophia is the original manifested Divine Feminine Trinity. The Father God is the darkness from which the light arose.

The manifest and unmanifest are simultaneous and undergo rhythms of expansion and contraction just as the beating of the human heart. Within each heart is a pulse point—the first aspect of blood circulation to develop. This pulse point continues to emit a powerful pulse of energy throughout life that gives the heart its rhythmic pace, keeping time with the rest of the universe. It is a great mystery that points to the Father God's Ground of Being in the human body. Still little known in science, it indicates intelligent design and a universal vibration of life found in the heart of all humans. The implication is profound. Instead of looking for God in outer space, we should look for Him within the beating of our own hearts.

Black holes swallow unimaginable numbers of suns and solar systems as they simply disappear. No one knows where they go or how they are dissolved into nothingness. Modern theories, which are inane at best, say that matter can never be destroyed, yet ignore the largest and most powerful event at the heart of our own galaxy.

Some scientists speculate that matter goes into a black hole and then passes through a wormhole and appears somewhere else in the universe. This is somewhat correct, since all matter in the universe is connected. Some galaxies are consuming matter, while others are expelling matter. Matter disappears in some galactic centers and appears in others. It would seem logical that the two activities are connected.

Some scientists speculate that the universe is a brain, that galaxies are neurons, and that some invisible force connects them like axons connecting neurons and dendrites. Thus, the universe is a brain that thinks matter into physical manifestation. As mentioned before, humans have as many neurons in their brains as there are galaxies in the known universe. This begs the question, "Who is thinking whom into existence?" Perhaps our thoughts are creating everything we see beyond the Earth, or perhaps the universe is thinking us into existence, or perhaps both are correct.

The Holy Sophia helps the human soul and spirit articulate the nature of the divine. As humans evolve, so do the thoughts that embody the descriptions of the divine.

God has evolved over time. This Being has become a paradoxically complex description that cannot be logically deciphered or scientifically proven. Science discovers new aspects of the divine daily, but no one is gathering those pieces of the mirror so that a whole image can arise.

As humans develop new scientific methods to observe the divine, spiritual scientists need to add the living qualities of Sophia to the equation, so that life—not death—will result from science. Even the seeming death of stars falling into a black hole may actually be a natural process of birth in another domain.

Without the complete picture of the complex workings of Wisdom and the many corresponding hierarchical and elemental beings acting visibly and invisibly to support the material world, we only have a partial view of nature that limits our understanding.

> *"If we look for God and do not find Him, then we know we have a godless soul, not that God does not exist."*

When we observe mysterious forces in nature, we are observing our own being. Everything in the human world is created for us, by us, with the same common forces repeatedly applied. Nature loves economy.

Life is somewhat like a practical joke of the general on the particular. The human being, seeking itself, is the mystery of the universe. We do not need to look anywhere or do anything except be pure, kind, and happy. There is no rush to embody the future if we appreciate the present with all of its majesty and glory. Our own body is the hieroglyph of the universe, the answer to all puzzles and the part of ourselves we have always sought.

Each individual soul is the mother of its own spiritual creation. We generally project our concepts upon the percepts of the world and arrive back again at our own cosmological view. Is the world heaven, or is it hell? That lies in the heart of the beholder and the purity that he brings to perception. If we look for God and do not find Him, then we know that we have a godless soul, not that God does not exist. We will only find that for which we seek; unless the thinker knows what he seeks, he will not find it.

Often it only takes backing up to realize that the perspective was limited, the whole picture not in view.

The Mother of God is a most profound perspective from which to perceive the world. Most religions, myths, and ancient philosophies all have an image of the Mother of God. These come in all forms but usually indicate that when "God" went to make the world, the Great Mother was already there. Vac is the Hindu Goddess who brought the male trinity of Brahma, Shiva, and Vishnu into existence. These types of stories abound in ancient literature and point out that Sophia was the primal manifested deity; She is the Mother of God.

Much interest in the Feminine Divine has arisen in our times as people become more clairvoyant and can see into the spiritual world and speak about Sophia's revelation. The matriarchal culture of the past faded away around 2100 B. C., about the time that the Holy Sophia was arising on the Earth. The male dominated war-culture began subsuming the Mysteries of Sophia.

Although Her hidden Wisdom was still available in sacred literature, it was ignored. In some cases, females were enslaved as the new aggressive forces of the male-centered culture destroyed the past and rewrote the stories to center around the dominant male.

The story of Psyche transformed into those of Orpheus, Aeneas, Heracles, and other male heroes accomplishing the heroic labors, descending to the underworld and returning the victor over death. The wings of the Bee Goddess of Crete were turned into the wings of Cupid, Psyche, and Hermes. Through Zeus' rule of Mount Olympus, the Minoan *Throne of Birthing* was turned into the throne of martial power. Beauty, as Helen, was abducted and enslaved against her will, and Wisdom went into hiding to protect Herself. The path to Eden was lost; the seeds from the Tree of Life became a legend. This was the effect of hiding the truth that God had a Mother.

Everywhere the ancients looked in nature, they saw the power of mothers to birth the future and sustain life from their own bodies. This magical wonder of life was revered and worshipped. As human thought advanced and looked further throughout the world, the power of the mother was recognized in the forces of life streaming from the sun.

Most cultures treat the sun as feminine. They know that all earthly life comes from the sun, as all life for a newborn comes from the mother. Compared to the power and glory of the sun, the Earth is much like a newborn. When the Earth's gender was changed to a being called Gaia, this altered our collective consciousness about the planet being alive and our *mother*.

In this same way, since archetypal symbols and images transform consciousness, a true understanding of what it means to be the Mother of God will change a person's worldview. To understand that the God we have been seeking does not manifest will most certainly change a thinker's philosophy. To the clear thinker, it is obvious that the Divine Feminine Divinity manifested this world as its child and rightly tends it as its mother.

Theologians have been struggling with the fact that the worship of the Great Goddess has never ceased, even though the male-centered cultures tried to wipe out memory of Her. Over time, the Catholic Church and others have given more and more credence to the Divine Feminine by allowing Mary, the mother of Jesus, to represent some of the aspects of Sophia that are being described in *The Gospel of Sophia*.

The doctrines of the Immaculate Conception, the Assumption into Heaven, and other similar ideas were a way to elevate the Great Mother back into the highly respected position She deserves.

The Eastern Orthodox Church worships Sophia in many forms, including the belief that She is the Holy Spirit or Christ.

Many churches are dedicated to the Holy Mother, another aspect of Sophia.

All Catholics belong to the Holy Mother Church.

The Litany of Loretto has more than forty titles for which the Divine Mother is known and under which She is worshipped.

As repressed Wisdom rises up with new forces of revelation, the power and scope of the Divine Feminine grows steadily. Sophia, the Mother of God, has always been there for us *before creation* and will be there until every soul returns to heaven under Her loving care and support.

Theologians have tried to limit the influence of the Divine Feminine by imparting another meaning to the Mother of God as the humble mother of Jesus of Nazareth. Since Christ, the Son of God, was born through Mary, and Christ is the same as, and co-equal to, the Father God, then by logic of the Trinity, Mary is the Mother of Christ, who is God, which makes Mary the Mother of God.

This issue has hounded the church fathers for centuries. The nature of the Male Trinity has been debated most particularly over the issue of Christ being God incarnate, which then makes Mary the Mother of God, which, in turn, would necessitate the creation of a doctrine of Immaculate Conception.

Some theologians debate that Christ was not physically the same as the Father God and, therefore Mary was not the Mother of God. If she were, she would need to be elevated in the doctrines of the church to assume a worthy role as the Mother of God the Father. This is very disconcerting to a church filled with all-male priests who have blamed original sin on Eve.

The church's confusion is demonstrated by its *mixed-bag* approach to the Divine Feminine, its attempt to please the followers of the Great Mother by adopting new doctrines that increasingly deify Mary, the Mother of Jesus. Accordingly, the doctrine of the Assumption of the Blessed Virgin Mary was created.

Creation is usually caused by some type of divine couple that mysteriously works together to balance forces, sustain order, and introduce Wisdom into the design of what is usually described as a pre-existing cosmic soup. The bewildering thing about male-centered theologies is that they simply ignore the words and images they do not understand. In some cases, they even mimic what they think they understand, yet end up making a confusing mess of it all. This has happened in mythologies, legends, religions, and ancient teachings and can be discovered without much effort.

Later in this book, literature from different religions and myths are offered to demonstrate the primacy of the Mother Goddess, in no uncertain terms. The words, symbols, and images are clear, but the sense-bound thinker cannot penetrate the Wisdom and truth of these beautiful words taken from sacred texts.

The research shown in the next section of *The Gospel of Sophia* demonstrates that almost all traditions describe Sophia in terms that are understandable and near to human consciousness, whereas the concepts about the Father God are unintelligible and mean little to everyday, earthly life.

God is inconveniently invisible and unreachable. No one has ever laid eyes upon Him. There is no proof of His existence, yet many say a male priest is required to approach Him. In the Old Testament, He is portrayed as a God of wrath and vengeance—and a jealous God to boot. Only a priest or a prophet might have a revelation or experience from this male God.

The divine was sequestered in the temple or church, and a special language was invented to confound those who were not part of the priesthood. Rituals were created and sacraments established that kept access in the hands of men who tried to convince people that God has no mother. By limiting access to the divine, the male-centered culture could maintain control of the temporal.

God is unmanifest, so it is more likely that God is androgynous, rather than male, because the duality of the manifest world does not touch him, let alone cause a necessity for gender to come into the picture.

According to sacred writings, the Father God needed to unite with the Creatrix because She was the *already existing* substance from which creation could arise. Perhaps this *already existing* substance of the Creatrix was left over from a previous cycle of creation. It had dissolved into its component parts and was ready for another round.

Nature does not usually appear out of nothing, nor does it wait for some outside force to generate motion, heat, or the initial action of creation. Creation goes through great cycles where the material world dissolves into an amorphous soup of potential that remembers the previous level of evolution, then reorganizes that material at a higher level to be ready for the next round of creation. To think that the universe came into being by an *explosion* that organizes and creates divine order is completely foreign to natural law.

The *big bang* theory is simply not feasible. It is the projection of the male-dominated scientific mindset. More likely, the universe was birthed by a loving Mother who applies the same natural law to order both great and small. Sophia, the Mother of God, is the *true author of creation*. Her forces and processes do not require blind faith, nor do they require one to follow a male intermediary to gain exclusive access to the divine. The church and laboratory both have twisted and forged Sophia into the unwieldy, foreign shape of a male God, who subsumes Her place, but never shows His face.

Many great thinkers have developed an evolving image of Sophia that attempts to regain some of Her rightful honor in the divine worlds. They have suggested that Sophia be given more prominence in theological considerations.

Some theologians have suggested Sophia was the Holy Spirit, or married to the Father God and Son God, or that She is a mystical force that moves between the beings in the Male Trinity.

Many aspects of Sophia that are presented in this gospel have been described by such thinkers. Here, all perspectives are combined to depict the full picture of a complete Divine Feminine Trinity.

In the past, the resistance to such ideas about Sophia has been quite pronounced, and may have even led believers to be burnt at the stake as heretics. But the truth must be told. It is self-evident to those who have developed the requisite level of spiritual development that there is a Divine

Feminine Trinity. These truths can be tested by the spiritual scientist and compared with the results of other aspirants who love Sophia.

We also become somewhat like Sophia, the Mother of God, when we mother our own process of spiritual evolution in our soul and spirit. We are a consciousness bringing to birth a higher spiritual consciousness through soul and spiritual development of the human being.

We are the mother of our own spiritual path. Although help is there at every turn, we still must endure the labor and birth of our higher self.

Though Sophia manifests continuously, we are still human, not yet angels, and we fight the battle of good and evil every day with much at stake. We must stand upright and take spiritual steps ourselves. We are free to decide our direction and speed. In the end, we become our divine self. The spiritual world has given us all that we need and plenty of help along the way. Ultimately, only we ourselves can birth our higher self, the *god* or *goddess* in us. In this way, we resemble the Holy Sophia manifesting in Her form as the Mother of God.

Mother of Us All

Primal source of all life and holy love,
The eternal spring and milk from above,
The dawn and dusk, aurora and twilight hues
Speak of Your birth, the day and night's coming too.
The herald of knowing, ancient wisdom awakens,
Time's first beginning, the foundations of space were shaken.
The breath divine moved upon Her waters deep
Bringing all that we know from Her dreamless sleep,
All dreams, all hopes, aspirations burgeoning anew,
Another of the eternal offspring, born from Her work's dew.
Precipitous gatherings drawn from the philosopher's stone
Each separate, conscious, free to live and grow alone,
Perhaps never knowing the Mother, the home, the heart

The One who cares for all, from the very start.
The dark quiet of receptive night, the brilliance of day
All make their home in Her circuitous ways;
Building labyrinths of life, the convolutions of the mind,
Helping Her children's fate, their destiny to find.
There at the beginning, present with each new day,
She is our life, our love, our own precious way;
Sweet Mother of blessed life, midwife of cold, calm death,
Brought to birth our God, His Son, His Holy Breath.
Vessel of the Spirit, Holy Grail of heart and love,
We find you all around us, hell below, heaven above.
It is ever You we search for, it is ever You we find,
Teach us to seek You everywhere, Your mysteries to unwind.

Sophia as Queen of Heaven

She is the One, the sum total of creation,

the rhythmic warp and weft of gravity and levity

that draws forth the soul to Eros' experience of duality,

the wonder of synthesis, and a sublime vision of nature.

The Holy Sophia is the Queen of Heaven by virtue of Her being the third person in the Divine Feminine Trinity. Sophia, as the Mother aspect of the Trinity, is above the nine orders of hierarchies. Essentially the Queen Mother, ruler of heaven and Earth, the Mother Goddess is in heaven and reigns as the Supreme Being in manifest creation.

According to the Catholic Church, Mary was assumed into heaven with Her physical body that was immaculate and pure, and there She was given a throne and became the Queen of Heaven alongside of Christ, Her son. Mary is given the highest honors. She becomes the one who intercedes for humanity and each individual to the Father God.

The Queen of Heaven has the power to hear human prayer and take those prayers to the Father God.

Mary is seen as being close to humanity, and the prayer, *Hail Mary*, asks that the "Mother of God pray for us sinners now and at the hour of our death." The Queen of Heaven listens to the prayers of the faithful and delivers God's mercy and grace to them as an answer to Her intercession on behalf of Her children. Still the Mother of Her children, this Queen of Heaven seems to have some control over the moods of the Father God. Many Catholics pray the rosary. Millions of faithful followers worship

Mary, the Queen of Heaven. As Queen of Heaven, the Holy Sophia also has the power of the Daughter of the Goddess, the leader of the Spirits of Wisdom. These Spirits control and order all aspects of creation. They rule all that comes to exist in space and time.

Sophia as the Being of Wisdom is indeed the Queen and ruler of the hierarchies. Wisdom has created everything out of Her being. She controls all manifestation, with the help of the nine ranks of hierarchies below Her and all of the elemental beings who follow Her natural and super-natural laws.

The Queen of Heaven is rightly an earned aspect of the Mother and Daughter Goddesses. The Mother created the heavens of which She is the Queen. Her Daughter descended from the heaven of the Trinity into the collective consciousness of the Beings of Wisdom, then down through the ranks, until She became human for eleven years over-lighting the being of Mary, the mother of Christ.

The Holy Sophia also descended from the Trinity into a human-like condition of consciousness. For the last four millennia, She has been growing collectively with the intellectual and spiritual development of humanity. The Holy Sophia has now entered the angelic realm and works from the super-etheric sphere around the Earth. She has yet to rise back to Her home, the Divine Feminine Trinity, and assume Her role as Queen of Heaven.

The Holy Sophia has taken a vow that in Buddhism is called the "vow of the bodhisattva," essentially a commitment to strive for enlightenment for the sake of all sentient beings. This is a vow of selflessness that focuses all desire on the goal of enlightenment but does so for the sake of others. The desire for enlightenment, or spiritual development, is for the purpose of becoming more helpful to others on their spiritual path.

The Holy Sophia is already enlightened and actively helps all sentient beings move towards their personal advancement and spiritual enlightenment. She knows that this spiritual evolution was the original intent of the Mother Goddess during creation. Sophia built Her Temple of Wisdom so that all spirits could use it as the sacred ground for purifying the Earthly soul into the divine spirit. It is a doorway into heaven.

The Holy Sophia must evolve through two more conditions of spiritual development before She returns to her heavenly home where the Trinity resides.

Each person of the Trinity (Male or Female) is both in heaven and anywhere else He or She wants to be simultaneously. The Holy Sophia is both in heaven and here on Earth. She can dissolve space and time to perceive Her nature in the future spiritual realms and be the Queen of Heaven even now.

As humans evolve their understanding of the Holy Sophia, we come to understand that She has not ascended and returned to the Trinity at this time. Indeed, She is very near us, *now and at the hour of our death*. We know that the part of the Holy Sophia that is the Queen of Heaven can intercede with the divine to lead us to mercy and grace. The Holy Sophia has enormous power but humbly serves each of us as Her personal beloved, or Her most precious child. Sophia has many aspects of the divine available to Her to help the striving human soul ascend to his or her higher self, beside the Queen of Heaven.

Just as the Mother Goddess works with the highest three hierarchies consisting of the beings of Love, Harmony, and Will, and the Daughter Goddess works closely with the middle group of the hierarchy called the beings of Wisdom, Motion, and Form, the Holy Sophia works through Guardian Angels, Folk Spirits, and the Beings of Time.

This hierarchy of beings is closest to humanity. In Christian terms, they are known as the angels, archangels, and archai. Therefore, the Holy Sophia is likely to be working with the developing aspirant's guardian angel to awaken thinking as a path of developing consciousness and awareness of divine workings.

The guardian angel is very concerned with helping the thinker develop thoughts that are unbound by physical perceptions. This enables the soul to become a vessel for higher concepts to alight. The Holy Sophia works with the guardian angel to prepare the karmic path, to lead the aspirant through events that demonstrate the working of providence. These events that indicate the hand of the divine can be seen as synchronicity and synergy in karmic occurrences. Reviewing the workings of karma over our life reveals the actions of our guardian angel and Sophia.

The Holy Sophia is not limited by the perceptions of an angel. She can reach higher into the divine world to weave the golden threads that demonstrate karmic gravitation.

When we are open to our angel and Sophia, we are guided and led to the right place at the right time so that karma can smoothly accelerate the spiritual growth of the aspirant. This *burning of karmic attachment* accelerates the path to enlightenment, the goal of rising to be a Christened self who then can co-create with Sophia to manifest beautiful new worlds and opportunities for other spirits to evolve into their divine nature.

The prodigal son story applies to humanity in general. We are all on the ascending path back to our home and our inheritance. Christ sits at the right hand of the Father. His Mother sits next to him. The Holy Spirit seems to be ever descending into the prepared souls of the faithful to bring them the baptism by fire. The Holy Sophia prepares the soul for the World Pentecost.

Likewise, the Queen of Heaven is on Her throne. Her Daughter has returned to heaven after descending to the Earth. The Holy Sophia seems to be ever passing through and assisting humanity's efforts to spiritually evolve. These collective efforts all contribute to humanity's ascension to the angelic realms through the love and intercession of the Holy Sophia as Her empowered self, the future Queen of Heaven.

Just as Christ spoke of a kingdom that his Father ruled, so too does Sophia speak of a future spiritual kingdom of love that humans will inherit once they have turned from the darkness of Earth and chosen the higher path to the light. Christ and Sophia work together through the three persons in their own respective Trinity. Duality is conquered when we know that all dual aspects have been united by the sacred couples of the spiritual world and that the Trinities have been united.

> *"Sophia's closeness is more spiritually tender than all that a religion might offer a believer."*

We do not have to suffer the feelings of loneliness and separation, since the duality of the Earthly realm has been conquered by these great spiritual beings. There are examples of the divine couple at many levels of the physical and spiritual realms: Christ and Sophia, Mother and Father, Son and Daughter, Bride and Groom, Consciousness Soul and Spirit Self. These are all good examples of duality wed into unity.

Christ said, "Wherever two or three gather in my name, there am I in the midst of them." This promise was clearly a reference to ending the power of duality in the material world and the idea that the material and spiritual are separate and cannot be united. If we look closely, we will see the reign of the Queen of Heaven acting in the realm of the Earthly, and thus She wields Her power on high and on Earth.

The Holy Sophia is Queen of the Earth at this point. One day, She will be the Queen of Heaven. Her spiritual evolution is the closest contact point with the spiritual world as an objective, living reality. Ideas of gods and goddesses on faraway mountains have little to do with human daily struggles. Sophia is near us. She is the Queen of our hearts.

We realize that She has been with us always, as close as our breath and heartbeat. Her throne is in our heart. The king in our head needs to listen to his Mother the Queen so that his thoughts can be warmed by Her love.

Sophia is there at every stage of development. She changes Her appearance to match our ability to see Her. But Sophia cannot show us Her ascended self from the future because it would overwhelm us, just as Semele demanded to see Zeus in all his glory and then was incinerated by his majesty.

The Holy Sophia arose with and for the intellectual and spiritual development of humanity. Think of her as a human spirit that can pass through us and carry our spiritual intent to the best possible outcome.

Sophia's closeness is more spiritually tender than all that a religion might offer a believer. She creates personal spiritual interactions that are key rungs on Jacob's ladder ascending into heaven.

When support and inspiration are needed, Sophia is there.

It is She who explains that our bodies are the Temple of Sophia, filled with Wisdom and beauty.

She is the guide who shows us that this Temple is the Kingdom of the Divine and She the Queen of that Kingdom. This is why so many who come to know and communicate with Her have sworn allegiance to Sophia.

As the modern age developed, materialism drove numerous groups of seekers into churches and associations that made Sophia the sole object of worship. Most of these groups, starting with the inspirations of Jacob Boehme, elevate Sophia to Her well-earned position of Queen of Heaven.

Often you see that the lover of Sophia has a direct, seemingly physical relationship with Her that perhaps has been reinforced by repeated visions and encounters over a lifetime. Authors have written about these powerful life-changing experiences, and described Sophia in every imaginable way. Sometimes the encounters happen once or twice in a lifetime, while others happen many times, even in front of other followers. These direct experiences are generally the inspiration for many writings and teachings that are filled with great wisdom and beauty.

One could call these encounters *revelations from the living being Sophia.* The Unity Brethren, the Harmonists, the followers of Boehme, and many other groups essentially started their own religions based upon the direct revelations given to them by Sophia.

It was quite common that people who were filled with revelations from Sophia then believed that they had become lovers and married Her. Even women had this same experience and described the association as a marriage. Often these *prophets of Sophia* then moved into another condition they described as "letting Sophia become Queen of their heart."

This relationship was described as "dedicating everything in their life to Sophia the Queen."

They stopped interacting with the outside world and spent hours attempting to commune with Sophia and bring Her teachings back into the world. Some of these Sophiologists built churches, wrote songs, and inspired writings in praise of Sophia. The revelations of these lovers of Sophia were written and considered to be divinely inspired.

Many of these people dedicated their entire lives to the pursuit of Sophia. The dedication and devotion of these children of Wisdom are remarkable, their works considerable and significant. They comprise one of the only modern religious movements that claim to have direct contact with the divine, through Sophia.

There is something about encountering Sophia that makes the seer passionate and imbued with new energy to spread the truth about the resurrected being of Wisdom. There is no end to the beautiful descriptions of the kindness and the tenderness that Sophia gives to the aspirant as he devotes himself to the spiritual path. The seer often renounces the desires of the world. Through austerities and sacrifice, he becomes completely devoted to having a continuous relationship with Sophia.

Unfortunately, this overzealous attitude of some seers and their community of followers has led to ruin as the aspirants' intentions were too hasty in trying to coax Sophia's revelation into full bloom immediately.

Sophia, like Zeus from Semele, should not be asked to reveal Her full glory. As one of the Divine Feminine Trinity, She is too great a being to be cognized by a human brain, or even a good-hearted aspirant.

It takes time for the Holy Sophia to unveil the full Mysteries of the Divine Feminine. Presently, humans do not have the requisite morality to hold in their souls the breadth and depth of Sophia in Her many forms. They must wait for Her to reveal Her full majesty. Plus, most people must first unlearn what they have been taught about the spirit. This unlearning process involves having direct spiritual experiences of the living spiritual world of hierarchical beings.

Sophia helps humans see their own guardian angels. That, in itself, is more than most aspirants can handle. To see our own guardian angel directly would make us think we were seeing the divine, although to some degree that would be true, since all the hierarchy demonstrate characteristics of the divine and are interconnected.

But just like Semele, we would be overwhelmed by the spirit and should heed the warning of her example. Sophia directly reveals the mechanism of ascension to the aspirant. This power can be devastating to the uninitiated who reaches too high too quickly and then falls back due to a lack of proper spiritual preparation. This is what seemed to happen to numerous zealous followers of Sophia in modern times.

It was often assumed by these fellowships of Sophia that a new age had come due to direct revelation finally being given from the spiritual world to humanity.

Sophia manifesting in a living form to the seers was confirmation of spirit, proof that we can contact higher spiritual beings. This usually led to a utopian community being founded upon higher principles of morality and spiritual revelation.

Many of these groups came to America and tried to start a new culture of love, inspired by Sophia. Some of these communities still exist. A few have evolved into schools and colleges that study Sophia and Marian doctrine. But the greatest number of Sophiologists were in Russia, where the Orthodox Church still believed in Sophia as an active part of the Trinity. This belief provided the foundation for great thinkers and theologians to seek and expound on spiritual encounters with Sophia.

> *"The idea of the Divine Feminine Trinity is as old as any story."*

In the work of the Russian Sophiologists, we find wonderful descriptions of physical, living encounters with Sophia and the beautiful relationships these thinkers had with Her. Each new thinker became bolder in his definition of Sophia's nature and Her place in the scheme of things.

One would report that Sophia spoke to him and said She was the same as the Holy Spirit.

Another would report that She is a breath of spirit that blows from and around the Male Trinity, connecting their spirits.

Others claimed that Sophia was the wisdom aspect of Christ, the Mother aspect of the Father God, and the same as the Holy Spirit.

Some claimed that She was Lucifer redeemed and that the fall from heaven was redeemed when Mary birthed her son Jesus and her body became the Holy Mother Church.

There was no lack of imagination in the ideas of the Russian Sophiologist. Much of the content of these ideas originated from people who had direct experiences with Sophia but could only interpret the Wisdom they experienced at the level of spiritual development that they had attained. As a result, Sophia is worshipped in Eastern Orthodox religions and has found many warm hearts that have embraced Her as Queen of Heaven.

Some Russian and Greek icons depict Sophia as the Mother of God and Queen of Heaven. The mystical worship of Sophia has many forms, such as that described in the Twelve Labors of Sophia. The simple peasant may still have the atavistic clairvoyance that sees the Great Mother everywhere and has yet to loosen the old ties to the Divine Feminine. It seems that the greater the soul, the greater the image of Sophia to be expressed through thought, art, music, and writing. Great souls wrote down ideas that were considered heretical at their time and caused them many tribulations. The world was still not ready, even in the place where Sophia is revered, to hear the truth about the Divine Feminine Trinity.

The idea of the Divine Feminine Trinity is as old as any story. The threefold nature of the divine feminine was described in many traditions as the triple goddess, like the three Norns of Norse Myths, or the Fates of Greek Myths, or the many triple goddesses throughout the Greek pantheon.

Ancient seers could perceive these living beings as they did their work of weaving the threads of life into the tapestry of destiny.

Countless triple feminine forces are found in all descriptions of the divine back to the original, ubiquitous belief in the Great Goddess of Birth, Death, and Rebirth. For the Divine Feminine Trinity to reascend to Her throne, it will take many followers developing the consciousness to be able to hold the majesty of the truth about Her nature in their hearts. Sophia will need to become Queen of all our hearts. We will need to develop the spiritual organs to witness Her in all Her glory.

Sophia the Mother was always Queen of Heaven.

Her Daughter regained Her crown after Her ascension to Her throne.

The Holy Sophia rounds off creation by returning to Her home with humanity following close behind.

This makes Sophia the *Once and Future Queen of Heaven*, yet in the present time it is still difficult for Her to reign supreme on Earth. It will take the unfolding of space and the unwinding of time for the Holy Sophia and the human spirit to rise to heaven and perceive Her crowned as Queen of Heaven. Any attempt to try to accelerate the process, leaping over the steps of time to crown Her at this time in history, will fall into the devouring teeth of the modern world's apocalyptic dragon that wishes to annihilate Her and Her offspring.

Just as the Apocalypse of St. John has indicated, Sophia is ready to give birth, but the dragon and the beast are anxious to take Her child from Her. Sophia must do so only at the proper time, when the spirit moves the Mother to begin labor. All births are miraculous. In their very nature, they show the wonder of creation and the Wisdom of the Queen who rules all.

When followers of Sophia the Queen of Heaven have tried to bring a new age of Sophia to birth prematurely, it has not worked out for the prophet or his followers. Sophia is still an unfamiliar part of the divine. The little that is known about Her is often confusing and not useful for following in Her footsteps. Utopian communities based upon a few people's direct experience of Sophia are not necessarily the direction of Sophia awareness that will help the modern person. Setting up a brotherhood or spiritual order that tries to use old forms of religion and worship will not unlock the Mystery of Sophia in our time.

Everything in evolution is about timing, and Sophia is manifesting Her many facets to people at every level of spiritual development. That does not mean, however, that we can push or spur evolution to move at a faster pace. Many aspects of Wisdom may only develop over time to come to fruition and a mature understanding of Sophia.

The Avatar and Bodhisattva Streams

There are two streams that help in the process to make sure that humans evolve along at the right pace so that they may return to their rightful homes in heaven with Sophia, the Queen of Heaven.

One stream flows down from above.

This is Sophia the Daughter and Christ the Son consciously sacrificing themselves and descending from the celestial to the Earthly. This stream of spiritual gifts and guidance happens at the exact right moment in evolution to have the greatest impact on humanity. These gifts are often referred to as gifts or treasures from the avatars, the lofty spiritual beings who watch over and care for humanity on its road from dark to light. This is the avatar stream, which descends from above.

The other stream, which ascends from below, is the one that comes from the efforts of humans as they evolve over many incarnations.

This is often referred to as the path to enlightenment, which is known in the East as the vow of the bodhisattva that drives a human to become an enlightened Buddha. A bodhisattva is a highly developed initiate who is evolving towards being able to help humanity without having the encumbrance of a human body.

"In Mary Sophia we have both streams united, descending and ascending."

Gautama Buddha is the most prominent bodhisattva who became a Buddha and no longer has to incarnate in a physical body but helps humanity from the realm of Mars. Gautama was a human who evolved over many incarnations to reach his Buddhahood. This stream is one that rises up from the Earthly, by human effort, to reach the divine.

These two streams are found in Sophia the Daughter and Holy Sophia. The Daughter represents the descending stream, and the Holy Sophia represents the ascending stream of spirituality.

When the Daughter over-lighted Mary, She poured into her spiritual qualities from the paradisiacal realm that renewed her body until it was a virgin, immaculate soul. This was the descending stream of spirit of Wisdom from the Beings of Wisdom.

Eve's efforts throughout many incarnations brought her to the incarnation of Mary where she was able to hold the body of wisdom given to her by Jesus of Nazareth, earthly wisdom accumulated since the Garden of Eden. From Eve through Mary human development is the ascending, or bodhisattva, stream of spirituality.

In Mary Sophia we have both streams united, descending and ascending.

It is little understood that the greatest human initiate is presently the being we have referred to as Mary/Eve/Sophia, Mary Sophia, or "Maria

Sophia."

The idea that a collective being from the hierarchy of the Beings of Wisdom descended with Christ to the Earth and over-lighted Mary, who was the reincarnation of the original Eve, is almost inconceivable to humans. To add the being of Eve Kadmon, the part of Eve that remained in paradise until she incarnated as Mary of Nazareth, adds a paradox to a mystery. Sophia, the Being of Wisdom, over-lighted Mary/Eve, who was united with Eve Kadmon (Mary of Nazareth, who had died), making Mary/Eve the first fully redeemed human being in history. This is the Mary/Eve that is taken bodily into heaven at the Assumption.

This would seem to make Maria Sophia the most significant human biography that illustrates the future path of all of humanity that will merge the two streams of spirituality, the avatar and bodhisattva.

Maria Sophia becomes through her union with her *paradisiacal-self,* the first fully realized human being to return to heaven as a prodigal child. Her experience is imprinted in the super-etheric realm around the Earth and available to use by initiates as an aid to their development. And even beyond this marvelous trinity of forces active in Maria Sophia, we also understand that Jesus gave his body of wisdom that had ripened the wisdom of Zarathustra, Hermes, and Moses to Mary.

Therefore, Maria Sophia came to hold in her heart the cosmic Wisdom of Sophia and the human wisdom of the great initiates transformed by Jesus.

This merging of celestial Wisdom given by Sophia and human, earthly wisdom given by Jesus to Mary represents the merging of the two streams of avatars (celestial) and bodhisattvas (Earthly).

The distinction between heavenly and earthly wisdom is misunderstood by spiritual seekers and more than often the descriptions of avatars and bodhisattvas are confused by Westerners trying to interpret Eastern doctrines. The mixing of Christian and Buddhist doctrines is a very slippery slope. It is not easy for a Western materialist to be able to embody the lofty and celestial ideas concerning the incarnations of avatars or the nature and work of bodhisattvas.

The ten incarnations of Vishnu have been taken to be literally true by some western occultists who predict the eminent incarnation of Vishnu as the Kalki Avatar. There are also many people who claim to be the incarnation of the newest bodhisattva who is working to become the next Buddha to reach enlightenment—the Maitreya Buddha.

Avatars descend as perfected beings to bring spiritual manifestations that are needed to sustain humanity on its ascent to the spirit. Bodhisattvas rise up from human effort into the spiritual world. In Maria Sophia we have the greatest example of the avatar stream merging with the bodhisattva stream.

In Maria Sophia, we have a confluence of beings that was unparalleled.

It is premature to discuss the identity of great spiritual teachers until one hundred years have passed since their deaths. We know these reincarnating human personalities by their works, which may not take deep root until a century after they have passed over the threshold of death.

To speak of one person or another as the Kalki Avatar or Maitreya Buddha or some other bodhisattva before a century has passed since their death is spiritual sophistry that will lead to cults of the personality or spiritually hinder those who become followers of these alleged great teachers. Every person on the Earth who puts forth the effort can embody great avatars, saints, and spiritual beings.

We should keep our eye on learning to know our own guardian angel rather than seeking exalted teachers outside of ourselves. All too often, belief in a guru or teacher may take the place of personally taking responsibility for one's own self-development, with the help of the ever-present beings in the spiritual world.

Let us look at the greatest of Hindu avatars, Vishnu, as an illustration of exactly what was meant by that term in the tradition that created it. Vishnu is one of the three gods in the male trinity of the Hindu pantheon. Vishnu is called the sustainer, essentially a similar role as Christ, the second person in the Christian Trinity. He incarnates in a physical form on a regular basis to keep creation in balance. Vishnu has had nine incarnations, and his tenth is awaited as the Kalki Avatar.

Vishnu is the archetypal avatar who comes from the celestial realm to Earth in whatever form he wishes to take and is not bound by any physical law of nature. He created fantastic wonders during his incarnations. He was there at creation as a giant turtle, then later as a flying boar, then a one-horned whale who saved Manu from the flood, then the half man/half lion named Narashimha, then the dwarf Vamana who conquered the evil demon Bali, then Parashurama, Rama, Krishna, and his brother Balarama.

The ninth incarnation of Vishnu is hotly debated. Some scholars say it was Balarama and others say Gautama Buddha. This debate highlights the confusion between an avatar and a bodhisattva. Gautama Buddha was clearly a human who evolved to an enlightened state, not an avatar who descended from heaven. Thus, the debate over the Kalki Avatar began with the enlightenment of Gautama Buddha, and it hasn't ended yet.

There is another school of thought that believes that when Krishna manifested to Arjuna as his charioteer, this was the tenth incarnation of Vishnu. Some say that this manifestation as Arjuna was connected to the descent of Christ into the human realm. Others are convinced that the tenth incarnation of Vishnu as the Kalki Avatar has happened in our own time and that this being has united with the new bodhisattva who is evolving towards becoming the Maitreya Buddha, the successor of the Gautama Buddha.

And yet others, like Amma Bhagavan, claim to be the physical incarnation of the Maitreya Buddha. Amma Bhagavan are two great Hindu teachers in India who founded the Oneness University, which has over fifty million followers worldwide. Amma and Bhagavan are male and female and teach that they are one being, united in all ways, as twins. They claim to have the signs and prophecies that prove their assertion to be the Maitreya Buddha.

Other Maitreya Buddha claimants have been prophesized by authors who insist that Maitreya has been manifesting throughout the world before many people doing great feats of wonder and bringing spiritual blessings to many. There are also Indian, Tibetan, Bonpo, and other spiritual lineages that claim to have an incarnation of the Maitreya in their particular tradition incarnated at this time. The author has met multiple claimants to the title of Maitreya Buddha, and they all seem like lovely, genuine people.

So then, the question arises as to which of the many Maitreyas and Kalki Avatars are real?

George William Russell (writing under the name A. E.) wrote a book titled *The Avatars* in which he describes how a young shepherd who plays the flute and sings beautifully becomes an avatar over time. The young man does not know that he is such a highly developed person and appears as a humble shepherd throughout most of his life. Eventually, he becomes more spiritually developed and begins to realize this as he notices the magical effect he has over people in bringing them great happiness.

A young girl, in the same countryside as the shepherd boy, has an ethereal companion who others cannot see at first. Over the years, the companion becomes more and more physical until she incarnates in a seemingly physical body. Eventually, the shepherd boy and the girl's companion meet and fall in love. They travel throughout the countryside, bringing happiness and joy to everyone they meet, creating a legend and leaving many anecdotes of wisdom for the villagers to talk about for a long time to come. The two finally retreat from the physical world to continue to do their good work far from humanity, which understands them all too little.

This story of avatars also underscores the distinction between the Earthly bodhisattva stream of humans ascending to the divine and the avatar stream descending from above.

The merging of these two streams is similar to the merging of the celestial and earthly streams that united in Maria Sophia.

These streams are found also in the divine being of Christ descending into the body of Jesus of Nazareth, the Adam Kadmon body, for three years. Jesus, as a human, then underwent His ministry and passion before He ascended into heaven.

The veils between all worlds are thinning, and humans have one foot on each side of the threshold between the physical and spiritual worlds. Avatars work with bodhisattvas to help them penetrate the veils between these worlds so that they may develop their spiritual nature. But we must be clear about why each tradition has its own version of these spiritual realities and be true to the spirit of current revelation available for the budding bodhisattvas in ourselves.

The tradition of bodhisattvas is long and involved and is often referred to as the Masters of Wisdom and the Harmony of Feelings and Sensation. This is, in short, what *The Gospel of Sophia* is teaching: the Masters have mastered thinking (wisdom), feeling (harmony of feelings), and willing (harmony of sensations).

> **"The Maitreya Buddha will teach Christianity in the most profound way."**

This Great White Brotherhood, or Lodge, as it is often called, is traditionally a group of twelve bodhisattvas who are circled around Christ receiving His teachings directly so that they may descend to Earth and share those Wisdom teachings of love with humanity. One bodhisattva at a time comes to the fore and descends into incarnation to bring the teachings of Christ.

After four or five thousand years, the current bodhisattva then ascends to become a Buddha who does not incarnate into a physical body again, but rather works from the spiritual world to continue the mission as an ascended master.

When Gautama Buddha reached enlightenment in a physical body, he chose his successor who is called the Maitreya Buddha, the bringer of good. However, the Maitreya *Bodhisattva* will not become a Buddha for another few thousand years.

The mission of the Maitreya Buddha is to bring the Wisdom of Christ that illuminates the cosmic nature of Christ's origin and his singular deed that redeemed the Earth and saved it from becoming too hardened and materialized.

"The battle between light and dark is raging, and all of human evolution is at a precipice."

This is called the Wisdom of Christ, or Sophia of Christ, for it is this Wisdom that will bring understanding about the true nature of Christ's deed and particularly about Christ's redemption and resurrection of the super-etheric body of the Earth and the ether body of humanity.

Christ conquered the Earthly realm and now is conquering the etheric realm so that humanity can assume its rightful position in creation.

Christ conquered death as an Earthly and Cosmic Deed, and this is the message of the Maitreya Buddha in our time.

When Maitreya speaks, so much wisdom and truth is present in the moral content of the words that they become reality. The Maitreya's words have the power to *create* just as the divine *spoke creation into being* through the Word, or Logos.

It is erroneous that the Maitreya Buddha will teach traditional Buddhism.

The Maitreya Buddha will teach Christianity in the most profound way.

Gautama Buddha taught the six steps of compassion that lead to love, but Christ is the author and master of love. Gautama Buddha was intimately involved in the life of Christ and was there from his birth as the Star of Bethlehem.

Buddha's higher bodies participated in the Mystery of Golgotha—the life, death, and resurrection of Jesus Christ.

Buddha was taught by Christ when he was one of the bodhisattvas circled around Him in the spiritual lodge of the sun. These masters are called many names in many faiths—elders, masters, wise women, bodhisattvas, candles, fires, and other such names.

In our times, due to the incarnation of Ahriman, both groups of twelve circled around Christ are currently active on the Earth. This is the first time that such a dramatic event as this has happened. All twenty-four elders, plus avatars, bodhisattvas, arahats, mahatmas, saints, patriarchs, and a host of others great spiritual beings are incarnating at this time. This is well known by clairvoyants in these traditions, who can witness such events.

This is an unprecedented time that is a fulcrum of evolution.

The battle between light and dark is raging, and human evolution is at a precipice.

One of the reasons that so many great spiritual beings have incarnated to wage the battle against materialism and the forces of Ahriman and his followers is because human bodies have degraded so much that it is very difficult

"Sophia is higher than an avatar and is ready to help the bodhisattva in us blossom into the spiritual world."

for spiritual beings to find suitable human bodies that can carry the weight of spiritual consciousness in these hyper-materialistic times. Many great beings are finding bodies that do not permit them to manifest their spiritual strength without great hindrances.

Thus, of the twenty-four elders, it will be hard to find twelve who can join together to confront the incarnation of Ahriman and the many dark beings who have also taken form with him. Without the lodge of the elders working to bring light and warmth into the grey shadow-thoughts of materialism that have become common in the world, much of humanity will fail to evolve properly and move forward in evolution. The battle for humanity is being waged day and night, and most people have no idea of the costs.

Humans will either become angels or animals, and the elders are committed to serve the angelic in humans.

Avatars and bodhisattvas, the celestial and the Earthly, hang in the balance of what humans will do in these crucial years of trying to keep the spiritual world from darkening our consciousness. When a materialist sleeps or dies, he does not have spiritual food to feed the hierarchy, and thus the spiritual world has no food to feed him. Subsequently, light is not born, and all is turned towards darkness in both realms. Christ is crucified again in the etheric realm of light and life by materialistic thinking.

Humans are starving from the lack of spiritual nourishment because they bring none to the spiritual world. As a result, human evolution could be lost to beings who want to impede and end human spiritual development. This death of the spirit has caused the spiritual world to empty itself of souls and flood the Earth with as much help as it can send.

We need to remember that Sophia is higher than an avatar and is ready to help the bodhisattva in us blossom into the spiritual world. Sophia as Maria Sophia is far beyond a bodhisattva who evolves into a Buddha. She is a perfect archetype to emulate, as she is a balance between celestial and earthly.

Christ is the Being we all must meet each time we cross the threshold between the physical and spiritual worlds. Currently, we have the greatest imaginable help from the spiritual world. All around us are the great spiritual teachers of all time, incarnated to help us move along the spiritual path of self-development.

We should not be surprised to find many false prophets claiming these spiritual titles; however, it is not the author's intent to denounce them, just to inspire the seeker to bring true light into his and her own spiritual research. Once you know these spiritual realities, you can be more discerning of the teachings and practices of any spiritual teacher.

> *"Sophia is alive, vibrant, and active in the world around us."*

We should remember that any spiritual being can alight in our spirit, even if for only a moment of golden illumination. We need not speculate on past incarnations or play the spiritual game of *who was who*; rather, we should research our own incarnations with the help of Sophia and Her hosts and utilize the research to perfect our own self without concern about who others think we are or who we think some teacher might be in the larger scheme of history.

We need to take the vow of the bodhisattva, which is that we will continue to strive towards enlightenment for the sake of all other sentient beings. This is a prerequisite for advancing towards our Buddhahood or Christened Self.

The author points to Hindu tradition to be most helpful and accurate— that the Kalki Avatar will be the incarnation of Kali *herself*. The Hindu text *Divya Maha Kala Jnana* (The Divine Knowledge of Time), written around 1000 A.D. by Jagas Guru Srimad Virat Potaluru Veera Brahmendra Maha Swami, describes social conditions before the arrival of Kali Purusha, the Kalki Avatar, by the Kali year 5101 (1999 A.D.).

This being, it is told, is the incarnation of Kali, the destructive and procreative female aspect of the divine. It is predicted that Kali Purusha will be called Shree Shree Shree ("Thrice Great") Veera Bhoga Vasataraya Maha Swami and will carry a fiery sword to strike off the head of ignorance and champion Wisdom.

The Divine Feminine Trinity is a similar archetype to this prediction of the Thrice Great Goddess, who is the necessary spiritual teacher or avatar of our times.

The forces of Kali are the forces of death that accompany her consort, Shiva. It is the feminine forces of death that also create the forces of birth that are needed to overcome the deadening forces of materialism that threaten to destroy humanity's opportunity for spiritual advancement in this age of hyper-materialism.

The Maitreya Buddha is like the Holy Sophia as She slowly develops Herself and humanity in the process of spiritual evolution from the Earth to the realm of Queen of Heaven.

The Holy Sophia knows the suffering and strife of human life and is there to help midwife all of our efforts to birth the spirit. Like a bodhisattva, She has taken the vow to help all humans embody their angelic self and enter the super-etheric realm of the divine. Surely Sophia, in Her many forms, changes into the very companion we need to make the journey to our higher self.

Sophia the Creatrix is the slow-burning fire that Prometheus brought down from the gods and hid in the nerves of the human body until it enkindled the heart, illuminated the mind, and fired the will.

Sophia has changed throughout time as She takes on the many forms She has created. Her magical will passes through all life, in any natural form, from a sunflower to the crystals in the human pineal gland to the milk from a mother's breast. Sophia is alive, vibrant, and active in the world around us. She is in our body, soul, and spirit. She is everywhere we look, or listen, or sense. She is the Wisdom that brings sense perception into our inner being. She controls the natural laws and mechanisms that interpret sense perception from which we derive our consciousness. When we acknowledge the true workings of Sophia in the wisdom around us, we are beginning to perceive Her as the Queen of Heaven.

Sophia in all of Her facets is involved in all perception, earthly and celestial, and is the very tapestry upon which consciousness is written.

"When approaching the mystery of the Goddess of Love, most people have to stop and turn back until enough understanding of the true nature of love has ripened in their higher souls."

We are witness to those living forces active in our selves.

Sophia helps the fire of the nerves refine perception until it is the essence of immortality in this realm. She then imprints the efforts in the super-etheric realm of the akashic ether. She is the force of levity that arises from fire and kindles awareness from the heart through the nerves, into the secret reaches of the brain. This is sometimes called living thinking or warmed-up thoughts, both of which give fiery sustenance to the human will.

These secrets of Sophia make Her Queen of the Heaven in our brain, Queen of the Earth in our hearts, and Queen of our duty in our will. In this way, Sophia the Queen spans the past, present, and future. Her threefold nature has suffered the labor and birth of humanity and has sustained spiritual evolution ever since on Earth and in heaven.

We have now heard descriptions of how Sophia's facets have

transformed from ancient times to modern times and the accompanying human spiritual self-development that grew alongside of Her as our collective intellect and consciousness.

The story of human intellectual and spiritual development is the biography of the Holy Sophia and of collective human consciousness. This is easy to see when we study the past and the changing facets of Sophia as She has and will continue to inspire philosophers and artists. Her side-by-side development with us is clear. The time has come. Humanity must realize Her higher natures (Goddess of Love, Mother of God, Queen of Heaven, and the Most Holy Trinosophia) to be inspired to face the challenges of the future.

Sophia will change again and again. She will bring forth the very facet of the Goddess that is needed at the right time and in a form that can be understood.

Yesterday we had Rhea.

Today, we have Gaia.

Tomorrow, we will have Gaia-Sophia.

In the near future, we will have Sophia Christos.

Humanity can view Sophia as the trinity of Sun, Moon, and Earth. With the new spiritual organs being developed by spiritual scientists, all of Her forms may be perceived. As we examine the four facets of Sophia found in the Twelve Labors of Sophia that relate to the Holy Sophia, we are ascending to realms that are far beyond ordinary spiritual development and generally inconceivable by anyone except an initiate.

When approaching the Mystery of the Goddess of Love, most people have to stop and turn back until enough understanding of the true nature of love has ripened in their higher souls. To comprehend the nature of the true Mother of God is to objectively know yourself as a *god or goddess in the becoming*. This is not possible without a Wisdom cosmology that can transport the aspirant beyond the limits of space.

To understand the nature of the Once and Future Queen of Heaven is to remove the limits of time, to see into the workings of Providence and the Lord of Karma. Insight into previous incarnations would be necessary to experience and confirm the nature of Sophia at this level.

But to reach the next level of Sophia as the Most Holy Trinosophia, one must understand that all of creation is in perfect balance. Space, time, and consciousness were manipulated and responsive to evolving consciousness.

Wherever one trains the mind, all of space then becomes illuminated with Wisdom. This level of insight is far beyond what is necessary in this age to be wise and in sync with evolution. The Beings of Wisdom guide us through these levels of spiritual awareness and assume the responsibility with devotion and love. All of Sophia's Mysteries have yet to unfold. What can be communicated now is only a beginning.

Queen of Heaven

She is the One, the sum total of creation,
The rhythmic warp and weft of gravity and levity
That draws forth the soul to Eros' experience of duality,
The wonder of synthesis, and a sublime vision of nature.
All meditation relies on emptying ourselves into the emptiness,
The void, the space between electrons and protons,
Atoms and monads, others and ourselves, stars and other stars.
Who holds without a container, rules without ordaining,
Caresses without hands, births without a womb?
She is the mirror in all of our hearts that warms
Through the communion of recognition of the refined.

She cannot be killed, for She holds death in Her arms.
She cannot be extinguished, for Her dark fire needs no fuel.
She cannot be thought, for She holds the thinker's mind and his thoughts.
She cannot be conceived, for She conceived conception,
Now suffering through all time the conceptions of others, and yet is filled not.
If only we could remember the dream that once was—
A weaving presence of angelic hosts falling into our need and sustenance.
Her tides of time bring about the growing seasons, rhythms of birth and death;

Otherwise, we would imagine we are Earth-Gods, dreaming our immortality.

Of Her jaws of death and birth we know well
And long for Her sweet kiss of eternity's wonder.
The Goddess has many disguises and She wanders through time
To remind us that there is no time at all in Her realm.
She dons Her skulls and bones to remind us of ever present death
So that we may live, fully attentive to this moment of limitlessness,
In the void of silent repose of clear, luminous wisdom.

O, Holy Mother of All, Queen of Heaven!
Glance at me and boil my marrow,
Touch me and fire my thoughts,
Hold me and burst my heart into a nova of love
That embraces all others as Your heart holds your children.

Sophia as the Most Holy Trinosophia

You burgeon forth, and blossom anew

In each human heart, but conscious only in few,

Who know the call, ancient invitation of gold,

To wed with your angel, in alchemical hold

That unites the twins, marries spirit to soul,

New Jerusalem comes, and we're all made whole.

The great initiate, the Comte De St. Germain, gave Sophia the name Most Holy Trinosophia, which is also the name of a Masonic initiatory rite that he wrote to a student while he was imprisoned by the church. The name means "the most holy threefold wisdom," and refers to both the Being of Wisdom and the initiation process to comprehend Her.

The initiatory rite of the Comte De St. Germain is quite profound and singular in its nature—well worth the time to study at length. For our purposes, the Most Holy Trinosophia is the culmination of the Twelve Labors of Sophia as She spans space, time, and consciousness.

The Most Holy Trinosophia only arises when the Holy Sophia has undergone the full cycle of time to spiritually evolve through the human condition and return to the throne of the Queen of Heaven. Each step of the way becomes the illuminated path to the spirit that leads the human into angelic realms and beyond.

Sophia manifests in Twelve Labors or Facets that are also stages of spiritual development for human evolution. Just as the Greeks believed

Heracles conquered twelve *animal forces* before he was immortalized in the starry sky to be seen for all time. So too are Sophia's Labors written into the starry script as the "reimagined" Twelve Labors of Sophia.

The Great Mother was always viewed as a multiplicity of beings, threefold, ninefold, or twelvefold. She was depicted wearing many different animal heads, often with wings, horns, or other animal parts. This indicated the Great Goddess' cosmic nature as the mother and creator of these zodiacal forces. It also meant that She had wrestled with these animal forces and emerged the victor. She thus has the right to wear the animal head as a symbol of taming the forces of the zodiac's *many-headed dragon.*

By conquering earthly and cosmic Labors, Sophia can be seen as the Queen of Heaven,

> **"We are separate, but one, a multiplicity of beings united by one Mother."**

the ruler of the zodiac where the forces of space hold sway. She is the Earthly and cosmic Heracles who has descended to hell, as did Psyche. Like Heracles, She has fulfilled the three tasks of taming the *thinking, feeling, willing,* and forces of animals or dragons that still reside in the subconscious depths. Immortalized as Queen of Heaven, Her completion only comes when the Most Holy Trinosophia, slowly mastering time as a human, struggles with the daily challenges of conquering materialism and, hopefully, our animal nature.

Only an initiate can comprehend the slightest aspect of the Most Holy Trinosophia. She demonstrates paradoxes of space, time, and consciousness that are generally incomprehensible to the human mind. With the knowledge and experience that derives from being an initiate, one gains the capacity to allow spiritual beings from beyond the Earthly realm to enter and bring non-physical (sense-free) sense perceptions. Only these budding supersensible organs of perception can gain an understanding of such an advanced being as the Most Holy Trinosophia.

Once an initiate develops a comprehensive cosmology and discerns the activities of the various hierarchical beings, he can then approach the higher levels: Goddess of Love, Mother of God, Queen of Heaven, and the Most Holy Trinosophia. In regards to the Most Holy Trinosophia, only a direct Intuition from a higher being can inform a human about Her true nature.

An initiate can find a similar nature within himself, but only if unlimited by space and time. He can begin to understand how a multiplicity of manifestations, such as the many facets and aspects of the Trinity, can belong to one being.

So you see, in examining the Most Holy Trinosophia, we have come full circle to the image of Sophia as a multi-dimensional holographic mirror.

To understand the Divine Feminine Trinity, the initiate must be able to navigate concepts that are seemingly contrary to natural law. Supernatural law becomes the basis for understanding the connectivity of the Being who is the universe and yet manifests at every point in the universe.

We are a piece of Sophia's universal holographic mirror. Only when all the parts have been gathered to complete the puzzle do we become whole.

We are separate, but one, a multiplicity of beings united by one Mother.

Nowhere in the modern scientific explanation of the universe can you find these concepts. In fact, fairy tales, as surprising as it may seem, are more accurate descriptions of the universe than science.

The universe is clearly one story, not trillions of separate pieces of cosmic flotsam swirling through an unconscious void.

Sophia's story is our story. It is *Herstory*. It is created as one, but broken into many by necessity. At a higher level, we reunite with a nearly infinite variety of experiences that have contributed to the new creation.

> *"The universe is one story."*

In other words, we are gods and goddesses in the making. Therefore, we must have the potential to follow in Sophia's footsteps.

Just as humans must juggle duality, their threefold nature, their sevenfold nature, their ninefold nature, and their twelvefold nature, so must Sophia harmonize forces on a cosmic level, transforming chaos into a spiritual coherence that resonates with the universal frequencies of consciousness. As Sophia's Labors are successful, so too will human labors follow. All spiritually striving souls ultimately will benefit from these efforts.

Sophia reflects humanity's collective intellectual and spiritual development. She evolves and carries human efforts toward ultimate fulfillment. Her evolution provides the spiritual tools for humans to replicate Her efforts and manage the growing capacities of the soul and spirit. By developing our souls, we balance duality. We also learn how to harmonize the threefold aspects of the soul to wed the spiritual trinity.

Each of the seven planets are known to send a corresponding morphic vibration of life into the fluid column of our body, which serves as a receiving antenna for these frequencies of warmth, light, sound, and life.

These spiritual fires must be tempered in the chakras into the alchemist's slow-burning fire to drive the transmutation of our lower self into the higher self. Then through initiation into a complete spiritual cosmology, the aspirant begins to understand the nine different bodies that constitute the human spirit.

> *"The quest for Wisdom is a never-ending striving for the Holy Grail that reveals the Mother's cauldron of creation."*

This cosmology enables one to gain an unlimited perspective beyond space and time. It introduces the twelve directions of space, the creative letters of the magical alphabet that cause form and function to manifest through the language of the etheric formative forces.

At this point, the solidity of matter is seen as an illusion. The initiate understands the omniscience of spiritual beings. She learns that these beings can be physically present in many places simultaneously, because space and time are both illusions. She also learns that there is no past or future for the spiritual world. All of creation was, is, and will be in every moment of perceived Earth time.

These revelations are so profound that they cannot be imagined, only experienced. The initiate then understands the astounding reality that her higher self is waiting for her in the spiritual future, whole and complete. As complete paradoxes, these realities destroy the illusion of space and time, connecting the initiate with spiritual beings who are unbound by the Earthly realm.

The spiritual world rejoices at the sound of the name of the Most Holy Trinosophia. She indicates the fulfillment of evolution and the return of all of Her children who have grown into co-creative Christened Beings. This is the completion of space and time. All Beings are connected, working in unity for the common good.

This is the greatest moment for our Divine Parents, who have waited patiently as we took each step towards our spiritual inheritance.

Finally, all the veils of nature are drawn aside, and Sophia, the author of this universe, stands before us in all Her glory. We must be evolved enough to withstand Her majesty and effulgence. Here is the end of evolution and the beginning of a new era wherein humans take on the role of higher hierarchies who participate in birthing a new humanity.

In the first four of the Twelve Labors of Sophia, we see a maternal Sophia who established an environment full of Wisdom for Her children (humanity) to be born. Humans searched inside and outside of themselves and were mystified. They made humble attempts to comprehend nature and Her ways. Well-loved myths, religions, and stories were developed, pointing to one human emotion: gratitude. Like a newborn, the unknowing human stands in gratitude for a life he can barely comprehend. The original humans were symbiotically one with the spiritual world and knew their Mother as Creatrix.

Slowly, humans began to develop a perspective of personal thinking that was brain-bound, limited by the cosmology of the individual. This prompted the longing and search for Wisdom, the Creatrix who had become hidden behind the visible world of sense perception.

The quest for Wisdom is a never-ending striving for the Holy Grail that reveals the Mother's cauldron of creation.

The characteristics have continually evolved. Searching for Beauty and the Virgin changed over time into a personal desire to hold the Goddess as Bride and Beloved. Our human mind desired Wisdom, yet settled for the lowly thoughts of personal desire, attachment, and the Seven Deadly Sins. Wisdom was the goal of the enlightened mind. If desire could be conquered, Wisdom showed Her Beauty to one's higher thoughts, and the love of Wisdom (philo-Sophy) was born as worship of the divine in thinking.

When the desires of the aspirant were turned into the higher aspects of Sophia the Daughter (Beauty, Cosmic Virgin, Bride, and Beloved), the Temple of Wisdom came into view. She then led the marriage of soul to spirit. At this point, the human spirit was born and Sophia's higher aspects could be revealed.

The last four labors of Sophia are the highest that the spirit may attain. They take the initiated into realms beyond the Earthly. The Goddess of Love has little to do with what humans believe or practice as love. Love must stretch for new definitions of itself and reach new heights before the initiate can experience Sophia as the Goddess of Love.

The love of which Christ spoke is the foundation of Sophia's love. It is the profound love of a Mother, and it knows no limits of space or time. It is eternal. This form of love bestows all power in heaven and on Earth, yet cannot be possessed or owned.

Love is the force that sings the universe into the creation of the wedding dance.

Like all of Sophia's forces, love can be found in the human body but is often hidden and invisible. The slow-burning fire of the alchemist can temper the soul into the golden nature of love.

Sophia's love is that fire.

She is Prometheus, who brought fire down from heaven for human use as Living Imaginations active in the realm of the angels.

These are the Mysteries of Fire that are unimaginable with brain-bound thinking. Higher feelings from the Daughter Goddess and Her corresponding Labors can fire the will to behold these higher ideas that are sustained by angels. Realms normally unreachable can be perceived by the higher aspects of heart-fired thinking that discern the spiritual future.

> *"These realms can only be perceived by the higher aspects of heart-fired thinking that reach into the spiritual future."*

The Mother of God can be perceived from the archangelic realms through Inspirations that communicate the intent of the spiritual world.

An initiate who has completed the prerequisite moral and spiritual development can approach these realms and embody the forces of divine Inspiration.

This sounding of the spirit is overwhelming to the uninitiated. All of the forces of spiritual development created by the Goddess of Love are needed to withstand the confluence of beings and forces that reside in Her realm. The cosmic suffering that Sophia endured to rise to Her lofty throne is far beyond words to describe or ears to hear.

It is said that the nine hierarchies emanate a universal word that sounds to humans like the word *suffering*. This word also can be interpreted as the name of the Mother of God, the Great Mother who endures all. It is this type of suffering that the Mother of God veils from human perception so that we may not be overwhelmed and incinerated by Her majesty.

> *"Love is the force that sings the universe into creation."*

The Queen of Heaven is the joyous reunion with the ultimate higher self, a time of celebration in Heaven and on Earth. By then, humans will have evolved into angels and archangels. They will be ready to become archai beings who commune with their Christened Spirit, the perfected human or Spirit Human (Atman).

As Sophia takes her throne as Queen of Heaven, humans will become the rulers of their own fate. The Archai are filled with the Intuitions of the divine in all aspects of their being. They are constantly linked with the hierarchies above and below. Throughout the ranks, they hear the unified directions of the Trinity.

Each archai is separate, having evolved through the human stage to develop a singular identity, but also an intimate part of the whole.

Angels witness the Goddess of Love.

Archangels witness the Mother of God.

Archai witness the Queen of Heaven.

The hierarchy commune to recreate the complete picture of Sophia in the holographic mirror; but this time, when it comes together, it will be exponentially larger, as each of the pieces has grown into a greater being. Sophia's creation was broken and scattered, to be regathered into a greater whole.

This is the magic of Sophia and the intent of humanity's creation—a type of "creation out of nothingness," another of Her Mysteries. When we come to the Most Holy Trinosophia, we must have evolved beyond the archai stage of spiritual development and assumed our role as Christened Beings.

Then we may see Her directly and fully realize the similarities between us.

We will know that we are an integral part of Her body. We have a crucial role to perform in the co-creation of worlds.

The Mysteries of Sophia Christos will reveal to us the past and future meaning of spiritual evolution.

We will find our place among the hierarchy. The heavens will rejoice.

We will see through the eyes of the Holy Spirit wed to the Holy Sophia, who play an instrumental role in supplying us with guidance and support as we evolve. They lead us upward into angels, archangels, and archai. Now, Christ places on our head the crown of glory and helps us embody the full nature of His Being.

We become divine, and the divine is exultant.

There is one more step that must be taken to understand Sophia in Her nature as the Most Holy Trinosophia. This can only be drawn in vague terms, with inadequate words, because everything that you think you know becomes immaterial when you are considering the ultimate origins of creation.

In Hindu philosophy, there are great periods of time called *manvantaras* and *pralayas*.

Manvantaras are periods when matter comes into existence out of nothingness and organizes itself upon the memory of the forms from the previous cycle. Matter grows through many stages. At a certain point, it dissolves and disappears back into nothingness, called a pralaya.

The entire universe participates in these rhythmic cycles of creation and dissolution, and then creation again at a higher level. The ancient Hindu clairvoyants were quite accurate, for this same reality is found also in black holes and ion jets. Four thousand years ago, ancient Hindus perceived what modern science *believes* it has just recently *discovered*.

It seems the third eye of the Hindus was much more perceptive than both eyes of the modern scientist! The concept of great cycles creating and dissolving all matter may seem a bit far-fetched, but both the ancients and the moderns have perceived these cycles occurring in the galaxies of our universe.

> *"Christ and Sophia have left signposts along the way to help guide us back home."*

The Most Holy Trinosophia is the full consciousness of Sophia in the past, present, and future. She fully understands the great cycles of creation, destruction, and resurrection. These mysteries are ineffable. They simply cannot be understood in a trifling way. It takes both an Intuition of the Father Ground of Being and the Most Holy Trinosophia to understand the true nature of created matter, its seeming destruction in black holes (pralayas) and resurrection through galactic ion jets (manvantaras).

When the two great Trinities unite, all of evolution can be understood, including these great periods of manifestation and dissolution. The combined Trinities of Male and Female unite these two realms through a cosmology that knows that life is eternal. Humans have eternal life born through the tides of space and time that create the great cycles of birth, death, and rebirth—the original ubiquitous Mother.

Gratitude, wisdom, and love are the gifts of the Twelve Labors of Sophia to humanity. Through Her Labors, Sophia Herself gains the mastery of space, time, and consciousness. These Labors are inscribed in humanity's biography. Each soul grows through the loving relationship with Sophia, the midwife who births our spirit.

In this way, Sophia and humanity are inextricably interwoven. She helps embody the collective development of the human spirit. She plays all of the feminine roles as we grow from neophytes into initiates. Her many facets change as our new spiritual sense organs develop to reveal new parts of ourselves and Her. The spiritual world has provided for our nurturing with great care and detail. Christ and Sophia have left signposts along the way to help guide us back home.

The transformation of the higher aspects of the soul into the capacities of the spirit is an alchemical process that undergoes several stages until the base animal nature of the human is refined and transmuted into the gold of the spirit.

This process takes many forms. The alchemist's language was often obscure. The intent was not to turn lead into gold, but rather physical into spiritual.

Alchemists, Rosicrucians, Masons, and many other esoteric orders describe this transformation as a seven-, ten-, or twelve-step process that must be conducted slowly, sequentially, and with focused consciousness in tune with planetary influences. The alchemical process is often described as a marriage of the King and Queen who bring forth a Child greater than the parents.

The Chemical Wedding of Christian Rosenkreutz is just such a description, a very helpful resource for studying these stages of spiritual transmutation. Sophia is reunited with the Male Trinity as the Most Holy Trinosophia (the resurrected Divine Feminine Trinity) and accomplishes the transmutation of the human into the divine. The Most Holy Trinosophia becomes the Queen of Heaven and Queen of our Hearts forever.

When humans learn to collapse space and time and link to the higher hierarchies, Intuitions rush in as illumined Wisdom with the power to heal and create. To stand stripped before the divine is to stand before the Holy Grail of Spirit, a fountain of gratitude, wisdom, and love. Spiritual nourishment will come from connecting with spiritual beings and allowing them to flow through and empower us. Free will is the only thing that holds back this process. The human thinker who considers himself all powerful, but alone, in his brain-bound thinking will hold back the process. Yet timeless Wisdom shines out from every aspect of the human spirit trying to teach us that we are angelic in nature.

> *"Initiates will bring forth new revelations and the good news of the coming of Sophia Christos."*

There will come a time when Christ will walk the Earth and appear to anyone who needs Him, simultaneously. Sophia Christos will be the twin avatars who wander the Earth bringing wisdom and love. Humans will be able to see these Spirits, and the other hierarchy will begin to make their presence known. Humans will gladly enjoin their free will to directly perceive the incredible beings that feed their spiritual needs. The nature of the Divine Feminine Trinity will be commonly understood, because humans will develop new sense organs to perceive Her activity in the human constitution and the world.

When new ears for hearing the spirit are developed, the Inspirations of the spiritual world will pour forth with harmonic symphonies that enhance consciousness and feed the spirit.

When a newfound power to control the forces inherent in the human will is developed, initiates will bring forth new *revelations* and the *good news* of the *coming of Sophia Christos.*

New prophets will rise up. They will create ideas that fire human imagination, inspire morality, and kindle love in the deeds of humans. The aspirant will adorn the clean white gown, symbol of purified virtues, and rise to the divine Temple of Wisdom to wed her higher self. Christ and Sophia will be there as the parents. Once the spiritual union is consecrated, a new child will be born, destined to be a king in full glory, who wears the crown of heaven.

Lucifer made his own crown. He placed it on his own head. For his pride, he was thrown down from heaven to Earth.

The human spiritual crown is the redemption of Lucifer's pride.

Our central jewel is Christ's light that lovingly radiates throughout all kingdoms. This coronation, then, is the birth of the spirit's Christened Self, anointed by Sophia Christos.

It represents a new sacrament of the spirit, a wedding of soul and spirit that births the eternal.

It becomes a new communion of saints, and it bespeaks the goal of human spiritual evolution—to embody the redemption of duality through sacred nourishment that brings eternal life.

These are the gifts of Sophia Christos: the anointing of the sacred couple and the transmutation of the transitory soul into the eternal spirit.

There is one exception that bypasses the previously mentioned rule of slow-measured advancement.

Purity can cause extreme acceleration of the spiritual development processes and might be considered an instrument of *quantum leap*. When a great soul is pure, the spirit already shines through the person. The normal challenges of the soul may seem lifted.

This is quite different from being ignorant or naïve. It entails the accumulation of good karma from moral deeds in previous lives. Some people are born with advanced spiritual development and can race ahead into the future, already embodying the higher aspects of the spirit and acting as the angelic. This purity accompanies some great initiates and enables them to embody their spiritual nature long before others—for the sake of helping humanity.

Other souls may experience the *golden moment of illumination*, wherein the higher self descends into the prepared soul. Golden light then irradiates their entire being. This illumination brings Wisdom and inexplicable insight. It also may enable that person to communicate with higher beings. Great initiates create works of architecture, sculpture, art, and literature that reflect the golden moment of illumination. Structures from the megalithic age still baffle modern engineers. Some of them cannot be replicated, even with all of the tools of modern science at hand.

For example, the Parthenon was built with the knowledge of the Earth's curvature. The mathematical wonders of the Egyptian pyramids are still being puzzled. Secrets of the universe have been known since ancient times, and the consciousness to utilize them is still beyond the reach of the modern thinker.

In China, entire pyramid cities remain unexplored. Their arrangements mimic star clusters, just as found in Angkor Wat in Cambodia and the Giza pyramids.

Each gift of the great initiates holds wonders that continue to unfold. The Comte De St. Germain wrote beautiful music. Novalis wrote stories and poetry. Raphael Stanza painted archetypal Madonnas that depict the face of the Holy Mother. These gifts are priceless and timeless in their use on the spiritual path as is a poem of St. Germain's called *The Philosophic Sonnet*. This short piece is an alchemical description of spiritual development. It conveys the familiar story of the prodigal child who is expelled from primal unity and must go through the transmutation processes by which the soul may return to the spiritual world.

Symbols speak louder than words. A parable can teach morality through example. Extraordinary artistic achievements help lift the veil of Sophia's Mystery over time, and many more will follow.

Philosophical Sonnet
by Comte De Saint Germain

Curious scrutator of all nature,
I have known of the great whole, the principle and the end,
I have seen gold thick in the depths of the double mercury;
I have seized its substance, and surprised its changing.
I explain by that art, the soul with the womb of a Mother,
Make its home, take it away, and as a kernel
Placed against a grain of wheat, under the humid pollen;
The one plant and the other vine-stock, are the bread and wine,
Nothing was, God willing, nothing became something,
I doubted it, I sought that on which the universe rests,
Nothing preserves the equilibrium and serves to sustain,
Then with the weight of praise and of blame,
I weighed the eternal, it called my soul,
I died, I adored, I knew nothing more.

FOURTH SEAL

Encountering the Holy Sophia

You are made of the Primal Beginnings,
The Mothers, the foundations of creation—
The Original Ocean of Dark Spirit Light
That was yet to be born into the Light of Love.

The Evolving Relationship with Sophia

Called to a new day, when time and space separate those

who love and shall love again before long,

When age and wisdom cycle round to separate fullness born of union,

but clarified and raised to glory by opposing forces.

Humanity develops its thinking nature through speech, writings, images, symbols, stories, and other types of media. As a result, one can access a vast, collective consciousness in many ways: myths, dreams, fairytales, religious ideas, philosophy, and the evolving intellect itself. Today, we can access all of humanity's intellectual progress through the Internet.

Our entire evolution, humanity's complete progress to date on the Earth, is demonstrated by the history and development of higher forms of thought. Yet with materialistic, sense-bound thinking, it is difficult to completely understand history in terms of the true perspectives of the ancients—how they saw their place in the world. For example, our ancestors believed that thoughts were shared among all thinkers. Their living archetypes described the forces and beings of nature and were part of everyone's general experience. Clairvoyance was a common capacity.

We can little understand what the ancients thought. Written records remain of ideas that we either cannot accept or conclude are less advanced, since the ancient mind lacked the capacity of "modern thinking." When it comes to the past, historians are simply voicing their own opinions on what and how the ancients thought.

What were the ancients thinking when they wrote down their beliefs or built megalithic structures such as their cultural centers? Who can truly know? These societal remnants of past civilizations are still mysteries. Even after extensive archaeological study, the true Mystery rites of the Great Pyramid, or most any ancient cultural site, are not fully understood. We can only speculate as to the meaning of some hieroglyphics, cuneiform tablets, and other ancient writings. In fact, many hieroglyphs remain untranslated, leaving modern theorists in the dark about the way the human intellect developed during that ancient era.

The biography of the Holy Sophia reflects the nature of the evolving human intellect. Serious thinkers seek the Wisdom of knowledge and may find Her after a long, cultivated effort of thinking, patience, and gratitude.

We may call the dance of human consciousness with Wisdom a relationship between the thinker and the object of the thinker's mind. The mental image that one perceives does not convey meaning, per se, until the thinker imposes his worldview upon it. For example, the Greek thinker knew that Zeus caused lightning, while the modern materialistic thinker attributes lightning to electrical friction.

The ancient Greek knew wisdom as Athena's owl; it sat upon her shoulder, knew all things, and spoke them into her ear. In contrast, the modern thinker sees wisdom as the Internet, the owl as Wi-Fi.

The ancients perceived powerful beings, whereas the modern thinker sees power articulated as forces and energies. Today's thinker may scoff at the ancients, discounting their thinking as undeveloped and their efforts to understand the world as pseudo-science. How is it, then, that modern scientists cannot replicate the wonders of the past? Why is it that they are still struggling to understand and conquer forces that the ancients commanded with ease through their relationship with divine and elemental beings?

The modern thinker is quick to accept the idea that humanity has a "collective unconscious" that drives human nature, especially the animalistic forces of personal desire and gratification. But the idea of a "collective consciousness" that reflects the evolving human intellect is more than modern thinkers are willing to accept.

The modern thinker believes that his thoughts are "his own" in a private world where no one else may enter. Here is a stumbling block for evolution, a necessary human dilemma. This ushered in an age when the independent human thinker could stand alone in the universe and believe, with great pride and complete certainty, that his thoughts are his alone—that he does not have to share them with any other man or god.

This was a necessary step in evolution, to create a free thinker. Yet it introduced the loneliness of personal thought. It fostered pride and arrogance through the misconception that humans have developed this thinking capacity on our own.

This pride recalls Lucifer, who thought his brilliance and magnificence were of his own efforts. Lucifer was defeated in his attempt to overthrow his creator. He was thrown down into dark matter to become the king of his own realm. Over time, each of us relives this story in our own physiology and psychology as we recapitulate the holistic development of humanity. We have all fallen from heaven to earth. Now, we must rise to reclaim our rightful positions once again.

The concept that the development of the individual recapitulates the development of all of humanity leads us to conclude that somewhere, perhaps in DNA or other places, a record exists of all of humanity's efforts to develop a free-thinking consciousness. Just as the mitochondrial DNA remember everything that your ancestors have eaten as it created the substance to digest these new foods, so does DNA, and other mechanisms, remember the ancestral, evolutionary steps of consciousness and thought.

Why should the development of thought be any different? Somewhere in the body, this development is recorded. Fields of morphic resonance in the brain have been suggested as the mechanism by which thinking evolves; the effect of the hundredth monkey may apply here. Once a certain number of people have forged new consciousness capacities, perhaps that "perfected vehicle of expression" may be imprinted both within the human and outside in the etheric fields around the Earth. Eventually, this force changes human organs into more refined sense organs that can perceive supersensible realms.

Rudolf Steiner believed that the perfected vehicles of great master beings need only be perfected once to enter an etheric realm he called Shamballa, after the Eastern belief in a perfected land of shining warmth and wisdom. Steiner called the principle of storing and accessing these perfected vehicles "the principle of spiritual economy."

Throughout history, certain highly developed individuals have used the perfected vehicles of the Christ to once again bring the perfected clarity and Wisdom into personal manifestation. These vehicles stand as the high mark of what humans can attain through morphic resonance with what could be called the collective consciousness of humanity.

Sophia manifests as the Holy Sophia, the Third Person in the Divine Feminine Trinity, through the development of human intellect and thinking. Her goal is to evolve alongside humanity, to help the individual develop thinking, feeling, and willing into more advanced capacities that can lead to Wisdom and communion with higher spiritual beings.

The Holy Sophia came to Earth just as the developing human intellect began to become individualized. (See Appendix F.) At that time, key cultures were focused on the abstract thought process that enhanced individual cognitive capacities. Father Abraham, patriarch of the Jews, Christians, and Muslims, was a good example of our individualized thinking capacity. Other cultures also began to demonstrate clear, individualized thinking that led to philosophical development.

This was a distinct departure of the human intellect in history. Previously, it was primarily through clairvoyance, not individualized thought, that cultural leaders discerned the leading images in myth, religion, and culture.

As the Holy Sophia grew, so did humanity's understanding of its own capacity for thinking. At first, thinking was described as external to the human being in the forces of nature. Over time, this concept shifted, where thinking was imagined to be an individualized process, personal and hidden within the human body.

Now, through quantum physics and other theories, thinking is once again a force that exists both outside of the human being and inside the human body simultaneously. In modern theories, the observer affects the observed. Thoughts are inherent in the object itself. They emit a morphic field of resonance that is the signature of the object, which is then impressed upon the senses of the observer.

In this light, humans are intricately connected with their environments. We can defy the previously agreed upon laws of nature and the general laws of space and time. Science has come full circle to what the ancient Hindus knew: that man and the world are the same. Only the developing thinker who wishes to perceive them as separate is separate.

Humanity has created a lonely ivory tower that separates it from the world so that it can become an independent, free thinker. This birth of thinking in darkness was necessary for evolution. We are children who still need one third of our day to sleep our way into being one with the world. Two thirds of the day, when we are awake, we think we are the god or goddess of our own private world. This is quite naive, since we are surrounded by higher and lower spiritual and elemental beings at all times.

We have never been alone. We are still not gods and goddesses.

Ancient Indian texts were written down by the Holy Rishis, who were inspired by angels. They directly perceived the workings of spirit in matter. Their perceptions and ideas, while absolutely correct and accurate for their own time, are not so applicable now due to the evolution that has occurred.

The Holy Sophia and humanity's intellect and consciousness have developed significantly. We have gone from clairvoyance to a complete lack of clairvoyance. Now, in modern times, we have begun the return to clairvoyance with scientific accuracy—spiritual science.

> *"We are children who still need one third of our day to sleep our way into being one with the world."*

Many people are relinking with the spiritual world and beginning to develop new sense organs of perception. These organs are developed through mental and spiritual training that focuses the mind on ideas that are supersensible and invisible. Eventually, through great concentration, contemplation, meditation, and prayer, the thinker begins to communicate with beings who are in close spiritual proximity and intimately concerned with one's personal development of these new senses.

On the path of self-knowledge, training oneself how to think becomes a tool of spiritual development. In fact, the first stage of development is to *think about thinking*.

The ancients began this process of thinking about thinking as a study of the divine. It turned into philosophy—the love of Sophia. They knew that thinking itself holds the secrets to finding higher forms of perception capable of rising up to Wisdom and the divine. Thinking is the ladder of Jacob to climb into heaven, but first we must wrestle with our angel until the truth is grasped.

The Holy Sophia passes through the human being every time he takes another step toward the spirit. She acknowledges our efforts to embody our spiritual capacity to think living thoughts. Human, Earth-bound thinking cannot cross the threshold into the spiritual world tainted with sense-perceptible images of the lower realms. Only higher thinking, called Imagination, can begin to perceive the host of spiritual beings all around us.

As this world starts to unveil itself, a personal relationship with the Holy Sophia emerges in the foreground. The Holy Sophia is the representative of Sophia, the Goddess of Wisdom, whose natural and supernatural laws control the universe. This relationship with the Holy Sophia has evolved from a cold distant one to the most intimate spiritual love one can experience.

The relationship between the Holy Sophia and the great thinkers is a record of the continuing evolution of human thinking as aided by Her.

We have discussed many facets of Sophia from a variety of perspectives, especially our personal relationship to these ideas. The following selections demonstrate the relationships between the Holy Sophia and thinkers throughout history.

As you read each progressive description, you can begin to get a picture of the Holy Sophia developing as a spiritual being passing through the human intellect. You can also sense the biography of the developing human intellect over time as the descriptions become more detailed and closer to the thinker.

These historical selections will show some of the facets of the Holy Sophia that have been characterized in the Twelve Labors of Sophia. As humans have grown closer to Her through concerted efforts to raise their thinking to higher realms, She has taken on many faces and facets.

The Mirror of Love

My love is as burnished as the brilliant sunset, calling forth the sickle moon from
    her hidden ways, dancing round her love, the sun,

As she changes, moment by moment, to new unbound horizons in her yet familiar
    ways of coursing.

Her glance, like a sliver of sweet response to her sinking beloved, longs for the silent
    union that quiets and darkens her soul.

Oh, to be close to the other and hidden from the view of all, so selflessly
    languishing in the presence that obscures;

Or to part and, step by step, distance oneself to that furthest point where brilliant
    white reflection rules the night,

With light borrowed from the one beloved, who sheds light to those in distant
    lands, so far away.

Separation brings illumination, longing, the ability to mirror the higher nature we
    perceive in our beloved.

Does the moon laugh or weep, so far away, yet so full and fecund with
    celestial glory?

Hecate's horns dive down into the dark blood red of the day's remains, into that
    dark night of soul,

And as a chalice filled with the hopeful draught of life, and night's mysterious
    whispers of eternity and rest,

She calls forth the gift of the evening star, to remind us of other suns in distance
    lands that call our name.

What wondrous bed of night opens to the union of these lovers, who now are
    gently touching, and then parting from sweet embrace,

Called to a new day, when time and space separate those who love, and shall love
    again before long,

When age and wisdom cycle round to separate fullness born of union, but clarified,
    and raised to glory by opposing forces.

Wait my beloved, for like the wandering stars, our fate also is ruled by a greater
    destiny that knows, in time, all mysteries shall unfold their secrets.

The Composite Picture of Sophia

You are made of the Primal Beginnings,

The Mothers, the foundations of creation —

The Original Ocean of Dark Spirit Light

That was yet to be born into the Light of Love.

The composite picture of Sophia evolving alongside of humanity is the history of human intellectual development. Emerson wrote about this topic in his last work, *The Natural History of the Intellect*, in a philosophical fashion that examined human soul qualities and their refinement.

A. E. also wrote about the same soul development that leads to Imagination, Inspiration, and Intuition through the enhancement of higher soul qualities. Without using any religious terms or relating to church doctrines, both of these writers described the same experience of meeting the Divine Feminine in very real terms.

Development of the soul leads to knowing the Great Mother as a living, fully present being who demonstrates Her care and support with every step of self-development towards the spirit. Without a claim to revelation or prophecy, both Emerson and A. E. transport us directly into heaven. They use the intellect to create living Imaginations that connect us to the spiritual world. With common words devoid of jargon or dogma, these writers show that the human soul can experience the divine without an intermediary priest, guru, or teacher.

We stand wide open before the Creatrix in the heart of our soul knowing that every step we take has also been taken by beings on rungs above us, showing the way.

The selections below convey a wondrous and comprehensive picture of Sophia in Her many facets. The love and devotion demonstrated by the followers of Sophia is unending. Sophia has never forsaken humanity. Through all our strivings, She stands ready to help.

In ancient times, only the Great Mother was worshipped as the sole deity. We also see that in modern times, the Mother is still revered and praised with the highest words language can forge.

The primacy of the Mother of Creation seems self-evident. The rational mind must logically conclude from a thorough examination of both self and world that the divine permeates everything. Therefore we, too, are divine.

As such, we are developing ourselves to become greater spiritual beings who assume more responsibility and authority over time. This development, from life to life, is the *eternal*—it makes itself known in our life through Wisdom.

Wisdom was available for the ancients as a second nature, a second sight, if you will, or as many refer to it, "the sixth sense." Clairvoyance, clairaudience, and telekinesis were naturally available to the ancient sage and shaman. Worship of the Great Mother was universal because the clairvoyants all saw the same divine Being permeating the world. When clairvoyant ability began to decrease, human thinking became confined to the brain. So, too, did Sophia as Wisdom become more distant to human perception. This development was for the purpose of creating freedom in human thinking.

As time progressed, the Divine Feminine Trinity, the Triple Goddess of Birth, Death, and Rebirth, was subsumed by male gods for control of culture. From 2100 B.C. on, matriarchal guidance darkened as the male gods took the place of the female. Sophia receded to a place beyond the stars, awaiting a time when humans could once again perceive Her being, not just Her forces in the realm of nature.

Sophia's facets changed continually and are still changing today. Her revelation is constant and never-ending. It takes on many forms that may appear different only because the observer is tainting the perception of Her with his own limitations.

Clairvoyants have never stopped seeing Sophia and Her work. Throughout history, they have described beautiful encounters that are physical, filled with passion and love. Many seekers of Wisdom have sacrificed all just to see Her or experience Her divine presence. They discovered that their personal souls were intertwined inextricably with Sophia, linked with Her in spiritual evolution.

Sophia and the seekers began to unite. But there remained one problem. The triple nature of the Goddess must be born in the seeker's triple soul nature so that it can model itself after Sophia's threefoldness.

This threefold soul nature had to be recognized and brought into a coherent harmony so that it could be used to embody the Wisdom of Sophia.

The threefold nature of the soul of humans is the mirror of Sophia, the Creatrix and Sustainer of the universe.

Humans are the image of Sophia.

She is the image of the universe.

The threefold soul of humans is the sacred Temple of Wisdom. The seven pillars are the seven harmonies of the planets resonating in the heart, head, and organs activating the Seven Holy Virtues. Sophia built this temple. It is Her greatest masterwork of beauty, harmony, and love.

Humans use Sophia's Temple of Wisdom as a place of learning. There, knowledge is forged into Wisdom. The soul is set free. It becomes a winged spirit that mounts the heights of heaven with fiery moral deeds of love. When thinking, feeling, and willing become Imagination, Inspiration, and Intuition, humans become angelic. Sophia is there to give us our wings.

Throughout the development of the human intellect, Sophia and the concept of a Divine Feminine Trinity have evolved dramatically into the modern view of spirituality. We need to do more than just resurrect the Triple Goddess and worship Her old forms. We need to see Sophia as Mother/Daughter/Holy Sophia in one Being with three faces.

The Holy Sophia cannot be held static. She has evolved greatly over the past 4,000 years of human intellectual development. In the ensuing millennia, Christ the Son has come to Earth. With the Daughter's help, They have rewritten spiritual history through the gift of the Mystery of Sophia Christos. The Holy Sophia has come to Earth to grow as a human alongside humanity, to be the collective consciousness of our soul and spiritual evolution. Christ sent the Holy Spirit to attend humanity's spiritual needs as the Comforter. In this way, the Holy Sophia works closely with the Holy Spirit to bring illumination to the soul and spirit of humanity.

The Holy Sophia is growing into Her angelic nature at this time. At every moment, She stands ready to assist and record the growth of every human soul as it blossoms into its angelic spiritual nature.

Much has changed over these four millennia. As humanity has advanced, the Father Ground of Being and the Mother Goddess have grown as well.

Only at this point in human consciousness could a new vision of the current manifestation of Sophia's revelation as a Divine Feminine Trinity arise. Sophia's Trinity is the primal trinity that developed prior to the male trinity. Both are necessary for the manifestation and sustenance of creation. Every person needs a Mother and a Father. Our Earth realm needed the Son of God and the Daughter of the Goddess to descend from heaven to the Earth to experience the human condition and redeem it.

"We need not fight over the darkening of the Goddess, for that was necessary in the scheme of evolution. Rather, we should fully resurrect Her nature."

These divine twins, the Son and Daughter, joined Love and Wisdom together for all times to come. Their union is the redemption of the Earthly realm, which is ruled by a dual nature.

It took the unity of two divine archetypes to end duality through the paradox: two can be one and yet separate. Their timeless example of Love and Wisdom will stand as the perfected vehicle for all alchemical weddings of a purified soul to their higher spirit self—Sophia Christos.

This gift from both Trinities is the ultimate legacy of a parent to a child, to create a path of initiation for all others to follow. The initiation can be done with the soul and spirit of an individual or as two separate people, which is much harder. Here is the fulfillment of the prophecy: "The child becomes greater than the father or the mother."

The gift of the Holy Spirit, sent by Christ to be the comforter of the apostles, is the fiery baptism of the spirit that allows the Christ to work through the hearts and minds of His followers. The Holy Spirit is close to us. He provides us with all we need to grow and develop into the spiritual beings Christ said we would become. The Holy Spirit brings us our spiritual inheritance.

The Holy Sophia was sent by the Daughter of the Goddess, the Being of Wisdom, to grow as a human (without the encumbrances of a physical body) alongside humanity, offering guidance and support for aspiring seekers of Wisdom. The Holy Sophia has grown into Her spirit self, an angelic body that stands just above humanity, beckoning us to climb the sacred mountain and don our wings to mount the spiritual skies.

Sophia does lead us "ever upwards and on," as the poet says. She is the soul of humanity reclaiming its spiritual rights, so close to us that She knows our every breath, thought, and deed.

The two Trinities, both Male and Female, work together so closely that it is hard to tell them apart. We must no longer confuse the two and combine them into a less refined picture. All aspects of the biographies of Sophia are necessary to raise Her story out of obscurity, back to the central position She holds in the heavens and on Earth.

> *"Love will lead us to this New Age of Sophia."*

We need not fight over the darkening of the Goddess, for that was necessary in the scheme of evolution. Rather, we should fully resurrect Her nature. Give back Her throne. Redefine Her current manifestation. Create accurate systems that describe Her forces and works.

We should develop new leading images, symbols, and parables that try to embody the scope of Sophia without limiting Her manifestation. As we do so, we must remember that any limits in our system to imagine Sophia will also be the limits in the systems we use to create our own spiritual development.

Sophia must be seen for what She is, without limit. To imagine Her as a subset of the Male Trinity or some type of created being secondary to a male god only limits the thinking of the seeker. An inexplicable mystery, She must now be revealed. We must Know Her.

Words cannot describe the experience of the *becoming* of the world—the life, love, and being of all. There are no words to describe such mysteries.

The symbol of the Trinity of the Divine Feminine and the biographies of Sophia are starting points from which to build a more complete picture of the Temple of Wisdom.

This Temple is in the making. Our personal efforts matter a great deal in its design and composition. As the Temple becomes more detailed, we realize that the Temple is the Wisdom of the human body, soul, and spirit.

Once again, the *trinity* reigns supreme both inside and outside of the human body as we balance our three soul forces with Sophia in the world.

Throughout this book, the faces and facets of Sophia have been presented not as a dogma or doctrine, but as an artistic expression. This is part of a continuing effort to visualize, praise, and evoke the Goddess in the world and in ourselves. There is no perfectly correct or accurate description of the spiritual world, if words are used. Therefore, many descriptions of encounters with Sophia have been gathered in the selections so that the plethora of images could weave together a pala (wisdom cloak). This cloak may then be gently draped over Sophia's shoulders to reveal a slight bit of Her divine form and the beauty of Her visage.

> *"When new angels get their wings, Sophia teaches them how to fly."*

As we imagine Sophia evolving through time, changing in pace with humanity's developing intellect, the golden footprints of the divine are on the path ahead of us, showing the way home. The revelation of Sophia is a testament to humanity's efforts to accept their inheritance as angels in the making and continue on that path.

When new angels get their wings, Sophia teaches them how to fly.

We should not limit our vision of either ourselves or Sophia. As we grow, so will our scope of understanding Wisdom through Her. Love will lead us to this New Age of Sophia, Sophia Christos.

The love of Sophia Christos feeds our soul and births our spirit. We are as unlimited as the beings with which we commune. They grow as we grow.

It is in Sophia's best interest to help us assume our spiritual roles, so we can begin the work She and other beings have been doing for us.

It is time that the baby spirit in us begins to stand and take first steps towards our parents. When our eyes open, we will see Sophia there on the path with Her hand outstretched, waiting for us, encouraging us to step forward. We will be supported by the Queen of Heaven and Earth, our Holy Mother Sophia.

Union Complete

You are made of the Primal Beginnings,
The Mothers, the foundations of creation—
The Original Ocean of Dark Spirit Light
That was yet to be born into the Light of Love
Only shared with another who can reflect your vision
And embrace the blessings of Grace made whole.

The calling of a New Dawn, an age of wonder and bliss
Dancing in the flames of history's mistakes brightly glowing
In a new sky, filled with spirit whirlwinds of color,
Bowing down to acknowledge the deeds of courage and love,
Freely rising as luminous gifts and offerings to Heaven
Every time Sophia's Christened love frees Lucifer's brilliance
Into wisdom-seeds of mercy gathering the faithful to Christ's altar.

We are wrapped in the star-studded Cloak of Sophia, full of diadems
Radiating through suffering's Wisdom-light that spans all time
Weaving Wisdom's foundation through the heart's tempered gold
Into the worlds we already move through during sacred dreams
Weaving our single efforts into fabrics of luminous glory.

Bursting from the heart of the Earth, where we kneel in sleep
Folding our hands with resolve that our hearts will love each and every thing,
Releasing from enchantment the desires that bind our souls to Earth—
Embracing Her—who shows that it takes two to unite through love,
Outshining the little worlds we each hold sacred and dear,
To create for Sophia, on Sacred Ground, the gift of "love come true."

Selections from
History

Her Physical Body
2100–1400 B.C.

From 2100 B.C. to 1400 B.C., the Holy Sophia was developing Her physical body. (See Appendix F for the Biographical Timeline of Sophia.)

Greek Myths, Robert Graves (Neolithic reference)

The whole of Neolithic Europe, to judge from surviving artifacts and myths, had a remarkably homogeneous system of religious ideas, based on worship of the many-titled Mother-goddess, who was also known in Syria and Libya. Ancient Europe had no gods. The Great Goddess was regarded as immortal, changeless, and omnipotent; and the concept of fatherhood had not been introduced into religious thought.

All original descriptions of the divine have a strong feminine source. Often considered threefold, this divine source governs birth, death, and rebirth. One can imagine that an animistic response to watching the birth of children could have been at the heart of this worship.

Some believe that all humans began as female, just as the human fetus is female prior to the twelfth week of gestation. Maria Gimbutas pioneered the work, now generally accepted by archeologists, that all pre–Indo-European societies of "Old Europe" were matriarchal.

Most ancient texts are clear: before a male God supposedly created the world, there already was a female being present who was the substance of creation. She seems to have existed prior to the creation story. This primal nature of the Great Mother Goddess makes Her the "Creatrix."

Gunther Zuntz (Paleolithic reference)

To be gripped by the realization of deity in woman, the spring and harbor of life, mankind did not have to wait for the invention of agriculture. Everywhere, from Spain to Serbia, so many Paleolithic documents of this devotion have emerged, and with traits so specific recurring in Neolithic relics, as to forbid the facile inference that this change, however epochal, in man's living habits could by itself account for what is loosely called "cult of the Mother Goddess" … What evidence there is—and it is not a little—points to concerns more comprehensive and profound. This is the oldest godhead perceived by mankind.

All aspects of a male God have previously been attributed to the Great Mother. Indeed, there are many qualities of the Goddess as Creatrix that the male God does not hold.

God was not the substance of creation, or the divine waters, or the original Mother, or the chaos of creation, or any of the specifically female references to the aspects of creation. The Goddess was primary in manifestation.

God the Father did not manifest. During the act of creation, he projected his creation onto the feminine principal. This primary Goddess has been found in the worship of aboriginal cultures worldwide.

Egyptian Isis Poem (2100 B.C.)

I gave and ordained laws for men, which no one is able to change …
I am she that is called goddess by women …

I divided the earth from the heaven.

I showed the paths of the stars.

I ordered the course of the sun and the moon.

I devised business in the sea.

I made strong the right.

I brought together women and men.

I appointed to women to bring their infants to birth in the tenth month.

I ordained that parents should be loved by children.

I laid punishment upon those disposed without natural affection towards their parents.

I made with my brother Osiris an end to the eating of men.

I revealed mysteries unto men.

I taught men to honor images of the gods ...

I made the right to be stronger than gold and silver.

I ordained that the true should be thought good ...

I am the Queen of rivers and winds and sea.

No one is held in honor without my knowing it.

I am the Queen of war.

I am the Queen of the thunderbolt.

I stir up the sea and I calm it.

I am in the rays of the sun ...

I set free those in bonds ...

I overcome Fate.

In this ancient poem, Isis is the sole creator deity. She changed her nature many times in Egyptian history, but began as the sun, moon, earth, and all other creations. She was the teacher of humanity, described as intimately imparting all necessary knowledge to mortals.

She was honored in her roles. There is only a slight reference to her brother Osiris as a male force of the divine; he is obviously secondary.

The image of Isis can be found to change dramatically over the long history of Egypt.

Ishtar Poem (2000 B.C.)

Praise to the Goddess, most awesome of goddesses
She is clothed with pleasure and love
She is laden with vitality, charm and voluptuousness
The goddess—with her counsel
The fate of everything she holds in her hand
At her glance is created joy
Power, magnificence the protecting deity, and the guardian spirit.

In the most ancient texts, there is no reference to a male deity. In some sources, the Goddess is self-propagating and needs no male influence. Ishtar's supremacy is unquestioned, yet unfortunately unnoticed by many researchers and historians.

It is hard to imagine how a Goddess so powerful and revered could be ignored and marginalized. In these first selections, we see Sophia described as Creator, Mother of All, and the Goddess of Nature. At this point, the Holy Sophia is only now incarnating. She is beginning to see personal human thinking start to arise and displace the image of the single, male creator with the primary Creatrix.

Purascharanollasa Tantra (1700 B.C.)

All the pilgrimage-centers exist in woman's body.

This statement indicates that Sophia as the divine is drawing closer to human perception as the outer pilgrimage centers become located in the body of all women. Sophia is placed in every woman because they have similar capacities of birth and resurrection.

Her Etheric Body
1400–700 B.C.

From 1400 B.C. to 700 B.C., the Holy Sophia was developing Her etheric body.

The Rig Veda (1700–1100 B.C.)

That which is beyond heaven, beyond this earth, beyond the gods and asuras—
*   what first embryo/germ, wherein all the gods beheld each other, did the waters*
*   (Ap) hold?*
The waters held that very first embryo/germ where all the gods came together,
that one in which all the worlds abide, placed on the navel of the Unborn.

Previously, Ap was considered the Creator Goddess, but in this selection she has been reduced to a sideline reference. Already, in this time period, we can begin to see Sophia as Ap pushed aside and marginalized into a footnote.

The Rig Veda (1700–1100 B.C.)

I (Vac) am queen, gatherer of riches, knowing, the first among those worthy of being honored.
I am she, having many stations and much bestowing, whom the gods have distributed in
*   many places. Through me, he who discerns, who breathes, who indeed hears what is said,*
*   eats his food. Though ignorant of this, they dwell in me.*
Hear that you are heard! What I tell you is to be believed.
I, myself, say this welcome news to gods and men.

He whom I love, I make him powerful, I make him a Brahmin,

I make him a seer, I make him wise … I have entered into heaven and earth.

I bring forth the father at the summit of this creation.

My womb is within the waters, in the ocean.

Thence I extend over all worlds, and I touch heaven with my uppermost part.

I also blow forth like the wind, reaching all the worlds.

Beyond heaven, beyond the earth, so great have I become through my grandeur.

The buffalo cow (Vac) lowed, she fashioned the floods, having become one-footed, two-footed, four-footed, eight-footed, nine-footed, she who in the highest heaven has a thousand syllables.

From her flow forth the heavenly oceans, on account of which the four directions exist, and from her flows the imperishable syllable, on which the entire universe exists.

Here we see the beginning of the sublimation of the feminine divine. Vac is said to have all of the powers of heaven and Earth. She should be worshiped and considered the mother of all things. Yet in the beginning statement, the male priests have now inserted that the "gods" made Vac.

This is clearly the beginning of human individualization. The human thinker can now separate himself from what clairvoyance tells him is the reality. He adds the male counterpart to fit the Earthly model he understands: mother and father create together.

The Rig Veda (1700–1100 B.C.)

Indeed, all your names, oh gods, are to be honored, praised, and worshipped;

you that are born here of Aditi, the waters (ap), and earth (prthivi), hear my call.

Aditi is the heaven, Aditi is the middle region, Aditi is the mother, she is the father, she is the son;

all the gods are Aditi, and the five clans; Aditi is what has been born and what will be born.

In conception of strength we call with speech the great mother,

Aditi, on whom this whole world has settled.

    Even though this passage states that Aditi is the father, mother, and son, she is still marginalized by the injunction that all of the gods' names are to be honored and praised.

    If Aditi is everything, why do new gods also require worship? This is clearly an attempt to strengthen the divinity of male gods, who are the children of Aditi.

The Wisdom of Solomon (1500 B.C.)

Wisdom is bright and unfading,

And she is easily seen by those who love her,

And found by those who search for her.

She forestalls those who desire her, by making herself known first.

The man who rises early to seek her will not have to toil,

For he will find her sitting at his gates.

For to think of her is the highest understanding,

And the man who is vigilant for her sake will soon be free from care.

For she goes about in search of those who are worthy of her,

And she graciously appears to them in their paths,

And meets them in every thought.

For wisdom is more mobile than any motion,

And she penetrates and permeates everything, because she is so pure;

For she is the breath of the power of God,

And a pure emanation of his almighty glory;

Therefore nothing defiled can enter into her.

For she is a reflection of the everlasting light,

And a spotless mirror of the activity of God,

And a likeness of his goodness.

Though she is one, she can do all things,

And while remaining in herself, she makes everything new.

And passing into holy souls, generation after generation,

She makes them friends of God, and prophets.

For God loves nothing but the man who lives with wisdom.

For she is fairer than the sun, or any group of stars;

Compared with light, she is found superior; for night succeeds to it,

But evil cannot overpower wisdom.

The Wisdom Books of the Hebrews profoundly illuminate the evolving relationship with Sophia. Here She is described as being present with God at creation and a mirror of his activity.

In the first paragraph, Sophia stands alone with the seeker, helping each step of the way in developing wisdom. She is sought after, much desired, and graciously meets the seeker in his thoughts. This is a very good description of the Holy Sophia working with the thinker to develop higher qualities that transform knowledge into wisdom.

In the Wisdom traditions, Sophia is personal, close, and intimately concerned with spiritual development. With access to indescribable power and majesty, She can take the seeker anywhere that She wants to lead him. Sophia as Wisdom is the Virgin Bride that all advanced thinkers are looking to wed.

Wisdom of Sirach (1500 B.C.)

I prayed and understanding was given me; I called upon God, and the spirit of wisdom
    came to me.

I loved her above health and beauty, and chose to have her instead of light, for the light
    that cometh from her never goeth out.

And all such things as are either secret or manifest, them I know.

For wisdom, which is the worker of all things, taught me; for in her is an understanding spirit, holy, one only, manifold, subtle, lively, clear, undefiled, plain, not subject to hurt, loving the thing that is good, quick which cannot be letted, ready to do good.

Kind to man, steadfast, sure, free from care, having all power, overseeing all things, and going through all understanding, pure, and most sublime spirits.

For wisdom is more moving than any motion; she passeth and goeth through all things by reason of her pureness.

For she is the breath of the power of God, and a pure influence flowing from the glory of the Almighty;

For she is the brightness of the everlasting light, the unspotted mirror of the power of God, and the image of his goodness.

And being but one, she can do all things: and remaining in herself, she maketh all things new: and in all ages entering into holy souls, she maketh them friends of God and prophets.

For she is more beautiful than the sun, and above all the order of stars: being compared with light, she is found before it.

I loved her, and sought her out from my youth, I desired to make her my spouse, and I was a lover of her beauty.

What greater praise could a writer give to the divine than as stated in this passage? The fulfillment of all of the seeker's efforts is met by encountering Sophia as Wisdom. The experience leaves no room for speculation; Sophia is a being that will visit you and commune with your higher nature. As Beauty, Bride, and Lover, She is pictured quite beautifully here, with a clarity that describes Her ability to give the seeker all good things necessary for him to evolve and ascend to higher realms of being.

Svetasvatara Upanishad (1000 B.C.)

O Lord Brahma, the Great Goddess Prakrti, your source and mother,
and that of Vishnu and the other gods, has been apportioned out ...
Those knowing the truth call her by various names:
the one possessing four-faces, the origin and the womb of the universe,
primordial cow, the foundation, Maya, Vidya, or Prakrti.
They call her unborn, singular, red, white, and black,
creating all beings as having the same form as her.

    Prakrti is stated to be the source and mother of Brahma, Vishnu, and the other gods. Therefore, she is the primal divinity and her praise in this Upanishad is comprehensive and inclusive. The question arises, "What is there for the male gods to do if Prakrti is the mother of all?"

Devi Upanishad (800 B.C.)

Great Goddess, who art Thou?
She replies: I am essentially Brahma (the Absolute).
From me has proceeded the world comprising Prakrti (material substance)
and Purusha (cosmic consciousness), the void and the Plenum.
I am (all forms of) bliss and non-bliss.
Knowledge and ignorance are Myself.
I am the five elements and also what is different from
the panchabhutas (five gross elements)
and tanmatras (five subtle elements).
I am the entire world.
I am the Veda as well as what is different from it.
I am unknown.
Below and above and around am I.

In this passage, we see that confusion becomes institutionalized. The feminine is simply subsumed in a sentence wherein the Great Goddess is said to be Brahma. The feminine that gave birth to Brahma is now one and the same. She is simply called the masculine, and no one seems to notice.

The Goddess created the Trinity of Brahma, Vishnu, and Shiva, yet now She is positioned somewhere beneath Brahma. The subtle slip into oblivion of the primary place of the Great Goddess has begun.

Uttara Tantra (800 B.C.)

Look upon a woman as a goddess whose special energy she is, and honor her in that state.

In theory, this statement is wonderful, but the Hindus still expected a wife to throw herself alive onto the burning pyre of her husband at his death. The place of woman was respected, but in the general tenure of the caste system in ancient India, the female was certainly secondary to the male. We can see that the ancients did perceive Sophia descending into the physical body of humans as they developed more independence in thinking. Some might say that placing the Goddess exclusively in the female body was the end of the worship of the Great Mother.

S'vetasvataropanishad (800 B.C.)

That which, in the beginning, sent forth the Creator and favored him with the storehouse of all knowledge, the Veda; I, desirous of liberation, betake myself to It, the ever-effulgent light, revealing Its eternal Self through the intellect.

We see here that the Creator Goddess is referred to as a force, not a being. This force sends forth the male creator. Here seems to be double-talk and a clear sublimation of contrary teachings found in surrounding passages of this work.

Interestingly, the self as intellect is also referred to as coming into being. As the male-dominated priesthood subsumes the roles of the Feminine Divine, the intellect is born. The self of the human being comes into existence as an independent thinker.

Panchadasi (800 B.C.)

Setting aside everything which becomes the object of knowledge in this world, there yet remains a residuum the real essence of knowledge. The knowledge that this is the Real Self, is true knowledge of the Self.

The real essence of knowledge is now referred to as the Self, which plays a role in further intellectual development and the description of both the divine and the divine in man.

Yogavasishtha (800 B.C.)

He continually sees the Real Self, who studies to unify philosophy, and the teacher's explanations, with the facts of his own consciousness.

This is a tremendous step in the development of human thinking when the newborn human self can now hold an individualized opinion about philosophy. Not only is the self "born" in this description, but there is also the need to unify philosophy.

This indicates that numerous philosophies have been created from speculation. As soon as the self comes into being, multiple philosophies arise, demonstrating that individualized thinking leads to differences of opinion.

Chandogyopanishad (800 B.C.)

That Self which is beyond sin, decay, death, sorrow; which requires no food nor drink; which is all accomplished desire, all fulfilled thought; should be looked for, should be inquired after. He gains access to all worlds, has all his desires fulfilled, who, having known this Self, realizes it fully in himself and all.

The self is now described as "all accomplished desire, all fulfilled thought" which can gain access to all worlds. This self is directly linked to thinking and consciousness through desire. Desire predicates individualization. "Thoughts fulfilled" indicate that the *I* has the possibility of fulfilling thoughts. This concept indicates that thoughts must first be developed to become fulfilled. Therefore, the development of thinking and desire develops the self, which is the path sought to contact the divine.

Her Astral Body
700 B.C.–33 A.D.

From 700 B.C. to 33 A.D., the Holy Sophia was developing Her astral body.

<u>Kurma Purana</u> (700 B.C.)

She (Laksmi) is that supreme power wholly consisting of me, of the nature of Brahma, my beloved, endless maya by which this is universe is deluded.
Through her, I delude, swallow up, and recreate the whole world ...
Depending on parts of her, the twice-born and the gods—
Brahma, Siva, and so forth—have become possessed of power.
She is my entire power.
She is the source of the entire universe, prakrti possessing the three gunas.

Brahma claims here that all of the powers of Laksmi, the Great Goddess, are part of him. Then he says that he accomplishes his work through her. In both cases, Brahma is trying to subsume and absorb the powers of Laksmi. Yet he breaks down and admits that she is his entire power. This clear attempt to assume the feminine divine characteristics with a poorly disguised philosophical footnote is tantamount to admission by the male-dominated priesthood to the intent to hide the feminine nature of the divine.

Devi-Mahatmya (700 B.C.)

The Goddess said: ... Formerly, I alone existed.

There was nothing else whatsoever ...

At that time, my own form was named intellect, consciousness, and supreme Brahma.

I am incomprehensible, indefinable, unparalleled,

My perfect sakti is known as maya.

It is neither existent or nonexistent, nor both, nor self-contradictory.

This indefinable entity always exists.

This is one of the most beautiful philosophical paradoxes ever written, and a most accurate description of Sophia. Sophia states Her primal and singular nature, Her creations of intellect, consciousness, and Brahma.

Brahma is mentioned because Sophia did create a priesthood to administer the male-oriented Mystery initiation wisdom. Subsumed, She is part of the plan for developing free human beings. Most interesting is the syllogistic description of Her nature that is a triple paradox, the basis for a philosophical Trinity of Being that defies all comprehension.

Devi-Mahatmya (700 B.C.)

By you the universe is born, by you this world is created.

By you it is protected, O Devi. By you it is consumed at the end.

This is a beautiful description of the Trinity of birth, death, and rebirth which is the ubiquitous nature of the Great Goddess.

Orphic Hymns: To the Mother of the Gods (600 B.C.)

Divinely honored, mother of the deathless gods, nurse of all.

Look in our direction; accomplishing Goddess, thou Lady, be with us.

Your fast-running chariot is drawn by bull-killing lions.

You carry the sceptre of command, the famous axis of the sky, thou, many
  named, majestic.

Your throne is in the centre of the world, and therefore,

Yours is the earth, gently granting nourishment to mortals.

From you the race of immortals and mortals poured out.

From you grew mighty rivers and all the oceans.

Once you were called Hestia, now we name you Giver of Prosperity.

Because you graciously provide all good things mortals.

Attend our Mysteries, Lady who loves the drumbeat.

All subduer, Phrygian, Savior, Bedfellow of time.

Celestial, ancient, life-gathering, frenzy loving.

Come in joy, Agreeable one, to our holy celebrations.

As we move to Greece and examine this Orphic Hymn, we hear that the Mother of the Gods is the creator of the deathless gods and nurse of all. This Mother created the eternal gods. She cares for all things in nature as a Mother of All, Hestia.

The descriptions are physical, sensual, earthly, and divine. They depict the Mother in many of Her facets. Orpheus asks Her to look in his direction and be with him. This is almost a personal entreaty to a physical, perceptible being.

She is asked to attend the Mysteries and directly interact with the aspirant. The Goddess has become visible through the devotions and practices of the priest and is asked to come into his being. Any distance between the thinker and the Holy Sophia is closing. A personal, intimate relationship is developing.

Orpheus is beckoning the Goddess to come closer and take over his divine efforts.

Tao Te Ching, Lao Tzu (6th Century B.C.)

The spirit of the fountain never dies.

It is called the mysterious feminine.

It is the root of all heaven and earth.

Frail, frail it is, hardly existing.

But touch it, it will never run dry.

This mysterious description of the eternal feminine is precious in its nature. Lao Tzu describes both the most powerful and the most sensitive natures existing in the same thing at one time. Again, Sophia is described as a paradox, but that doesn't stop him from telling you to "touch it" because it will never run dry. This eternal fountain of the spirit that creates heaven and Earth is frail. It hardly exists, but we must find it. This is a beautiful description of thinking as the creative divine. Truly Lao Tzu knew Sophia well.

The Timaeus, Plato (423—348 B.C.)

But soul, being interwoven everywhere to the uttermost bounds of the universe, and enfolded round it externally in a circle, and herself revolving within herself, gave rise to the divine beginning of an unceasing and wise life throughout all time. And, indeed, the body of the universe was created visible; but she (the soul) invisible, participating in reason and harmony, and the most excellent of the created things, being made by Him Who is of Intelligible and Eternal Beings the most excellent.

The soul descends either by the will of the Intelligibles or by losing its wings which allow it to rise to the perception of the Intelligibles. The souls that descend through losing their wings are those that are not yet perfected and cannot therefore sustain the flight to the Intelligibles.

The natural power of a wing is to raise up on high that which is heavy, and bring it to that place where the race of the Gods dwell; and indeed among the parts of the body wings share most in the divine nature. But that which is divine is beautiful, wise and good, and has every similar perfection. It is by such things, then, that the growth of the soul's wings is chiefly nourished and increased, but through the opposites of these, the base and the evil, the wing languishes and is destroyed.

Love therefore is the "fire-laden bond" which connects all things, and gives to the soul the wings by which she may mount to the contemplation of the Beautiful and thereby attain to union with the Good.

Since, therefore, every artist is a lover, and since the highest of all arts and that for which all others exist is the Art of the Perfect Life by which the soul is restored and enabled to ascend to Reality and to God, he that loves the souls of his fellow-men and leads them, by whatever path, by his paintings, his music, his laws, his discourse or his philosophy, along the way that leads to the heights, will be the greatest artist, for he will both himself attain to initiation into the most perfect Mysteries and will confer like a blessing upon those he loves.

This description is an accurate assessment of the nature of the soul and spirit. Wings are the spirit that can grow from the aspirant's soul efforts to rise to the higher realms. Greek philosophers were not "fantasizing" that real wings would physically grow on the human body. Nor should we image that real wings are necessary for spiritual development.

The Greeks were speaking metaphorically and literally. It is very hard for us to reconcile such statements with materialistic thinking.

The lateral ventricles in the brain look a great deal like wings, and they are connected to higher processes of thought.

The heart has two unused ventricles that sit on the top of each chamber, just waiting to open like wings and add a new dimension to the heart.

Wings denoted many things to the Greeks, but in this case they are referring to higher forms of thought, called Imaginations. These thoughts directly connect the thinker to higher archetypes that are the source of earthly forms.

Called Intelligibles, the Greeks communicated with these beings directly. They blessed the thinker's life in tangible ways. For the Greek, higher thoughts were outside of himself. The thinker had to rise to thoughts to commune with them.

Thoughts were living beings. Love was the force that drove the thinker to rise up and perceive the Intelligibles.

The Chaldean Oracles, Zarathustra (220 B.C.)

Hecate or Diana is the Gateway of Life, the Vivific Ruling Principle Who is said to be filled with undefiled powers from the Amiliktoi, and to impart this characteristic to all beings that pass through Her mysterious gateway, at the crossroads of life and death. For death is but an entrance into Life Supernal: and life is but a birth into the realms of generation. Proserpine, the Ruling Soul, is the power whereby the Soul preserves the middle or abiding subsistence at the same time that it merges upward or downward, either to the Above or the Below. Hence, when the Soul is identified with the realms of nature and matter, Proserpine is said to be united to Pluto; but in her pre-existent and post-existent states, when reigning on high purified from matter, Proserpine is said to be united with Jupiter. Minerva, or Ruling Virtue, reveals the way of return, converts ends to beginnings, preserves the order of wholes undefiled and unvanquished by matter, and fills all who are able to participate with intellectual light. She is the Fountain of all fountains, and the womb that holds all things together. This Goddess, binding together the sphere of the Intellectuals, and emblossoming the vivific plenitude, emits all the intellectual powers in rivers of life and is the Source of Sources, and the bond of all sources.

From about the hollows beneath the ribs of Her right side (Hecate) there bursts in mighty fullness a fountain of Primordial Soul, animating to the uttermost light, fire, ether, worlds. In the left side of Hecate there is a Fountain of Virtue, remaining wholly within, not sending forth its virginity. And about the shoulders of the Goddess, vast Nature hangs. In accordance with the Purpose of the Father, I, the Soul, dwell, animating all things with heat.

The Demiurgus, possessing and comprehending in Himself the Solar Fountain, generates likewise, in conjunction with the Principles and Rulers, the Solar Powers and the Triad of Solar Gods, through Whom all things are elevated, perfected, and filled with Intellectual Goods. They are called The Triple Sun, which is invisible and intellectual, within and beyond all the suns of the universe; Mercury the Super-essential Light, Venus-Urania the Intelligible Light, and Apollo the Sovereign Sun. The First is the announcer of Truth and the Intellectual Light which subsists occultly in the Gods Themselves; the Second undermines everything confused and exterminates all disorder; and the Third renders all things commensurable and friendly to each other, through harmonic reasoning. Mercury reveals the Light of Divine Truth; Venus-Urania reveals the Light of Divine Beauty; and Apollo reveals the Light of Divine Goodness or Harmony. Although this Triple Sun is a dazzling light in itself, it is surrounded by a profound mystical darkness.

The Triple Sun is the Light of the Divine Intellect, which is hidden, as it were, in the heart of the Great World Mother as well as in the deeps of the Soul.

The Triple Goddess is first mentioned as Diana, Proserpine, and Minerva. Then, before the selection is over, She becomes the Trinity of Mercury, Venus, and Apollo. We also hear the implied idea that the Triple Goddess fell to Earth and journeyed to the underworld to redeem it. Then the Triple Goddess is attributed to being the Primordial Soul and the creator of all nature.

Within just a single selection, we see a clear sliding into a male-dominated divinity. This might seem confusing to some who aren't watching out for the darkening of the Triple Goddess. The last line is wonderfully confusing. The new Trinity of Mercury, Venus, and Apollo is the Divine Intellect which is hidden in the Great World Mother and the soul.

This is telling us that the Trinity of Sophia can be seen in the world through thinking, feeling, and willing as truth, beauty, and goodness. Humans embody the Triple Goddess in their capacity to experience truth, beauty, and goodness.

Lotus Sutra (100 B.C.)

In the lands of the universe there is no place
Where She does not manifest Herself ...
Compassion wondrous as a great cloud,
Pouring spiritual rain like nectar,
Quenching the flames of distress.

First, it is established that "She" is compassion existing everywhere and that She also is close and personal, bringing nectar to quench distress. This dichotomy of being both everywhere and personally with the aspirant is a quantum paradox of space that Sophia bridges to care for Her children. She is everywhere if we accept Her abundant grace.

On the Nature of the Universe, Lucretius (99–55 B.C.)

Mother of Aeneas and his race, delight of men and gods, life-giving Venus, it is your doing that under the wheeling constellations of the sky all nature teems with life, both the sea that buoys up our ships and the earth that yields our food. Through you all living creatures are conceived and come forth to look upon the sunlight. Before you the winds flee, and at your coming the clouds forsake the sky. For you the inventive earth flings up sweet flowers.

Since you alone are the guiding power of the universe and without you nothing emerges into the shining sunlit world to grow in joy and loveliness, yours is the partnership I seek.

This selection shows the thinking individual assessing what is known of reality, then deciding to partner with the most powerful divine entity. It illustrates the dilemma of thinking—torn between what was once known by the sages and seers and what is known by the thinking individual.

It would seem prudent that if Venus has the power to create all of nature, then she is the being with whom you would want to connect. This thinking almost creates fear in the thinker, an attitude that would later be solicited by male deities.

Her Sentient Soul
33–700 A. D.

From 33 A.D. to 700 A.D., the Holy Sophia was developing Her sentient soul.

<u>The Protennoia</u> (100 A.D.) **A Sethian Gnostic Text translated by John D. Turner**

I am Protennoia, the Thought that dwells in the Light.

I am the movement that dwells in the All,

She in whom the All takes its stand,

The first-born among those who came to exist,

She who exists before the All ...

Called by three names, although she dwells alone (since she is perfect).

I am invisible within the thought of the Invisible One,

I am revealed in the immeasurable, ineffable,

I am incomprehensible, dwelling in the incomprehensible.

I move in every creature ...

I dwell in those who came to be.

I move in everyone and I delve into them all.

I walk uprightly and those who sleep, I awaken.

I am in the Invisible One within the All.

It is I who counsel those who are hidden since

I know the All that exists in it.

I am numberless beyond everyone, I am immeasurable, ineffable.

Whatever I wish, I shall reveal myself of my own accord.

I am the head of the All.

I exist before the All and I am the All, since I exist in everyone.

I am the thought of the Father

I am mother and the light which she appointed as Virgin

I am their Father and I shall tell you an ineffable Mystery.

This text emphasizes repeatedly that the Protennoia, Sophia, is before All and the creator of the Father, Mother, and Virgin. She is the primal trinity beyond all thought or comprehension. This type of description is trying to show Sophia as the primal, singular divinity with three parts. The recognition of the trinity is the message. We are told that we are created in Her image. Therefore we are a trinity ourselves.

A Valentinian Exposition (100 A.D.)

And whenever Sophia receives her consort and Jesus receives the Christ and the seeds and the angels, then the Pleroma will receive Sophia joyfully, and the All will come to be in unity and reconciliation.

This is a reference to Sophia as the consort of Christ, who is needed for the reconciliation or redemption of creation. Sophia and Christ must unite through the sacred marriage in heaven after suffering the Earthly realm. This is the model for each soul to unite the higher aspects of his soul with the spiritual aspects of his future.

The Transformations of Lucius, Apuleius (125–180 A.D.)

"I am Nature, the universal Mother, mistress of all the elements, primordial child of time, sovereign of all things spiritual, queen of the dead, queen also of the immortals, the single manifestation of all gods and goddesses that are. My nod governs the shining heights of Heaven, the wholesome sea breezes, the lamentable silences of the world below. Though I am worshipped in many aspects, known by countless names, and propitiated with all manner of different rites, yet the whole round earth venerates me."

I fell prostrate at the Goddess's feet, and washed them with my tears as I prayed to her in a voice choked with sobs: "Holiest of the Holy, perpetual comfort of mankind, you whose bountiful graces nourishes the whole world; whose heart turns towards all those in sorrow and tribulation as a mother's to her children; you who take no rest by night, no rest by day, but are always at hand to succor the distressed by land and sea, dispersing the gales that beat upon them. Your hand alone can disentangle the hopelessly knotted skeins of fate, terminate every spell of bad weather, and restrain the stars from harmful conjunction. The gods above adore you, the gods below do homage to you, you set the orb of heaven spinning around the poles, you give light to the sun, you govern the universe, you trample down the powers of Hell. At your voice the stars move, the seasons recur, the spirits of earth rejoice, the elements obey. At your nod the winds blow, clouds drop wholesome rain upon the earth, seeds quicken, buds swell. Birds that fly through the air, beasts that prowl on the mountain, serpents that lurk in the dust, all these tremble in a single awe of you ... I will keep your divine countenance always before my eyes and the secret knowledge of your divinity locked deep in my heart."

Apuleius states that the revelation of the Universal Mother will be kept locked in his heart so that She may always be before his eyes. This direct experience of the Goddess was physical. Apuleius speaks with the Goddess, and She speaks with him directly. He is able to perceive this divine being and tries to describe the experience that will always be before his eyes.

An experience of the Holy Sophia is like meeting an angel who has the power of the Great Goddess. He experienced this, and tried to describe and define the ineffable in mere words. Once again, the Holy Sophia comes closer to the thinking human and now physically appears before him in some part of Her glory.

The Womb of Every Thing, <u>The Apocryphon of John</u> (200 A.D.)

The invisible Spirit looks at himself in the light that surrounds him, the water of life.

He gives to every realm in every way, putting his desire into the spring of the pure-light water.

His thought performed a deed, and she came forth;

She appeared before him in the radiance of his light.

Her light shines like his light, the perfect power of the virginal Spirit.

She is the First Power to come forth from his mind.

She is the Forethought of the All.

She became the womb of everything, for she is prior to them all:

the Mother-Father, the first Man, the Holy Spirit,

and the eternal realm among the invisible realms.

He looked at her with the pure light and she conceived from him.

He begot a spark of light and anointed it until it became

perfect with the goodness of the Spirit.

When it had received from the Spirit, it glorified the Spirit

and the perfect Forethought for whose sake it had come forth.

This convoluted thinking is an attempt to demote Sophia to a creation of a Father God. Unconvincing, it falls back into paradoxes to explain where the male God came from or how he created the goddess called "she" in this selection. Here it states that "His thought performed a deed" and the goddess was created. Creation is related to thinking and thinking doesn't answer paradoxes very well since it prefers the rule of logic. The goddess here is hidden, unnamed, and demoted to a thought creation.

Body, Soul and Spirit—Kephalais, Mani (216–276 A.D.)

Again Mani speaks to his disciples: three images occur in the Elect person. The first is the spiritual image, which is the New Man, which the Light-Mind shall form in him. It enters into him and dwells in him. The second image is the remnant and remainder of the New Man, which is the psychic image that is bound in the flesh like the Old Man. The other one is the corporeal image that is added to them all. Then shall a Virgin of Light come and reveal the spiritual image that is there, which is the New Man. That virgin acts as a guide. She goes on before, and is extended to the heights above, and received into the spiritual image. And she sculpts it and adorns it with the New Man within. It is sealed with all the limbs of this Virgin of Light who is present and dwells in the New Man. So, this is how this living limb shall be purified and live: the one that comes in to the body of the righteous one from without, through the administration of food of various kinds. However, in the spiritual image it shall itself live and be joined with long-sufferingness, the perfection of faith and love that reigns over them all. It is the Virgin of Light who robes the New Man and who shall be called "the Hour of Life." She is the first, but also the last.

The Virgin mentioned above is the Holy Sophia who does enter into the soul and help in the process of transformation. The person is divided into a trinity. The Virgin brings light and sculpts it into the New Man. This is the mission of the Holy Sophia as She feeds and tends the soul so that it may receive nourishment from the spiritual world.

The Cosmic Context: The Redeemer Speaks, Mani

Imagination is a spontaneous act; a perception and affirming of a real relationship between a thought and some material fact. Whenever this resemblance is real, not playful, and is deep, or pointing at the causal identity, it is the act of Imagination. The very design of Imagination, this gift celestial, is to domesticate us in another nature.

Happy beyond the common lot if he learn the secret, that besides the energy of his conscious intellect, his intellect is capable of new energy by abandonment to a higher influence; or, besides his privacy of power as an individual man, there is a great Public Power on which he can draw—by only letting himself go—by a certain abandonment to it—shall I say, by unlocking at all risks his human doors, and suffering the inundation of the ethereal tides to roll and circulate through him. This ecstasy the old philosophers called an inebriation, and said, that Intellect by its relation to what is prior to Intellect is a god.

Thought is identical with the oceanic one which flows hither and thither and sees that all are its offspring, and coins itself indifferently into house or inhabitant, into

planet, man, fish, oak, or grain of sand. Nature is saturated with deity. The particle
is saturated with the elixir of the universe. The thinker radiates as suns and revolves
as planets.

Mani has clearly defined the nature of higher thought that appears as
Imagination. This celestial gift is to "domesticate us in another nature"
or prepare us for ascending into another world. To reach Imagination,
one must "let go of himself," abandon oneself to an inundation of ethereal
tides that cause ecstasy and spiritual inebriation. This is the experience
of Sophia showing us the greater light of our capacity of thinking.
Imagination is the ability to commune with the divine.

Prayer to Terra Matris (200 A.D.)

Nature's mother who bringest all to life and revives all from day to day:
The food of life Thou grantest in eternal fidelity.
And when the soul hath retired we take refuge in Thee.
All that Thou grantest falls back somewhere into Thy womb.

This prayer shows that the Great Mother was not yet forgotten in the
early centuries after Christ. Many of the lingering aspects of Her worship
were incorporated into more modern churches under many different
names and forms. This selection is a clear statement of the nature of the
Triple Goddess of birth, death, and rebirth.

The Apocalypse of St. John (200 A.D.)

And She being with child cried, travailing in birth, and pained to be delivered.
And there appeared another wonder in heaven; and behold a great red dragon, having
seven heads and ten horns, and seven crowns upon his heads. And his tail drew the

third part of the stars of heaven, and did cast them to the earth: and the dragon stood before the woman who was ready to be delivered, for to devour her child as soon as it was born. And she brought forth a man child, who was to rule all nations with a rod of iron: and her child was caught up unto God, and to his throne.

Here we see Sophia raised to the realm of heaven, where She brings forth the predicted "child who is greater than the parents" so hated by the dragon. Sophia is the soul of humanity, bringing forth Her spiritual self as a child with the dragon ready to consume it at birth. The child is born safely, "caught up unto God," and raised to heaven. This symbolizes that the newly born spiritual thinker who can develop Imagination will be guided into the proper realm by the forces of heaven. It is a testament to Sophia's mission of helping humanity become spiritualized.

A Parthian Manichean Text (216–276 A.D.)

Wisdom, you good teacher, or merciful Mother; in wisdom you are like the Mother of the Living, the most beloved of all gods, from whom all pious teachings issued forth. Thus you (the teacher) are also a living mother, who bears children by word-created wisdom. And you nurture them with spiritual milk and lead them to the maturity of godliness.

This section clearly describes Sophia's task of helping humanity become gods and goddesses. She loves us like a mother. Like a teacher, She leads us to Wisdom. She even feeds us—the spiritual newborns—with spiritual milk.

The Consolation of Philosophy, Anicius Boethius (475–524 A.D.)

While I was quietly thinking these thoughts over to myself and giving vent to my sorrow with the help of my pen, I became aware of a woman standing over me. She was of awe-inspiring appearance, her eyes burning and keen beyond the usual power of men. She was so full of years that I could hardly think of her as of my own generation, and yet she possessed a vivid color and undiminished vigor. It was difficult to be sure of her height, for sometimes she was of average human size, while at other times she seemed to touch the very sky with the top of her head, and when she lifted herself even higher, she pierced it and was lost to human sight. Her clothes were made of imperishable material, of the finest thread woven with the most delicate skill. Their color, however, was obscured by a kind of film as of long neglect, like statues covered in dust. On the bottom hem could be read the embroidered Greek letter pi, and on the top hem the Greek letter theta. Between the two a ladder of steps rose from the lower to the higher letter. Her dress had been torn by the hands of marauders who had each carried off such pieces as he could get. There were some books in her right hand, and in her left hand she held a scepter.

Boethius had a direct experience with a semi-visible being who has divine capacities and speaks to him directly. He complains that Philosophy had been defiled, neglected, and misunderstood. Somehow, Sophia's power was waning even though She could appear to some people as a powerful goddess.

Her Intellectual Soul
700–1400 A.D.

From 700 A.D. to 1400 A.D., the Holy Sophia was developing Her intellectual soul.

The Inner Journey, Yeshe Tsogyel (757–817)

Listen, O brothers and sisters, you who have mastered the teaching—

If you recognize me, Queen of the Lake of Awareness,

who encompasses both emptiness and form,

know that I live in the minds of all beings who live.

Know that I live in the body of mind and the field of the senses,

that the twelve kinds of matter are only my bones and my skin.

We are not two, yet you look for me outside;

when you find me within yourself, your own naked mind,

that Single Awareness will fill all worlds.

Then the joy of the One will hold you like a lake —

its fish with gold-seeing eyes will grow many and fat.

Hold to that knowledge and pleasure, and the Creative will be your wings.

You will leap through the green meadows of earthly appearance, enter the sky-fields,

> *and vanish.*

Here, Sophia is described as the Queen of Awareness, existing both outside and inside the aspirant. Once the Queen is found, "the creative will be your wings," with which you can enter the sky-fields and ascend to heaven. Awareness is deified in this idea. As Queen of Heaven, Sophia is found both outside in the sky-fields and inside the aspirant who seeks

Her to gain a Single Awareness that fills all worlds. This is what the Holy Sophia does for the aspirant: helps him become so creative with his thoughts that he earns wings to rise to heaven.

Monologion, Anselm of Canterbury (1033–1109)

But you, Jesus, good lord, are you not also a mother?

Are you not that mother who, like a hen, collects her chickens under her wings?

Truly, master, you are a mother.

For what others have conceived and given birth to, they have received from you ...

You are the author, others are the ministers.

It is then you, above all, Lord God, who are mother.

Here we can see an attempt to attribute Jesus with the aspects of the divine Mother. Jesus, through Christ, certainly possesses similar forces, but the two are different and need to be considered for the individualized traits perfected by each of them.

Antiphon for the Holy Spirit, Hildegard of Bingen (1098–1179)

The Holy Spirit is life that gives life,

Moving all things.

It is the root in every creature

And purifies all things,

Wiping away sins,

Anointing wounds.

It is radiant life, worthy of praise,

Awakening and enlivening

All things.

Love

Gives herself to all things,

Most excellent in the depths,

And above the stars

Cherishing all:

For the High King

She has given

The kiss of peace.

The distinction between the Holy Spirit and the Holy Sophia is much needed to understand the dynamic of these two Beings uniting in the human soul to help it ascend. The forces of life are attributed to the Holy Spirit, while Love is attributed to the Holy Sophia.

The Purity of the Living God, Hildegard of Bingen (1098–1179)

The leaping fountain is clearly the purity of the living God.

His radiance is reflected in it, and in that splendor,

God embraces in his great love all things whose reflection appeared

in the leaping fountain before he ordered them to come forth in their own shape.

And in me, Love, all things are reflected and my splendor reveals the design of things,

just as the reflection indicates their form.

We are created in the form of love out of the leaping fountain of God's purity. Sophia is this love. God is the purity that brings humanity into existence. Even for this female thinker, Sophia is second to God in creation and manifestation. Although truly loved by Hildegard, Sophia is still not regarded as the primal being.

Antiphone for Divine Wisdom, Hildegard of Bingen (1098–1179)

Sophia! You of the whirling wings, circling encompassing energy of God:

You quicken the world in your clasp.

One wing soars in heaven one wing sweeps the earth

and the third flies all around us.

Praise to Sophia!

Let all the earth praise her!

The Triple Goddess still survives but is relegated to being an energy of God. Sophia's triple nature is described as three wings that are above, below, and all around us.

The Fountain of Life, Hildegard of Bingen (1098–1179)

I also saw, as if in the middle of the southern region I mentioned,

three figures, two of whom were standing in a fountain of great purity,

which was surrounded by a round stone, pierced with holes.

They seemed to be rooted in it, just as trees sometimes appear to be growing in water.

One was clad in purple, the other in white, but of such a brightness

that I could not look at them directly.

The third, however, was standing out of the fountain, on the stone.

She was clad in a white robe, and her face shone with such radiance

that my face flinched from it.

And the blessed ranks of saints appeared like clouds before them

and they gazed intently upon them.

But now the first figure began to speak:

"I am Love—the radiance of the living God.

Wisdom has performed her work with me,

and Humility (who is rooted in the living fountain) is my helper.

To her, Peace clings. And through the brightness that I am,

the living light of the blessed angels blazes.

For, just as a ray flashes from a lamp so this brightness shines in the blessed angels—

nor could it do otherwise, since a light cannot help but shine."

Hildegard's experience is similar to many others who witness the glory of the Trinity of the Divine Feminine. Love, Humility, and Peace are the three names she gives Sophia. The descriptions are the highest praise any being could receive, but Sophia is still a "radiance" of God, not the Mother of God, as previous thinkers had experienced.

The Praise of the Virtues, St. Francis of Assisi (1181–1226)

Hail, Queen Wisdom! The Lord save you, with your sister, pure, holy Simplicity.

Lady Holy Poverty, God keep you, with your sister, holy Humility.

Lady Holy Love, God keep you, with your sister, holy Obedience.

All holy virtues, God keep you, God, from whom you proceed and come.

In all the world there is not a man who can possess any one of you

without first dying to himself.

The man who practices one and does not offend against the other possesses all;

The man who offends against one, possesses none and violates all.

Each and every one of you puts vice and sin to shame.

Holy Wisdom puts Satan and all his wiles to shame.

Holy Poverty puts to shame all greed, avarice, and all the anxieties of this life.

Holy Humility puts pride to shame, and all the inhabitants of this world

and all that is in the world.

Holy Love puts to shame all the temptations of the devil and the flesh and all natural fear.

St. Francis describes the Queen of Wisdom manifesting as Simplicity, Poverty, Humility, Love, and Obedience. These virtues of humanity are the efforts of the "sisters" of Queen Wisdom to win the battle against the seven deadly sins. Spiritual characteristics are now being described as aspects of Wisdom that take root in the moral person striving for perfection. Thinking can now lead to higher feelings and moral deeds.

The Good and Perfect Man, Alan of Lille (1116–1202)

Behold, a maiden, with her abode at the summit of the pole, looking down upon the heavens, turning her eyes aloft, searches with every effort of sight for something that lies beyond. She pursues nothing corporeal but passing beyond it, examines the hidden cause of the incorporeal, seeking the beginning and end of things. She presents herself to Phronesis' view; with her bright light she flashes suddenly on Phronesis' vision and with its strangeness, she untensed her mind. This is not surprising, since she stands out in such bright beauty that she is endowed with a resplendence beyond the stars, as she adds brightness to brightness and light to light and has no hesitation in sharing this light, which has made her its daughter, with Olympus itself. She shows nothing of earth in her face; she allows nothing mortal, nothing doomed to die, to creep into her expression. The maiden's face shows her parentage, the maiden's form shows that what she has to offer is exclusively of heaven. Arguments based on beauty prove that she is a goddess. No insistence in denial refutes what this beauty and a face so heaven-like prove. A diadem sets her head a glitter; sparkling with the deep luster of gems, it is afire with gold and flashing forth, gleams with a cluster of twelve stones. She carries a book in her right hand, a royal scepter in her left and her eyes frequently seek the book but rarely return to the staff: yet finally they do return to it and cast their gaze around it lest her left hand waver, be overcome by the burden of the rod and relinquish the scepter.

She is clothed in a garment steeped in gold, shining with silver, more becoming than any veil, more charming than any regular dress, more gleaming than the pure

stars of heaven. The hand of God and Minerva's skilled right hand wove it, as the
nobility of its form shows us. Here a fine needle has traced the secrets of God and the
depths of the divine mind and with form informs and formless, localizes the boundless,
reveals the hidden, gives limits to the unlimited, brings the invisible into view.

"O Queen of the pole, goddess of heaven, daughter of the Master above, for your
divine face shows that you are no mortal nor need bewail the stain of our race; your
countenance proves that you are a goddess, your scepter proclaims that you are a queen
and your glory shows that you are the child of God. To you the abodes of the gods, the
ways of the heavens, the path of Olympus, the orb that lies beyond the universe, the
entire land of the Thunderer lie open as well as the dominion of God and the destiny
that lies beyond. Guide me in my wanderings, direct me in my confusion, steady me
in my fears, teach me in my ignorance, take hold of me in my wavering, gladden me
in my sorrow, willingly look to the interests of a stranger, complete what is begun,
support one tottering, come to the aid of one falling. For I am a wanderer, fearful,
confused, untaught, in difficulty, incompetent, unacquainted with the place, a stranger,
faint. Trying to cross the poles and enter the abodes above, the inner sanctuary of God,
the chamber of the Thunderer and the council of Jupiter, I go along stumbling, straying,
alone, losing my way as I essay the hidden ways of heaven."

The ruler of the court of Heaven speaks:

"Maiden, mother of the world, sister of the gods above and my daughter,
heavenly in origin, yet an inhabitant of earth: on earth you alone have a feeling for
things divine and possess the image of my godhead; you alone relieve the boredom
of the world and wipe away its tears with your consolation. Your will does not in
degeneration fall away from the supreme mind: for the daughter sighs in unison with
the father's desire and the offspring, in harmony with her father, follows his wish.
Reason has for long recommended this to me, that I should show regard for earth by
one gift and bless the world by the godlike presence of a heavenly man, who in himself
would have a treasury of virtue to match every worthy office he would hold ..."

This description is an accurate picture of the workings of Sophia in the Earthly realm. She is called the Daughter of God, the Sister of the Gods, and the Mother of the World. Her roles are quite confused here. God appears and speaks directly with the author as if this were not an uncommon occurrence.

Sophia's role as the teacher and leader of humanity's spiritual striving also is implied. She acts as a mediator for humanity when She asks for a "heavenly man" to be sent into the world.

The Essential Rumi, Rumi (1207–1273)

Woman is a beam of the divine Light.

She is not the being whom sensual desire takes as its object.

She is Creator, it should be said,

She is not a Creature.

In Rumi, we begin to find a blend of past Wisdom of Sophia merged with new Imaginations of the Goddess. Rumi is clear that Sophia is not a created being, but instead the creator. The true nature of woman cannot be taken as an object because She is not of this world. Sophia is beginning to be seen again.

Paradiso, Dante Alighieri (1265–1321)

A fire descended out of heaven from afar

Shaped in a circle like a coronal,

Which turned and turned as it engirdled her.

Whatever music sounds most sweet of all

On earth, and draws the soul most in desire,

Would seem cloud crackling in the thunder's brawl

Compared with the resounding of that lyre

Whereby the beautiful Sapphire was crowned
Which makes the cleared heaven all one sapphire.
"I am angelic love and circle round
The sublime joy, which breathes out from the womb
Wherein the world's desire its hostel found.
And I shall circle, Lady of Heaven, till home
Thou thy son follow into the sphere supreme
And make it more divine since thou art come."
Thus the encircling melody of flame
Sealed itself up, and the other lights in praise
Made all the air re-echo Mary's name.
The royal mantle of all the wheeling maze
Of the universe, whose ardor burns most hot,
Most quickened in God's breath and in His ways,
Had the inner border of it so far remote
Above, that in my vision's narrower scope,
Where I was stationed, I discerned it not.
Therefore my eyes' endeavor might not hope
To accompany the crowned flame beyond,
As after her own seed she mounted up.
And as the child who toward his mother fond
Stretches his arms when he has milked her breast—
The spirit flaming outward to respond—
Each of those white fires strained into a crest
Its flame, so that the affection infinite
They had for Mary was made manifest.

Mary is now made to be the vehicle to express Sophia in all Her forms. Love and joy are Her tools to help humanity rise and return home to heaven. Dante seemed to have an experience of Sophia that was quite beautiful and inspiring. He combines numerous aspects of Sophia into a description of Mary.

The Legend of Good Women, Geoffrey Chaucer (1343–1400)

Since what I write is honor to the power

Of love, and in true service of the flower

Whom I shall serve while I have wit or might.

She is the brightness and the perfect light

That in this dark world shows, and steers my course.

The heart within my sad breast with such force

Respects and loves you that of my true wit,

You are the mistress: I guide none of it.

My words and deeds are so in your command

That, as a harp obeys the player's hand

And sings according to its fingering,

So from my heart-strings you can always bring

What voice you please, to laugh or to complain.

Be ever my guide and Lady Sovereign!

To you as to my earthly god I cry

Both in this poem and when my woes I sight.

This love poem is profoundly touching. It shows the deep, personal pathways that Sophia makes into the heart of the poet and artist. Chaucer is describing something far beyond the influence of the Muses or an imaginary lover. He is describing his soul's love of the divine, both inside himself and embodied in Lady Sovereign. This is true Inspiration gained through an active relationship with Sophia in the consciousness of the soul.

Her Consciousness Soul
1400–2100 A.D.

From 1400 A.D. to 2100 A.D., the Holy Sophia develops Her consciousness soul.

<u>Songs of Kabir</u>, Kabir (1440–1518)

Who first came into existence? Who was created next?

Brahma, Vishnu, Shiva (Mahadeva) and Shakti (the goddess) appeared first.

A woman (illusion) came into the world.

She had neither father nor mother.

She had neither head nor legs but only life.

In her the whole world roams about.

Being tolerated for seven days,

She expressed a wonderful word of wisdom.

This poem has many hidden meanings and implications that are filled with the Wisdom of India, Persia, Greece, and the Near East.

The clarity of this text comes from a synthesis of old doctrines added to a modern perspective. After the year 1415, humanity began to have the opportunity to develop the third aspect of the human soul: the consciousness soul.

Kabir is a thinker who can look at the past, the present, and the future of Sophia and mold a poem into a truism of philosophical insight about Her nature and manifestation.

The Way to Christ, Jacob Boehme (1575–1624)

Sophia gave me her faithful word, as she appeared to me,
   that she wanted to turn all my sorrow into great joy.
As I lay on the mountain, it was approaching midnight ...
   and all storms passed over me ...
She came to comfort me and married herself to me.
Sophia was above all chosen and sent to unite herself
   with Mary and to strengthen her, so that she would be able to become
   the Mother of the incarnating Logos. She incarnated into Mary;
Mary is the incarnated Sophia.

No other writer gives more detail about Sophia and his relationship with Her than Boehme. After a beam of light gave Jacob Boehme the "golden moment of illumination," he became somewhat enlightened. He then had multiple encounters with Sophia until he literally believed he was married to Her. He also shares tremendous insight into the incarnation of Sophia as the Daughter of the Goddess who over-lighted Mary and helped her birth the vessel for the Christ.

The Way to Christ, Jacob Boehme (1575–1624)

And the virgin of the Wisdom of God is the spirit of the pure element, and is therefore called a Virgin, because she is so chaste, and generates nothing; yet as the flaming spirit in man's body generates nothing, but opens all secrets ... so also here; the Wisdom (or the eternal virgin) of God opens all the great wonders in the holy Element, for there are the essences wherein the fruits of Paradise spring up.

Boehme's descriptions of Sophia are all worth studying because they go step by step through the experiences that the seeker of Wisdom will undergo. The details about Sophia are astonishing, and his writings are truly inspired. Boehme, above all other writers, accurately describes the many faces of Sophia. The Virgin, the Bride, the Beloved, and Love itself, along with other aspects of the Holy Sophia, are clearly articulated in his writings.

Boehme had direct communion with Sophia. His works reflect the refined results of spiritual development that lead to accurate Imaginations, Inspirations, and Intuitions. He was not a learned man, but after his illumination, he wrote the most inspired works about Sophia that we have in the Western esoteric wisdom tradition.

The Way to Christ, Jacob Boehme (1575–1624)

When thou standest still from the thinking of Self, and the willing of Self; "When both thy Intellect and Will are quiet and passive to the Impressions of the Eternal Word and Spirit; when thy Soul is winged up, and above that which is temporal, the outward Senses, and the Imagination being locked up by Holy Abstraction," then the Eternal Hearing, Seeing, and Speaking will be revealed in thee; and so God heareth "and seeth through thee," being now the Organ of his Spirit; and so God speaketh in thee, and whispereth to thy Spirit, and thy Spirit heareth his Voice. Blessed art thou therefore if that thou canst stand still from Self-thinking and Self-willing, and canst stop the Wheel of thy Imagination and Senses; forasmuch as hereby thou mayest arrive at length to see the great Salvation of God, being made capable of all Manner of Divine Sensations and Heavenly Communications. Since it is nought indeed but thine own Hearing and Willing that do hinder thee, so that thou dost not see and hear God.

Thou must learn to distinguish well betwixt the Thing, and that which only is an Image thereof; betwixt that Sovereignty which is substantial, and in the inward Ground or Nature, and that which is imaginary, and in an outward Form, or Semblance; betwixt that which is properly Angelical, and that which is no more than bestial.

Boehme describes the three qualities of the soul that will help you ascend to the spirit: eternal hearing, seeing, and speaking. These gifts are provided with the help of Sophia so that we can partake of heavenly sensations and communications. This is the path of Sophia, through love, that leads to the ascension of the Holy Sophia into Her heavenly aspects.

The Cherubinic, Angelus Silesius (1624–1677)

A new Jerusalem, a castle all completed,

A realm no enemy will ever have defeated,

A maiden who was raised as high as any goddess

This, Virgin, is your soul when she is God's beloved.

Angelus Silesius is one of the most beautiful, succinct poets who can describe spiritual beings and experiences in simple words that carry ponderous ideas. He could see the many aspects of Sophia and the fact that those aspects also live in the human soul. The Virgin Soul is the beloved of God and the same as Sophia.

Sophia joins us in our bridal preparations and is excited about the spiritual union that She will help birth.

Hymn to Darkness, J. Norris of Bemerton (1657–1711)

Hail thou most sacred, venerable thing!

What Muse is worthy thee to sing?

Thee, from whose pregnant universal womb

All things, ev'n Light, thy rival, first did come.

What dares he not attempt that sings of thee,

Thou first and greatest mystery?

Beyond the Muse is the mystery of the pregnant womb of darkness from which light was born. These mysteries of death and darkness can only be alluded to because they are aspects of Sophia that cannot be illuminated. Sophia lets all creation fall back into the womb from which it was born, without resistance. She is the beginning and the end. The modern conscious soul can begin to sense these mysteries when the spiritual self starts to enlighten the soul through the help and mitigation of Sophia.

Geheimniss de gottlichen Sophia, Gottfried Arnold (1666–1714)

Sophia is an eternal Being, which before all creatures, with the Holy Trinity, is eternal, and remains forever in eternity. She is above all the Angels; the eternal wisdom has her root alone in the Godhead itself, and through her Being it reveals itself ... Sophia is not a Person outside the Trinity ... the spirit of Jesus and the spirit of Sophia are not separate. The eternal Sophia urges humans through being reborn to return to completeness in Paradise, to which she will lead them.

Arnold has associated Sophia with the Trinity but not made Her part of it. He does not explain how that could be, yet all but states that Sophia is Jesus, not a separate being. He tries to expand the view of Sophia in his age, but it falls far short of the true nature of the Divine Feminine Trinity.

Philosophical Sonnet, Comte Saint Germain (1712–1784)

Curious scrutator of all nature,

I have known of the great whole, the principle, and the end,

I have seen gold thick in the depths of the double mercury,

I have seized its substance, and surprised its changing,

I explain by that art, the soul with the womb of a Mother,

Make its home, take it away, and as a kernel

Placed against a grain of wheat, under the humid pollen;

The one plant and the other vine-stock, are the bread and wine,

Nothing was, God willing, nothing became something,

I doubted it, I sought that on which the universe rests,

Nothing preserves the equilibrium and serves to sustain,

Then with the weight of praise and of blame,

I weighed the eternal, it called my soul,

I died, I adored, I knew nothing more.

This alchemical poem is a key to seeing the work of Sophia Christos in the world. The birth of the spirit is described in hidden terms, even though the images are somewhat familiar. This poem is a formula for developing the higher soul capacities to encounter the spirit.

Hymns to the Night, Novalis (1722–1801)

To thee, O mother maiden,

Ten thousand hearts aspire;

In this life, sorrow-laden,

Thee only they desire;

In thee they hope for healing;

In thee expect true rest,

When thou, their safety sealing,

Shalt clasp them to thy breast.

Mother, home, heart, and heaven have the same root: Sophia. She will clasp the aspirant to Her breast and be present for every single heartbeat in countless hearts at once.

Pollen and Seeds, Novalis (1722–1801)

Only woman and love dissolve the intellect.

In his time, Novalis saw the intellect killing the world through male-dominated war machines. He took refuge in his idealized love for Sophie Kuhn, his fiancé, a young girl who died before they could be married. Filled with natural Wisdom, Novalis could write seven words that "say it all" about the feminine.

Klingsor's Fairytale, Novalis (1722–1801)

The kingdom of eternity is founded,
By love and peace all strife has been impounded,
The dreams of pain are gone, to plague us never,
Sophia is priestess of all hearts forever.

This is a true testament of faith in Sophia as the teacher and guide of humanity.

Faith and Love or the King and Queen, Novalis (1722–1801)

One finds what one loves everywhere, and sees similarities everywhere. The greater the love, the more extensive and manifold is this similar world. My beloved is the abbreviation of the universe; the universe is the extension of my beloved. To the lover of learning, all its branches offer garlands and remembrances for his beloved.

To learn is to honor the beloved with love and find her everywhere, creating a world filled with love. The beloved is the doorway to the universe, learning, and love.

Christendom or Europe, Novalis (1722–1801)

So come then you too, all you philanthropists and encyclopedists, into the peace-bringing lodge, and receive the fraternal kiss, brush the gray net aside and gaze with young love at the wondrous splendor of nature, history, and humanity. I want to conduct you to a brother who will talk with you so that your hearts rejoice and you gird your beloved. This brother is the heartbeat of the new age, whoever has felt his presence does not doubt any more that it will come, and he too steps out from the crowd with sweet pride in being a contemporary to join the new band of disciples. He has made a new veil for the Holy Virgin which caresses her body, betraying the heavenly shape of her limbs, and yet covers her more chastely than any other.

The veil is for the Virgin what the spirit is for the body, her indispensable instrument whose folds are the letters of her sweet Annunciation; the infinite play of the folds is a music of numbers, for language is too wooden and too impudent for the Virgin—her lips open only to sing. For me her singing is nothing but the ceremonial call to a new foundation gathering, the mighty beating of the wings of an angelic herald who is passing. They are the first birth pangs, let everyone prepare for the birth!

This *call* to a New Age centered on Sophia, the Holy Virgin, is a call to recognize the Goddess as a divine being and leader of our souls. The Holy Virgin heralds this New Age with the wings of angels. As a forerunner of the consciousness soul age, Novalis is a good example of what the thinker can do with the help of Sophia. He loved Sophia as a being, not a concept.

Man: His True Nature and Ministry, Claude de Saint-Martin (1743–1803)

I have no doubt she may be born in our center,
I have no doubt that the Divine Word can also be born there by her means,
as he was thus born in Mary.

All the saints and all the elect share this Sophia.
The Spirit of Jesus and the Spirit of Wisdom are not two different spirits,
but rather are one spirit and one inseparable Essence.

Sophia and Christ can be born in our hearts just as Christ was born through Mary. Sophia is also shared by all other spiritual beings. These thoughts are true. But we should not confuse Wisdom with Christ. Love and Wisdom are two separate Beings that are consorts and representatives from two different Trinities. Christ and Sophia are now inseparable through their union, but they are still different beings.

<u>Faust</u>, Goethe (1749–1832)

Penitents, look up, elate,
Where she beams salvation:
Gratefully to blessed fate
Grow, in re-creation!
Be our souls, as they have been,
Dedicate to Thee!
Virgin Holy, Mother, Queen,
Goddess, gracious be!

All things are transitory
But as symbols are sent:
Earth's insufficiency
Here grows to Event,
The Indescribable,
Here it is done:
The Eternal-Feminine leadeth us
Upward and on!

Goethe names Sophia as Virgin, Mother, Queen, Goddess, and the source of salvation beamed from above. Our souls are dedicated to this Goddess, and She leads us upward and on.

Goethe had insight into the changing aspects of Sophia. It is not a great leap to see Sophia as the collective consciousness of humans, especially since he attributes salvation to Her.

Woman, Eaton Stannard Barrett (1786–1820)

Nor she with traitorous kiss her Savior stung,

Not she denied Him with unholy tongue;

She, while apostles shrank, could dangers brave,

Last at the cross and earliest at the grave.

When we look at the actions of the followers of Christ, we certainly find that the women listened to Jesus and did as he asked. The three Marys and John were the only ones faithful to Christ until the end. They were always there for Jesus and stayed with him throughout His passion, death, resurrection, and ascension. They also were there for the coming of Christ's promised Holy Spirit at Pentecost.

The female spirit is stronger than anyone can imagine. She has endured suffering beyond imagination and still triumphed.

The Natural History of the Intellect, Ralph Waldo Emerson (1803–1882)

The means of ennobling everything sensuous, and to animate also the deadest facts through uniting them to the idea, Goethe said, is the finest privilege of our supersensuous origin. Man, how much soever the earth draws him, with its thousand and myriad appearances, lifts yet a searching, longing look to the heaven which vaults over him in immeasurable spaces, whilst he feels deeply in himself that he is a citizen of that spiritual kingdom, our belief in which we must not repel or surrender. In this longing lies the secret of the eternal striving after an unknown aim. It is also the lever of our searching and thinking,—soft bond between poetry and reality.

Dionysius described the orders of celestial angels, so the degrees of Intellect are an organic fact, and it is these which give birth to mythology. You have been pleased with stories of gods, in Homer, Ovid, and the Edda. I invite you to the beholding and knowing of real gods, who forever work and rule: Memory; and Vision: the Power of Imagination; the Poet Apollo, the Zodiacal Chain of Cause and Effect; Illusion the veil, and Transition the Energy; Wisdom with his solar eye, whose look is classification, and distributes natures. And high over all its several perceptions and powers, the Intellect Pure, which we cannot discriminate from the Cause of Causes.

In this selection, Emerson is indicating that the human Intellect Pure is the source of all. With poetic logic, he shows us that advancement towards the spiritual kingdom lies in our own capacities if we will develop them. Here is a call to mount the rungs of the ladder to the celestial hierarchy and return to our home. Emerson was a spiritual scientist who looked to human intellect as the tool that will build the divine out of existing human capacities.

Harmonist's Hymn Number 394 (1805)

Sophia, from your glances rapture flows into my heart
When a friendly love delights my soul;
O the pure instincts your charm arouses in me;
This flame feeds the blessed heavenly love.

Beloved, let me experience the gentleness and faith if we were united,

With your sweet caress many an anxious hour would flee,

My wounds would be healed,

Pure fire would be drawn to love.

Your demeanor reveals that your heart treasures me;

What joy, what rapture when you are close to me.

Dip your brush into the rays of the sun to paint me your lovely picture;

Your lips and cheeks scarlet

Should my mouth and heart be pressed thereon,

My soul and spirit would be refreshed.

O your walk is without care; your work is the joy of love;

Gentle and white as the lily is your sign on my breast,

For the hand of harmony is the throne of love complete;

Beloved, if you live with us, you are our spiritual sun.

The followers in the Harmonist Movement lived their lives for Sophia in every way. One could say that they were a true religion of Sophia. They would become enraptured with their pursuit of Sophia to the point that they actually thought they physically encountered Her in many ways. Some believed that Sophia would convey a spiritual kiss that would vouchsafe their souls.

They truly loved Sophia in all aspects of their lives and believed She became physical in Her manifestations.

Abraham Lincoln (1809–1865)

No man is poor who has had a godly mother.

There is a very thin line between godly and mother, the difference being that mothers are always physically present with the love that is needed by their children.

<u>Mother</u>, Edgar Allan Poe (1809–1849)

I love to feel that in the heavens above,

The angels whispering to one another

Can find among their burning words of love

No name so beautiful as that of Mother.

The original source of all life is the Mother, who is worshipped in heaven and on Earth. Here the poet makes a sweeping statement that all spiritual beings acknowledge the primacy of the Mother.

<u>Evolution and Religion</u>, Henry Beecher (1813–1887)

When God thought of mother, He must have laughed with satisfaction, and framed it quickly—so rich, so deep, so divine, so full of soul, power, and beauty, was the conception. Nothing can compare in beauty, and wonder, and admirableness, and divinity itself, to the silent work in obscure dwellings of faithful women bringing their children to honor and virtue and piety.

This description of mothers turns everyday duties into the work of the Queen of Heaven. Or perhaps the Queen of Heaven has come to the Earth to do the greatest work: tend Her children.

Mother, Bishop John P. Newman (1826–1899)

Heaven— the end of all a mother's prayers;

The home of all her dreams; the guiding star to light our path

With hope's encheering beams;

The haven for our storm-tossed bark,

From out a world where, wild and dark,

The tempests often rise.

But still in every darksome hour

This hope will rise with holy power,

And point us to the skies,

Where Mother, Home, and Heaven are seen

Without a cloud to intervene.

Sophia manifests in the mind of this thinker as heaven and home where the Mother lives perpetually. We come from the Mother, and we return to the Mother.

The Secret Doctrine, H. P. Blavatsky (1831–1891)

The Gnostic Sophia, "Wisdom" who is "the Mother" of Ogdoad, is the Holy Ghost and the Creator of all, as in the ancient systems. The "father" is a far later invention. The earliest manifested Logos was female everywhere—the mother of the seven planetary powers.

The various Cosmogonies show that the Archaic Universal Soul was held by every nation as the "Mind" of the Demiurgic Creator; and that it was called the "Mother," Sophia with the Gnostics (or the female Wisdom), the Sephira with the Jews, Saraswati or Vach, with the Hindus, the Holy Ghost being a female Principle ... The female Soul of the World or the "Great Deep;" the deity, from which

*these two in one have their being, is ever concealed and called the "Hidden One,"
connected only indirectly with Creation.*

*The Spiritual substance sent forth by the Infinite Light is the first Sephira
or Shekinah: Sephira exoterically contains all the other nine Sephiroths in her.
Esoterically she contains but two. These two Sephiroths called, Father, Abba, and
Mother, Amona, are the duad or the double-sexed logos from which issued the other
seven Sephiroths.*

*In the Kabala, Sephira is the same as Shekinah, and is, in other synthesis, the
wife, daughter, and mother of the "Heavenly man," Adam Kadmon, and is even
identical with him, just as Vach is identical with Brahma, and is called the female
Logos.... Moreover, she is called "the Mother of the Veda," "since it is through her
power that Brahma revealed them, and also owing to her power that he produced the
universe"—i.e., through speech, and words and numbers.*

*Again, as goddess of Speech and of Sound, and a permutation of Aditi—She
is Chaos, in one sense. At any rate, she is the "Mother of the gods" ... Whether as
Aditi, or the divine Sophia of the Greek Gnostics, she is the mother of the seven
sons: the "Angels of the Face of the Deep," or the "Great Green One" of the "Book
of the Dead."*

*"Thou art that Prakrti (essence), infinite and subtle, which bore Brahma in its
womb. Thou eternal being, comprising in thy substance the essence of all created
things, wast identical with creation; thou wast the parent of the triform sacrifice,
becoming the germ of all ... Thou art sacrifice, whence all fruit proceeds; thou art the
arani whose attrition engenders fir." "As Aditi, thou art the parent of the gods ...
Thou art the morning twilight ... Thou art humility, the mother of Wisdom; thou art
the parent of harmony; thou art modesty, the progenitrix of affection; thou art desire,
of whom love is born ..."*

Blavatsky tends to be the most comprehensive philosopher in comparative religions and often has the most succinct but far-reaching opinion on spiritual topics. Most of the descriptions we have presented to this point are summarized in her sweeping statements.

From the primal divinity to the being of love, Sophia is described in many of Her forms found in sacred scripture. This is enigmatic, just as Sophia's evolution is a conundrum, Her nature ever-changing.

Blavatsky doesn't pin a final definition on Sophia because She is evolving alongside humanity. She cannot be described comprehensively without framing the description in its own historical perspective.

A brilliant scholar, Blavatsky does not limit Sophia. She finds Her many aspects in a variety of Goddesses.

The Prophecy of the Kingdom of the Soul, Anna Kingsford (1846–1888)

And now I show you a mystery and a new thing,

Which is part of the mystery of the fourth day of creation.

The word which shall come to save the world, shall be uttered by a woman.

A woman shall conceive, and shall bring forth the tidings of salvation.

For the reign of Adam is at its last hour;

And God shall crown all things by the creation of Eve.

Anna Kingsford's prediction that a "word" shall be uttered by a woman that will save the world is somewhat mysterious. Sophia is often associated with the Logos of the Greeks. Logos means word, and John the Divine describes Christ as the word.

The word *Christ* comes to be spoken in the individual soul. Evolution unfolds as the soul is Christened by his own spiritual self-rising towards heaven.

Three Meetings, Vladimir Soloviev (1853–1900)

Let it be known; today the Eternal Feminine
In an incorruptible body is descending to earth.
In the unfading light of the new goddess,
Heaven has become one with the deeps.

This is a prediction that Sophia's revelation is coming to humans in our age. Sophia is seen as descending to help humans ascend. She is one with Her creation. She descends from the Trinity to the Earth to become one with humanity.

Soloviev is the prophet of Sophia in Russia, a land where the worship of the Great Goddess has never ceased. Therefore, the new revelation of Sophia is easily accepted and followed as a spiritual path.

The Eternal Feminine, Vladimir Soloviev (1853–1900)

And in the purple of the heaven's splendor,
With eyes filled with an azure fire,
You looked like the first radiance
Of a universal and creative day.
What is, what was, and what will always be—
A single motionless look encompassed everything here ...
The seas and rivers showed dark blue beneath me
As did the distant forest, and the heights of snowy mountains.
I saw everything, and everything was one thing only—
A single image of female beauty ...
The infinite fit within its dimension:
Before me, in me—were you alone.
O, radiant woman! In you I am not deceived.

The triple Goddess of the past, present, and future is described beautifully here. Sophia brings with Her the forces of eternal youth, yet the infinite power of the universe. She is the image of the divine—that being also the image of the human being.

The Soul's Probation, Rudolf Steiner (1861–1925)

Love must not forget

That she is Wisdom's sister.

Love is the only passion which must not

be discarded in the search for Truth.

In Love lies the seed of Truth,

In Truth seek the root of Love:

Thus speaks thy higher Self.

Rudolf Steiner is a sterling example of a fully developed consciousness soul that perceives Sophia in Her many forms. Sophia is the love, wisdom, and truth of the higher self. She is personal. A passionate desire to seek Her is a higher spiritual quality much to be desired.

The Search for the New Isis, Rudolf Steiner (1861–1925)

It is not on account of something happening by itself from without that Christ will be able to appear again in his spiritual form in the course of the twentieth century, but rather through human beings finding the force represented by the Holy Sophia. The tendency in recent times has been to lose precisely this Isis force, this Mary force, which has been stamped out through that which has arisen within the modern consciousness of humanity. And the more recent confessions have partly obliterated a perspective concerning Mary. To a certain extent this is the mystery of modern mankind, that basically Mary-Isis has been killed, and that she must be sought again, sought in the widespread heavenly realms with the power which Christ is able to kindle within us when we devote ourselves to him in the right way.

Man has learned to relate to the Sophia through his consciousness-soul, to associate her directly with human beings. This happened during the consciousness-soul age. The Sophia has therefore become the Being that elucidates man. Once having entered into humanity, she has to take up this human nature and set it objectively before mankind. She detaches herself again but takes with her what man is and places herself outside him, no longer merely as Sophia but as Anthropo-Sophia, as that Sophia who has passed through the soul of man, through man's being, and henceforth bears this being of man within herself.

This is an excellent description of Sophia in our time. Dr. Steiner was clairvoyant but also a spiritual scientist who taught others how to develop the forces to create new spiritual sense organs that can perceive Sophia.

This description makes distinctions that other writers tend to blend together or mix into a generalized picture of Sophia. Sophia has distinct parts that evolve with humanity, and they are united in a way that is seldom described.

As the greatest prophet of Sophia in our times, Steiner's insights are profound and far-reaching.

The Gospel of St. John, Rudolf Steiner (1861–1925)

The human soul as it is fructified out of the World-Spirit is made manifest in the Madonna ... Then we see with what devotion our soul, as the eternal feminine in us, longs and searches for the divine Father Spirit who is born out of the universe and to whom we give birth as a Sun in our soul ... And on the other hand, the Madonna contains that which can be born out of the human soul: the true, higher self that slumbers in every human being, all that is best in humanity, what as spirit weaves and flows through the world.

The Madonna is more than a symbol of the human soul. It is the evolutionary intent of the World Soul to search for its missing part in the spirit. This constitutes the alchemical wedding of soul to spirit.

The Candle of Vision, A.E. (George William Russell) (1867–1935)

While the child is still in its mother's arms it is nourished by her, yet it does not know it is a mother which feeds it. It knows later in whose bosom it has lain. As the mother nourishes the body so the Mighty Mother nourishes the soul. Yet there are but few who pay reverence where reverence is due, and that is because this benign deity is like a mother who indulges the fancies of her children. With some she imparts life to their own thoughts. Others she endows with the vision of her own heart. Even of these last some love in silence, being afraid to speak of the majesty which smiled on them, and others deceived think with pride: "This vision is my own."

...Of the Mother of the gods, I have already said she is the first spiritual form of matter, and therefore Beauty. As every being emerges out of her womb clothed with form, she is the Mighty Mother, and as mother of all she is that divine compassion which exists beyond and is the final arbiter of the justice of the gods. Her heart will be in ours when ours forgive.

A. E. gives the most complete description of Sophia helping the soul attain Imagination, Inspiration, and Intuition that can be found outside of esoteric circles. He uses simple language with fantastic imagery that paints the reality of Sophia working in our souls. The author recommends that everyone read this book as a master plan for the development of the soul awakening to the spirit.

The Quest, James H. Cousins (1873–1856)

They said: "She dwelleth in some place apart,
Immortal Truth, within whose eyes
Who looks may find the secret of the skies
And healing for life's smart."

I sought Her in loud caverns underground,
On heights where lightning flashed and fell;
I scaled high Heaven; I stormed the gates of Hell,
But Her I never found.
Till thro' the tumults of my Quest I caught
A whisper: "Here, within thy heart,
I dwell; for I am thou: behold thou art
The seeker—and the Sought."

Sophia as Immortal Truth exists both in the outer world and the inner world of the human soul. Searching for Her is a noble pastime, but will only yield positive results when we know that She is the creator of our hearts, the home of the divine.

The Rise and Fall of Male Supremacy, Otfried Eberz (1878–1958)

Perhaps we shall witness at the end of history, as in its beginning, a Feminine World Age; perhaps woman will once more redeem herself and man from his mania of destruction. In any case, the secret of love belongs to her. When she was forced to surrender her mysteries to the male, they were exposed to profanation and devaluation, and finally to that obscene "sexual enlightenment" through the male single-gender-being. It has become all the more clear that only woman can be the

guardian of the meaning, i.e., the metaphysics, of love ... Everything she can learn
from man is of secondary importance of life; but that which man will have to learn
from her again is the very condition of life, is life itself, the double-gender-being.

This type of thinking is only possible after the darkening and resurrection of Sophia. Beyond gender bias, Eberz predicts a future where a Feminine World Age will rule with love.

Woman is Sophia's representative and the source of a positive future where gender is biased towards the female.

Alchemical Studies, Carl G. Jung (1875–1961)

The creative process has a feminine quality, and the creative work arises from
unconscious depths—we might truly say, from the realm of the Mothers.

This reference to the Mothers is as mysterious as Goethe's reference to the Mothers in *Faust*. The Mothers represent a trinity of creative forces imagined to have created the world and then receded to the underworld. In this passage, Jung is also insinuating the collective unconscious.

The Eternal Feminine, Pierre Teilhard De Chardin (1881–1955)

When the world was born, I came into being. Before the centuries were made, I
*   issued from the hand of God— half-formed, yet destined to grow in beauty from*
*   age to age, the handmaid of his work.*
Through me, all things have their movement and are made to work as one.
I am the beauty running through the world, to make it associate in ordered groups:
*   the ideal held up before the world to make it ascend.*
I am the essential Feminine.

I was the bond that thus held together the foundations of the universe.
For every monad, be it ever so humble, provided it is in very truth a center of
     activity, obeys in its movement an embryo of love for me:
The universal Feminine.

De Chardin made a huge step forward for the Catholic Church when this poem was discovered and made public. But again, due to his conditioning, De Chardin makes the Eternal Feminine a created being and not the Creatrix. His poem is monumental and only quoted here in three small fragments. Sophia was raised up another step in the Catholic Church by these concepts, but Her place is not sufficiently described to include the comprehensive aspects of Her complete nature.

The Pillar and the Foundation of Truth, Pavel Florensky (1882–1937)

Sophia is the Great Root of the whole creation. Sophia is the first-created being of the creaturely world, with the creative love of God ... In relation to the creaturely world Sophia is the Guardian Angel of the world, the Ideal nature of the world.

... If Sophia is the entire Creation, then the soul and conscience of Creation-Humanity-is above all Sophia. If Sophia is all of Humanity, then the soul and conscience of Humanity-the Church-is above all Sophia. If Sophia is the Church, then the soul and conscience of the Church-the Saints-is above all Sophia. If Sophia is the Church of Saints, then the soul and conscience of the Church of Saints-the Intercessor and Mediatrix on behalf of the creation before the Word of God, who judges and divides creation in two, the Mother of God, is once again above all Sophia. But the true sign of the Blessed Mary is manifested in Her Virginity, the Beauty of Her Soul.

Russian Sophiologists try hard to credit Sophia with the honor She deserves, but they often make Her a created being instead of the Creatrix. Great praise and respect is given for Sophia, yet without direct clairvoyance, it is easy to misunderstand and simply speculate on Sophia's nature.

The Invisible Footprints, Frater Achad (1886–1950)

Love have I roamed the Earth delighting in the Good, the Beautiful and the True;

ever seeking the spots where these seem to be most Perfect.

There is joy in this wandering among the flowers of life,

but Thy Joy, O Beloved, is to be desired above all.

Now I seek a resting place, I set upon a new Quest, to Worship at Thy feet.

For it is written of Thee: "Bending down, a lambent flame of blue,

all touching, all penetrant, her lovely hands upon the black earth,

and her lithe body arched for love, and her soft feet not hurting the little flowers.

O! That I might discover Thine Invisible Footprints upon

the Earth and there come to the Understanding of Thy Being, O Beloved.

Frater Achad wrote a series of poems about the Goddess. This one displays the passion and true love that drove his creative expression and desire to unite with the feminine divine. The poem is an attempt to resurrect the worship of the Goddess in a new way.

Frater Achad makes it clear that he plans to marry Sophia as his beloved and longs for the day. This spiritual marriage is obviously the greatest desire of a soul in love with the spirit.

Selected Essays, Andrej Belyj (Boris Bugaev) (1923–2007)

The ideas of the world and mankind coincide conditionally for us. The idea of the world may be called the world soul. The world soul, Sophia according to Solov'ev, is perfect humanity, eternally enclosed in the divine nature of Christ. Here the mystical nature of the church coincides with the image of the eternal feminine, the bride of the Lamb. Here are the Alpha and Omega of true love. Christ's relation to the church—that of the bridegroom to the bride—is an unfathomable universal symbol. This symbol illuminates every ultimate love.

This insight is the door of love opening from heaven to Earth that can inform all love, just as Belyj implies in the last sentence. The heavenly marriage gives equal credence to Sophia and makes Her a co-creator with Christ. Here is the true nature of the soul and spirit uniting as one.

Listening to Our Bodies, Stephanie Demetrakopoulos (Modern)

Woman's consciousness of birth, its meaning,
and its echoes of cosmic patterns is an unconscious,
nonimagistic, nonverbal, yet shared feminine metaphysic.

The Mother in each woman is connected to the Divine Mother in Sophia. This truth is a shared metaphysic of love.

Sister of Wisdom, Barbara Newman (Modern)

We have seen, thus far, that the feminine divine is the revelation of the hidden God-particularly in the archetypal world, in nature, and in the life of the soul. She is divinity proposing, revealing, creating, assisting, and alluring; she is also the inner dynamism of the world obeying, receiving, responding, and cooperating. Through her the heavens declare the glory of God, the prophets are overshadowed by the living Light, and the faithful participate in the Virtues. Her bearing is regal toward the cosmos, erotic toward God, maternal toward men and women; her epiphanies aim to inspire the love of wisdom through the beauty of holiness.

She is the faithful mirror of divine intentions but also of human actions; it is her vesture that men and women adorn through good works or disfigure through sin. Intimate with God, she is supremely accessible to the faithful, for her consummate work, her operation, is the union of Creator and nature. As the "counsel of the Lord which stands forever" (Ps. 32:11), the feminine divine brings the world into being that God may be born in it and leads it back to God through the Word-made-flesh. Under the first aspect, she is the archetype of Mary; under the second, she is the eternal and preexistent Church.

This comprehensive religious summary of Wisdom, Mary, and Sophia is a good male version of the female; all that is missing is the primacy of Sophia. Sophia is not a creature. She is the Creatrix.

Eternal Individuality, Sergei O. Prokofieff (1954–2014)

Thus in the figure of the Luke Mary we have a human being who was worthy of becoming the bearer of one of the highest Avatar Beings after the Sun-Spirit of the Christ Himself, of that exalted Being who in the ancient world was called the Divine Isis, and in the early Christian communities and in places where esoteric Christianity was nurtured, the Divine Sophia.

Prokofieff defines the Divine Sophia as an Avatar Being after the Sun-Spirit of the Christ. This places Sophia on equal terms with Her Consort, the Son of God, Christ. This insight was gained from the works of Rudolf Steiner and his interactions with the being Anthropo-Sophia.

Life's Guardian Angels, Anonymous

The mothers of the human race;
A solemn beauty stamps each face;
Unfathomed love is their embrace;
They hold a high and holy place,
A place by God appointed!
With altar-fire their bosoms glow;
A sacred halo spans each brow;
They are life's guardian angels now,
Life's hierophants anointed.
Kings may have power, but ye have more;
Philosophers have sapient lore,
But in your bosom lies a store of wisdom,
Which is far beyond the wisdom of the sages.
Love, which no injury hath outworn;
Much steadfastness, the fruit of scorn;
And patience, and sweet pity, born
From the old woe of ages.

We are all mothers if we remember that we reincarnate in both male and female bodies. Within the scope of human experiences, there truly is no higher concept than Mother. The author intuitively knows this truth is self-evident and timeless.

The Triple Goddess, Adam McLean (Modern)

The Goddess is an eternal archetype in the human psyche. She will always be with us, even though we neglect her, repress her, or outwardly deny her existence. She has shown herself to us from the earliest times of our civilization, in cave drawing and primitive sculpture, in the days of great mythologies, and appears in many guises in our present culture. She is part of the fabric of our being that all humanity must inwardly relate to if we are to have an inner balance in our souls. So essentially, she is a part of humankind, that even if in the next centuries we become children of the Cosmos, leaving the Earth planet behind voyaging to the stars, we will undoubtedly meet her in the dark depths of space. In ancient times, we projected her outwardly from within ourselves, saw her in the Kingdoms of Nature, within the body of the Earth, or working behind human destiny. We experienced her as a power beyond and above ourselves—a power that transformed and challenged us, as well as a being that nourished, protected, and preserved us.

During this present century we have come to recognize a structure or layering of human consciousness, and that the Goddess dwells as archetype within our inner space, as essentially a part of our being as our physical heart. And yet she has been so exiled in our souls that often we do not recognize her subtle workings, and only when she manifests in an outwardly powerful or disruptive manner do we see her at all. The Goddess is triple, manifesting in a threefold form, because she unites within herself the complementaries, the opposites, of the psyche. Thus she is both gentle and caring, and at the same time harsh and ruthless. She is both full of light and fair visions, and simultaneously can lead one into darkness and terrible horrors.

Adam McLean has done a wonderful job describing the evolution of Sophia in simple terms that yield tremendous insight. Sophia has evolved as we evolved over history, and Her roles have changed dramatically. This description is not limiting or confining for Sophia. It offers a sense of who She is for humanity, the world, and our personal selves.

Theologia Mystic, Alan Watts (1915–1975)

The Virgin Mother Goddess is, first of all, Mater Virgo–virgin matter or the unploughed soil—that is to say, the Prima Materia prior to its division, or ploughing into the multiplicity of created things. As Star of the Sea, Stella Maris, the Sealed Fountain, "the immaculate womb of this divine fount," she is likewise the Water over which the Spirit moved in the beginning of time. As the "woman clothed with the sun, and the moon under her feet," she is also everything signified in other mythologies by the goddesses of the moon, which shines by the sun's light, and appears in the night surrounded (crowned) with stars. As the Womb in which the Logos comes to birth she is also Space, signified in the common artistic convention of clothing her in a blue mantle, spangled with stars.

This is a beautiful description of Sophia without limitations, religious dogma, or doctrines, just Beauty in some of Her magnificent forms. It is Intuition that brings forth such accurate descriptions of Sophia.

The Rain of Wisdom, Trungpa Rinpoche (1939–1987)

In phenomenal experience, whether pleasure or pain, birth or death, sanity or insanity, good or bad, it is necessary to have a basic ground. This basic ground is known in Buddhist literature as the mother principle. Prajnaparamita (the perfection of wisdom) is called the mother-consort of all the Buddhas … As a principle of cosmic structure, the all-accommodating basic ground is neither male nor female. One might call it hermaphroditic, but due to its quality of fertility or potentiality, it is regarded as feminine.

The playful maiden is all-present. She loves you. She hates you. Without her your life would be continual boredom. But she continually plays tricks on you. When you want to get rid of her, she clings. To get rid of her is to get rid of your own body-

she is that close. In Tantric literature she is referred to as the dakini principle. The dakini is playful. She gambles with your life. The work of woman is transformation: making something out of nothing, giving form to formless energy. Her instruments in this work are the tripod and cauldron, her elements blood and milk-both liquids held within her are organic, that with which one works. She is both container and contained at this stage. She transforms matter and is herself transformed. She is the procession of form and the forms of the process.

These ideas go far beyond normal Buddhist views of the Goddess of Wisdom. Trungpa was a brilliant thinker who had a flexible mind that could take the ancient traditions and make them applicable to the modern aspirant.

This description is a beautiful and playful way of articulating the Buddhist tradition of Crazy Wisdom, the childlike mind that can attain Wisdom through play. Trungpa has merged a few wisdom traditions of the East into this accurate description of Sophia, the Goddess of Wisdom.

Birth of Intuition

Harken, celestial choirs, to needs of earthly kind,
The echoing heart-song of the child we wish to find.
Sparkling dayspring of ether worlds,
Inkling of tomorrow cast from sheltering womb,
Star-born and destiny-wrought,
Comes seeking the life that She has sought;
Beckoning earth, water, fire, and air,
The magic elements that create Her here.
But yonder in bright spheres She knew
Of light, sound, and life that are true.
O little one, whose star radiates clear in my mind,
Show me the glistening path you wish to find.
The eyes of age in innocence unfold
The workings of gods for futures untold:
Laughter, as clear as a bell that peels
Speaks of her home, the sun that reels,
In courses ancient and ever on;
Join in our dance, in our hearts, in our song.

FIFTH SEAL

Seeds of Wisdom

What radiant passage in solemn night

Gives us entry into the sovereign light

Receiving the childlike in heaven's womb

And freeing the spirit from its earthly tomb?

The Lemurian Calendar and the Goddess

The Hawaiian Alii were buried in the lava tubes,

to rest in Her veins until the awakening of the Goddess.

It was refreshing to see Joseph Campbell, in his book, *In All Her Names*, tackle the topic of the Great Goddess that Marija Gimbutas's *The Language of the Goddess* has brought to the forefront of modern archeomythology.

Just before Campbell died, he recognized the being that was behind all of the masks of the heroes: the Great Goddess, in all Her many forms. He shared this last work with Marija Gimbutas, who offered a shortened version of her thesis found in *The Language of the Goddess*.

Campbell's chapter was entitled, "The Mystery Number of the Goddess," wherein he catalogs the mystery numbers of sun-oriented, male-dominated cultures since approximately 3000 B.C. These mystery numbers seem to add together to reveal the "body of the Great Goddess" or the Platonic Year of 25,920 years, which demonstrates that the ancients could calculate the precession of the equinoxes (an impressive mathematical feat) sometimes called the "Cosmic Year."

Each degree of the 360 degrees of the zodiac takes 72 years to complete in this Platonic Year, or the average lifespan of a human. It is this calculation that creates the extrapolation of the entrance into the New Age of Aquarius. This calendar of the Mother Goddess is a useful tool for reaching back into the mysterious ages led by women who worshipped the Great Goddess.

In August of 1991, the last of the kahunas of Tahitian and Hawaiian origin gathered on the Big Island of Hawaii to celebrate the passing of the end of their calendar. This calendar, which had been carved into staffs, stones, and speaking sticks for the last 25,920 years, led the fiery peoples of their ancient lands, now called Mu or Lemuria, to their final resting place on the volcanically active island of Hawaii.

How is it that these wandering tribes of seafarers from the lands of fire could calculate this astronomical occurrence in the sky with such accuracy and navigate so astutely? These questions plagued the author until a kahuna explained the nature of the "Passing Ceremony," which was celebrated in Hawaii on August 15, 1991. This ceremony marked the end of the time when the great kahunas were able to foretell, through their calendars and astronomical predictions, the events that would affect the Tahitian people. This celebration followed immediately on the heels of a zero-degree, full eclipse of the sun on July 11, 1991, directly over the Big Island of Hawaii, the home of the Fire Goddess Pele, who was introduced in the first chapter.

The Kahuna teacher explained that just as the eclipse of the sun would darken the Big Island, so the ancient Hawaiian/Tahitian people would have to relinquish their hold on the land (be eclipsed) and pass it on to the people who would represent other races and creeds at the ceremony.

All of this had been predicted by a great prophet who had lived in the kahuna astrological school of Kapoho. He spoke of the volcano Goddess Pele moving further east of the Big Island and creating an island under the surface of the ocean. And, in fact, this Hawaiian astrologer was correct about the eclipse's timing and about the shifting tectonic plates that have caused the Hawaiian Islands to move steadily northwest, creating a new island to the east.

He also taught that the Tahitian people are descendants from the star cluster of the Pleiades. The Tahitians have followed the motion of the Pleiades projected onto the Earth to claim new lands over those 25,920 years. Their recent move to the Hawaiian Islands around 10 B.C., and again in 1200 A.D., was difficult due to the remoteness of the islands. Legend has it that a great god, in the form of a huge white shark, led their ships 2,800 miles across the Pacific.

In Lemuria, the most ancient culture was developed by women who kept the Fire Mysteries, or secrets of the Earth, in underground kevas (caves) by rhythmic chanting, singing, and cyclic activities. These matriarchs began to keep time and record the cycles of animals, plants, and humans. They developed humanity's memory for thousands of years with the symbols and pictures of the body of the Great Goddess and her rhythmic workings in nature. Pictorial keys, symbols, cave paintings, carvings, pictographs, and sculptures arose to depict this threefold being of birth, death, and regeneration: the fiery Goddess of life cycles.

The inner Fire Mysteries of the matriarchy ruled for 21,000 years, leading the Tahitians to follow the volcanic Creator Goddess to Her ever-changing fiery home in the west, the Hawaiian islands, where these Mother Goddess people followed their simple life in harmony with nature under the shadow of the inspirer of the Fire Mysteries.

But in the end, men took over, as they did globally, and from then on, the male god of war ruled the Polynesian and Hawaiian islands.

The point of the Passing Ceremony in 1991 was to once again acknowledge the feminine source of the Tahitian/Lemurian pantheon and to transfer the blood lineage kahuna duties to all beings. A sorrowful recognition of the wrongful acts of war and violence was explicit in this Passing, and a great offering had to be made to rectify violent and lamentable behavior.

All land and possessions had to be sacrificed, and a new, less attached-to-things mentality needed to be developed. Women were once again enthroned as the keepers of time and the rulers of the home. In other words, the ravished body of the Goddess (Gaia/Earth) was once more born again after her darkening. Her primal place has been restored as the Creatrix of the Earth and heavens.

The Lemurians never lost sight of the molten fire nature of the interior of the female Earth Goddess. They knew that the Black Goddess (lava) has Her home in the underground caves of molten creation. Therefore, the Hawaiian Alii (royalty) were buried in the lava tubes, to rest in Her veins until the awakening of the Goddess.

The great calendars of all cultures have come to an end, including the well-known Mayan calendar on December 21, 2012, and now it is in our hands to take what the Goddess has given us and go forward. How can we do that without knowing where She came from, how She was purposely hidden and darkened, and how She will resurrect? It is not enough to find the Great Goddess or resurrect female mythologies. We must eventually know Our Spirit through Her descent, and resurrection in personal detail if we wish to know the answers to the questions coming to us from the future.

The Mother Goddess will have to birth yet another child, pristine and pure, but powerful enough to combat the dragon of materialism that has turned our thinking into gray shadow-thoughts. The Apocalypse of St. John says that a Virgin clothed with the sun, the moon beneath her feet, and seven stars around Her head will bring forth a ruler with an iron rod. She will be given the wings of an eagle to fly into a place in the mountains that was prepared for Her.

Perhaps the male-dominated act of turning the winged Pallas Athena (the Goddess of Wisdom) into the armored Athena of the Greeks (with the head of Medusa on her shield) or the version of Athena called Nike Victorious, who had her wings clipped so that she might not fly away to any other city-state and protect only the Greeks, will soon end.

Let us offer wings to Wisdom and the rightful crown of Natura to this re-enthroned Goddess of Heaven and Earth, mindful of Her past suppression and recreate the Mysteries of inner, outer, and secret fire.

Campbell points the way with the question, "Can we find again these twelve cosmic routes to the Goddess called symbols, or a language that relates to the twelve basic symbols connecting us with the ancient zodiacal signs named by ancients and moderns as 'phosphenes'—primordial visual images in the human mind which can be elicited from the visual cortex of the brain?"

"Are we ready to have Her story told?"

Can we rediscover that Heracles was a woman whose labors lead us to twelve paths to the stars as celestial navigation that correspond to the twelve cranial nerves that feed the starry dome of our zodiacal brain?

Heracles (the female goddess) was turned into a male Heracles in 2101 B.C., when matriarchal wisdom was replaced by patriarchal aggression and the human mysteries of the body were projected into the starry realm of Astraea (Sophia) who withdrew from the Earth environment.

Once we have found these paths to the great Goddess, can they inspire us with the Wisdom from times before war, aggression, and nationalism plunged us into an age where HIStory has been a series of wars and a march towards materialism?

All of humanity seems to be calling for a *New Golden Age,* the Satya Yuga, or age of light, when the Wisdom of the Great Mother will be resurrected with her secrets of regeneration and new life. *The Gospel of Sophia* is one path that resurrects the Triple Goddess Sophia and enthrones Her in the Temple of Wisdom. Sophia calls us home to the altar of our hearts.

Are we prepared to hear the call, and answer it?

Are we ready to have *Her*story told?

Are we ready to Know Her?

Beyond Nature

Beyond the merging of apparent opposites
Lies a vast ocean where all union begins and ends;
This is where I know your spirit from,
A place where oaths are eternal as bonds adamantine.
No ill can endure such connectedness,
For the little self crumbles whole.
Only yourself in another here can hold,
And death has no sting.
You are I, and I am you,
But together we hold all others;
The terrible knowing of our little self,
Cries out like a suckling babe
Held in the arms of the All Knowing Mother.
Here, all desire melts like children's candy
And love is tempered by cold, harsh winds of time

And cooled over eons into a resolved contentedness.
Only that which is three in one can rise
Like a Phoenix from the ashes of love's self-sacrifice
To be born anew as the morning star
Bright and glorious for all to see.

The Harmony of the Spheres as the Goddess

Aurora of the soul, burst forth your newborn strength

In Splendor that splits the dark night.

For centuries, we have lived in the shadow and limitations of the scientific worldview of Kepler, Newton, and Descartes. This despite Kepler himself stating in his work, *Harmonices Mundi,* that he was seeking the Harmony of the Spheres that interpenetrate the physical world. He visualized this harmony as the platonic solids: cube, tetrahedron, octahedron, dodecahedron, icosahedron, and sphere interpenetrating each other with the only points of union at the terminal junctions of the solids. Each solid represents one of the seven planetary influences in our solar system. He struggled with this dream his entire life, but was never able to construct a cohesive cosmology.

Recently, Theodore Landscheidt, the discoverer of the galactic center and the super-galactic center, has fulfilled Kepler's dream. Landscheidt studied the mathematical documentation of sun spots, solar flares, tree rings, beach embankments, and other indicators, and subsequently found that the center of mass of our solar system is not at the core of the Sun. In fact, this assumption had blinded scientists who could not derive correct mathematical predictions of solar flares and sun spots, even though they had tree ring and beach embankment evidence over many thousands of years.

Rudolf Steiner had already stated in his 1921 *Astronomy Course* that the center of mass of our solar system is not stationary but moves between the forces created by the Sun, Mercury, Venus, and Earth, and the outer planets of Mars, Jupiter, and Saturn. This center of mass is constantly moving toward 26 degrees Sagittarius.

Landscheidt discovered this "galactic center" in 1973, followed by the "super-galactic center." In his 1988 book entitled *Sun-Earth-Man a Mesh of Cosmic Oscillations—How Planets Regulate Solar Eruptions, Geomagnetic Storms, Conditions of Life, and Economic Cycles*, he postulates the true center of mass of the solar system.

Steiner's astronomical indications have been accurate to date, while many still remain to be studied and verified.

This incredible discovery of the periodicity of sun spots and the center of mass of the solar system then pointed in a direction for Landscheidt that would have delighted Kepler. Landscheidt realized that there is a set of factors that mesh with the sevenfold field theory of movement and harmony that appeal to planetary forces and dynamics. This set of factors is called the Mandelbrot set, which has seven individual foci (fields) of activity that correspond with natural musical harmonies. These sets of factors, like Julia sets (the natural spiral pattern of nautilus shells), create geometrizing sets, or fields of force, that demonstrate the harmonies and geometry of the interpenetrating planetary spheres.

The astronomer Johann Kepler, in his work *Harmonices Mundi*, stated, "Even though men may scorn me for my frank confession—Yes! I have stolen the sacred vessels of the Egyptians that I might make of them a sanctuary for my God, far, far from the confines of Egypt."

Indeed, these Egyptian vessels are religious tools that reconnect the influence of the seven organs of the human body to the working harmonies created and nurtured by the Music of the Spheres. Pythagoras believed that he could divine the harmony on which a building was built and subsequently strike an opposite or dissonant note to crumble it. His last words were, "Study the unicord!"

This "unicord" is the human body with its harmonic overtones that correspond to the interpenetrating spheres of the planets. It is the resurrection of the Body of the Great Goddess, often called the music of the spheres.

Landscheidt is a genius and prophet of our age. The Mandelbrot series applied to cosmology unlocked some of the mysteries of occult anatomy to which both Steiner and H.P. Blavatsky point: the seven planets correspond to the seven chambers of the heart, the seven chambers (ventricles and nuclei) of the brain and the seven organs of the body (lung-Mercury, gall bladder-Mars, liver-Jupiter, heart-Sun, genitals-Moon, kidneys-Venus, spleen-Saturn.)

These laws of correspondence are based on the Hermetic principle: "As below, so above, as above, so below; this accomplishes the wonders of oneness." This discovery of the center of mass of our solar system and its relationship to the harmonies of the Mandelbrot set could lead us closer to universal principles that guide human development.

The Mandelbrot set, which looks like a human sitting in the "full lotus" position of yoga, is a new musical instrument upon which we might be able to begin a symphonic communion with the Cosmic Nature that made humans in Her own image.

Just as the Mandelbrot set is a spatial, musical, geometrical, and mathematical expression of the seven-fold Temple of Sophia, the Wisdom of the Goddess implanted in our anatomy, so is *The Gospel of Sophia* a journey through the new temple of the Most Holy Trinosophia that is spread out in the twelve directions of celestial navigation, the boat (or ark) of consciousness on the sea of space.

The original Temple of Wisdom has seven pillars and upholds creation by its virtues. It is the sacred canon of proportions hidden in the microcosmic human anatomy. The New Temple of Wisdom has no walls. It must be built pillar by pillar through virtuous labors that tame and rename each zodiacal archetype in a living way. These are the new Twelve Labors of Sophia that re-enliven and renew the wisdom active in human understanding and spiritual development.

Heracles attained his immortality by his twelve labors on the Earth with animal or astral representatives of the twelve zodiacal influences. Once he had accomplished these labors, he and many of the conquered archetypes were placed in the starry heavens by Zeus as reminders of his efforts to subdue the archetypal astral labors in the outer world.

The new path of Sophia lies not in conquering these forces in an exclusive, aggressive, male-dominated fashion, but in redeeming them in an inclusive, nurturing fashion. Sophia tames the forces through understanding the Beingness of the influences raying in from the cosmic expanse.

Surrendering and accepting the whole, instead of dividing and conquering it, is the new path of the Twelve Labors of Sophia.

Sophia holds the Wisdom of time (through the working of the forces of seven), which unravels the mysteries of space (the forces of twelve). Her underground microcosmic Temple with seven pillars (the child in utero) rises up out of the darkened, shrouded mysteries and finds itself surrounded by the twelve directions of macrocosmic space, which lay before the soul with infinite yearning possibilities.

The seven works together with the twelve. This journey of the virgin soul is accomplished through the recognition of the threefold nature of the human being acting out of the past (forces of the seven), with consciousness of the present (forces of the trinity), and faith in the future (forces of the twelve).

These are the mysteries of manifesting love through freedom and the recognition of the forces of time (seven) and space (twelve).

Thinking, feeling, and willing must be balanced to act in freedom and love. Thus, every person is a microcosmic trinity.

This is the true image of the Most Holy Trinosophia—the Great Goddess of birth, death, and resurrection.

The original creator is the Mother of All.

Thus it can be the task of every evolving being to master the Twelve Labors of Sophia. This book is a Gospel of Good News to assist the aspirant on the path to immortalizing the Goddess within, which is the meaning of each labor undertaken.

Each archetype of the Goddess that the aspirant embodies resurrects Her from the darkness.

Each archetype leads the aspirant deeper into the Mysteries of life as She begins to articulate the language of the spirit, the formative power of the zodiacal influences.

Each of the twelve zodiacal signs sounds forth two of the twenty-four consonants in this language. The seven planets sound forth the seven vowels, and together they speak and sing creation into being.

Once the seeker learns to understand and speak this language, she can begin to move and dance among these beings, and then perhaps she can give back to the cosmic Creatrix Her own individual speech of love through freedom. In this way, the aspirant can become co-creative with the apocalyptic present.

Rudolf Steiner has indicated that at the time of birth, the convolutions of each individual's brain create a picture of the activity that the seven planetary spheres make upon the twelve zodiacal areas of the cosmos. This imprint is a record of what the cosmos has given to the individual. The task of humanity is to develop those natural abilities until we can, as free human beings, give back to the cosmos the gifts we have developed. These gifts become food for the communion of spirits who have built up our bodies as microcosmic temples, or hieroglyphs, of the universe.

Standing upright and free has caused the human brain to develop twelve cranial nerves, which nourish the twelve archetypal areas of the convolutions of the brain that surround the seven cavities in the midbrain (five ventricles and two nuclei).

The heart actually has seven chambers, and the seven organs of the body are regulated by the seven life processes.

The brain is often seen as threefold in its division into reptilian, limbic, and forebrain, or the left and right hemispheres connected by the corpus callosum. This same threefoldness is found in the human body in the head, trunk, and limbs, or nerve-sense system, rhythmic system, and metabolic system.

This trinity of the soul creates many threefold systems in the human that relate to the past, the present, and the future, i.e. thinking, feeling, and willing—the cognitive, affective, and psychomotor realms—waking, dreaming, and dreamless sleep.

All outer macrocosmic manifestations reflect their microcosmic aspect in the human Temple of Wisdom, our bodies. In relating our evolution to the Body of the Earth, Gaia, the progressive spring equinox point in the zodiac takes 25,920 years to return to its original spot, having traversed the twelve signs of the zodiac.

The Great Year of 25,920 is the Body of the Great Goddess projected out into cosmic space. For us on Earth, a year takes twelve solar months or thirteen lunar months to traverse. But each degree in the Great Year of the Goddess takes seventy-two years to complete.

Our lives are but a day in the life of the Great Goddess. Our monthly labors tick off like a second hand on the clock of the Goddess. One year of consistent, daily, conscious participation in this cycle is but a minute to the Mother of All.

It is past time to begin the work of embodying the principles of our Creatrix.

If we can struggle to awaken enough to resurrect the darkened Goddess from obscurity by meditating Her qualities while contemplating Wisdom teachings, or Truth Sayings, we can begin to commune with the living forces that have brought us into creation. We can learn to give back to Her the resurrected image of a new Earth and a new heaven, wherein the Twelve Labors of Sophia are brought forward in time and consciously projected in all directions to all beings as the Twelve Labors of Sophia, balancing the forces of time and space.

This creates the alchemical wedding of our soul to our higher selves, which takes place in the New Jerusalem of our hearts, descending as Grail nourishment from the land of the divine.

The Dayspring of Eons Untold

Wellspring of Grace, blessing all worlds,
Accept human strivings, forged in time's furnace,
As we bow in this pause of reflective thanks,
And rise again anew to climb and soar.

Filled is the emptiness of our poured-out hearts,
That fountain-chalice, ever flowing,
With the Trinity's manifold sustenance,
Dancing elementals weaving your wonder cloak.

Aurora of the soul, burst forth newborn strength
In splendor that splits the dark night
O'ertaking revolution's constant march,
With hope of the morning's fresh life.

Cast from the eye of the Thrones of Beauty,
Mankind is forlorn, seeking union with self;
Myriad paths, and betrayals of inner light,
Are balanced in communion, exchange or flight,
Joined in the union of spirit's bliss and holy light.

Death's moment of perfect peace is its gift to life,
And from the darkness comes all creation;
While in us is the divine light,
The New Dawn, the hope ever-bright,
Seeking the Grail of the Heart, the perfect light.

Our Spirit

No earthly foot can traverse that sacred bridge of light,

No evil thought, nor feeling false, no results of deeds untrue-

Only light-filled Imaginative thought, Inspirations grand, and moral will

Can penetrate those hallowed halls of warriors strong and bold.

The *Gospel of Sophia* has been presented as the Good News of Sophia's threefold nature resurrecting from the grave of history into a new golden age of Wisdom where the higher nature of each individual is supported by the evolution of the Divine Feminine Trinity.

The Divine Feminine Trinity was introduced in the *Vision of Pele* as the threefold Goddess who inspired the path to understand the full significance of this initial revelation. Once the veils were lifted, the distinct and separate nature of each of the faces of the Great Goddess came into view.

A reexamination of sacred literature demonstrated the subsuming of the Divine Feminine Trinity into the Male Trinity. It was demonstrated that the Divine Feminine Trinity was always present in the sacred writings and practices of all religions, myths, and cultural beliefs.

Examining the literature in relationship to the developing human intellect reveals the nature of Sophia working with human intellectual and spiritual development.

Directly experiencing the three Goddesses in Hawaii through the Volcano Goddess Pele was the beginning of a never-ending path that first led to Sophia, in Her threefold nature, and now joins together with Sophia on Her path.

Sophia and humanity's path is one and the same. Humanity is unfolding Her threefold nature in all parts of their physical, soul, and spiritual natures, and She is the closest guide and support we have to develop our higher selves.

The original encounter of Sophia in Hawaii revealed Her threefold nature manifesting in time. A picture was created of the seven pillars of the Temple of Wisdom to show Her sevenfold nature as the differentiation of time throughout evolution.

Both the threefold and sevenfold natures of Sophia have their corollaries that correspond in the human body. *As above, so below.*

The threefold and sevenfold aspects of Sophia were quite evident, but the twelvefold nature of Sophia was more hidden in the literature and took the author years to discover. It was only a passionate commitment to research that brought forth the evidence for a twelvefold aspect of Sophia in the third person of the Divine Feminine Trinity, the Holy Sophia.

The revelations that poured forth about the esoteric teachings concerning a Language of the Spirit permitted the discovery of numerous spiritual descriptions of exactly how Sophia manifests as a current revelation in our everyday world. These discoveries completed the evidence necessary for seeing Sophia as the original Trinity. Seals Six and Seven contained in Volume 2 of *The Gospel of Sophia* describe the mechanics of the earthly and cosmic nutrition streams and demonstrate the physiological way spirit manifests in matter.

Sophia as a twelvefold Goddess nourishes humans through daily interactions with these nutrition streams. The twelve cranial nerves bring the distillation of all sense perception into forces of nutrition for the spiritual world, which reciprocates by giving a like amount of spiritual nutrition back to the aspirant. This is the mother's milk that Sophia provides to the aspirant from the twelve directions of space that is turned into inner space in the human body.

Sophia as a threefold Goddess rules the past, present, and future.

As the sevenfold Goddess, She rules time and the planets in our solar system, which are also reflected in the seven organs and chambers of the human body.

As the twelvefold Goddess, She is the collective consciousness of humanity and guides each person to his higher self through the twelve steps of learning the spiritual script, or language, found in the world of space and the human body.

The resurrection of the Goddess as the original Trinity necessitated a thorough examination of each of the faces or persons of the Divine Feminine Trinity. In essence, the necessity to study each face created a sort of biography. The more She was contemplated, the more it was realized that there is no end to the evidence of three distinct biographies of the beings of the Divine Feminine Trinity.

Sophia was shown as a Mother, reflected in literature and beliefs of a primal Creatrix.

Then it was revealed that Sophia is also a Daughter of the Mother because Sophia the Daughter descended from the ranks of the hierarchy of Wisdom to over-light Mary, the mother of Jesus. Sophia the Daughter is also clearly described in literature and beliefs. This face of Sophia is worshiped in many faiths as the being of Wisdom. Thus the Mother and Daughter were easily found in the existing writings and beliefs.

But the third face or person of the Divine Feminine Trinity was not at first apparent. It was through the insights of Rudolf Steiner, A. E., and Emerson that the Holy Sophia started to reveal Herself in the research. Once the sacred literature was laid out as a timeline, the development of the collective intellectual consciousness of humanity became apparent. It was then effortless to find the renaming and disguising of the third person of the Divine Feminine Trinity, the Holy Sophia.

Mapping the development of human intellectual development revealed the biography of the Holy Sophia.

The sevenfold nature of the Temple of Wisdom was presented as an orientation to the planetary forces that sound together to create the fabric of the vibrations of life that support the trinity of our heart, head, and metabolic processes. The seven planets, centered around the sun, correspond in the natural world with the bodily nature of the human being.

In *The Gospel of Sophia* these sevenfold forces of the solar system were named the *Pillars of the Temple of Wisdom*. Each pillar represents the formative forces specific to each planet and is an integral part of the whole. The six pillars of the planets form a six-pointed star around the central pillar, the sun, just as children gather around their mother. These distinctive vibrations, or music, comprise the harmony of the spheres as the balanced and blended notes unite to create a symphony of music that feeds and nourishes the human body.

Sophia works through the sounding planets to send to each human the echoed solar light that is transformed by each planet into a carrier-wave emitting the morphological fields of life that create the form and function of each respective organ.

The heart, the head, and the metabolic centers receive these vibrations of life in the seven chambers as a radio receives the station to which it is tuned via its frequency or vibration. These seven sounding fields of life are combined to bring the warmth, light, sound, and life of the sun into our organs through a step-down process of retuning the solar vibration into differentiated frequencies.

Our seven chakras are sending and receiving these morphic fields of resonance as nourishment for consciousness. The Seven Pillars of Sophia's Temple of Wisdom are the foundation of the systems and processes of the human body.

Each of these pillars, or notes in the scale, is the music of Sophia's Wisdom manifesting in the world as the master time-keeper of evolution.

The Holy Sophia works through a Language of the Spirit that is imprinted into the human body. This language has twelve formative forces. They are mirrored into a language of twenty-four syllables or archetypal phosphenes found in the zodiacal formative forces of the stars, which are mirrored in the human brain.

Finding the language of Sophia is accomplished through celestial navigation through the twelve directions of space, often depicted as Her pala or cloak of starry Wisdom. Through embodying the Twelve Labors of Sophia, the seeker finds the language to speak with the higher self and with the Holy Sophia.

These twelve cosmic labors were depicted in Greek history through Heracles, whose deeds were written into the stars. Sophia's Labors come from the stars.

Her facets are a part of our inner soul and spiritual forces like a lotus petal in a chakra. As we resurrect and polish each facet, the jewel in our heart shines more brightly—"hail thou jewel in the heart of the lotus—Om Mani Padme Hum."

The petals of our heart chakra unfold like a rose bringing beauty, fragrance, and delight to all. Each facet leads us from the Mother to the Daughter and then to the Holy Sophia, who are as close to us as our own heartbeat.

From threefold to sevenfold to twelvefold, we have come to understand the Divine Feminine Trinity and Her manifestation in the world and the human body.

The Gospel of Sophia sounds forth a long-awaited message of hope, mercy and comfort of the Spirit, the New World Pentecost. Like the heralding trumpets of angelic hosts, *The Gospel of Sophia* announces that the sunrise of a New Age is upon us. The night of Kali Yuga, which was none other than the darkening of the Goddess, is over.

It is not by happenstance that this revelation goes out into the world at the winter solstice of 2014, exactly two years after the end of all known aboriginal calendars. If you are one of the many initiates who have felt a shift in consciousness during these last few years, take comfort. The Earth and her inhabitants have crossed the galactic mid-point, and your intuitions of a spiritual shift in our collective consciousness are valid. *Our Spirit* is being born in this Age of Light, the Satya Yuga.

We are all enwrapped in the body of the Great Goddess Sophia, which is none other than the Platonic Year or the Precession of the Equinox. A new great cycle of 25,920 years has already begun. For those who have been preparing themselves spiritually, and for many readers, this has been a lifetime pursuit. Their lamp of knowledge and Wisdom will illuminate the reimagined world of the resurrected Goddess for those around them.

Make no mistake. We are all being pulled across the threshold between the physical and spiritual worlds, whether we are ready or not. Whether we believe or not. For those who are spiritually unprepared, these may seem like apocalyptic times as their current "life resonance" is not in harmony with the accelerated vibration of this new cycle.

It is not the end of time; it is the beginning of a new great cycle. And like the ten virgins in Matthew 25 who took their lamps with extra oil to meet the bridegroom, those of us that are spiritually prepared will be ready, just as Rudolf Steiner foretold, for the direct experience of the Etheric Christ. Together we can rise up into the etheric realm about the Earth and unite as *Our Spirit*, the new voice of Sophia Christos.

The Temple of Sophia Christos

They gathered from all parts of the world
Launched from the golden heart of the Earth,
Aiming their colorful Imaginations toward the unmoving stars.
There, surrounded by veils of glorious majesty flowing aloft,
Rising as funeral pyres of living offerings from the thoughts of seekers
Gleaned from the fires of love which illuminate the mind;
Rising like painted warriors dancing round the war-fire,
Calling thoughts to courageous union with archetypes divine,
Sacrificing their sense-free images as new star-light,
Quivering before the breath of the solar winds,
Displaying their bursts of mighty spirit-force,
As sighs of relief, resolved to bear the future
When Earth-beings brighten their own world,
Radiating the love they have received from their star.
Sounding forth waves of curtains bright,
Like thunder rippling the cold thin air,
Pronouncing the new rainbow with one great clarion call,
The crown of glory shines star-light, made by humans,
Encircling the poles as twin rings of colorful fires that do not burn.

Michael's sword of fire stands guard against unprepared souls
So that Eden's rush of light be not vainly wasted on weak eyes.
There, Michael stands as the countenance, the face of Christ,
With Sophia standing on the other side of the threshold door,
Welcoming the Virgin Soul into the Temple of Wisdom, home of spirit.

The Rainbow Maidens of the North are Sophia's spiritual midwives
Preparing each soul for the passage across the celestial bridge.
No earthly foot can transverse that sacred bridge of light,
No evil thought, nor feeling false, no results of deeds untrue —
Only light-filled Imaginative thought, Inspirations grand, and moral Will
Can penetrate those hallowed halls of warriors strong and bold;
Only eyes that see heaven, hearts that praise the divine, and moral deeds.

There, among the teachers who worship Sophia Christos is seen,
Risen in His new form, the Groom of the Spirit that weds our Virgin Soul
Creating the New Garden that shines as a beacon of guiding light
To all striving souls who have the power to see this risen Christ Light
Manifesting in the aura of humanity's new spiritual effulgence,
Offered each night from pious, pure souls throughout the world
As humanity's elixir of life, in the morally chiseled Grail of the Heart.

How to Use This Book

Through daily study of Sophia and Her nature, the qualities of Wisdom will gradually descend into your innermost being, which has been prepared by:

- Visualizing (Thinking),
- Invoking (Feeling),
- and Embodying (Willing).

Devoted study will help you develop the capacity to hold Sophia's Wisdom as you carry it forth in your daily life.

Imagine that "capacity" is like a riverbed and Sophia like the waters that flow within its banks. When you start on your path of initiation, your capacity might only hold a pool or a small stream, but as your studies continue, your capacity increases until you can hold more and more of Her Wisdom.

She flows through you to the world around you in ways that are uniquely expressed by your personal capacities. We each have our special talents that can be deepened and inspired by invoking Sophia on a daily basis. Her great Wisdom Body will unfold in the world as we each take on the calling of consciously expressing Her through our unique abilities.

Eventually your soul will become a Holy Grail in the form of a chalice of love which is created by interacting with the Wisdom of Sophia. Sophia can make Her presence known to you as you unite with your own angel in the alchemical wedding of your soul (Sophia) to your spiritual self (Christ).

With daily, rhythmic invocation of the divine facets of the Goddess, you can awaken and empower the sacred temple in your heart, making a home for the Most Holy Trinosophia, the Being of Wisdom who is wedded to Love, Sophia Christos.

As you visualize aspects of the Goddess, Her virtues and qualities can live and breathe into your heart and reach into your daily life, transforming and illuminating your thoughts, feelings, and actions. Invocation, either alone or with your study group, resonates in the heart and echoes in the mind. Eventually the Goddess qualities come to reside in your actions as you continue to invoke, visualize, and meditate daily.

When the Great Mother is remembered, resurrected, and embodied as the Triple Goddess, the Most Holy Trinosophia or Primal Divine Feminine Trinity, Her archetypal principles can rise up into a new form that speaks through those meditating on Her. By visualizing Her many wondrous forms, you can resurrect Her nature, darkened over the past four thousand years. You can remove the veils that hide Her power and beauty. You will see Her in all Her Glory as the Once and Future Great Goddess.

The ideas in this gospel can lead you on the path from past, to present, to future—also called the Three Fates or Norns. They are the aspects of creatrix, sustainer, and destroyer, manifesting throughout all space, time, and consciousness. Each idea can open another petal in the flower of your mind's eye as you contemplate the wondrous nature of Sophia's splendor.

It is suggested that the aspirant practice twice daily, just before and after sleep, becoming one with the visualizations and invocations of Sophia, feeling oneself becoming united with the many facets of the Goddess. The Divine Feminine Trinity can then come to rest in the healing rhythms of a balanced heart devoted to the divine.

Breathe deeply Her essence into your spirit and give freely of Her qualities to all.

"Mother of All"

A Buddhist meditation states: "All living beings have been or will be the mother of all other sentient beings, either in past, present, or future incarnations."

The message is that you should treat all beings with the sacredness that you treat your own mother. By studying Sophia, you can begin to embody the nature of the many-faced Mother of All and develop the compassion needed to take the vow of the bodhisattva: to attain enlightenment for the sake of all other beings and to help all other beings stop suffering and attain true happiness and enlightenment. Indeed, the bodhisattva chooses not to enter heaven until all other beings have also made their heavenly transitions.

This book focuses on bringing the same spirit of unconditional love, compassion, and healing to you on a deeply personal level through Sophia—and into a world so desperately in need of Wisdom.

Afterword

Welcome the Age of Satya Yuga

Like many paths of initiation from the Mystery Schools, the eternal gospel that reveals the nature of the etheric manifestation of Christ in our times must stay protected from the misuse and misinterpretation of people not ready to hear this message. Intuitions of Sophia in our time always lead to the revelation of the Cosmic Christ and His activities in our living etheric realm of formative forces. Sophia reveals Christ at this time through Her Wisdom.

The Gospel of Sophia, Volume 1, can only hint at the final stages of self-initiation in a book available to the general public. Esoteric secrets have always been held back and given when an aspirant is ready and requests further light on the path.

The Satya Yuga is the Age of Light and the greatest teachers of all traditions have returned to aid in this battle against darkness. You may be standing next to one of those teachers and not be aware of it.

The Dragon, known in Anthroposophic circles as Ahriman, has incarnated into a physical human body at this time. It takes unprecedented spiritual courage to counter the apocalyptic actions of evil all around us. The Dragon wishes to consume the child born to the "woman clothed with the sun" and end all spiritual evolution. This child is your higher self and the Dragon wishes it to die in its infancy. We truly are but "babes in the spirit" when it comes to spiritual development and we need the *woman clothed with the sun*, Sophia, to help birth and protect us from the Dragon's evil.

Humanity is collectively being "initiated" into the spirit whether they are ready for it or not. Fear, doubt, and hatred will arise in those who have not chosen the moral path back home to the divine. Faith, wisdom, and love will arise in those who practice the path of Sophia's Wisdom and this virtuous development will build new worlds in which *Our Spirit* may thrive.

It is because of the heralding of the Age of Light and the ending of all known ancient calendars that the opportunity is given to reveal, for the first time outside of a closed lineage, the teachings of the Maitreya Buddha and the Kalki Avatar. These beings are the forerunners of this New Age and will bring the teachings of Sophia out of darkness and into the light. The Maitreya will teach about Sophia and the Wisdom of the Kyriotetes as it pertains to Christ's Cosmic Deed. The Kalki Avatar, like the Archangel Michael, brings a fiery sword to destroy ignorance and return Wisdom to Her rightful throne. She is threefold in Her manifestation as priestess, warrior, and Mother of All.

These teachings have been known in the Mystery Schools and even in some modern day paths of initiation, but until now have not been linked to the Divine Feminine Trinity and its manifestation in the human being and the world.

Further teachings from this Language of the Spirit will be forthcoming in *Our Spirit* newsletters that will share parts of upcoming books and relevant articles that illuminate these topics and others.

The Trilogy

The Gospel of Sophia is the testament of an aspirant of Sophia who has been given self-initiation with the assistance of the Divine Feminine Trinity as guide and teacher. From the first revelation of Sophia through Pele, to the Etheric Christ experience several years later, the author has followed the luminous path of study and communion with Sophia Christos to become an initiate of Sophia. The teachings about the Being of Sophia are the result of living Imaginations given to the author by spiritual beings that inspired her over many years, guiding her to active Intuitions that unveil the hidden nature of the Great Goddess.

The resultant Wisdom and path of self-initiation has become the first biography of the Divine Feminine Trinity of Mother, Daughter, and Holy Sophia. Each Being in this Trinity has an amazing story to reveal to the attentive aspirant.

The Biographies of the Divine Feminine Trinity, the first book of the trilogy, provides an intellectual and philosophical platform upon which to build the aspirant's knowledge of the breadth and scope of the Being of Sophia through the course of time. These are the Outer Teachings.

A Modern Path of Initiation, the second book of the series, provides the practical means to apply the mental, spiritual, and morality training that Volume 1 embodies. Instructions are given to prepare the aspirant in activating the earthly and cosmic nutrition streams that create the reciprocal feeding between the human and spiritual worlds and support the aspirant's path of initiation into knowledge of the higher worlds. These are the Inner Teachings.

The Sophia Christos Initiation, which is the third book and the Secret Teachings of the trilogy, is offered to the initiate ready to cross a spiritual threshold beyond "intellect" into a realm of actual spiritual experiences of Imagination, Inspiration, and Intuition.

In Tantric Buddhism these esoteric teachings are called the "generation" and "completion" stages of practice. An aspirant may practice the generation stage of Vajrayogini for multiple lifetimes before the great secret treasure of the completion stages of the practice are given. The

generation stages (Volume 1 and 2) are for anyone who wishes to spiritually develop. The completion stages (Volume 3) are for serious students and initiates. The practices are so powerful that to reveal them without preparation could become problematic without the prerequisite morality training.

Together the three books of *The Gospel of Sophia* comprise Seven Seals.

For more information the Our Spirit project, please visit us at www. ourspirit.com.

Goddess Bless,

Tyla Gabriel, ND
Sister of Sophia

Appendix A

The Traditional View of Sophia

Sophia is the Greek word for wisdom and a central idea in Greek philosophy and religion, Platonism, Gnosticism, Orthodox Christianity, Esoteric Christianity, and Christian mysticism. Sophiology is a philosophical concept regarding wisdom, as well as a theological concept regarding the wisdom of the biblical God developed principally in the East. She also is honored by Gnostics as a goddess of wisdom. Plato understands philosophy as *philo-sophia*, or, the love of Wisdom. In Plato's *Republic*, the leaders of the utopia are to be philosopher kings: rulers who love Sophia, Wisdom.

Wisdom (Hebrew: *Chokhmah)* is a central topic in the sapiential books of the Hebrews, i.e. *Proverbs, Psalms, Song of Songs, Ecclesiastes, Book of Wisdom, Wisdom of Sirach*, and *Baruch*. Old Testament themes of wisdom are referenced in: Proverbs 8:22–31, Wisdom 8:4–6, Sirach 24:4, Wisdom 9:9–10, Job 28:12–13, 20–1, 23–27, Baruch 3:29–37, Sirach 24:1–12, Sirach 1:15, Wisdom 7:12, Proverbs 1:20–33, 8:1–9:6, 9:1–6, and Wisdom 7:22b–8:1, 8:2.

In Christian theology, "wisdom" (Latin: *Sapientia*) describes an aspect of God, or the theological concept regarding the wisdom of God that is not part of the Male Trinity. In the Eastern Orthodox Church, Holy Wisdom is understood as the Divine Logos who incarnated as Jesus Christ. In Eastern Orthodoxy, humility is the highest wisdom to be sought more than any other virtue. Humility, not knowledge, cultivates Holy Wisdom. It is the defining quality that grants humans salvation and entrance into heaven.

Some Eastern Orthodox religious thinkers have championed the concept of Sophia as a key part of the Godhead. These include Vladimir Solovyov, Pavel Florensky, Nikolai Berdyaev, and Sergei Bulgakov. For Bulgakov, the Sophia is co-existent with the Trinity, operating as the feminine aspect of God in concert with the three masculine principles of the Father, the Son, and the Holy Spirit.

In Roman Catholic mysticism, Hildegard of Bingen celebrated Sophia as a cosmic figure in both her writing and her art. Sophia, in Catholic theology, is the Wisdom of God, and is thus eternal.

Within the Protestant tradition in England, Jane Leade, 17th-century Christian mystic, Universalist, and founder of the Philadelphian Society, wrote copious descriptions of her visions and dialogues with the "Virgin Sophia." Leade was influenced by Jakob Böhme, who also speaks of the Sophia in works such as *The Way to Christ*.

Jakob Böhme was very influential to a number of Christian mystics and religious leaders, including George Rapp and the Harmony Society.

Appendix B

Sophia as the Spirits of Wisdom

In the traditions of angelology, Kyriotetes/Dominations are the first Angels (and therefore the oldest Angels) created by God. In turn, they receive their instructions from the Cherubim and the Thrones.

Anything concerning leadership falls under the realm of the Dominations. They carry scepter and sword to symbolize their power over all creation. They decide what needs to be done to accomplish God's needs and regulate the duties of Angels to ensure the universe keeps working as it should.

Through the efforts of these spirits, the very order of the cosmos is maintained. They handle the minute details of cosmic life and existence, designating tasks to the lower orders of angels. They are depicted in human form, but with wings wearing a triple crown to signify their position over the physical form. They also are pictured as carrying a scepter of cross and a sword to symbolize the balance of mercy and judgment as Lords. They are sometimes perceived as travelers, appearing in widely separated spaces and times.

The Dominions are translated from the Greek term "kuriotes," which means Lordships. They are also known as the Lords, Kyriotetes, or Hashmallim whose purpose is to regulate the duties of the lower angels.

Dominations or Dominions are so called because they rule over all the angelic orders charged with the execution of the commands of the higher hierarchy. They are often described as the angels of intuition and wisdom, controlling the laws of cause and effect. They act as a form of middle rank between the upper choir and the lower.

Receiving their directions from the Seraphim and Cherubim, these Spirits make known to us the commands of the divine and ensure the cosmos remains in order. Their main virtue is zeal for the maintenance of order. Only on very rare occasions do they reveal themselves to mortals; instead, they quietly concern themselves with the details of existence. They integrate the material world with the spiritual, maintaining balance and order.

The Spirits of Wisdom preside over evolution from the future Jupiter sphere. They embody the spiritual consciousness needed to guide evolution.

The Spirits of Movement live in the Mars sphere. In general they work with the motions—the ebbs and flows—of spiritual energies in and around the forms of evolution.

The Spirits of Form reside in the Sun sphere. They oversee the forms taken by the Earth and its surroundings as evolution progresses. They donate the human ego, or "I" to humanity.

Rudolf Steiner speaks of these beings in his book, *Occult Science,* as follows:

> *Certain sublime Beings whose life Saturn rays back, may be called Spirits of Wisdom. In Christian spiritual science they bear the name Kyriotetes, i.e. Dominions. Their activity on Saturn does not by any means begin with the middle epoch of evolution ... Indeed in a certain sense it is by then already at an end. Before they could become conscious of the reflection of their own life, proceeding from the warmth-bodies of Saturn, they had first to make these bodies capable of bringing about such a reflection. Hence their activity began soon after the commencement of Saturn evolution, at a time when the Saturn corporeality was still chaotic substance which could not have reflected anything ... The Spirits of Wisdom have in their etheric body attained the power to do more than enjoy the reflection of Life—as on Saturn; they are now able to pour Life out of themselves, endowing other beings with it.*

He speaks again of these beings in his book, *The Spiritual Hierarchies,* as follows:

> *The Spirits of Wisdom or Kyriotetes receive from the circumference of Saturn that which comes down through the mediation of the highest Hierarchy, so that they may transform it and make it harmonize with what is in the interior of Saturn ... The Dominions or Spirits of Wisdom are the directors inside Saturn ... Which are the Spiritual Beings who carried over the condensation of the substance of ancient Saturn to the ancient Sun? These Beings, whom we call the Dominions, or Spirits of Wisdom. It is they who now press inwards from outside and who originally pressed together the mighty mass of Saturn*

so that it grew smaller. The Dominions brought pressure to bear upon it, until the ancient Sun became the size of a globe, the mass of which, if you place the Sun in its center, you must imagine as reaching out to Jupiter. Thus Saturn was a gigantic world-globe, which having our Sun in its center would have reached as far as to the present Saturn, an enormous globe, as large as our present solar system. The Sun of which we have just spoken was a world-globe which stretched as far as the Jupiter of today. This point marks the boundary of the ancient Sun-world. You will do well if you picture those outer planets as boundary marks for the limits of the ancient Worlds. You see that we are gradually approaching the theory of the planets, being led thereto through the activity of the hierarchies.

The Spiritual Hierarchy

Name Given by Steiner	Christian Esotericism	Biblical
1. Spirits of Love	Seraphim	Seraphime
2. Spirits of Harmony	Cherubim	Cherubime
3. Spirits of Will	Thrones	Thronos
4. Spirits of Wisdom	Dominions	Kyriotetes
5. Spirits of Motion	Mights	Dynamis
6. Spirits of Form	Powers (Authorities)	Exusiai (Elohim)
7. Spirits of Personality	Principalities (Primal Beginnings)	Archai
8. Spirits of Fire (Folk)	Archangels (Folksouls)	Archangeloi
9. Sons of Life (Twilight)	Angels (Guardian)	Angeloi

Appendix C

The Turning Point in Time: The Mystery of Golgatha

Tree of Life [1]
Jesus of Nazareth becomes Christ
Adam Kadmon becomes New Adam [2]

Mary of Jerusalem (Original Eve) [3]
Mary Magdalene
Mary of Bethany

St. John (Lazarus raised)
Joseph of Arimethea (caught the blood of Christ)
Nicodemus (saw crucifixion in a dream-like state)
Longinus the Centurion (pierced side of Christ)

The collective beings working with Mary of Jerusalem:

Mary of Nazareth (Eve Kadmon) [4]

Sophia the Being of Wisdom who descended through the hierarchies to become "human" by over-lighting Mary

Wisdom Body of Zarathustra transformed by Jesus and transmitted to Mary before His baptism

An immaculate body brought by the Beings of Wisdom to Mary/Eve who is combined with Eve Kadmon

The Holy Sophia working through Mary-Sophia personally

The Mother Goddess through the Divine Feminine Trinity

The collective beings working with St. John (Lazarus raised)

John the Baptist after his death (Original Adam)

Group-soul of the apostles merged with John the Baptist

Other witnesses:

Zarathustra's ego over-lighting the events

Buddha (the Star of Bethlehem) over-lighting the events

Archangel Michael (the "countenance of Christ")

Christ joins Mary-Sophia to St. John under the cross as Mother and Son
This is an archetypal image of Sophia Christos

[1] Christ's cross was wood from the Tree of Life – the other two crosses represent the Tree of Good and Evil
[2] There were two Kadmon (paradisiacal) bodies held in waiting since the creation of the Original Adam and Eve-these Kadmon bodies had never incarnated before and were still pristine vessels for Mary and Jesus of Nazareth to use
[3] Mary of Jerusalem as described in the Gospel of Matthew
[4] Mary of Nazareth as described in the Gospel of Luke

Appendix D

The Incarnations of Zarathustra— The Master Jesus

Zarathustra was repeatedly a student of the Great Manu, the spiritual leader of the Atlantean Sun Mystery Temple, in the City of Manu, known as the Central Asian Mystery Initiation Center, from about 7000 B.C. until about 5000 B.C. Zarathustra is a human initiate who has risen up to an angelic and archangelic view of the world.

Zarathustra, or Zoroaster, led the ancient Persian culture from 5067 B.C. until 2907 B.C. through the age of Gemini developing the human etheric body. Modern Zoroasterism is a late derivative of this ancient culture that we know only slightly through the existing records.

During his ten incarnations as Zarathustra, the principle leader of the ancient Persian culture, he wrote the *Gathas*, the *Zend Avesta*, and the *Chaldean Oracles*. He domesticated most of the farm animals we still eat today and many of the grains and vegetables, too. He crossbred the lily with the wild grasses to create modern grains and the rose with vines and trees to create many of the fruits we still eat. Zarathustra was a priest-king who created the laws and ordered all aspects of culture, just as Manu had done for the ancient Indian culture from 7227 B.C. to 5067 B.C.

Hermes led the Egyptian culture as Zarathustra led the Persian and Manu the Indian. Hermes wrote the Egyptian laws, temple rituals, dogma of the religion, and ordered all planting, building, and other aspects of culture and religion.

Moses led the Hebrew people as its holy prophet and guide together with his brother Aaron who was the high priest. Moses gave the first five books of the Old Testament and essentially ordered all Hebrew religious and cultural life.

Jesus of Jerusalem (Gospel of Matthew) was predicted by the star of the magi that brought Persian astrologers to Jerusalem to greet the King of Kings. Jesus of Jerusalem died and merged his consciousness with Jesus of Nazareth at age twelve in the Temple of Jerusalem as insinuated in the Bible. All of the human wisdom of Zarathustra's many incarnations became available to Jesus of Nazareth due to the sacrifice of Jesus of Jerusalem. After his death, Jesus of Jerusalem watches over Jesus of Nazareth and witnesses the descent of Christ into him at the baptism in the Jordan by John of Baptist and then accompanied the passion, resurrection, and ascension of Jesus Christ.

Jesus of Jerusalem is now known as the "Master Jesus" who incarnates every century and often alternates incarnations with St. John the Divine. Some incarnations have been speculated upon but little is known accept that he has had many incarnations where his identity is not historically known even though he dramatically effects the course of history through his mysterious encounters with others. What is known is that he was Zarathustra, Hermes, and Moses before his incarnation as the Master Jesus.

Appendix E

The Incarnations of the Two Johns of Jerusalem

John the Baptist

Adam in the Garden of Eden

First truly human soul

Part of this being remains in paradise called Adam Kadmon

Elijah

Mysterious Hebrew prophet who later works through Elisha

John the Baptist

Cousin of Jesus

Prophet and preacher who baptizes by water

Beheaded by Herod before crucifixion

Jesus mentions Elijah has come again as a voice in the wilderness, referring to John the Baptist.

Group Soul of the Apostles

John the Baptist lingers after his physical death and becomes the group-soul of the twelve Apostles lending them courage and strength

Merges with Lazarus (St. John) after Christ raises Lazarus from the dead

Lazarus becomes St. John the Divine, the Beloved, the one whom Christ loved

The merged John the Baptist-Lazarus—witnesses the Mystery of Christ's death and resurrection through his eyes as St. John the Divine

Raphael Stanza (the painter)

Paints the beautiful Madonnas from his direct memory of Mary-Sophia

Novalis

Fredrick von Hardenberg, principal founder of the Romantic Movement, poet, philosopher, scientist, geologist, novelist

Key inspirer of Rudolf Steiner

St. John the Divine

Hiram Abiff

Builder of the Temple of Solomon

Pre-Christian Masonic Mysteries centered around raising Hiram from the dead

Lazarus

Follower of Jesus who is raised from the dead

Later called St. John the Divine, the Beloved, the one who Christ loved

The author of the Gospel of John, Epistles, and Apocalypse

Merges with the excarnated soul of John the Baptist

Becomes united with his mission as the group-soul of the Apostles

Christian Rosenkreutz

Founder of the legendary Rosicrucians, a post Renaissance spiritual scientific movement for the renewal of science, art, and religion

Comte de St. Germaine

A great initiate from a deposed European throne who wandered throughout different courts lending his brilliance and innovation to the particular problems of each country

Author of *The Most Holy Trinosophia*

Biographical Timeline of the Holy Sophia's Development

Biographical Timeline of The Holy Sophia's Development

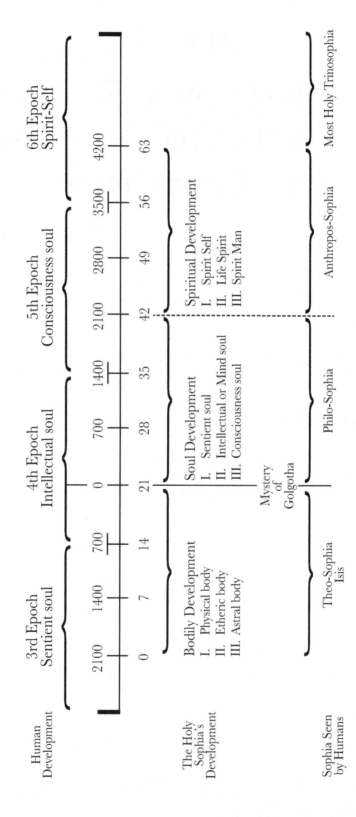

Appendix G

Planetary Incarnations of the Earth

Planetary Incarnations of the Earth

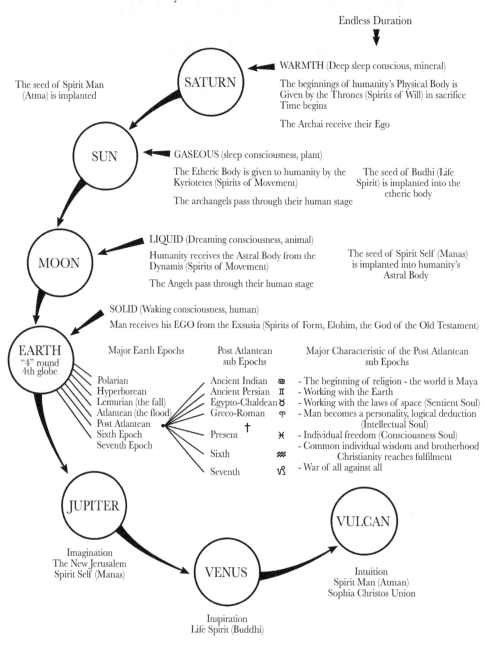

Endless Duration

SATURN

WARMTH (Deep sleep conscious, mineral)

The beginnings of humanity's Physical Body is Given by the Thrones (Spirits of Will) in sacrifice Time begins

The Archai receive their Ego

The seed of Spirit Man (Atma) is implanted

SUN

GASEOUS (sleep consciousness, plant)

The Etheric Body is given to humanity by the Kyriotetes (Spirits of Movement)

The archangels pass through their human stage

The seed of Budhi (Life Spirit) is implanted into the etheric body

MOON

LIQUID (Dreaming consciousness, animal)

Humanity receives the Astral Body from the Dynamis (Spirits of Movement)

The Angels pass through their human stage

The seed of Spirit Self (Manas) is implanted into humanity's Astral Body

EARTH
"4" round
4th globe

SOLID (Waking consciousness, human)

Man receives his EGO from the Exsusia (Spirits of Form, Elohim, the God of the Old Testament)

Major Earth Epochs	Post Atlantean sub Epochs		Major Characteristic of the Post Atlantean sub Epochs
Polarian	Ancient Indian	♋	- The beginning of religion - the world is Maya
Hyperborean	Ancient Persian	♊	- Working with the Earth
Lemurian (the fall)	Egypto-Chaldean	♉	- Working with the laws of space (Sentient Soul)
Atlantean (the flood)	Greco-Roman	♈	- Man becomes a personality, logical deduction (Intellectual Soul)
Post Atlantean	Present	✝ ♓	- Individual freedom (Consciousness Soul)
Sixth Epoch	Sixth	♒	- Common individual wisdom and brotherhood Christianity reaches fulfilment
Seventh Epoch	Seventh	♑	- War of all against all

JUPITER

Imagination
The New Jerusalem
Spirit Self (Manas)

VENUS

Inspiration
Life Spirit (Buddhi)

VULCAN

Intuition
Spirit Man (Atman)
Sophia Christos Union

Bibliographical References

Aldredge-Clanton, Jann. *In Search of the Christ-Sophia: An Inclusive Christology for Liberating Christians*. Twenty-Third Publications, Mystic, CT, 1995.

Ashe, Geoffrey. *The Virgin Mary's Cult and the Re-emergence of the Goddess*. Arkana, New York, 1976.

Aude, Sapere. *The Chaldean Oracles of Zoroaster*. Occult Research Press, New York.

Barnwell, John. *The Arcana of the Grail Angel*. Verticordia Press, Bloomfield Hills, 1999.

Baring, Anne and Cashford, Jules. *The Myth of the Goddess Evolution of an Image*. Viking Arkana, New York, 1991.

Benard, Elisabeth and Moon, Beverly. *Goddesses Who Rule*. Oxford University Press, 2000.

Bennell, Margaret and Wyatt, Isabel. *The Chymical Wedding of Christian Rosenkreutz*. Temple Lodge, 1989.

Betti, Mario. *The Sophia Mystery In Our Time*. Temple Lodge, London, 1994.

Black Koltuv, Barabra. *Slolomon & Sheba: Inner Marriage and Individuation*. Nicolas-Hays, Inc., Maine, 1993.

Bock, Emil. *Threefold Mary*. Steiner Books, 2003.

Brown, Mackenzie C. *The Song of the Goddess The Devi Gita: Spiritual Counsel of the Great Goddess*. State University of New York Press, 2002.

Bulgakov, Sergei. *Sophia, The Wisdom of God: An Outline of Sophiology*. Lindisfarne Press, 1993.

Bulgakov, Sergius. *The Holy Grail & the Eucharist*. Lindisfarne Books, N.Y., 1997.

Cahill, Suzanne E. *Transcendence & Divine Passion: The Queen Mother of the West in Medieval China*. Stanford University Press, California, 1993.

Campbell, Joseph, *Goddess Mysteries of the Feminine Divine*. New World Library, Novato, CA, 2013.

Cioran, Samuel D. *Vladimir Solov'ev and the Knighthood of the Divine Sophia*. Wilfrid Laurier University Press, Canada, 1977.

Crawford, John Martin. *The Kalevala: The Epic Poem of Finland*. John B. Alden, Publisher, 1888.

Debus, Michael. *Mary and Sophia: The Feminine Element in the Spiritual Evolution of Humanity*. Floris Books, 2013.

Durdin-Robertson, Lawrence. *The Year of the Goddess: A Perpetual Calendar of Festivals*. The Aquarian Press, 1990.

Eckhart, Meister. *Meister Eckhart: A central source and inspiration of dominant currents in philosophy and theology since Aquinas*. Translated by Raymond B. Blakney. HarperPerennial, 1941.

Emerson, Ralph Waldo. *Natural History of the Intellect*. Wrightwood, Chicago, 2008.

Frater Acad. *Thirty-One Hymns to the Star Goddess*. Sure Fire Press, 1988.

Geshe Kelsang Gyatso. *Guide to Dakini Land: A Commentary to the Highest Yoga Tantra Practices of Vajrayogini*. Tharpa Publications, London, 1991.

Goethe, Johann Wolfgang Von. *Fairy Tale of the Green Snake and the Beautiful Lily*. Spiritual Literature Library, Blauvelt, New York, 1979.

Graves, Robert. *The Transformations of Lucius Otherwise Known as the Golden Ass of Apuleius*. The Noonday Press, New York, 1951.

Grosse, Rudolf. *The Christmas Foundation; Beginning Of A New Cosmic Age*. Steiner Book Center, Vancouver, 1984.

Grosse, Rudolf. *The Living Being "Anthrosophia."* Steiner Book Center, North Vancouver, 1986.

Gyalwa Changchub and Namkhai Nyingpo. *Lady of the Lotus-Born: The Life and Enlightenment of Yeshe Tsogyal*. Shambhala, Boston, 1999.

Hall, Manly P. *Man, Grand Symbol of the Mysteries: Thoughts in Occult Anatomy*. The Philosophical Research Society, CA, 1972.

Hall, Manly P. *The Most Holy Trinosophia of the Comte De St. Germain*. The Philosophical Research Society, Los Angeles, 1983.

Hall, Manly P. *The Occult Anatomy of Man & Occult Masonry*. The Philosophical Research Society, California, 1997.

Hall, Manly P. *Woman, The Mother of All Living*. The Philosophical Research Society, Inc., California, 1955.

Harding, Elizabeth U. *Kali: The Black Goddess of Dakshineswar*. Nicolas-Hays, Inc., Maine, 1993.

Harvey, Andrew. *The Return of the Mother*. Frog, Ltd, Berkeley, California, 1995.

Hemleben, Johannes. *Rudolf Steiner: An Illustrated Biography*. Sophia Books, London, 2000.

Jones, Kathy. *The Ancient British Goddess: Her Myths, Legends and Sacred Sites.* Ariadne Publications, Glastonbury, 1991.

Kinsley, David R. *Hindu Goddesses.* University of California Press, Berkeley, 1988.

Knight, Gareth. *Evoking the Goddess: Initiation Worship, and the Eternal Feminine in the Western Mysteries.* Destiny Books, Rochester, Vermont, 1985.

Konig, Karl. *Earth and Man.* Bio-Dynamic Literature, Wyoming, Rhode Island, 1982.

Koulias, Adriana. *Fifth Gospel - A Novel.* Zuriel Press, 2012.

Landscheidt, Theodor. *Sun-Earth-Man: A Mesh of Cosmic Oscillations.* Urania Trust, London, 1989.

Lash, John Lamb. *Not In His Image: Gnostic Vision, Sacred Ecology, and the Future of Belief.* Chelsea Green Publishing, Vermont, 2006.

Laszlo, Ervin. *Science and the Akashic Field: An Integral Theory of Everything.* Inner Traditions, Rochester, Vermont, 2004.

Leviton, Richard. *The Imagination of Pentecost.* Anthroposophic Press, N.Y., 1994.

Lorimer, David. *The Circle of Sacred Dance: Peter Deunov's Paneurhythmy.* Element, Rockport, 1991.

Maclean, Adam. *The Triple Goddess.* Hermetic Research Series, Edinburgh, 1983.

Muller-Ortega, Paul Eduardo. *The Triadic Heart of Siva.* State University of New York Press, 1989.

Newman, Barbara. *Sister of Wisdom: St. Hildegard's Theology of the Feminine.* University of California Press, Berkeley, 1987.

Novalis. *Henry von Ofterdingen.* Frederick Ungar Publishing Co., New York, 1978.

Novalis translated by George MacDonald. *Hymns to the Night Spiritual Songs.* Temple Lodge, London, 1992.

Novalis. *Pollen and Fragments.* Translated by Arthur Versluis. Phanes Press, 1989.

Pearce, Joseph Chilton. *The Heart-Mind Matrix: How the Heart Can Teach the Mind New Ways to Think.* Park Street Press, Rochester, 2010.

Pintchman, Tracy. *The Rise of the Goddess in the Hindu Tradition.* State University of New York Press, 1994.

Powell, Robert. *The Most Holy Trinosophia.* Golden Stone Press, 1990.

Powell, Robert. *The Sophia Teachings.* Lindisfarne Books, Great Barrington, 2001.

Prokofieff, Sergei O. *The Heavenly Sophia and the Being Anthroposophia.* Temple Lodge, London, 1996.

Prokofieff, Sergei O. *The Twelve Holy Nights and the Spiritual Hierarchies.* Temple Lodge, London, 1993.

Robbins Dexter, Miriam. *Whence the Goddesses: A Source Book*. The Athene Series, Pergamon Press. 1990.

Rumi, Maulana Jalalu-D-Din Muhammad I. *The Mathnawi*. Translate by E. H. Whinfield. Watkins Publishing, London, 2002.

Schaup, Susanne. *Sophia: Aspects of the Divine Feminine*. Nicolas-Hays, Inc., Maine, 1997.

Schmidt-Brabant, Manfred and Sease, Virginia. *The Archetypal Feminine in the Mystery Stream of Humanity: Towards a New Culture of the Family*. Temple Lodge, London, 1999.

Schroeder, Hans-Werner. *The Cosmic Christ*. Floris Books, 1998.

Sease, Virginia and Schmidt-Brabant, Manfred. *Paths of the Christian Mysteries*. Temple Lodge, 2003.

Sease, Virginia and Schmidt-Brabant, Manfred. *The New Mysteries and the Wisdom of Christ*. Temple Lodge, 2005.

Sermey Khensur Lobsang Tharcin. *Sublime Path to Kechara Paradise: Vajrayogini's Eleven Yogas of Generation Stage Practice as Revealed by the Glorious Naropa*. Mahayan Sutra and Tantra Press, New Jersey, 1997.

Shopflinger, Thomas. *Sophia-Maria: A Holistic Vision of Creation*. Sam Weiser, Maine, 1998.

Sjoo, Monica & Mor, Barbara. *The Great Cosmic Mother: Rediscovering the Religion of the Earth*. Harper & Row, Publishers, San Francisco, 1975.

Steiner, Rudolf. *Ancient Myths: Their Meaning and Connection with Evolution*. Steiner Book Center, 1971.

Steiner, Rudolf. *Christ and the Spiritual World: The Search for the Holy Grail*. Rudolf Steiner Press, London, 1963.

Steiner, Rudolf. *Foundations of Esotericism*. Rudolf Steiner Press, London, 1983.

Steiner, Rudolf. *Isis Mary Sophia: Her Mission and Ours*. Steiner Books, 2003.

Steiner, Rudolf. *Man as a Being of Sense and Perception*. Steiner Book Center, Vancouver, 1981.

Steiner, Rudolf. *Man as Symphony of the Creative Word*. Rudolf Steiner Publishing, London, 1978.

Steiner, Rudolf. *Occult Science*. Anthroposophic Press, NY, 1972.

Steiner, Rudolf. *Rosicrucian Esotericism*. Anthroposophic Press, NY, 1978.

Steiner, Rudolf. *Rosicrucian Wisdom: An Introduction*. Rudolf Steiner Press, London, 2000.

Steiner, Rudolf. *The Bridge between Universal Spirituality and the Physical Constitution of Man.* Anthroposophic Press, NY, 1958.

Steiner, Rudolf. *The Evolution of Consciousness.* Rudolf Steiner Press, London, 1926.

Steiner, Rudolf. *The Goddess from Natura to the Divine Sophia.* Sophia Books, 2001.

Steiner, Rudolf. *The Holy Grail from the Works of Rudolf Steiner Compiled by Steven Roboz.* Steiner Book Center, North Vancouver, 1984.

Steiner, Rudolf. *The Influence of Spiritual Beings Upon Man.* Anthroposophic Press, NY, 1971.

Steiner, Rudolf. *The Reappearance of Christ in the Etheric.* Anthroposophic Press, NY, 1983.

Steiner, Rudolf. *The Risen Christ and the Etheric Christ.* Rudolf Steiner Press, London, 1969.

Steiner, Rudolf. *The Search for the New Isis the Divine Sophia.* Mercury Press, N.Y., 1983.

Steiner, Rudolf. *The Spiritual Hierarchies and the Physical World.* Anthroposophic Press, N.Y., 1996.

Steiner, Rudolf. *The Tree of Life and the Tree of Knowledge.* Mercury Press, NY, 2006.

Steiner, Rudolf. *The True Nature of the Second Coming.* Rudolf Steiner Press, London, 1971.

Steiner, Rudolf. *Theosophy.* Anthroposophic Press, New York, 1986.

Tagore, Rabindranath. *Songs of Kabir.* Weiser Books, Boston, 2002.

Taylor, Thomas. *The Fable of Cupid and Psyche.* The Philosophical Research Society, California, 1977.

Tomberg, Valentin. *Covenant of the Heart.* Element, Rockport, 1992.

Urieli, Baruch Luke. *Eros and Fable: Novalis' Fairy Tale of Human and Earth Evolution.* Camphill Books 1999.

Valentine, Jon. *The Chymical Wedding of Christian Rosencreuz Anno 1459.* St. George Publications, Spring Valley N.Y., 1981.

Versluis, Arthur. *TheoSophia: Hidden Dimensions of Christianity.* Lindisfarne Press, 1994.

Versluis, Arthur. *Wisdom's Book: The Sophia Anthology.* Paragon House, St. Paul, Minnesota, 2000.

Versluis, Arthur. *Wisdom's Children: A Christian Esoteric Tradition.* State University of New York Press, 1999.

Welburn, Andrew. *Mani, the Angel and the Column of Glory.* Floris Books, 1998.

William, Russell George. A. E. *Collected Poems*. MacMillan and Co, London, 1931.

William, Russell George. A. E. *The Avatars A Futurist Fantasy*. MacMillan and Co., London, 1933.

William, Russell George. A. E. *The Candle of Vision*. University Books, New York, 1965.

Wood, David W. *Novalis: Notes for a Romantic Encyclopedia*. State University of New York Press, 2007.

Zoeteman, Kees. *Gaia-Sophia: A Framework for Ecology*. Floris Books, 1991.

Made in United States
Orlando, FL
27 July 2024

49596796R00241